THE INTELLECTUAL REVOLUTION OF THE SEVENTEENTH CENTURY

Past and Present Series

GENERAL EDITOR: TREVOR ASTON

CONTRIBUTORS

G. E. Aylmer   William Lamont
David E. Brewster   C. B. Macpherson
Bernard Capp   S. F. Mason
J. C. Davis   Lotte Mulligan
Margaret 'Espinasse   John F. H. New
J. A. W. Gunn   Theodore K. Rabb
Christopher Hill   Barbara J. Shapiro
Roger Howell Jr   Keith Thomas
H. F. Kearney   Charles Webster
   Gweneth Whitteridge

Already published in this series
Studies in Ancient Society
edited by M. I. Finley

THE INTELLECTUAL REVOLUTION OF THE SEVENTEENTH CENTURY

Past and Present Series

GENERAL EDITOR: TREVOR ASTON

Edited by
CHARLES WEBSTER

ROUTLEDGE & KEGAN PAUL
London and Boston

First published in 1974
by Routledge & Kegan Paul Ltd
Broadway House, 68–74 Carter Lane,
London EC4V 5EL and
9 Park Street,
Boston, Mass. 02108, U.S.A.
Set in Monotype Garamond
and printed in Great Britain by
Butler & Tanner Ltd, Frome and London
ISBN 0 7100 7844 7

CONTENTS

CONTENTS

Debate

vii

CONTENTS

PREFACE

This anthology collects together a series of articles relating to various aspects of seventeenth-century intellectual history, contributed to *Past and Present* between 1953 and May 1973. In many ways it complements the first *Past and Present* anthology, *Crisis in Europe 1560–1660* the editor of which, Trevor Aston, drew attention to some of the material reprinted below. The present volume adopts a slightly different perspective, to concentrate on political theory, natural philosophy and theology in the seventeenth century. The original articles and debates included, focus on James Harrington, the Levellers, the social relations of early modern science and the role of millennial or utopian doctrines. The *Past and Present* debates on these subjects have attracted such wide interest that readers will find it useful to have them collected into a single volume. Apart from avoiding overlap with the previous anthology, every article or debate contribution on these themes appearing in *Past and Present* has been reprinted here.

The articles have been extensively corrected and reduced to uniform *Past and Present* style, and where possible quotations are given with original spelling, italicization, capitalization and punctuation. Substantial alterations have not been allowed. Cross-references within the text are made where relevant. Current addresses given for contributors are in many cases different from those originally supplied. The Editor is deeply indebted to Margaret Pelling for assistance in correcting the text and in preparing the index. The introduction to this anthology aims to provide the reader with an impression of the context of the debates and a guide to relevant literature published before January 1973.

Wellcome Unit for the History of Medicine,   CHARLES WEBSTER
  Oxford

I

INTRODUCTION

Charles Webster

The seventeenth century marked a turning point in western thought. Between the humanists of the sixteenth century, and Locke, Leibniz and Newton, ideas about nature and society underwent a radical transformation. The foundations of the modern world-view were laid during this period; an intellectual revolution was accomplished. The great progressive achievements in political theory, economics and natural philosophy have been charted in lavish detail. Major innovators and classic texts have been subjected to microscopic examination; specialist history of ideas journals have explored lines of influence and unearthed neglected sources. But the exegetical approach and excitement over relevance to modern beliefs have inevitably introduced an anachronistic element into interpretation; specialists have fallen too easily into the belief that their subject could be adequately comprehended without reference to historical context. This tendency has been to a certain extent encouraged by the insensitivity of historians and historical journals to many aspects of intellectual history. *Past and Present* has tended to attract articles on seventeenth-century political theory, science and theology which consciously attempt to restore historical perspective by placing major figures and developments firmly in their context. The papers included in this volume, which are largely concerned with English intellectual history, are almost invariably representative of this point of view.

The fertile developments in theology, philosophy and science which distinguish the seventeenth century took place within a complex and fluctuating historical framework. England's assumption of political importance and imperial status was accompanied by an increasing intellectual ascendancy. Contributors to *Past and Present* whose papers are collected in this volume have been involved in reassessing the classic developments in theology, political thought and science which are such a conspicuous feature of the seventeenth century. No tidy solutions have emerged; heroic figures have not been eulogized; but moves have been made towards genuine historical explanations and an integrated view of history. The debates in *Past and Present* should make it more difficult for historians to pursue any specialized branch of intellectual history *in vacuo*, or to lay claim to an understanding of any historical phase without reference to a whole spectrum of topics ranging from medicine to theology. It is only by avoiding these limiting tendencies that the historian will arrive at an adequate understanding of human motivations.

As Frances Yates has aptly remarked, at the outset of the reign of James I 'the English Renaissance was at a high point of splendour, developing into the dawning intellectual promise of the seventeenth century'.[1] Such figures as Bacon, Gilbert and Harvey established a mood of self-confidence which persisted into the age of Newton. Although deeply imbued with the spirit of humanistic learning, and thoroughly acquainted with the doctrines of antiquity, scholars were not tempted to relapse into the condition of commentators. A new spirit of inquiry emerged which found expression in critical scrutiny of the classical intellectual legacy and in suspicion of authority, as well as in the conviction that the moderns were equipped to climb higher and see further than any previous generation since the fall of Adam. There was an inclination to look forward to a new era of spiritual and intellectual enlightenment which would bring about the resumption of man's dominion over nature and provide the conditions for a religious settlement. Equipped with Bacon's blueprint for reform, the *Instauratio Magna*, and Hakewill's guarantee that innovation was sanctioned by divine providence, the new generation was confident that the seventeenth century would be favoured with supreme intellectual achievement and that England was destined to play a leading role in this process. A revival in learning analogous to the discovery of the new world was anticipated which

[1] F. A. Yates, *The Rosicrucian Enlightenment* (London, 1972), p. 1.

would lead to the unseating of received opinions 'in Divinitie, Philosophy, Ecclesiasticall Historie, in Civil and National Historie, in Natural Historie'.[2] John Goodwin's views were eagerly embraced by the puritan movement and shared by many others besides. Once innovation was found to be consistent with the search for primitive purity in religion, and to have the authoritative support of Biblical prophecy, there existed a licence for active participation in the quest for reconstruction. A new methodology, applicable to all 'sciences', was provided by Bacon's *Novum Organum*. Bacon relied heavily on experimental science and technology to illustrate the fertility of his inductive method, with the result that natural philosophy became the model to which all other sciences were referred.[3] His methods demanded unremitting dedication and absolute liberation from prejudice. The promised reward was a gradual accumulation of certain knowledge, which would lay the foundations for a new philosophy.

The efficacy of the empiricist approach (subsequently seen as a vindication of Bacon's views) was demonstrated by model investigations of magnetism by William Gilbert and of cardio-vascular circulation by William Harvey. Success in these spheres encouraged others in the search for incontrovertible knowledge in more complex and controversial fields. Hobbes, Harrington and Petty approached economics and politics with the feeling that the state could be anatomized with the same success as its microcosm, the human body.

Thus the seventeenth-century search for the Kingdom of God, and for completion of religious reform was accompanied by equally dedicated efforts towards general intellectual reform. The new philosophy promised a more effective exploitation of nature, to yield both agricultural and technological innovations. When reinforced by economic policies established according to rational criteria the way seemed clear for major social reconstruction and some amelioration of the condition of the poorer classes. Indeed the prospects seemed utopian, if both man and society could be analysed with scientific precision and models constructed for the

[2] John Goodwin, *Imputatio Fidei* (London, 1642), Preface, sig. C1v.
[3] Francis Bacon, *Novum Organum*, I, Aph. 127. Bacon asserted that his method should be applied to 'other sciences, logic, ethic and politics' besides natural philosophy.

guidance of legislators. This optimism was heightened by wide-spread speculations about the millennium, and there was a tendency to express intellectual aspirations in terms of utopian programmes. Bacon's *New Atlantis*, a direct descendant of the *Utopia* of Thomas More, was published in 1628. Then during the English Revolution *Macaria*, *Leviathan*, *Law of Freedom* and *Oceana* made their appearance. In each case there were specific reasons for adopting the utopian framework, but all conceived their systems of social organization in the spirit of the new philosophy.

James Harrington's *Oceana* has proved to be both enigmatic and intractable. On the whole, Harrington has been a figure to avoid, although it is generally conceded that behind his rambling archaisms lie important political ideas. About the nature of his originality there is much disagreement. He has been characterized as the prophet of widely divergent modern theories, and as the advocate of classical doctrines.[4] It is very noticeable that reviewers of Macpherson's *Possessive Individualism* uniformly ignored that author's long essay on Harrington, except in one case where the reviewer mentions the 'overrated' Harrington only to deride Macpherson's concern with him. Hall has adopted a similarly dismissive attitude to scientific and technological utopias.[5] The utopian genre may not appeal to modern theorists but its use is no necessary reflection of inferior intellectual quality or lack of intrinsic historical interest. Harrington defies categorization and his example warns us away from simplistic estimates of the seventeenth-century innovators. He was at once deeply read in classical and renaissance literature, convinced of the possibility of evolving a new scientific theory of the state and absorbed in the constitutional crisis of the Protectorate.

Most exponents of the new philosophy were both involved in ideological conflicts and indebted to the intellectual legacy of antiquity, an indebtedness which it was sometimes necessary for

[4] For an excellent digest of interpretations of Harrington, see F. Raab, *The English Face of Machiavelli* (London, 1964), pp. 185–6.
[5] P. Laslett, 'Market society and political theory [Review of C. B. Macpherson, *The Political Theory of Possessive Individualism, Hobbes to Locke*]', *Historical Journal*, vii (1964), p. 152; A. R. Hall, 'Science, technology and utopia in the seventeenth century' in *Science and Society 1600–1900*, ed. P. Mathias (Cambridge, 1972), pp. 33–53.

them to conceal in the course of the 'ancients *versus* moderns' debate. Hobbes, Bacon and their followers felt impelled to pour scorn on ancient learning in order to stimulate a spirit of critical inquiry, whereas others such as Harvey, Harrington and the Neoplatonists selectively absorbed doctrines from the past without any inhibition or sense of conflict. Harrington was as thoroughly versed in the arguments of classical republicanism, the *lex agraria* and the cyclical view of history, as in the politics of Machiavelli. But his contemporaries, Hobbes and Harvey, inspired him to construct a 'Model of Government' based on a scientific 'political anatomy' as demonstrable as Harveian physiology. Only by this means could the state be rescued from the inevitable tendency to decay and the course of history be arrested to secure the establishment of an immortal commonwealth. Central to Harrington's system was the 'Doctrine of Balance', a principle which was intended to infuse mathematical certainty into political theory, and which his first biographer thought as important as the discovery of the circulation of blood.[6] The Principle of Balance was derived from a quantitative analysis of changes in ownership of property during recent centuries, and complemented the statistical works of Harrington's Rota associate, William Petty, who was equally motivated by the belief that 'there is a *Political Arithmetic*, and a *Geometrical Justice* to be yet further cultivated in the World'.[7] Thus, Hobbes had powerful rivals in the attempt to construct a science of politics. This approach continued to attract adherents, as illustrated by a previously neglected but substantial writer, Peter Paxton, who represents the continuity of the Harringtonian tradition into the eighteenth century. Writing on anatomy and politics, Paxton sought to solve all problems by a 'plain historical Method, extending my proofs to such things only as are well known by Experience, or have the immediate Evidence of Sense, or are clear deductions from such'.[8]

[6] James Harrington, *Works*, ed. Toland (London, 1737), pp. xviii, 197–8.
[7] William Petty, *The Discourse made before the Royal Society . . . concerning the Use of Duplicate Proportion* (London, 1674), sig. A10v. For Petty see W. Letwin, *The Origins of Scientific Economics* (London, 1963), chap. 5.
[8] Peter Paxton, *An Essay concerning the Body of Man* (London, 1701), sig. A2v; J. A. W. Gunn, 'The *Civil Polity* of Peter Paxton', pp. 142–59 in this volume. For further work on Paxton, see Gunn, *Politics and Public Interest in the Seventeenth Century* (London, 1969), pp. 312–17.

Harrington's Principle of Balance was conceived with mathematical simplicity, but in expression it was shrouded in impene-
trable complexity and ambiguity. Macpherson has undertaken a
daring analysis of Balance and the operation of the Agrarian, in
order to explain apparent inconsistencies in Harrington's thought
in terms of his intuitive acceptance of 'bourgeois' or 'possessive
market' relations. In reply, New has put forward a rival interpretation of the Agrarian which is intended to buttress the 'utopian'
or 'social and political idealist' aspect of Harrington's thought,
while denying the central importance of his desire to facilitate a
possessive market economy.[9] Examining Harrington from a
different perspective, Pocock has emphasized the relevance of
Oceana to the constitutional debates of the Protectorate. The
Principle of Balance may have been specifically designed to display
the weakness of a second House recruited from the old peerage or
from military grandees.[10] Macpherson's interpretation of Hobbes
in 'bourgeois' terms has attracted rather more comment and
criticism.[11] The demonstration that *Leviathan* amalgamated advanced economic ideas with conventional and romantic or aristocratic elements, while also having relevance to the ideological
conflict of 1649–50 on *de facto* government and the Engagement,
provides a suggestive parallel to the debate over Harrington.[12]

Macpherson's *Possessive Individualism*, ever the source for
controversial interpretations, assailed the traditional doctrine that
the Levellers were pioneer advocates of universal manhood

[9] Macpherson, 'Harrington's Opportunity State', pp. 23–53 in this
volume, reproduced with slight modifications in Macpherson, *The Political
Theory of Possessive Individualism: Hobbes to Locke* (Oxford, 1962), pp. 160–
192. New, 'Harrington, a realist?'; Macpherson, 'Harrington as realist: a
rejoinder'; New, 'Harrington's Agrarian'; pp. 54–69 in this volume.
[10] J. G. A. Pocock, 'James Harrington and the Good Old Cause: a study
of the ideological context of his writings', *Journal of British Studies*, x (1970),
pp. 30–48.
[11] Macpherson, *Possessive Individualism*, pp. 9–106.
[12] Keith Thomas, 'The social origins of Hobbes's political thought' in
Hobbes Studies, ed. K. C. Brown (Oxford, 1965), pp. 185–236; Q. Skinner,
'The ideological context of Hobbes's political thought', *Historical Journal*,
ix (1966), pp. 286–317——, 'Conquest and consent: Thomas Hobbes and
the Engagement controversy' in *The Interregnum: The Quest for Settlement
1646–1662*, ed. G. E. Aylmer (London, 1972), pp. 79–98. For a generally
favourable review of Macpherson, see Hill, *Past and Present*, no. 24 (April
1963), pp. 86–9.

suffrage. The Levellers believed that all men had a natural right to vote, but Macpherson suggests that they consistently intended to exclude servants and alms-takers from the franchise. On his calculations, implementation of the Leveller proposals would have left two-thirds of the adult male population disfranchised; such a conclusion would severely qualify any claim that the Levellers were democrats in the modern sense.[13] None the less, the Levellers were, in Macpherson's view, consistent, since their notion of 'freedom as the active proprietorship of one's person and capacities' involved confining political rights to those who had not 'alienated the use of their capacities by entering a wage-contract'.[14] Thus there was, underlying the diverse writings of the Leveller party, a consistency of principle intelligible in terms of market relations. In response Davis argues that Macpherson's view of the Levellers may be correct if Maximilian Petty is taken as their representative, but that Rainsborough, who also spoke in the Putney debates, exhibits much more strongly democratic inclinations. Equally a wide selection of evidence from the *Moderate* has been cited to indicate awareness of the rights of the servant class.[15] Detailed examination of the Leveller movement indicates the need to take account of variations of opinion and the modification of policy according to political expediency. There may have been an underlying consensus of opinion among the Levellers, but some of its constituents are difficult to define. Nevertheless, the majority opinion undoubtedly envisaged a more liberal settlement than that designated by Macpherson. After embracing various social reforms, the commonwealth would evolve to the position where only apprentices, temporary household servants and possibly elderly or indigent persons dependent on public relief would be excluded from the vote.[16]

[13] Macpherson, *Possessive Individualism*, pp. 107–59, 290–2.
[14] *Ibid.*, pp. 142–4.
[15] J. C. Davis, 'The Levellers and democracy', pp. 70–8 in this volume. Roger Howell Jr and David E. Brewster, 'Reconsidering the Levellers: the evidence of the *Moderate*', pp. 79–100 in this volume.
[16] For an excellent exposition of this point of view see Keith Thomas, 'The Levellers and the franchise' in *The Interregnum: The Quest for Settlement*, ed. Aylmer, pp. 57–78.
See also A. L. Morton, *Leveller Democracy—Fact or Myth? (Our History*, pamphlet no. 51, 1968; reprinted in his *The World of The Ranters* (London, 1970), pp. 197–219).

Collective biography and bibliography of the Levellers and the Diggers is severely handicapped by lack of evidence about these shadowy figures who moved briefly into the public gaze during the mid-century constitutional crisis. Professor Aylmer has collated existing information on Leveller biography and provided a guide to sources which might serve as the basis for study of related problems.[17] New material is occasionally discovered. An edition of *A Declaration why the poor Inhabitants of Iver have begun to digge* (1650) sheds further light on the rapid spread of digging in 1649 and 1650. In addition to the five colonies previously known, the tract edited by Keith Thomas proves the existence of colonies in five more localities, and also provides evidence about supporters of the Iver petitioners.[18] Aylmer has edited *Englands Spirit Unfoulded* (1650?), composed by Winstanley himself with the intention of promoting acquiescence to the Engagement. Thus Winstanley (aligned with Dury, John Goodwin, Hobbes and Lilburne) tentatively expressed confidence in the republican regime, hoping that the Commonwealth might evolve into an effective vehicle for social reform. While in the short term the Diggers were willing to confine their activities to digging in commons and wastes, respecting customary rights of private property, they looked forward to the ultimate Kingdom of Christ under which the institution of private property would wither away. Hence there was no necessary incompatibility between the conformist *Englands Spirit Unfoulded* and the apocalyptic *Fire in the Bush*. Similarly, Dury, one of the staunchest supporters of the Engagement, predicted imminent apocalyptic turmoil, before the establishment of a final age of peace and harmony.[19] For long, the dating of *Fire in the Bush* was unsettled but Thomas establishes that it must have been composed at the beginning of March 1650.[20] The exact date of *Englands Spirit* remains obscure.

Dury was a puritan churchman, Winstanley a separatist. Both

[17] G. E. Aylmer, 'Gentlemen Levellers?', pp. 101–8 in this volume.
[18] Keith Thomas, 'Another Digger broadside', pp. 124–37 in this volume.
[19] 'Epistolical Discourse' by Dury in [anon.], *Clavis apocalyptica* (London, 1651).
[20] G. E. Aylmer, '*Englands Spirit Unfoulded*', pp. 109–23 in this volume; Keith Thomas, 'The date of Gerrard Winstanley's *Fire in the Bush*', pp. 138–41 in this volume. For the Engagement controversy, see J. M. Wallace, *Destiny his Choice: The Loyalism of Andrew Marvell* (Cambridge, 1968), chap. 1.

were millenarians. They are representative of the wide spectrum
of opinion which embraced millennial doctrines during the
Puritan Revolution. Fascination with the doctrine of the millennium linked academic theologians with mechanic preachers, or
parliamentary leaders with the humble Fifth Monarchists. Beyond
this common feeling there was great diversity on matters of
interpretation, although the millennium undoubtedly played a
cohesive role during the early stages of the Civil War, uniting the
parliamentary forces in the struggle with Antichrist and instilling
confidence in a successful outcome. Although general interest
among historians in puritan eschatology is a very recent phenomenon, millennial inspiration in the puritan party has long been
recognized. As Woodhouse commented, 'Daniel and Revelation
afforded a key to events, past and present, a vision of the future.
From these books the Millenarians derived a view of history and
a motive of revolution. And the pattern exhibited coloured the
thought of many who could not be described as active adherents,
so that one may speak of Millenarian doctrine as in a sense
typical.' Writing on Milton, Barker warned 'To disregard that
conception [millenarianism] would be to ignore one of the chief
sources of seventeenth-century idealism.'[21] As in post-apostolic
times, the promise of the millennium acted as an incentive to
prepare conditions on earth for the anticipated return of Christ.
Hence the unprecedented outburst of concern with social
planning during the Puritan Revolution. Ambitious proposals
were announced in utopian terms, which can often be related to
chiliastic motivation. *Macaria* (1641) was one of the first reform
tracts to adopt a utopian framework. The literary inspiration for
Macaria was provided by Caspar Stiblinus, the plan for state
regulation of technology and economic innovation by Gabriel
Plattes. But the general context was supplied by Samuel Hartlib,
close associate of Joseph Mede (author of the influential *Clavis
apocalyptica*) and editor of John Stoughton's rhapsodic *Felicitas
Ultimi Saeculi* (1640).[22] That millenarianism inspired *Macaria* will

[21] A. S. P. Woodhouse (ed.), *Puritanism and Liberty*, 2nd edn. (London,
1951), p. [41]. A. E. Barker, *Milton and The Puritan Dilemma* (Toronto,
1942), p. 194. Barker's interpretation is extended by M. Fixler, *Milton and
the Kingdoms of God* (London, 1964).
[22] Webster, 'The authorship and significance of *Macaria*', pp. 369–85 in
this volume. The editor is indebted to Miss Frances Yates for bringing to

cause no surprise, but Pocock's elucidation of the millennial framework of *Leviathan* establishes a perspective difficult to reconcile with current estimates of Hobbes's political philosophy.[23] Among recent studies which have drawn attention to the importance of millenarianism, Lamont's *Godly Rule* has made ambitious use of eschatology to discriminate between conflicting approaches to religious settlement between 1603 and 1660.[24] In order to facilitate comparison between groups as disparate as the Laudians and the Independents, Lamont elected to adopt Thrupp's general and figurative use of the term millennium for 'any conception of a perfect age to come, or of a perfect land to be made accessible'.[25] Given this definition millenarianism may be applied to all societies, periods or political visions however conservative or radical. Capp has appealed for a more restrained approach to millenarianism in which application of the term is restricted to those groups which in seventeenth-century theological usage would have been designated millenarian.[26] It may be freely admitted that apocalyptic imagery was widely employed and that curiosity about the millennium was pervasive, but belief in the imminent personal reign of Christ on earth for a thousand years

his notice the following brief survey of the life and writings of Stiblinus and facsimile reproduction of his utopia: Luigi Firpo, *Kaspar Stiblin utopista con il testo originale del de Eudaemonensium Republica* (Turin, 1959).
[23] J. G. A. Pocock, 'Time, history and eschatology in the thought of Thomas Hobbes' in *The Diversity of History: Essays in honour of Sir Herbert Butterfield*, eds J. H. Elliott and H. G. Koenigsberger (London, 1970), pp. 149-98.
[24] W. M. Lamont, *Godly Rule: Politics and Religion, 1603-60* (London, 1969); see also his 'Puritanism as history and historiography: some further thoughts', *Past and Present*, no. 44 (Aug. 1969), pp. 133-46. See also C. Webster (ed.), *Samuel Hartlib and the Advancement of Learning* (Cambridge 1970); C. Hill, *Antichrist in Seventeenth-Century England* (London, 1971); F. A. Yates, *The Rosicrucian Enlightenment* (London, 1972); B. S. Capp, *The Fifth Monarchy Men* (London, 1972). For a general consideration of prophecy, see Keith Thomas, *Religion and the Decline of Magic* (London, 1971), chap. 5.
[25] S. Thrupp (ed.), *Millennial Dreams in Action* (The Hague, 1962), Introduction, p. 12, where the author admits that the term is 'applied figuratively'.
[26] B. S. Capp, '*Godly Rule* and English millenarianism', pp. 386-98 in this volume. W. M. Lamont, 'Richard Baxter, the Apocalypse and the Mad Major', pp. 399-426 in this volume. Capp, 'The millennium and eschatology in England', pp. 427-34 in this volume.

was restricted to limited and transient groups. Between this extreme and a general belief in progress lay a whole spectrum of opinion more or less influenced by millennial doctrine. Unless attention is paid to such distinctions, the role of millenarianism in seventeenth-century thought will not be precisely understood.

Whatever the disagreements over the extent of adherence to millennial doctrine, it is now recognized that this doctrine played a leading part in securing dedication to wholesale social and political reform between 1640 and 1660. Thereafter, it is generally alleged, millenarianism was rapidly extinguished following the last desperate flourish of the Fifth Monarchy Men in 1659. The emergence of political stability and the control of separatism, superintended by the ordered world-view of the Royal Society and of Newton, are thought to have stultified millenarian expression. With the Restoration, the nation appears to embark on an age of reason and progress. On the other hand, as Capp recognizes, it was occasionally found necessary to repress millenarians after 1660. Lamont has provided detailed evidence for Richard Baxter's investigations of the Apocalypse in 1686, while Hill has described the apocalyptic speculations of the Cambridge scholar John Mason.[27] At a popular level millenarianism exerted a slight but continuous influence, giving comfort to the oppressed classes and, occasionally, providing the inspiration for protest.[28] Baptists, Muggletonians and Huguenot refugees periodically became fired with millennial zeal during the latter part of the seventeenth century. What is more surprising is the intense attraction which the millennium had for Anglican intellectuals and advocates of the new science. The tradition of interpretation of Daniel and Revelation stemming from Joseph Mede went on to culminate in Isaac Newton's *Observations upon the Prophecies of Daniel and the Apocalypse of St. John*. Geological and astronomical theories were applied to provide a scientific basis for the story of creation and the final conflagration; chronology was investigated with mathematical precision. Then, during the reign of James II the millennium assumed an added political significance, inspiring

[27] Capp, 'The millennium and eschatology in England', p. 432 in this volume. Lamont, pp. 399–426 in this volume. Christopher Hill, 'John Mason and the end of the world', in *Puritanism and Revolution* (London, 1958), pp. 323–36.
[28] E. P. Thompson, *The Making of the English Working Class*, revised edn (London, 1968), pp. 52–8.

the Anglican church to opposition with the assurance that Babylon would be defeated and a messianic monarchy established.[29]

The transformation in natural philosophy which took place in the seventeenth century is generally called the 'Scientific Revolution'. Of the scale of this modification in world-view and the acceleration in positive development of the specialized sciences, from mathematics to natural history, there can be no doubt. But the causes contributing to the Scientific Revolution and the spectacular rise of English science in the seventeenth century have been the subject of protracted dispute. By concentrating on the case-history approach, historians of science have been able to describe the emergence of important facets of modern science without making more than incidental reference to the wider historical context. General histories of early modern science have almost invariably been composed from this point of view, although increasing reference to methodological or metaphysical factors, or recognition of the complexities of outlook among major innovators has ensured that this branch of history of ideas does not wholly lack distinction. But having a little extended their horizons, historians of science have generally not been willing to concede that science was integrally related to a range of other developments. Even the close interaction between science and technology in the seventeenth century has been disputed in order to maintain the complete and aristocratic autonomy of modern science.[30] Historians of science have fallen into the fallacy

[29] E. Tuveson, *Millennium and Utopia: A Study in the Background of the Idea of Progress* (New York, 1964); F. E. Manuel, *A Portrait of Isaac Newton* (Cambridge, Mass., 1968), pp. 206–9, 361–80. M. C. Jacob and W. A. Lockwood, 'Political millenarianism and Burnet's *Sacred Theory*', *Science Studies*, ii (1972), pp. 265–79.

[30] For recent defences of this position see: A. R. Hall, 'Merton revisited; or science and society in the seventeenth century', *History of Science*, ii (1963), pp. 1–16; ——, 'On the historical singularity of the Scientific Revolution of the seventeenth century' in Elliott and Koenigsberger (eds), *op. cit.*, pp. 199–221; ——, 'Science, technology and utopia in the seventeenth century' in Mathias (ed.), *op. cit.*, pp. 33–53; M. Hesse, 'Hermeticism and historiography: an apology for internal history of science', *Minnesota Studies in the Philosophy of Science*, v (1970), pp. 134–60. For a debate on this subject between Rattansi and Hesse, see M. Teich and R. M. Young (eds), *Changing Perspectives in the History of Science* (London, 1973), pp. 127–66. For a summary of recent historiography of science see Kearney, 'Puritanism and science: problems of definition', pp. 219–21 in this volume.

of legislating for the past, of predetermining the scope of evidence required for the explanation of scientific change. This viewpoint has been termed 'restrictive history' in the context of the claim that utopian writings lacked serious scientific or technological commitment.[31] Restrictive history states that 'Utopian idealism in England . . . had nothing to do with science directly; it based no expectations on the hope of scientific progress'.[32] In a similar manner reference to millenarianism, Hermeticism, Neoplatonism, puritanism or other major religious, political, economic and technological movements has been rigorously excluded from the history of science. On minor technical issues this approach may be adequate; but it inevitably leads to distortion if major intellectual developments, scientific education or the emergence of scientific organizations are under consideration, or if an assessment is being made of the world-views of leading natural philosophers. The more attention is turned away from modern science towards a reconstruction of the idea of nature prevailing in the seventeenth century, the more important it becomes to abandon a restrictive point of view and to consider science and technology in terms of local religious and socio-economic developments. Science may then be seen in terms of priorities which the seventeenth century would have recognized.

Hessen's pioneer study of Newton has paved the way for social interpretations of other major innovators. By illustrating dependence on economic and technological developments or affiliation with the magical traditions of the renaissance, a new perspective has been provided on Bacon, Gilbert and Harvey.[33] Pagel high-

[31] Webster, 'The authorship and significance of *Macaria*', pp. 379–85 in this volume.
[32] A. R. Hall, 'Science, technology and utopia in the seventeenth century', in Mathias (ed.), *op. cit.*, p. 40.
[33] B. Hessen, 'The social and economic roots of Newton's *Principia*', in N. Bukharin (ed.), *Science at the Crossroads* (London, 1931), pp. 151–76.
B. Farrington, *Francis Bacon, Philosopher of Industrial Science* (New York, 1949); P. Rossi, *Francis Bacon: from Magic to Science* (London, 1968); E. Zilsel, 'The origins of William Gilbert's scientific method', *Jour. Hist. Ideas*, ii (1941), pp. 1–32.
P. Rossi, 'Sulla valutazione delle arti meccaniche nei secoli XVI e XVII', *Rivista critica di storia filosofia*, ii (1956), pp. 126–48; P. M. Rattansi, 'The social interpretation of science in the seventeenth century' in Mathias (ed.), *op. cit.*, pp. 1–32. For a valuable historical perspective see Keith Thomas, *Religion and the Decline of Magic*.

lighted Harvey's formulation of a consistent neo-Aristotelian biological philosophy while underlining his debt to renaissance circle symbolism.[34] In turning to the neglected question of the evolution of Harvey's ideas Hill warns 'that we should never consider ideas in abstraction from the social environment of the thinker'. In line with Curtis's perceptive observation that Harvey's *De motu cordis* (1628) placed emphasis on the primacy of the heart, while his later writings (1649 and 1651) favoured primacy of blood, Hill suggests that the transition was 'stimulated by the experience of living in a republic'.[35] His paper also suggests interesting relationships between Harvey, the parliamentarians and the prevalent heresy of mortalism.

These novel interpretations are not congenial to leading students of Harvey. Although Pagel and Whitteridge represent very different approaches to Harvey, they agree in asserting that on the subject of embryological and physiological primacy 'there was no basic change in the conclusions which he drew from his early embryological observation, throughout the thirty-five years that lay between the Lecture notes [1616] and the work *On generation* [1651]'.[36] Nevertheless, while the evidence cited indicates that Harvey had the germ of the idea of embryological primacy in 1616 and still maintained the important physiological role of the heart in 1651, both critics are obliged to accept Hill's basic point that there are distinct differences of emphasis between *De motu cordis* and *De generatione*. The drift away from Aristotelian heart-centred theory may have been caused primarily by the gradual maturation of Harvey's physiological ideas and in particular by the findings of his remarkable work on early chick embryology.[37]

[34] W. Pagel, *William Harvey's Biological Ideas* (Basel and New York, 1967); —, 'William Harvey Revisited', *History of Science*, viii (1969), pp. 1–31; ix (1970), pp. 1–41.

[35] Hill, 'William Harvey and the idea of monarchy', pp. 160–81 in this volume.

[36] Pagel, *William Harvey's Biological Ideas*, pp. 341–6; p. 342. G. Whitteridge, 'William Harvey: a royalist and no parliamentarian', pp. 182–8 in this volume; ——, *William Harvey and Circulation of the Blood* (London, 1971), pp. 215–19 for a fuller discussion of Harvey's dilemma over primacy. For Hill's reply see 'William Harvey (no parliamentarian, no heretic) and the idea of monarchy', pp. 189–96 in this volume.

[37] C. Webster, 'Harvey's *De generatione*: its origins and relevance to the theory of circulation', *British Journal for the History of Science*, iii (1967),

Hill's paper draws attention to the liberal use of analogy in the seventeenth century. It has been noted above that Harveian physiology exerted considerable influence on both Hobbes and Harrington. Conversely, political models were commonly used to support physiological beliefs. Continuing acceptance of a tightly-co-ordinated universe allowed a more flexible use of analogy than has been admitted in more recent science.[38]

Factors influencing continental and especially English science in its crucial formative phase are the subject of a group of papers by Mason, Kearney, Hill, Rabb and Shapiro. As the Reformation provided a backcloth to European science, so English science rose into prominence along with puritanism. A focus for debate has been provided by the hypothesis that experimental science, as a corollary of the protestant ethic, was one of the most important cultural manifestations of the Reformation. English society, strongly influenced by Calvinism and deeply involved in the development of science and scientific institutions, constitutes an ideal test case in which to examine the relations between science and religion. Reference to religious factors has naturally led to a consideration of social ethic, and thence, to a wide range of socio-economic factors. The foundations have been laid for a comprehensive social interpretation of early modern science.[39]

Although the 'protestantism/puritanism-science hypothesis'

---

pp. 262–74, cites evidence that *De generatione* was completed by the outset of the Civil Wars, suggesting that experience of living in a republic could not have caused the change in Harvey's views.

[38] For a typical example of a disputation discussing the primacy of the heart in terms of political analogy, see Albert Kyper, *Collegium Medicum* (Leyden, 1655), 'Disputatio physicis de principatu cordis'. For wider discussion see F. Oakley, 'Jacobean political theology: the absolute and ordinary powers of the king', *Jour. Hist. Ideas*, xxix (1968), pp. 323–46; J. E. McGuire, 'Atoms and the analogy of nature', *Studies in the History and Philosophy of Science*, i (1970), pp. 3–58.

[39] For the classic statement of this position derived from Weber and Tawney, see R. K. Merton, 'Science, technology and society in seventeenth century England', *Osiris*, iv (1938), pp. 414–565; published separately with a new introduction (New York, 1970). See also E. Zilsel, 'The sociological roots of science', *American Journal of Sociology*, xlvii (1942), pp. 544–62, and the other works cited in n. 32 above.

For a more cautious view, see G. N. Clark, *Science and Social Welfare in the Age of Newton* (Oxford, 1937; 2nd edn, 1949; reprinted with additions, 1970).

comprises one factor only in the wide-ranging socio-economic analyses of Merton and Hill, it has become a focal point for debate. Merton has described in detail the factors in protestant theology favourable to the active life and to participation in experimental science, using the writings of Baxter and Boyle to illustrate the explicit nature of this relationship. Mason has proceeded in a similar manner, citing Wilkins as evidence for the 'congruity between Calvinist theology and the new theories of modern science'.[40] On the whole, Merton has placed emphasis on the broad sanction given by Calvinism to experimental science, whereas other studies have suggested that Calvinist theology was instrumental in determining the formation of opinion on such specific questions as the status of laws of nature, and the theory of matter.[41] Thus in the early modern period religion not only influenced general social attitudes, but permeated science at all levels.

Following the Weber-Merton tradition, then, it appears that protestantism, or Calvinism in particular, provided a favourable environment for the development of experimental science in Western Europe. Nevertheless it must not be assumed axiomatically that the level of scientific achievement in areas under Catholic domination was negligible. Conditions in Catholic Europe were constantly changing, and local circumstances were sometimes favourable to productive scientific activity. It may even be claimed that the small English Catholic population contributed disproportionately to experimental science and to the growth of

[40] S. F. Mason, 'Science and religion in seventeenth century England', pp. 199–200; pp. 197–217 in this volume. For a fuller discussion see his 'The Scientific Revolution and the Protestant Reformation', *Annals of Science*, ix (1953), pp. 64–87, 154–75; also R. Hooykaas, *Religion and the Rise of Modern Science* (Edinburgh and London, 1972) and his earlier writings cited here. For a brief study of one Calvinist group see L. E. Loemker, 'Leibniz and the Herborn Encyclopaedists', *Jour. Hist. Ideas*, xxii (1961), pp. 323–38.

[41] M. B. Foster, 'The Christian doctrine of creation and the rise of modern natural science', *Mind*, xliii (1934), pp. 446–68; xliv (1935), pp. 439–66; xlv (1936), pp. 1–27. F. Oakley, 'Christian theology and Newtonian science: the rise of the concepts of laws of nature', *Church History*, xxx (1961), pp. 443–70. J. E. McGuire, 'Boyle's conception of nature', *Jour. Hist. Ideas*, xxxiii (1972), pp. 523–42.

E. Zilsel, 'The genesis of the concept of physical law', *Philosophical Review*, li (1942), pp. 245–79, adopts an economic interpretation.

Cartesianism. In the *Past and Present* debate, Rabb in particular has stressed the importance of the Catholic contribution to scientific discovery.[42] It is however often not clear whether such instances are cited to assert the autonomy of science, or whether it is claimed that religious and social factors operative in Catholic areas are relevant to the explanation of scientific change. Whatever point of view he adopts, the investigator must consider each specific historical situation on its merits. The explanation of the rise of experimental science in England by reference to the protestant ethic therefore in no way precludes reference to other factors in other situations.

Hill has been less concerned with the complex of positive scientific developments which are collectively known as the Scientific Revolution, than with the intellectual movements relevant to the English Revolution. Whatever their ultimate importance, Baconianism, Paracelsianism and Comenian pansophism must be seen as occupying an important position in the world-view of puritan intellectuals and artisans. The puritan social ethic, with its strong scientific and technological element, heightened by utopian and millenarian aspirations, shaped the intellectual development of the groups which laid the foundations of organized experimental science between 1640 and 1660. The London group founded by Haak, the Hartlib circle, the Cambridge Platonists and the Oxford Experimental Philosophy Club represent the major dimensions of the movement. Wilkins, Wallis, Goddard, Petty, Worsley, Hartlib, Boyle, More and Cudworth were some of its leading activists. Although Hill's Ford Lectures were primarily concerned with the period before 1640, they also provide a vivid impression of the rich intellectual legacy of pre-Civil War puritanism.[43]

In replies to Hill, considerable attention has been devoted to non-puritan aspects of English science. Kearney sees Gresham

[42] T. K. Rabb, 'Religion and the rise of modern science', pp. 262–79 in this volume. Kearney, p. 240 in this volume. F. Russo, 'Rôle respectif du catholicisme et du protestantisme dans le développement des sciences aux XVIe et XVIIe siècles', *Jl of World History*, iii (1957), pp. 854–80.

[43] C. Hill, *Intellectual Origins of the English Revolution*, (Oxford, 1965); The Ford Lectures 1962, reproduced in an abbreviated form in the *Listener*, 31 May, 7 June, 14 June, 21 June and 5 July 1962. See also D. Stimson, 'Puritanism and the new philosophy in seventeenth century England', *Bull. Inst. Hist. Med.*, iii (1935), pp. 321–34.

College not as a middle-class puritan educational venture, but as an institution dependent upon academics and the cultural traditions of universities.[44] Indeed Gresham may have had more varied fortunes than is generally supposed. After a high peak of activity before 1630 it may have declined, until Hartlib's associates pressed for drastic reforms aimed at bringing Gresham into line with puritan utilitarianism.[45] The non-puritan and non-protestant scientific contributions identified by Kearney and Rabb in no way diminish the scientific achievements of the puritan community.[46] From a historical point of view, puritan science constituted an important factor in the revolutionary situation and puritan natural philosophers came to play a conspicuous part in affairs during the Interregnum. It is only the relevance of puritanism to modern science which remains in question. The nature of the solution to this problem depends on the terms in which it is presented. In general there has been a tendency to depreciate the importance of puritanism and puritan intellectuals by asserting their lack of scientific sophistication, excessive utilitarianism, undue regard for theology and facile imitation of scientific undertakings which had their roots elsewhere. When pressed to an extreme, these arguments are used to affirm the absolute independence of scientific activity. Alternatively, other religious groups or theological positions have been held to have fostered the development of modern science. After taking account of the fragmentation and diversification of puritanism, Shapiro has claimed that the centre of gravity of the scientific movement lay with the 'firm alliance between religious moderates' which drew its membership from both the puritan and Anglican parties. But this 'Erasmian' or 'latitudinarian' position is defined so broadly as to embrace all but the extreme separatists, Laudians and Catholics.[47] Since latitudinarianism largely subsumes puritanism,

[44] Kearney, 'Puritanism, capitalism and the Scientific Revolution', pp. 225–9 in this volume. F. R. Johnson, 'Gresham College: precursor of the Royal Society', *Jour. Hist. Ideas*, i (1940), pp. 413–38.
[45] C. Webster (ed.), *Samuel Hartlib and the Advancement of Learning*, pp. 59–60.
[46] For the debate between Hill, Kearney and Rabb, see pp. 218–85 in this volume; T. K. Rabb, 'Puritanism and the rise of experimental science in England', *Jl of World History*, vii (1962), pp. 46–67.
[47] B. J. Shapiro, 'Latitudinarianism and science in seventeenth century England', pp. 286–316 in this volume; ——, *John Wilkins 1614–1672. An*

Hill's thesis is only slightly modified, and the religious associations of science are certainly not defined more precisely, by the introduction of a more diffuse category. All-embracing uses of 'millenarian' and 'Rosicrucian' by Lamont and Yates respectively have similarly tended to obscure fundamental divergences of outlook within these categories. It is also important to recognize the evolutionary character of puritanism during the English Revolution. As divergent attitudes developed, there emerged issues which united sections of the puritan movement with Anglicans and in opposition to more radical groups. In the important case of the defence of the universities as seminaries for the ministry, an alliance of this sort became involved in resistance to secularization and to a system of science-based higher education proposed by the radical puritan element. Hence, paradoxically, the famous Wilkins circle at Oxford became in at least one respect an obstruction to the advancement of experimental science.[48]

The Royal Society, established in 1660, overwhelmingly influences estimates of seventeenth-century English science. For the period before 1660, investigators of scientific organization have sought primarily to determine the origins of the Society; thereafter, the character of English science is discussed in terms of the researches conducted by the Fellows. There has been in consequence a great concentration of attention on Wilkins and his small group of associates, for the period from 1645 into the first, fertile decade of the Society. The latter as the first permanent scientific association has served as a test case for the various hypotheses concerning the social relations of science. No consensus has been reached. The Royal Society is seen variously as puritan, latitudinarian or Anglican in its inspiration. As a scientific organization its labours have been regarded as essentially utilitarian by Merton, and non-utilitarian by Purver. Apart from

---

Intellectual Biography (Berkeley and Los Angeles, 1969); D. S. Kemsley, 'Religious influences in the rise of modern science: a review and criticism, particularly of the "protestant-puritan ethic" theory', *Annals of Science,* xxiv (1968), pp. 199–226.

[48] A. G. Debus (ed.), *Science and Education in the Seventeenth Century* (London, 1970); C. Webster, 'William Dell and the idea of university' in Teich and Young, *op. cit.*, pp. 110–26; C. Hill, 'Radical critics of Oxford and Cambridge in the 1650s' in *Universities in Politics,* ed. J. W. Baldwin and C. Goldthwaite (Baltimore, 1972), pp. 107–32.

Merton's pioneer analysis of the *Philosophical Transactions*, most investigators have not relied on rigorously quantitative methods, although their conclusions have inevitably involved the use of quantitative terms. One might therefore expect a completely statistical approach to be attempted, and it is this method which has been adopted in the most recent *Past and Present* paper published in this anthology, 'Civil War politics, religion and the Royal Society', by Lotte Mulligan.[49] Mulligan sets out to examine the relationship between interest in science and political and religious attitudes in a simple quantitative way. Ideally such an exhaustive analysis should provide unambiguous evidence about the religious, political and social bias of the Royal Society. Recognizing the complexity of this question, the author has wisely focused on certain basic issues. The analysis has been limited to Fellows who were over sixteen in 1642. This group has been analysed with respect to (a) affiliation on 'politico-religious' issues between 1642 and 1644, (b) subject specialization in the Society. The typical science enthusiast of the 1660s, Mulligan concludes, emerged from a 'royalist, Anglican, university-educated gentleman' background. He was not 'middle-class, mercantile, puritan, politically radical, unacademic or utilitarian'.[50] The statistical results appear unequivocally to refute the puritanism- (or latitudinarianism)-science hypothesis, while generally supporting the view that science was the prerogative of the conservative Anglican gentry. At this point the author, rather than face the positive implications of her statistical results, falls back on the generally negative nature of her correlations to conclude that 'science correlated less with puritanism or latitudinarianism than with the waning role of religion'.[51] Hence Mulligan, at the end of her elaborate statistical study, appears to be drifting towards one of two long-cherished views, either that science is autonomous, or, alternatively, that it was generated by the stimulus of secularization.

Statistics may expose fundamental principles, or they can lead to conclusions which are self-evidently false. In the present instance, it is unlikely that *Past and Present* contributors will accept Mulligan's statistical apparatus as the last word on her

[49] pp. 317–46 in this volume.
[50] p. 336 in this volume.
[51] p. 339 in this volume.

subject. It may be argued that a balanced impression of the Royal Society is not obtained by giving equal weight to the 162 Fellows who had passed adolescence by 1642. The day-to-day activities of the Society are known in detail, and it is apparent that most Fellows gave only their names to the Society, withholding both their subscriptions and their attendance. Only a minority displayed distinctive scientific interests, and the chief impetus for research came from a small active nucleus of less than twenty members. There is consequently little point in assessing the social and religious bias of a society on the basis of its inactive, nominal, general membership. The other factor in Mulligan's correlation is politico-religious alignment. Here the primary categories are notoriously difficult to define. The author adopts the relatively straightforward criterion of 'parliamentarian' versus 'royalist' alignment for the period 1642–4. Critics will undoubtedly claim that there are some cases of wrong categorization. More seriously they will suggest that the estimate is made for a time when royalist support was at its greatest; after 1644, defection to parliament occurred on a large scale. This raises the problem of changing alignment, and demonstrates the limitation involved in analysing the situation in terms of two parties. Finally, as Hill has rightly insisted, it is not possible to use the terms parliamentarian and puritan (or royalist and Anglican) as synonyms. Mulligan moves too easily from statements about political alignment to conclusions about fundamental religious commitment. Before it is possible to produce a satisfying solution in statistical terms, it will be necessary to solve certain basic problems about the origins and early history of the Royal Society which are not recognized by Mulligan.[52] Then, it must be established whether the Royal Society, and its immediate precursors, were sufficiently dominant to merit exclusive attention in the investigation of the social origins of modern science!

Before 1660 the Wilkins circle was only one of a considerable network of groups of experimental philosophers operating in

[52] Thomas Sprat, *History of the Royal Society*, eds J. I. Cope and H. W. Jones (St Louis and London, 1956); M. Purver, *The Royal Society: Concept and Creation* (London, 1967); C. Webster, 'The origins of the Royal Society', *History of Science*, vi (1967), pp. 106–28; articles by A. R. Hall and M. B. Hall, C. Hill and P. M. Rattansi in *Notes and Records of the Royal Society*, vol. xxiii, no. 2 (1968); D. S. Kemsley, *op. cit.*

London, the university towns, the provinces and Ireland. Thereafter the picture was not essentially different. Fellows carried on their activities within various informal groups, as well as contributing to the Society's meetings and to the *Philosophical Transactions* issued in London. Even in its active early years, the Society was never able entirely to dominate the English scientific scene, although its continental reputation might have implied such an ascendancy. After little more than a decade, the Society suffered a rapid decline, both in membership and reputation; the *Philosophical Transactions* were interrupted, and its grand Baconian programme was not fulfilled. But the institutional weakness of the Royal Society has attracted remarkably little comment. Mrs 'Espinasse's brief but perceptive characterization of ideological reorientation among the Fellows almost alone provides a contrast to the more orthodox recitals of scientific accomplishment.[53] Such eminent Fellows as Hooke, Boyle, Ray and Newton were indeed responsible for striking advances in the specialized sciences, but it is important to recognize that their creative energies were only partly devoted to the Society. The Mechanical and Newtonian philosophies were the ultimate legacy of this period, but the immediate social impact and institutional success of the Royal Society depended upon its ability to sustain the momentum of the Baconian programme. Only during its first years were the optimistic goals of the *Instauratio Magna* constantly borne in mind. Only while inspired by the millennial zeal taken over from the Puritans could its supporters believe that the Society under its patron the messianic King Charles II, would lead the nation, and Christendom, towards a new utopia.[54]

[53] M. 'Espinasse, 'The decline and fall of Restoration science', pp. 347–68 in this volume. For literary criticisms of the Royal Society, see H. W. Jones, 'Mid-seventeenth century science: some polemics', *Osiris*, ix (1950), pp. 254–74; R. H. Syfret, 'Some early reactions to the Royal Society', *Notes and Records of the Royal Society*, vol. vii, no. 2 (1950), pp. 207–58; vol. viii, no. 1 (1951), pp. 20–64; J. I. Cope, *Joseph Glanvill, Anglican Apologist* (St Louis, 1956).

[54] Sprat, *op. cit.*, p. 437. 'But if . . . our *Nation* shall lay hold of this opportunity, to deserve the applause of Mankind, the force of this *Example* will be irresistably prevalent in all *Countries* round about us; the State of *Christendom* will soon obtain a new face; while this *Halcyon Knowledge* is breeding, all *Tempests* will cease.' See also pp. 2–3, 150–3, 436–8.

II

HARRINGTON'S 'OPPORTUNITY STATE'*

C. B. Macpherson

Until a few years ago Harrington's place in the history of political theory seemed secure. He had discovered a relation between property distribution and political power that had only been glimpsed by earlier writers, had formulated it systematically, and used it successfully to explain political change. He had shown not only that the relation did prevail in history, but also that it was a necessary relation; and that, in the measure that its necessity was understood, a permanently satisfactory frame of government could be fitted to any nation.

Harrington thought of himself as a scientist of politics rather than a philosopher, and the philosophers have generally left him alone. It has been the historians, not least the economic historians, who have given him his reputation. His handsome niche in the modern temple of fame was cemented and elegantly decorated by Professor Tawney's Raleigh Lecture of 1941: Harrington was 'the first English thinker to find the cause of political upheaval in antecedent social change'; his originality 'consisted primarily in his analysis of the constitutional consequences of English economic development in the century and a half preceding the Civil War'.[1] But in calling Harrington as a witness for what was to become a highly controversial interpretation of the economic changes of that period, Professor Tawney put him in an unexpectedly exposed position, and Harrington now seems in some danger

* From no. 17 (April 1960).
[1] 'Harrington's interpretation of his age', *Proc. Brit. Academy*, xxvii (1941), p. 200.

of being left a casualty of the battle over 'the rise of the gentry'. Mr Hill's valuable but too brief essay,[2] putting Harrington in longer historical perspective and emphasizing the place of the people in his theory, has done much to restore his position. But something remains to be done.

With all the attention Harrington has had in the last ten years, two central ambiguities in his theory have remained unexamined. First, in a theory which hinges almost entirely on the balance of property between the few and the many, the nobility and the people, Harrington is ambiguous as to whether the gentry are included in the former or in the latter. At different stages of his analysis he puts them now in one category, now in the other. Second, the central concept of the balance, or overbalance, is itself ambiguous to the point of apparent contradiction. In the statements of the general principle of the balance, and in the demonstration that England is ready for a commonwealth, it is the overbalance of property in the few or the many (i.e., possession of more than half the land by the few or the many) that determines the system of government, and a commonwealth is consistent only with the overbalance being in the many. But once Harrington's commonwealth is set up, a law which would enable one per cent of the citizens to acquire all the land is said to prevent them overbalancing the rest of the people, and this law is relied upon to secure the property basis of the commonwealth. The principle of the balance, used to establish the commonwealth, appears to be abrogated by the establishment of the commonwealth.

The two ambiguities do not cancel each other. But both are understandable on certain assumptions about the nature of seventeenth-century English society which Harrington can be shown, on other evidence, to have entertained. When the ambiguities are examined, Harrington's theory appears less systematic but perhaps more realistic than it has sometimes been made out to be. Harrington emerges neither as the illogical proponent of a declining gentry nor as the historian whose insight into English society, while novel, was limited to the effects of the disappearance of military tenure. I shall argue that Harrington thought that the gentry in 1656 had less than half the land, and based his case for a gentry-led commonwealth on that assumption; that he saw far enough into the bourgeois nature of English seventeenth-century

[2] Christopher Hill, *Puritanism and Revolution* (London, 1958), chap. 10.

society to assume that the gentry did, and always would, accept and support the bourgeois social order which then existed and which the rest of the people wanted; and that this assumption was essential to his whole political thought.

The term 'bourgeois' has become one of the least precise in historical and political writing. But since it stands for a concept that is central to the interpretation offered in this essay, it may be well to state now the sense in which it is being used. By bourgeois society I mean a society in which the relations between men are dominated by the market; in which, that is to say, land and labour, as well as moveable wealth and goods made for consumption, are treated as commodities to be bought and sold and contracted for with a view to profit and accumulation, and where men's relations to others are set largely by their ownership of these commodities and the success with which they utilize that ownership to their own profit. Alternatively, bourgeois society may be defined in terms of prevalent moral values, for a society cannot be dominated by the market unless the appropriate moral values are widely accepted. So defined, bourgeois society is one in which accumulation of wealth through the market (in the broad sense, including the market for land and labour) is regarded as honourable or even natural, and in which justice is the performance of contract rather than commutative or distributive justice.

I

THE BALANCE AND THE GENTRY

Harrington's principle of the balance seems quite straightforward. The location of political power, as between the rule ('empire') of one man, the few or the many, must, except for short-run periods of disequilibrium, correspond to the distribution of property (in most countries, of land) between the one, the few, and the many. Thus:[3]

> such (except it be in a city that has little or no land, and whose revenue is in trade) as is the proportion or balance

---

[3] *Oceana*, p. 37; cf. *Prerogative of Popular Government*, pp. 227, 270; *Art of Lawgiving*, p. 363; *System of Politics*, p. 467 (where the proportion is given as two-thirds). Page references throughout this article are to the 1771 edition of James Harrington, *The Oceana and Other Works*.

of dominion or property in land, such is the nature of the empire.

If one man be sole landlord of a territory, or overbalance the people, for example three parts in four, . . . his empire is absolute monarchy.

If the few or a nobility, or a nobility with the clergy be landlords, or overbalance the people to the like proportion, it makes the *Gothic* balance . . . and the empire is mix'd monarchy . . .

And if the whole people be landlords, or hold the lands so divided among them, that no one man, or number of men, within the compass of the *few* or *aristocracy*, overbalance them, the empire (without the interposition of force) is a commonwealth.

The necessary correspondence of the form of government with the distribution of property is presented as a deduction from self-evident propositions. Whichever of the one, the few, or the many has the power to dominate the others will do so. Since men must eat, whoever can feed them has their support. Whoever has the most land can feed and therefore command the largest army. Men depend upon riches 'not of choice . . . but of necessity and by the teeth: for as much as he who wants bread, is his servant that will feed him; if a man thus feeds a whole people, they are under his empire'.[4] Thus the distribution of property determines the distribution of political power. Disalignment between the two distributions may arise either through a group without the requisite proportion of property seizing political power, or through a change in the distribution of property not accompanied by the appropriate change in political power. In both cases, however, it follows from the postulates that an equilibrium (either the old or a new one) will be re-established. Harrington was mainly interested in the second of these kinds of change. Here he saw only one possible outcome: the old ruling class, without sufficient resources to maintain its rule, must sooner or later be overthrown by those who had the bulk of the property.

Hence, in order to have stable government, the balance of power must correspond to the balance of property. It was necessary also, for stable government, that the balance of property be

[4] *Oceana*, p. 37.

decisively in the one or the few or the many. They must have substantially more than half the property, for if one party has only about half and the rest have the other half 'the government becoms a very shambles', each constantly attempting to subdue the other.[5] And since the balance of property could shift from various causes unforeseen by human providence,[6] it was necessary, in order to perpetuate a stable government of any type, to impose some law which would prevent a decisive shift in the balance of property.

This is the substance of the famous theory of the balance. Although the principle is stated with complete generality ('such as is the proportion or balance of . . . property in land, such is the nature of the empire') the only application Harrington makes of it is as between one man, the few or a nobility, and the whole people. It is here that the first ambiguity enters. The few or the nobility is used sometimes to include, sometimes to exclude, the gentry.

In the statement of the general principle of the balance quoted above, while there is no definition of 'the few or a nobility', the small feudal nobility is presumably meant, for the overbalance of property in their hands is made to correspond to the Gothic balance, which is Harrington's term for the feudal order.

In the historical account of the change in the English balance of property from Henry VII to the Civil War it is quite clear that the nobility is limited to the feudal peerage at the beginning and the Stuart peerage at the end, never numbering more than two or three hundred men. Down to the reign of Henry VII, we are told, the balance of land was in the nobility, the great feudal lords who, having the military services of their tenants at their disposal, 'got the trick of . . . setting up and pulling down their kings according to their various interests. . .'.[7] Henry VII abated the power of the nobility by his statutes of population, of retainers, and of alienations. The first, by requiring the maintenance of houses of husbandry, did in effect 'amortize a great part of the lands to the hold and possession of the yeomanry or middle people', men 'of som substance, that might keep hinds and servants, and set the plow a going'; these men 'were much unlink'd from dependence upon their lords', who thus in effect lost their infantry.[8] The

[5] Ibid., p. 38; cf. System, p. 466.   [6] Prerogative, p. 270, Art of L., p. 364.
[7] Oceana, p. 64.   [8] Ibid., p. 64.

27

statute of retainers cut off their cavalry. The statute of alienations encouraged them to sell lands in order to keep up their positions, now rather as courtiers than as country nobility. The rest of the shift in the balance Harrington describes in two sentences: Henry VIII,[9]

> dissolving the abbys, brought with the declining state of the nobility so vast a prey to the industry of the people, that the balance of the commonwealth was too apparently in the popular party, to be unseen by the wise council of queen Parthenia [Elizabeth], who converting her reign thro the perpetual lovetricks that past between her and her people into a kind of romance, wholly neglected the nobility. And by these degrees came the house of commons to raise that head, which since has bin so high and formidable to their princes, that they have look'd pale upon those assemblys.

The balance of property had moved from the nobility to the people by the time of Elizabeth. The only class named as beneficiary of the shift is the yeomanry, but the reference to the House of Commons as the institutional beneficiary makes it clear that Harrington was including in 'the people' the gentry as well as the yeomanry.

The same analysis of the shift, with a few more strokes of detail, is given in *The Art of Lawgiving*: the growth of the city of London is linked with 'the declining of the balance to popularity'; parliaments were, by the time of James I, 'mere popular councils, and running to popularity of government like a bowl down a hill', and neither the new peerage which he created in abundance, nor the old, availed him anything against them; 'in our days . . . the lands in possession of the people overbalance those held by the nobility, at least, nine in ten'.[10] In neither of these accounts of the shift in the English balance is there any mention of the gentry. But there can be no doubt that here, as in the account in *Oceana*, the gentry were included in 'the people', as witness the description of James's parliaments as popular, and the estimate of the present holdings of the nobility as only one-tenth of the land.[11]

---

[9] *Oceana*, p. 65.   [10] *Art of L.*, pp. 364–6.

[11] Even if we could not assume that Harrington knew that gentry and nobility between them had much more than one-tenth, we have evidence that he thought the two or three hundred largest landowners alone held

When we go beyond the historical accounts of the shift in the English balance we do find explicit mention of the gentry. But whenever Harrington discusses them, whether in connection with his law of the balance, or with the application of that law to framing a system of government for contemporary England, he equates the gentry with the nobility and contrasts them with the people.

Thus in the first part of the Preliminaries of *Oceana*, where he is discussing government in general and the law of the balance, he follows Machiavelli in using gentry as synonymous with nobility —those who have lands, castles and treasures, whereby the rest are brought to dependence on them—while he corrects Machiavelli by saying that a nobility or gentry is destructive of popular government only if it has an overbalance of property.[12] A little farther on in the Preliminaries he argues that the gentry (still used synonymously with the nobility) and the people are as indispensable to each other in a commonwealth as are officers and soldiers in an army: the making, governing, and military leadership of a commonwealth require 'the genius of a gentleman', 'where there is not a nobility to hearten the people, they are slothful, regardless of the world, and of the public interest of liberty, as even those of *Rome* had bin without their gentry . . .'.[13] Gentry and people are separate classes, different in their nature and function, though necessary to each other.

When finally Harrington comes to fit a political superstructure to the existing balance of property in England, he again uses gentry as synonymous with nobility and distinct from the people. A 'nobility or gentry' is essential to a commonwealth, for politics cannot be mastered without study, and the people cannot have leisure to study; lawyers and divines, he adds, because of 'their incurable running upon their own narrow biass', are of no more use for this than are 'so many other tradesmen'. Since 'neither the people, nor divines, and lawyers, can be the aristocracy of a

---

something like one-tenth. The whole land of England he estimated as worth £10 million a year. There were, he said, at most 300 men who now had more than £2,000 a year in lands (*Oceana*, pp. 99–100). So the top 300 or so would alone account for something like £600,000 a year, and more probably, since the £2,000 is not an average but a minimum, for something like £1 million a year, i.e., one-tenth of the land.

[12] *Oceana*, pp. 39–40.   [13] *Ibid.*, p. 53.

nation, there remains only the nobility; in which stile, to avoid farther repetition, I shall understand the gentry also, as the *French* do by the word *noblesse*.'[14]

A nobility which holds an overbalance of property to the whole people, as did the feudal nobility, is incompatible with popular government. But a nobility which holds an underbalance to the people is 'not only safe, but necessary to the natural mixture of a well-order'd commonwealth'; nobility being here defined, again after Machiavelli, though now more broadly, as 'such as live upon their own revenues in plenty, without ingagement either to the tilling of their lands, or other work for their livelihood'.[15] It is in this context that England is said to be blessed in having exactly the right ingredients for a popular government: the balance of property is in the people, and at the same time there is an excellent 'nobility or gentry', well studied and well versed in military leadership, combining ancient riches with ancient virtue, ideally fitted to provide political leadership in the senate and offices of Oceana.[16]

In short, it is because the English 'nobility or gentry' do not possess an overbalance of property that they can safely be allowed the leadership in the proposed English republic. Harrington makes his whole case for the erection of a gentry-led commonwealth in England in 1656 rest on this. It is only, he insists, when a nobility or gentry have an underbalance of land that they can safely be permitted in a commonwealth; the English nobility or gentry, he insists equally, now are safe and necessary to the commonwealth.

Harrington is saying, then, that the nobility and gentry together held in 1656 less than half the land,[17] substantially less than half, for their underbalance is of such degree as to permit a stable commonwealth to be constructed on it, whereas whenever the balance between nobility and people is nearly equal there can be no stability.[18] And since he has said that the peers have not more than 10 per cent of the land, the distribution he believes to exist in 1656 is: peers, 10 per cent or less; gentry, substantially less than

[14] *Oceana*, p. 124. [15] *Ibid.*, p. 125. [16] *Ibid.*, pp. 123–5.
[17] This follows only if Harrington is here using underbalance in the sense required by his statements of the principle of the balance, not in the peculiar sense in which he later uses it. The ambiguity is examined below, p. 49 at note 67. [18] *Oceana*, p. 38.

40 per cent; yeomanry and townsmen, substantially more than 50 per cent.

How, then, it may be asked, could Harrington have written his account of the shift in the English balance in such a way as to leave the impression that the balance had shifted to the gentry? That he did leave this impression on some of his contemporaries and on some later scholars is evident in Professor Trevor-Roper's account, to which we shall turn in a moment. A sufficient reason for this impression is not difficult to see. The chief evidence Harrington offered for the shift away from the nobility to the people was the shift of power in the country and in parliament from the nobility to the independent commoners. The balance was so much in 'the popular party' by Elizabeth's time that she reigned by courting the people and neglecting the nobility, so that the House of Commons came to be dominant; James I's parliaments were 'mere popular councils'. Since it was obvious, then as now, that the Commons under Elizabeth and James were gentry rather than any lower rank, it was natural to conclude that Harrington meant that the balance of land was in the gentry. But the conclusion does not follow. For Harrington believed that the ordinary people, if not injured by 'the better sort', naturally defer to them,[19] and naturally elect as many of the better sort as they can,[20] so much so that he thought a special constitutional provision necessary to ensure that in the new commonwealth the main representative body would contain some of the lower sort.[21] All that follows from the description of Elizabethan and Jacobean parliaments as popular is that the balance of land was in the gentry and people together.

With this much elucidation of Harrington's own view of the gentry we may look briefly at the treatment he has had in the gentry controversy. We must look at it, for while the interpretation of Harrington is only marginal to the controversy, the controversy has become crucial to the interpretation of Harrington, and in a dangerously misleading way. Tawney, in using Harrington as a witness for the rise of the gentry, accurately described the shift that Harrington had seen as a shift from the nobility to the gentry and yeomanry, not to the gentry alone;[22] Harrington's statement was evidence for the rise of the gentry

[19] *Ibid.*, p. 133.
[21] *Valerius and Publicola*, pp. 449–50.
[20] *Art of L.*, p. 419.
[22] Tawney, *op. cit.*, p. 212.

31

only when taken together with the evidence of other observers as to the decline in the position of the yeomanry towards 1600 when long leases fell in.[23]

Trevor-Roper,[24] attacking Tawney's thesis, gives Harrington short shrift, first seeking to discredit him as a witness, then presenting his theory as the doctrine—demonstrably false—of the declining gentry in their hopeless struggle to restore their position. Both arguments depend on lumping together Harrington and several 'Harringtonians' who echoed or supported or used his theory for their own purposes: as arguments about Harrington's theory they are without foundation.

Take first Harrington's worth as a witness. We are told that a consistent doctrine was expressed or referred to by Harrington, Neville, Chaloner, Baynes, Ludlow and others, and that it included the proposition that a shift in the balance of property between social classes had taken place in England, that 'the Crown and nobility had lost their property and "the gentry have all the lands" '.[25] This doctrine is then discredited as evidence for the rise of the gentry between 1540 and 1640, on two grounds. First, these commentators 'were often obscure and sometimes self-contradictory' about the period in which the shift had occurred: its beginning was sometimes put two hundred or more years ago, sometimes in the reign of James I or even later. Hence the commentators could not be said to have been describing a historical process of 1540–1640; what they were doing was 'generalizing, over a vague tract of time, a process of which their only evidence is the violent change of the last decade' (i.e., 1640–50). Secondly, the commentators were not several independent observers but 'a group, almost a coterie, of active Republican politicians, who took their views from Harrington and Neville, themselves an inseparable combine'; their statements 'represent not a concurrence of observation but a repetition of dogma: the dogma of *Oceana*'.[26]

We may wonder how a coterie, repeating a dogma, could have been so vague and self-contradictory about the dates of the alleged shift, for Harrington was quite clear about it. The shift began

---

[23] Tawney, p. 216; and 'The rise of the gentry', *Econ. Hist. Rev.*, xi (1941), p. 5.

[24] *The Gentry*, 1540–1640, *Econ. Hist. Rev. Supplement* no. 1 (1953).

[25] *Ibid.*, p. 45.   [26] *Ibid.*, pp. 45–6.

about 1489 with Henry VII's legislation, was accelerated in 1536 with the dissolution of the monasteries, and had visibly tipped the balance by Elizabeth's reign.[27] It was not recently but in their great-grandfathers' time that the gentry had worn the blue coats of the nobility.[28] The reference to the nobility and clergy having the balance 'under the late monarchy' is to the time of the barons' wars.[29] True, when Harrington wants to show that a change in the balance can happen 'suddenly', he says that it had moved from monarchical to popular 'between the reign of Henry the SEVENTH, and that of Queen ELIZABETH, being under fifty years',[30] and when he wants to argue that it was not sudden he says that the government has been changing from aristocratical to popular for a hundred and forty years.[31] But there is no serious inconsistency here: the change in the balance starts about the beginning of the sixteenth century, the balance is tipped about the middle of the century, and it goes on moving down for another century. Harrington himself, then, was clear enough about the dates. And Harrington is not to be reproached with having generalized over that tract of time a process of which his only evidence was the violent change of 1640–50: the evidence on which he most relies he takes from Bacon's *History*, which had been published in 1622.

Harrington at any rate must be left out of the coterie. Whatever his disciples and those who made use of him said from time to time, Harrington did not say that 'the gentry have all the lands'. The shift he found was not from king and nobility to gentry but from king and nobility to the people, and in his usage the people always included the yeomanry and sometimes excluded the gentry.

The identification of Harrington's doctrine with the dicta of some of his followers leads Trevor-Roper even more unfortunately to describe Harrington's doctrine as false. The doctrine, he argues, providentially supplied just what the 'mere gentry' needed, and so became their slogan 'in their last losing struggle against the Court. The fact that they lost in that struggle is evidence of the falsity of the doctrine'.[32] But it was not Harrington's doctrine that property had shifted to, and power should therefore be vested in, the 'mere' gentry. He held, indeed, that property had

[27] *Oceana*, pp. 64–5; *Art of L.*, pp. 364–6. [28] *Prerogative*, p. 281.
[29] *Ibid.*, p. 246. [30] *Art of L.*, p. 408.
[31] *Pian Piano*, p. 528. [32] *The Gentry*, pp. 49–50.

shifted from nobility to gentry and people, and that power should shift accordingly. But even if we leave the people out of it, the gentry whom Harrington would invest with power included the 'greater gentry' and the 'improving gentry' as well as the mere or lesser or declining gentry. The greater or rising gentry, with incomes up to £2,000 or £3,000 a year,[33] would not be cramped by Harrington's agrarian limit of £2,000 a year lands in England (£4,500 in the British Isles, and possibly twice as much again in colonies) plus unlimited amounts from trade, and something from offices;[34] and the improving gentry are recognized in Harrington's endorsement of racking of rents.[35] Had Harrington postulated a preponderance of property in the mere gentry, their actual failure to win power would be evidence either that his factual postulate was wrong or that his theory was false. Trevor-Roper would have it both that Harrington's facts were wrong and that the theory was false. But since these were not Harrington's facts, neither conclusion follows.

There remains the question why Harrington was so ambiguous in placing the gentry now with the nobility and now with the people. Why did he use two different definitions of 'the few or a nobility', one excluding and one including the gentry, and was he inconsistent in doing so? It will be recalled that he used the narrow definition in describing the change from the Gothic to the modern balance, and the broad definition in discussing the position in 1656. The difference in usage is intelligible, and the two uses consistent, in view of the difference between feudal and post-feudal land tenure. When land was held on military tenure, it was only the nobility proper whose titles to land gave them the military power on which the balance of government depended; the knights and gentlemen who held of them were subordinate. But with the disappearance of feudal tenures the nobility proper got no more military benefit from their lands, acre for acre, than did any other landowner. Nobles and gentry, and even freeholders below the rank of gentry, were, in respect of the military potential given by land ownership, co-ordinate; each acre was of equal value in feeding an army. With this change, which was concurrent with the acquisition of a lot of land by the gentry and yeomanry, the old nobility was reduced so decisively that it became an insignificant class in calculations of the balance of property and

[33] *The Gentry*, p. 52. [34] *Prerogative*, p. 280. [35] *Oceana*, p. 165.

power. But the nobles still had qualities of leadership which were needed. So had the gentry. Thenceforth, nobles and gentry, as leisured rentiers able to give political leadership, could be treated as essentially the same class. The newly-significant dividing line for Harrington was that between the 'nobility or gentry' and the freeholders below that rank, who, working their land for a living, were by their way of life incapable of political leadership and so were classed with the mechanic 'people'.

It was not Harrington who moved the gentry from 'people' to 'nobility'; they moved themselves, by achieving independence of feudal status and acquiring substantial lands in their own right. In that sense at least, the gentry did in fact rise, and Harrington's double usage reflects that rise. This is not to say that Harrington made any such defence of his double usage. He made no defence of it at all. There is no indication that he was conscious of anything needing to be defended. He may well have assumed that the gentry readers for whom he was writing would not misunderstand his assessment of the facts, namely, that for purposes of government the gentry had, in the last century and a half, moved up a class. There is after all, nothing odd in the fact that Harrington never referred to the gentry as a separate class but always included them in another. The gentry had in fact never been a class capable of ruling on its own. It could share rule with the nobility and court, or with the yeomanry, but that was all. Harrington's double treatment of the gentry recognizes this, as does his proposal of a commonwealth in which gentry and yeomanry would share the power.

II

THE BOURGEOIS SOCIETY

We have seen that Harrington's ambiguous use of 'the few', or ambiguous placing of the gentry, is intelligible on his own terms of reference. The gentry had shared with the people a common subordination to the nobility; now, all landowners being co-ordinate, the gentry had more in common with the nobility than with the people. But to leave the analysis there would be to leave a misleading impression of Harrington's view of his own society. If he took an aristocratic view of the seventeenth-century gentry he also took, to a surprising extent, a bourgeois view of the seven-teenth-century aristocracy. Before we go on to look at the second central ambiguity in his theory we shall examine the extent to which he saw his England as a bourgeois society.

The orthodox post-Tawney view has credited Harrington with some insight into the nature of the change from feudal to bour-geois relations of production. Against this view Mr Pocock has entered a strong dissent. Harrington, he writes:[36]

> has no conception whatever that there exists a complex web of economic relationships between men which can be studied in itself and which determines the distribution of power among them. Compared to the best Tudor writers on social reform he is not so much ignorant of as uninterested in the realities of an agrarian political economy, and it has not occurred to him that the exchange of goods and services on an agrarian basis either can be studied in order to determine its own laws, or ought to be studied in its relation to political power. . . . His sole comment on the economic relations between men—and the sole foundation of all that he has to say about property as the basis of power—is, 'an army is a beast that hath a great belly and must be fed'; he that has the land can feed the soldiers.

The vigour of this attack is welcome. Some corrective was needed to the over-simple view that was coming to be taken of Harrington. It was improper to infer that because Harrington saw the fundamental political role of changes in the distribution of property between Henry VII and the Civil War, he also saw the nature of the change in the economic relations between men and classes that had taken place at the same time. To see the political effect of the disappearance of the system of dependent tenures—which Pocock holds to be Harrington's claim to originality as a political thinker, and one entitling him to high esteem—is not necessarily to see at all into the system of market relations which was replacing it.

Yet Pocock's corrective goes too far. There is evidence that Harrington was aware of the pervasiveness of market relations, even in the use of land; 'he that has the land can feed the soldiers'

[36] J. G. A. Pocock, *The Ancient Constitution and the Feudal Law* (Cambridge, 1957), pp. 128–9.

was not Harrington's sole comment on the economic relations between men. And, perhaps more important, Harrington's main defence of his political proposals rests on the assumption that the gentry are sufficiently bourgeois to administer an entrepreneurial society acceptably to the entrepreneurs.

Take first the evidence of Harrington's awareness and acceptance of market motivations and relations. There is his defence of usury, based on the postulates that private accumulations of capital should be made available for commercial enterprise, and that no man will venture his money but through hope of some gain. In a country as large as England, where money cannot overbalance land, usury 'is so far from being destructive that it is necessary'; it is 'of profit to the commonwealth', 'a mighty profit to the public', because it brings money into commercial circulation.[37] Moreover, accumulation is honourable and respectable. Estates are got by industry, not by 'covetousness and ambition'.[38] 'Industry of all things is the most accumulative, and accumulation of all things hates levelling: the revenue therefore of the people being the revenue of industry . . . [no people in the world] may be found to have bin levellers.'[39] The desire to accumulate, and the possibility of honest accumulation, are not of course presented as new in the seventeenth century, but one has only to compare the moral position revealed in these statements with the views of the seventeenth-century traditionalists to see how far Harrington has accepted bourgeois values.

His specific observations on the social economy of England recognize its fluid character. Upward class mobility based on commercial or industrial profits is commonplace: there are 'innumerable trades wherupon men live, not only better than others upon good shares of lands, but becom also purchasers of greater estates'; 'the revenue of industry in a nation, at least in this, is three or fourfold greater than that of the mere rent'.[40] The same postulate of mobility appears in the defence of the Agrarian Law, one of the merits of which is that under it the rich cannot 'exclude [the people's] industry or merit from attaining to the like estate, power, or honor'; to which he adds as a matter of course that the people will assume that the riches of the commonwealth should 'go according to the difference of mens industry'.[41]

[37] *Prerogative*, p. 229. [38] *Ibid.*, p. 278. [39] *System of Politics*, p. 471.
[40] *Oceana*, p. 154. [41] *Prerogative*, pp. 242–3.

To such indications that Harrington recognized the prevalence of bourgeois standards among 'the people' we may add that he had some notion of the elements of the market economy, and was not hostile to its social implications. He was not to be frightened by the prospect of a great increase in the size of mercantile cities: it would not disrupt but would strengthen the existing economy, for urban and rural were complementary parts of a single market society. Urban growth leads to rural growth and *vice versa*; in each case it is the natural operation of a law of supply and demand for commodities and labour that brings the secondary growth. Where the city grows first:[42]

> the more mouths there be in a city, the more meat of necessity must be vented by the country, and so there will be more corn, more cattel, and better markets; which breeding more laborers, more husbandmen, and richer farmers, bring the country so far from a commonwealth of cottagers, that . . . the husbandman, . . . his trade thus uninterrupted, in that his markets are certain, gos on with increase of children, of servants, of corn, and of cattel. . . . The country then growing more populous, and better stock'd with cattel, which also increases manure for the land, must proportionably increase in fruitfulness.

Likewise a populous countryside leads to a more populous city:

> for when the people increase so much, that the dug of earth can do no more, the overplus must seek som other way of livelihood: which is either arms, such were those of the *Goths* and *Vandals*; or merchandize and manufacture, for which ends it being necessary that they lay their heads and their stock together, this makes populous citys.

If this shows no mastery of political economy it does suggest some grasp of the essentials of a market economy; his remarks about the comparative advantages of English and Dutch trade[43] point in the same direction.

Harrington had, then, some idea of the market relations that prevailed among 'the people'. Yet for all we have seen so far he seems to have thought of the nobility and gentry as untouched by those relations. It is usually the contrast between the two ways of

[42] *Prerogative*, p. 279. [43] *Oceana*, p. 165.

life, and between the two sources of income, that he emphasizes. Incomes derived from trade, manufacture and husbandry come from effort intelligently applied to the production of commodities for the market, the incentive being the desire of accumulation. Income derived from ownership of land just flows in: 'that the rents and profits of a man's land in feesimple or property, com in naturally and easily, by common consent or concernment, that is, by virtue of the law founded upon the public interest, and therfore voluntarily establish'd by the whole people, is an apparent thing'.[44] No effort is required; the rentiers seem detached from the market society around them. But Harrington knew that their income did not arise from a traditional relation between landlord and tenant remote from the market relation. He knew that a capitalist relation had penetrated to the land, in the form of racking of rents, and he accepted it in principle, deploring only its excess: 'racking of rents is a vile thing in the richer sort, an uncharitable one to the poorer, a perfect mark of slavery, and nips your commonwealth in the fairest blossom. On the other side, if there should be too much ease given in this kind, it would occasion sloth, and so destroy industry, the principal nerve of a commonwealth'.[45] He professes himself insufficiently expert to say how far racking of rents should be allowed to go, but he is clear on the principle: far enough to keep the tenant yeomen from being slack but not so far as to destroy them, for they are the main strength of a commonwealth and 'the least turbulent or ambitious' of any class. Where upholders of traditional society could see nothing but evil and dissolvent effects in the racking of rents, Harrington saw its necessity as an incentive to industrious production. The economic function of the landlord was to enforce the industry of the tenant; by doing so he would keep alive, not destroy, a commonwealth of husbandmen.

Equally revealing of Harrington's view of the place of the landowner in capitalist society is his treatment of the advantages to be gained by military subjection of 'provinces'. He subsumes under one general theory of appropriation the labour of the entrepreneur and the labour of the armed nobility and gentry conquering lands and peoples for their private gain. In Harrington's labour justification of property, the labour that gives title to property is indifferently military or pacific. 'This donation of

[44] *Prerogative*, p. 231.   [45] *Oceana*, p. 165.

the earth to man', he writes, quoting the Psalms and Genesis, 'coms to a kind of selling it for INDUSTRY. . . . From the different kinds and successes of this industry, whether in arms, or in other exercises of the mind or body, derives the natural equity of dominion or property . . .'.[46] Oceana is to be:[47]

> a commonwealth for increase: the trade of a commonwealth for increase, is arms; arms are not born by merchants, but by noblemen and gentlemen. The nobility therfore having these arms in their hands, by which provinces are to be acquir'd, new provinces yield new estates; so whereas the merchant has his returns in silk or canvas, the soldier will have his return in land. . . . if ever the commonwealth attains to five new provinces (and such a commonwealth will have provinces enow) it is certain, that (besides the honors, magistracys, and the revenues annex'd) there will be more estates in the nobility of *Oceana*, of fourteen thousand pounds land a year, than ever were, or can otherwise be of four. . . .

The acquisition of such large estates by nobles and gentlemen who already had the maximum estates in England (and Ireland and Scotland)[48] would not endanger the popular balance of property or power at home, for the subjugated people were to be producers of revenue for, rather than potential military servitors of, their conquerors.

The trade of the nobility and gentry is arms, the labour by which they entitle themselves to their shares of God's donation of the earth to man is the labour of arms. The difference between the nobility-gentry and the people, of which Harrington makes so much when he is thinking of their political qualities, comes down to this: they have different trades, both accumulative, both yielding returns that increase the real capital of the nation. This is not to say that Harrington had in his own mind entirely assimilated the nobility-gentry into a bourgeois order, but it is at least to say that the contrast he so often draws between them and the mercantile and mechanic people is perfectly consistent with his seeing them as components of a bourgeois society.

---

[46] *Art of L.*, p. 363.   [47] *Prerogative*, p. 280.
[48] Under Harrington's Agrarian Law a man could hold up to £2,000 a year of land in England and as much again in Ireland, as well as £500 a year in Scotland (*Oceana*, p. 100).

We can go farther. A policy of colonial subjugation is, oj course, not peculiar to a bourgeois or capitalist society: it had been a normal method of building empires in the non-bourgeois states of the ancient world. But colonial subjugation, by which the surplus product of a people's labour could be made to flow in one form or another (as rents, or as profits of trade in the goods they produced) into the hands of the new owners, was in the sixteenth and seventeenth centuries one of the means by which the accumulations of wealth required to initiate modern capitalism were being provided. While we cannot be sure how clearly Harrington saw this, his views on Ireland are suggestive. He approved of its subjugation, regretted that it was not producing nearly as much revenue for England as it could do, and would have liked to see it repopulated with a more industrious and enterprising people, the Jews, whom he thought capable of improving Ireland's agriculture and increasing its trade to levels which produce £4 million a year 'dry rents', i.e., net surplus product over and above the wages of labour and the profits of enterprise. Of this surplus he modestly proposed that only £2 million a year (plus customs duties sufficient to maintain an army in Ireland) should be paid as tribute to England.[49] The scheme was unusual in that it involved granting the conquered lands to another outside people in return for an annual tribute. Harrington thought this unusual feature necessary because of the peculiar languor of the Irish climate, which had not only made the Irish people inveterately slothful but had similarly softened the English who had been planted there. Unique measures were needed to bring the cash returns to England up to a reasonable level. But it is clear from the remarks quoted above about the new estates to be yielded by new provinces, that in the lands still to be conquered Harrington envisaged the appropriation of the surplus taking place through the then more usual channels, chiefly as rents paid to the private English landlords.

We may say, then, that while Harrington certainly had no Marxian theory of 'primary accumulation' he saw plainly enough that the function of colonial peoples was to produce a surplus which would flow into English hands as disposable wealth. His models of the 'commonwealth for increase' came indeed from the ancient world. But if his head was stuffed with 'ancient prudence'

[49] *Oceana*, pp. 33–4.

his feet were on seventeenth-century ground. He saw the nobility and gentry making an economic as well as a political contribution to seventeenth-century England. In adding to their own wealth they would add very substantially to the wealth of the nation, for their new revenues could either be used to improve their estates or be lent at interest, in either case to the benefit of the commonwealth. So the nobility and gentry fitted usefully and smoothly into a society of predominantly free industrious entrepreneurs—husbandmen, tradesmen and merchants—in whom the balance now lay.

Before we leave Harrington's picture of his own society we should notice that he put one class right out of the picture. Wage-earners or 'servants' are not only denied citizenship (on the ground that they are not freemen and therefore are incapable of participating in the government of a commonwealth);[50] they are treated less as a class within the commonwealth than as a people outside it. No account is to be taken of them in constructing the balance of classes within the commonwealth: 'The causes of commotion in a commonwealth are either external or internal. External are from enemys, from subjects, or from servants'.[51]

III

THE EQUAL COMMONWEALTH AND THE EQUAL AGRARIAN

Upon this society Harrington proposed to erect a commonwealth that would last forever. He calls it an 'equal commonwealth' and he makes its permanence depend ultimately on the Agrarian Law which he calls an 'equal Agrarian'. But when we examine the proposals we find that the structure incorporates two legislative bodies, each with a veto in effect, made up of different social classes though both elected by the whole citizen body; that the two classes are, or may be, very unequal in their total landed wealth; and that the balance of property need not lie in that class which is numerically far the larger and which therefore can control the election of both legislative bodies. His attempts to explain why in spite of this the system will be everlasting—he scarcely tries to explain why it would work well from month to month or from year to year—are wildly confusing. We shall have to move

[50] *Oceana*, p. 77, *Art of L.*, p. 409.   [51] *Oceana*, p. 138.

a little way into this confusion in order to conjecture how Harrington could have thought he was being so clear. The argument essentially is that the commonwealth could not be overthrown as long as the Agrarian Law held, and that the Agrarian Law would hold because no class strong enough to alter it would have an interest in doing so. We shall see that neither of these propositions can be sustained without the assumption that both gentry and people are bourgeois; that he does in the course of the argument come close to stating this assumption but does not state it clearly or seem to see that it is needed; and that he is consequently involved in some striking contradictions. We shall first look briefly at the proposed constitutional structure, then at the more difficult problem of the Agrarian.

The essentials of the constitutional structure are: (1) a Senate of 300 members and a Representative of 1,050, both filled by indirect annual elections (one-third of the members elected each year for a three-year term, no member being eligible for successive terms) by secret ballot, the electors for both Senate and Representative being all men above the age of thirty, not servants or spendthrifts; candidacy for the Senate and for three-sevenths of the places in the Representative having a substantial property qualification; (2) a strict separation of powers between the two legislative bodies, the Senate debating and proposing legislation, the Representative approving or rejecting those proposals without debate; (3) election of civil, military and judicial officers, no incumbent being eligible for successive terms. A system so constituted (with the Agrarian to fix its property basis) would be immune from internal dissolution. It met the test of 'the perfection of government', namely, 'that no man or men in or under it can have the interest; or having the interest, can have the power to disturb it with sedition'.[52]

Where did the nobility-gentry and the people fit into this scheme? The nobility and gentry would fill the Senate, three-sevenths of the Representative, and the more important offices. They would fill them not as of right but elected by the whole people. The property qualification for these places (£100 a year in land, goods or money) would admit wealthier yeomen and townsmen as well as gentry. It was not on the property qualification but on the habitual deference of the people that Harrington

[52] *Ibid.*, p. 49; cf. *Prerogative*, p. 247, *Art of L.*, p. 433.

relied to fill these places with gentry. Indeed, the point of the property qualification (which was unusual in that it worked in both directions) was, he said, to ensure that the majority of the places in the Representative would be filled by men of under £100 a year.[53] To these men of 'the meaner sort', who made up the bulk of the people, were allotted four-sevenths of the places in the Representative, and the less important offices.

We thus have careful provision for two legislative bodies made up predominantly of two different classes. The argument by which the separation of powers between them is justified implies that they have to some extent different interests: just as two girls having to divide a cake between them, each wanting the most, will be equally served if one divides and the other chooses, so the Senate and the people, each wanting the most, will be equally served if one proposes legislative measures and the other chooses. Now it is not self-evident that a system which requires the concurrence of two such bodies would work harmoniously. Both, it is true, were to be elected by the whole citizen body, but there were to be no parties, no canvassing,[54] by which the people could make their wishes prevail; and the property qualification for the Senate would make it impossible for the middle and lower ranges of the people to put their own men in. Nor can the habitual deference of the people be treated as a sufficient condition for the harmonious operation of the system. The deference to which Harrington refers is an effect rather than a cause of harmony of interests: the people are deferential only when they do not feel themselves injured, and he assumes throughout that the people know their own interests.[55] He simply asserts that where the Senate is not confined to a hereditary order but is elected by the people, the interests of the Senate and the people are the same.[56]

In fact Harrington offered no proofs that the system would work. Presumably he thought that this was covered by his proofs of the more important proposition, i.e., that the system could never be overthrown by sedition. These proofs all come down to proof of the ability of the Agrarian Law to prevent any class having the interest and the power to overthrow the commonwealth.

[53] *Valerius*, pp. 449–50; cf. *Oceana*, p. 133, *Art of L.*, p. 419.
[54] *Oceana*, p. 144.
[55] E.g., *Prerogative*, p. 246, *Valerius*, p. 459.   [56] *Prerogative*, p. 244.

It is here that Harrington's argument becomes almost inexplicably confused. For the Agrarian, by Harrington's own account, would not prevent gross inequality of property. The Agrarian limit of £2,000 a year in land would, on his computation, allow all the land of England to fall into the hands of 5,000 men, leaving the rest of the 500,000 citizens with no land at all.[57] While he regarded it as highly improbable that the land would ever come into the hands of as few as 5,000 owners—'as improbable as any thing in the world that is not altogether impossible'—he held that even in that case there would still be a popular state and an equal balance:[58]

> the land coming to be in the possession of five thousand, falls not into a number that is within the compass of the few, or such a one as can be princes, either in regard of their number, or of their estates; but to such a one as cannot consent to abolish the agrarian, because that were to consent to rob one another: nor can they have any party among them, or against their common interest, strong enough to force them, or to break it; which remaining, the five thousand neither are nor can be any more than a popular state, and the balance remains every whit as equal, as if the land were in never so many more hands.

[57] *Oceana*, pp. 99, 154; *Prerogative*, pp. 243, 247. It is not clear what notion Harrington had of the size of the English population. At *Prerogative*, p. 247, he speaks of one million 'fathers of families', which appears to include labourers as well as citizens. This is a reasonable estimate, not far from Gregory King's figure of one and a third million 'families' as the total of all classes in 1688. At *Oceana*, p. 154, the number of men over 18 is given as one million, apparently heads of families; but it is not clear whether this is intended to include 'servants' or not. For the total of one million is here reached from the number of male 'elders' (age 30 and over) and 'youths' (age 18–30) 'upon the annual roll', which seems to mean citizens, not servants; but he immediately uses the figure one million to include day labourers. At *Art of Lawgiving*, p. 403, he speaks of England as a commonwealth of 'five hundred thousand men, or more', the context implying, though not clearly, that this is men above the level of servants. On the whole it seems likely that he thought of there being about 500,000 male citizens and an equal number of male servants. This also is not too far from King's estimate (511,000 families above the level of servants; 849,000 families of labouring people and out-servants, cottagers and paupers, and common seamen and soldiers).
[58] *Prerogative*, p. 247.

That the 5,000 would not consent to abolish the Agrarian may be granted, for if 5,000 had the whole £10 million a year of land, each of the 5,000 would under the Agrarian have exactly £2,000 a year of land, and if the Agrarian were abolished or raised any owner's gain would be another's loss. Yet the argument as a whole appears to be circular. The Agrarian would ensure the preservation of an equal balance, it is said, because the maximum concentration of ownership permitted by the Agrarian would not lead the owners to destroy the Agrarian. But this would only ensure the preservation of the equal balance if it was already assumed that the balance is equal as long as the Agrarian is unbroken.

Harrington has in fact already made and stated virtually this assumption:[59]

> where the rich are so bounded by an agrarian that they cannot overbalance (and therfore neither oppress the people, nor exclude their industry or merit from attaining to the like estate, power, or honor) the whole people have the whole riches of the nation already equally divided among them; for that the riches of a commonwealth should not go according to the difference of mens industry, but be distributed by the poll, were inequal.

Equality of riches, in Harrington's view, is not arithmetical equality, it is equality of opportunity of increasing one's riches. It is hence a sufficient basis for an 'equal commonwealth' that the rich should not be able to check the upward mobility of the middle class. The Agrarian is supposed to prevent them checking that mobility. Therefore, as long as the Agrarian is unbroken, the balance is 'equal'.

Thus when Harrington's concept of equality is brought into the reckoning the argument no longer appears circular. But the argument still involves an unstated assumption. For the Agrarian by itself would not prevent the rich from checking the upward mobility of the people. It would only do so on the assumption that any future class of the landed rich would be more interested in maintaining the market economy (which would incidentally permit industrious men from 'the people' to continue to accumulate and rise) than in banding together to oppose the people.

[59] *Prerogative*, pp. 242-3.

Harrington's defence of the Agrarian as a sufficient guarantee of an equal balance against attacks from the few rests, then, on a concept of equality that is characteristically bourgeois (equality of riches is equal opportunity to accumulate unequal amounts), and a concept of the gentry as sufficiently bourgeois to put first, in their own interests, the maintenance of a market economy.

The demonstration that the Agrarian is immune from attack from the other side rests on the same concept of equality and on some rudimentary concepts of capitalist economics. Why might not the people who had little land (or none at all, in the case of 5,000 having it all) seek to level the wealth, either seizing it by civil war or in effect confiscating it by legislation reducing the Agrarian limit? Harrington's most general answer is that they will not do it because they already have equal opportunity of accumulation, 'the whole riches of the nation already equally divided among them'. He reinforces this with an arithmetical argument designed to show that they would not wish to level because it would be against their own interest. The whole value of the land, as it is or might be rented, is £10 million a year. If the land were seized and divided equally among the one million heads of families it would bring each only £10 a year. But the meanest labourer at a shilling a day gets more than this already, and if the land were levelled he would lose his present income for 'there would be no body to set him on work'. The more prosperous tradesmen would lose even more, for the revenue of industry is three or four times greater than that of rent, and they would lose that revenue by raising civil war or even by constitutional levelling.[60]

The arithmetic does not seem very convincing. Why might not the labourer turned smallholder enjoy the £10 a year (which was the measure of the supposed productivity of his land over and above the yield of the labour on it) and the revenue of his labour as well? Why might not the tradesman, whose revenue from his industry had been enough to allow him to accumulate, continue to enjoy that revenue, which had never depended on his title to land? And why might not the middling yeoman, who indeed needed more land than he would get by complete levelling, still profit from a partial confiscation of the great estates by reducing the maximum from £2,000 to £1,000 or less? Harrington saw no such difficulties. But the questions answer themselves if some

[60] *Oceana*, pp. 154–5, *Prerogative*, p. 247.

rudimentary bourgeois economic notions are being assumed. The first objection disappears when it is assumed that the productivity of small holdings is much less than that of land worked as capital for a profit, or, which comes to the same thing, that the wage-labour structure is essential to maintain existing productivity. The second disappears when it is assumed that the profitability of trades depends on the profitable use of land. These assumptions are very much the ones we have already seen implied in Harring-ton's remarks on racking of rents and on the growth of cities. The third objection disappears when it is assumed (as we have seen Harrington does assume) that the equality the people want is equality of opportunity of profiting according to their enterprise: they would not risk weakening the sanctity of property by any confiscatory measures.

The whole of Harrington's defence of the Agrarian as a suffici-ent guarantee of an equal balance and a sufficient basis for a popular or equal commonwealth depends, we conclude, on a concept of the economy which takes for granted the necessity or at least the superiority of capitalist relations of production, and a concept of equality which is essentially bourgeois.

IV

THE SELF-CANCELLING BALANCE PRINCIPLE

It is only on these concepts that Harrington's extraordinary shift of meaning of the term overbalance makes any sense. In his general statements of the principle of the balance, and in his many examples of different historical balances and changes in balances, Harrington equates overbalance with possession of more than half the land. The prerequisite of a commonwealth is stated indifferently as possession of three-quarters (or two-thirds) of the land by the people, or where neither one man nor the few over-balance the people in land.[61] Yet now we find him saying that if all the land were to come into the hands of 5,000 proprietors (a tiny minority of the 500,000 citizens) the balance would still be a popular one; and not only that, but even that the Agrarian of Oceana, which would permit 5,000 to get all the land, would not

[61] E.g., *Oceana*, p. 37; *Prerogative*, pp. 227, 270; *Art of L.*, p. 363; *System of Politics*, p. 467.

permit 'the few or . . . the richer' (here defined as the 5,000) to overbalance the people (defined as 'the many or the poorer sort').[62]

It is hard to find any consistency in this. Everything seems to change its meaning. The few here are the 5,000; within a few pages it is said that 5,000 is not 'a number that is within the compass of the few'.[63] The balance is said to be in the people when all the land is in the 5,000-strong few. Overbalance does not mean what it did, for now the few, who would certainly have the overbalance of property, are 'not able to overbalance the people', in the sense of not having 'any power to disturb the commonwealth'.[64] Why not? Because even if they had an interest in doing so (which Harrington says they could not have, since they already have all the riches, all the liberty they want, and more power at the head of a commonwealth of a million men than they could have by excluding the million and reducing themselves to a commonwealth of 5,000, or thus spoiling their militia),[65] they would lack the power to do so, 'the people being equally possest of the government, of the arms, and far superior in number'.[66] The last vestige of the principle that the balance of power depends on the balance of property seems to have disappeared. Political power still depends on military power, but military power is now divorced from ownership of property.

What has happened to the principle of the balance? One thing is clear: however we may account for the inconsistency in the use of overbalance, and the apparent abandonment of the whole principle, the term overbalance is used in this contradictory sense only when Harrington is considering a hypothetical future condition that might arise after the establishment of the equal commonwealth. His use of overbalance in this special sense does not, therefore, invalidate the inference we made earlier[67] about his view of the distribution of land in 1656.

But how could Harrington have failed to see that he had contradicted himself in basing the need for the commonwealth on the principle of the balance, and then defending the very citadel of the commonwealth—the Agrarian—by arguments which deny the operation of the principle? He could do so if he was assuming that

[62] *Prerogative*, p. 243, cf. p. 242.   [63] *Ibid.*, p. 247, as quoted above.
[64] *Ibid.*, p. 243.   [65] *Oceana*, p. 99.
[66] *Prerogative*, pp. 243–4.   [67] Above, p. 30.

in any future condition in which 5,000 might come to have all the land, the 5,000 would differ in quality as well as in quantity from the few who had upheld the oligarchies of the ancient and feudal worlds. Assume that the English gentry are, and will be, substantially committed to the market economy, that they are bourgeois in their outlook, and the inconsistencies are no longer apparent. Such a 5,000 would not wish to impose institutions that would be oppressive to the people (who are only those above the level of wage-earners). They would have no interest in overbalancing the people in the sense of denying them co-ordinate political authority. Nor would they have the power to do so, for the people (who, at the outset of the commonwealth, enjoyed a wider diffusion of land and were armed to maintain the popular or equal balance) were still armed, and would use their arms to repel any attempt to exclude them from political authority (which they could only interpret as an attack on the 'equality' of property that they enjoyed as long as they were able to accumulate and to rise).

Harrington's unawareness of any inconsistency in his use of the principle of the balance is understandable, then, if he was thinking of the present gentry and the proposed commonwealth as essentially bourgeois. And the evidence we examined earlier suggests that that was how he thought of them. But to say this is still to accuse Harrington of contradiction. For the principle of the balance, asserted as universal, turns out to operate only down to the time the bourgeois commonwealth is established, when it is cancelled by that very step. In the past the balance had worked in every direction: as it moved it had brought down monarchies, oligarchies and commonwealths. But as soon as it has brought into being a bourgeois commonwealth it ceases to operate. Overbalance of land in a bourgeois few would not lead to overbalance of their political power. If Harrington's commonwealth were established, history would stop. Harrington was content that it should. His whole object was to stop it.

V

HARRINGTON'S STATURE

What becomes then of Harrington's high claims? 'The doctrin of the balance', he boasted, '. . . is that principle which makes the politics, not so before the invention of the same, to be undeniable throout, and . . . the most demonstrable of any whatsoever'.[68] He insisted that it was not merely a historical generalization but also a necessary principle. He denied that he was a mere empirical reasoner. While he was scornful of Hobbes's hanging a system by geometry,[69] it was not the deductive method he disdained. Deductive reasoning he thought the more 'honourable' argument, though it is by no means clear that he understood it.[70] He agreed with the geometricians of politics that law proceeds from the will, and that the mover of will is interest.[71] Where he quarrelled with them was in their imputing undifferentiated interests, and hence undifferentiated wills, to all men. Throughout history the few and the many had had different kinds of interests. Each had wanted to secure its own way of life. Class interests (i.e., the interests men had, as members of different classes, in attaining security for different ways of life and thus for different systems of property) were more important than the undifferentiated interests all men had in security *per se*. This was why you could not make kings (or commonwealths) merely by constructing a geometry of men's wills without constructing an anatomy of their property.[72] Whenever two classes wanted different kinds of security, different systems of property, each would have an interest in imposing its rule on the other, and would seek to do so. Whichever class got the bulk of the property would have the ability, as well as the will, to impose itself on the other, and would therefore do so. The principle of the balance was probably intended to state this necessary relation. Put in these terms, the principle is not contradicted by the divorce between class power and class property in the commonwealth. It simply ceases to be applicable because there are not now two classes who want different systems of property. But Harrington did not put it in these terms, and did contradict himself.

I have argued (1) that the reason Harrington was unaware of the inconsistencies between his principle of the balance and his defence of the Agrarian was that he was all along assuming that both the few and the many citizens were now essentially bourgeois; and (2) that if he had made this assumption clearly, and if he had been as good a deductive thinker as he pretended to be, he could

---

[68] *Prerogative*, p. 226.   [69] *Oceana*, p. 65.   [70] *Politicaster*, p. 560.
[71] *Ibid.*, p. 553.   [72] *Art of L.*, pp. 402–3.

have avoided the contradiction (by formulating the principle as operating only between two classes who wanted different systems of property).

To argue thus is to credit Harrington with a little more insight into seventeenth-century society, and with rather less logical ability, than has been customary. The weakness of his logic when he tries to turn a historically valid relationship into a necessary and universal principle is surely sufficiently demonstrated. The degree of his insight into seventeenth-century society is more open to question. Those who see Harrington as essentially a classical republican might argue that he was so enchanted with ancient prudence that he could easily force his own society into the ancient categories without seeing the illogic involved. If that were the case, it would be improper to infer that he could have failed to see the illogic only because he was taking for granted the bourgeois nature of seventeenth-century society. We have, however, seen evidence, apart from such inference, that Harrington thought of his society in what would now be called bourgeois concepts.

And it must be remembered also that Harrington took his ancient prudence from that learned disciple of the ancients, Machiavelli, 'the only politician of later ages',[73] and that the master had already seen that a bourgeois class was no threat to a commonwealth.[74] Starting from Machiavelli, Harrington was already half way into the modern age. And in understanding the modern age he made his own way somewhat farther. Where Machiavelli had drawn the line between those 'gentlemen' who were great landed proprietors and those whose wealth was in money and movable capital, and had allowed only the latter to be compatible with a commonwealth, Harrington had seen that a non-feudal landed gentry was also compatible with a commonwealth. In Machiavelli's Italy the monied men had been the bearers of capitalism; in Harrington's England the gentry were even more important in that role than were the merchants and financiers, and Harrington at least glimpsed this. The functions he saw the English gentry performing were capitalist functions, by which private accumulation would increase national wealth without at all endangering the 'equal' commonwealth. Private gain was public benefit.

[73] *Oceana*, p. 36.   [74] Machiavelli, *Discourses*, Bk. I, chap. 55.

Harrington had nothing like the insight of Hobbes into the nature of bourgeois society. He did not resolve all relations between men into relations of the market. If Harrington's gentry were bourgeois they were still gentry, with a sufficiently different way of life and code of behaviour that a separate place had to be found for them. Harrington found it, at the cost of some theoretical confusion. He cannot rank with Hobbes as a thinker. But just because he was less penetrating, because he abstracted less from the complexity of a society not yet entirely bourgeois, he may be counted the more realistic analyst of the transitional period.

III

HARRINGTON, A REALIST?*

John F. H. New

Recently the notion that Harrington was a thorough-going realist received vigorous support in *Past and Present*. The argument, both original and illuminating, falls into three parts: a demonstration of Harrington's ambiguous treatment of the gentry; a collation of his *obiter dicta* to reveal an understanding of his society as one dominated by market relations; and the revelation of the inconsistent analysis of the Agrarian Law, which inconsistency was explicable only in terms of Harrington's assuming a general acceptance and practice of bourgeois modes and attitudes. From this argument Harrington emerges as less logical but more realistic than recent critics had thought. Realism is explicitly equated with appreciation of the bourgeois nature of society in general and of the English gentry in particular—a realism deduced from Harrington's awareness that market relations governed economic, political and social relationships.

My paper hopes to show that this offers us a misleading view of Harrington's thought, that it misreads between Harrington's lines, that we should not be so eager to see inconsistencies and so quick to explain them by reference to Harrington's awareness of prevalent capitalist attitudes, lest we lose sight of an alternative hypothesis and overlook his own explicit explanations. Considerations that diminish and even counter the realist emphasis support the conclusion that, though Harrington recognized self-interest, he took pains to mitigate man's desire to accumulate; such pains, indeed, that to safeguard his provision against gross accumulation

* From no. 24 (April 1963).

he denied the absolute infallibility of his own first premise and fundamental law of history that power hinged upon the balance of property. Above all, he wished to limit and disperse property—his notion of justice was distributive—so he might be called a non-bourgeois idealist.

Harrington was certainly evasive on the gentry: he never offered a precise definition of them; and it is right to notice that they are equated with the people in the historical analyses of the shifting balance, but with the nobility in discussions of the ideal common-wealth. Harrington's explanation for this is explicit in his *A Discourse Shewing that the Spirit of Parliaments . . . is not to be trusted for a Settlement. . . :*[1]

> the House of Commons . . . consisted of about four hundred Deputies of the People, for the most Part Gentlemen, and old Stagers. . . . [This Assembly's Laws have] been much of the middle Way . . . while they [the gentry] were under a Nobility; but since, through the natural Decay of that Order, they came to a greater Height, it hath been to endure no Check. Wherefore as it hath been found under a King, that such an Assembly will endure no King, through the Check they apprehend from him; so it will be found that under a Commonwealth they will be addicted unto the Introduction of Monarchy, through the Check they apprehend from the People.

In the past, gentry had been neither fish nor fowl, nobility nor people. Under a king their interests stood close enough to the people's—yeomen and tenantry—for them to serve as 'Deputies for the People' in the Commons, though, at the same time, they remained 'too high and too narrow to descend wholly unto the true Interest of the People'.[2] But take some authority from above them and vest it below them and they would aspire to be aristocrats themselves. To be sure this was a slide, yet the reason for it was explicit: neither ambiguous nor dubious, but empirical. The slide simply mirrored what Harrington thought was happening to

---

[1] James Harrington, *The Oceana and Other Works*, ed. J. Toland *et al.* (London, 1737), pp. 609–10. (The 1737 and 1747 editions have the same pagination. Professor Macpherson used the 1771 edition with different pagination.)

[2] *A Discourse Shewing that the Spirit of Parliaments . . . is not to be trusted*, in *Works*, p. 609.

the gentry. When military power had been wrested from the
nobility by Henry VIII, it followed that in the power vacuum the
gentry would become more independent, and so more important
and self-conscious politically. This is to agree that Harrington
took an aristocratic view of the seventeenth-century gentry, but it
is to deny a charge of ambiguity and it avoids recourse to an
unstated assumption of Harrington's that the gentry were bourgeois-minded.

For the purpose of discussing his commonwealth Harrington
included gentry with nobility. Clearly he regarded nobility-
gentry as having divergent interests from the people. Give the
people some power and the nobility-gentry would be 'agin the
government' like Huck Finn's father. Harrington's crucial problem, therefore, was to cut them down to size, to divert and channel
their aristocratic inclinations in favour of the commonwealth, to
stifle their divisive tendencies for the unity and peace of the
nation. And his method to achieve this was the Agrarian Law.

Primogeniture was to be abolished, and a limit of £2,000 set on
incomes from land in England. (The limit was £4,500 for the
British Isles, and more in the colonies. Dowries were limited, but
incomes from office or business were unlimited. Harrington
regarded land as the primary source of wealth.) It is the limit of
£2,000 that gets Harrington into trouble, for, since he assumed the
total rental value of English land to be £10,000,000, it was possible
that 5,000 people might hold all the land. How then could he say
'the people' had the power?

One reason is that he defined his terms to suit himself: government by 5,000 or more citizens was government by the people.
5,000 was the lower limit, the point at which a popular government began to change into an aristocratical government:[3]

> In a Territory not exceding *England* in Revenue, if the
> Balance be in more hands than three hundred, it is declining
> from Monarchy; and if it be in fewer than five thousand
> hands, it is swerving from a Commonwealth.

Why is 5,000 chosen as the turning-point? As far as one can tell
the reason was simply that 5,000 became the quorum for the
Athenian Assembly, according to Thucydides:[4]

[3] *Art of Lawgiving*, p. 392.
[4] *Valerius and Publicola*, p. 479; see *Oceana*, p. 76.

Valerius. The *Athenian Quorum* was six thousand; which towards the latter end of that Commonwealth came to five.
Publicola. So, so, you may quote Authors: But you may remember also, that *Athens* was a small Commonwealth.
Val. How many would you advise for *England?*
Pub. Put the case I should say, ten thousand?
Val. They will laugh at you.
Pub. What can I help that? or how many would you advise?
Val. I would not go above five thousand.

If we appreciate that Harrington accepted 5,000 as an apt quorum for popular government then the difficulty that seems so glaring is obliterated. 5,000 might get all the land, but by definition government would still be by the people.

One may, of course, deplore Harrington's arbitrary and indiscriminate application of an Athenian standard to England. One may deplore his slavish reverence for classical models. One may even accuse him of imprecise writing, but not of wild contradictions. For, by playing at Humpty Dumpty, setting up his own criteria, he must be allowed to have avoided the brunt of the charge.

He is not entirely exonerated however, for when Harrington considered a hypothetical future danger he was led into temporary double-talk. What was to prevent the 5,000 people with all the land and hence the power from overthrowing both the Agrarian Law and the commonwealth at a blow. Here is the double-talk:

> thro the equality of the Balance, or of their Estates, they [the 5,000] can be no more by themselves than an equal Commonwealth, and that they were already with the People.[5]

By definition they were a popular government. Only they might become more narrowly popular than they should be. The whole problem, indeed, was hardly real to Harrington. It was asking 'Why shouldn't the few-many try to overthrow the many-many?' Harrington thought of 'the People' as an abstract unit, which underlines the strength of the influence of classical categories upon his thinking.

Anyway, to please his critics, Harrington offered three answers

[5] *Prerogative of Popular Government*, p. 261.

to the hypothetical, unlikely difficulty. Firstly, it would be against the interests of both the many-many or the few-many to alter the Agrarian Law. On the one hand the Agrarian would keep the opportunity of attaining property open to future generations. On the other hand, if 5,000 happened to acquire all the land, each would hold equal portions of it. Abolishing the Agrarian would permit one to gain more than another, at the expense of the other, so altering it would merely be granting licence to rob one another. As a collective group, the 5,000 would surely prefer equality to insecurity—a preference that does not seem particularly bourgeois. Altogether, an acquisitive, but a limited acquisitive self-interest would keep the Agrarian operating.

Secondly, the frame of the commonwealth's political structure provided against it. The Senate and a minority of the representative body were to be occupied by the 'natural aristocracy'. Harrington equated natural aristocracy with men affluent in landed property, that is, with the nobility-gentry, as only they had the leisure that freed them for political duty. However, a majority of the representative (variously 4:3 or 3:2) were to be specifically men of little property—men of the 'meaner sort'. Harrington assumed men knew their own interests. This being so the poorer majority would always block, having the power of veto, any attempt by a rich coterie to overthrow the Agrarian. This argument carries two implications that are worth emphasizing. Firstly, though by definition the 5,000 constituted a commonwealth, some of them might still want to overthrow the Agrarian. Their interests might still collide with the People's at large. The implication altogether precludes the assertion that Harrington assumed that nobility-gentry shared common attitudes with the many people. The truth is the reverse: Harrington envisaged the possibility of a class clash and provided for it, in the constitution, in advance. Secondly, providing for a majority of men of the meaner sort in the representative was, in effect, to vest an ultimate veto with them, which shows that the superstructure did not reflect the overbalance of property faithfully. Power could be exercised against and in spite of the overbalance. Clearly, with this argument, Harrington was entrenching somewhat upon his fundamental principle that the balance of power depended upon the balance of property. As clearly, he was so doing in order to maintain the Agrarian Law intact, and so to sustain the greater commonwealth.

Harrington's third argument involved a similar trespass on principle. 5,000 would not attempt to overthrow the greater commonwealth because the many people had superior numbers and arms. They could command superior force, 'the People being equally possest of the Government, of the Arms, and far superior in number'.[6] Power, here, was divorced from property. Force was recognized as an authority in itself, for it could capture power even though it was not based on the balance of property.

When Henry Neville and other Harringtonians argued in Parliament that 'the gentry do not now depend upon the peerage. The balance is in the gentry. They have all the lands',[7] one counter was Major Beake's:[8]

> The sword is there. Is not that . . . a good balance? He that has a regiment of foot to command in the army, he is as good a balance as any I know, and can do more.

It was unanswerable. Had not the Cromwellians risen to power without an overbalance of property, and were they not now setting up a House of Lords? The prospect moved Harrington close to despair.[9]

> If the House consists of new Peers only, it must consist of the chief Officers in the Army; which immediatly divides the Government into two distinct Governments: the one in the House of Commons, whose Foundation is the Body of the People; the other in the House of Peers, whose Foundation is the Army. This Army . . . they not only command the Commons, but make and unmake Kings as they please; or as ambitious Partys and Persons among themselves are diligent or fortunat.

In the real situation all Harrington could do was hope against hope. But in his model structure force was vested in the many, to be used if necessary against the few. Once again power was divorced from property, and once again, the discrepancy occurred

---

[6] *Prerogative of Popular Government*, p. 261; see *Art of Lawgiving*, p. 464; *A System of Politics*, p. 496.

[7] Thomas Burton, *Parliamentary Diary*, ed. J. T. Rutt, 4 vols (London, 1828), iii, p. 133.

[8] Burton, *Diary*, ii, p. 416.

[9] *A Word Concerning a House of Peers*, p. 470.

because Harrington wanted to safeguard the Agrarian Law against all contingencies.

If the Agrarian worked as it should, these safeguards would never be necessary. For it would be the rarest imaginable occurrence for all the land to fall into 5,000 hands. And it was so improbable because the Agrarian worked against the consolidation of large holdings in favour of their wider distribution. First, the Agrarian forbade primogeniture and provided for the equal, or near equal, distribution of property to all the children of a family. Secondly, Harrington assumed that the heirs would outnumber the benefactors, that the population would always be increasing.[10] The combination of these two circumstances had to result in wider distribution of property among the people. This Agrarian process would neither destroy private property, nor equalize or level it, but the process would distribute it to more people.[11]

> The Land thro which the River *Nilus* wanders in one stream,
> is barren; but where it parts into seven, it multiplys its
> fertil shores by distributing, yet keeping and improving such
> a Propriety and Nutrition, as is a prudent Agrarian to a well-
> order'd Commonwealth.

This distributive Agrarian was the real corner-stone of Harrington's ideal commonwealth. So much so, that as we have seen, he would diminish the applicability of his universal law to preserve it. It was the only way to tame the nobility-gentry. The size of their properties would be limited and they prevented from accumulating more. 'Popular Government requires ... that its Agrarian prevent accumulation.'[12] Distribution would occur in the next generation.

Such a scheme for limitation and dispersal of property can hardly be called bourgeois, for in principle it involved a negation of market relations, and an interference with private ownership. Neither, in view of his hopes, can Harrington be called a realist, for he believed that the Agrarian would work to obviate class divisions, guarantee political stability, achieve true liberty, justice, security, vast empire and national renown for ever.

[10] *Art of Lawgiving*, pp. 435 and 456–7; *Oceana*, pp. 107–8; *Prerogative of Popular Government*, pp. 300–1.
[11] *Oceana*, p. 108.
[12] *Art of Lawgiving*, p. 392.

But what of the second stage of the realist argument: the collation of *obiter dicta* to show Harrington's appreciation of market relations? Harrington's statements cannot be flatly denied. He did support usury within limits; he welcomed the social mobility resulting from the expansion of trade; he applauded industry, colonial expansion, and rent-raising. He had an elementary understanding of the inter-relationships between town and country, and he was certainly aware of market relations. All this is true. One can find a bit of the bourgeois in Harrington, and it is interesting for its own sake. But it is largely incidental to an overall appreciation of his thought, where the dominating strain was idealism: Harrington's conviction that he had divined the way to Utopia.

Does this interpretation suggest grosser inconsistencies than the realist approach discovered? No, rather it diminishes and delimits the contradictions. Harrington did maintain inconsistencies to protect his Agrarian Law, and these seem to contravene his fundamental thesis that power depended on the balance of property, yet the contrary provisions were for wholly unexpected and hypothetical occasions. His premise remained generally if not universally true. Like a biological law that states the norm but allows variations, Harrington's principle was applicable to most times but admitted of qualification in unusual cases. Harrington was neither highly illogical nor very realistic, but a Utopian who reasoned a dream on the basis of a distributive Agrarian.

IV

HARRINGTON AS REALIST: A REJOINDER *

C. B. Macpherson

The 'distributive Agrarian', the basis of Mr New's interpretation, requires attention first. The Agrarian, he says, 'provided for the equal, or near equal, distribution of property to all the children of a family'. It did nothing of the sort. Mr New has misread the inheritance provision of the Agrarian, which is:[1]

> that every man who is at present possest, or shall hereafter
> be possest of an estate in land exceeding the revenue of two
> thousand pounds a year, and having more than one son, shall
> leave his lands either equally divided among them, in case
> the lands amount to above 2000 l. a year to each; or so near
> equally in case they com under, that the greater part or
> portion of the same remaining to the eldest, excede not the
> value of two thousand pounds revenue.

This does *not* provide for the generally equal or near equal distribution of property to all the children of a family; nor even to all the sons of all the few families (fewer than 300 in all England) having estates of over £2,000 a year. The intention, and the effect, of the law is to divide these large estates not as equally as possible but as unequally as possible, i.e., as unequally as is consistent with the £2,000 a year upper limit. The eldest son is to have the full £2,000 a year land; the other sons are to divide what is left over.

* From no. 24 (April 1963).

[1] *Oceana*, p. 95 (102). Cf. *Prerogative of Popular Government*, p. 271 (291); *Art of Lawgiving*, p. 408 (435). Page references are to the 1771 edition of James Harrington, *The Oceana and Other Works*, with the page of the 1737 edition in brackets.

Only in the extreme case of an estate amounting to more than £2,000 a year for *each* son, is the division to be equal (unequal division not being needed, in that case, to give the eldest the full £2,000 a year). The purpose of the inheritance clause of the Agrarian was simply to reduce, into conformity with the £2,000 a year maximum (which was permanently established by the other main clause of the Agrarian), those few estates which now exceeded the maximum, and to do this in as painless (i.e. as unequal) a way as possible. The 'peculiar end' of the inheritance law was to 'prevent the growing of a monarchical nobility'[2] by preventing any new concentration of land in a small nobility.

The Agrarian neither 'forbade primogeniture' nor 'abolished' it. Primogeniture was left almost untouched. No one but the owner of an estate of more than £2,000 a year was forbidden to leave his entire estate to the eldest son. And within a few generations, as soon as the inheritance clause of the Agrarian had done its job of bringing the over-large estates within the maximum, there would be no obstacle whatever to primogeniture.

The Agrarian would indeed have the effect, in a few generations, of breaking up each estate of over £2,000 a year into two or more estates, one or more of which would be worth just £2,000 a year; but that is as far as the redistribution would go. I comment later on the implications of this much distribution. Harrington at least was sure that it would encourage, not discourage, enterprise and industry; the gentry-nobility, like the merchants, were expected to go on accumulating wealth.[3]

The Agrarian, then, affords no support (nor is there any other support) for Mr New's statements that Harrington 'took pains to mitigate man's desire to accumulate', that 'above all, he wished to limit and disperse property', and that 'his notion of justice was distributive'; nor does it merit the description 'a distributive Agrarian'. Yet it is on these propositions that Mr New's alternative hypothesis rests. I cannot therefore find that he has made any case for his view that Harrington was 'a non-bourgeois idealist' or 'a Utopian who reasoned a dream on the basis of a distributive Agrarian'.

Mr New's attempts to confute my interpretation may now be considered.

[2] *Art of L.*, p. 408 (435).
[3] *Oceana*, pp. 100-1 (108); *Prerogative*, p. 280 (301-2).

(1) About the ambiguous treatment of the gentry little need be said. Mr New admits the ambiguity. What he denies is historical inconsistency. I had already denied this (p. 34). Ambiguity is not the same as inconsistency.

(2) As to the relation between the gentry-nobility and the people in the proposed commonwealth, I agree (as I said, p. 44) that Harrington assumed they had different interests. But there is no evidence that Harrington thought the nobility-gentry in a popular commonwealth 'would be "agin the government" '. The evidence is all the other way: he thought that his system of concurrent powers for the two classes would work. He did not need to 'tame the nobility-gentry'. His 'crucial problem' was not 'to cut them down to size': he thought they were cut down to size already, as I showed (p. 30). They were no danger; they were 'not only safe, but necessary',[4] provided they held an underbalance of property, as they then did. Where the nobility-gentry do not overbalance the people in wealth, the people will willingly accept the leadership of a natural aristocracy:[5] 'the senat and the people in an equal commonwealth having but one and the same interest, never were nor can be at variance'; 'there being no possible cause of disagreement [in Oceana] between the few and the many, the senat and the people, there can be no such effect'.[6] The Agrarian was not a method of cutting them down to size; it was a method of preventing them ever getting an overbalance.

(3) Where Harrington gets into difficulty, as Mr New and I agree, is when he tries to show that even if the land all came into the hands of 5,000 owners there would still be a popular commonwealth or an 'equal balance', and that the Agrarian and the commonwealth would not be endangered. I found contradictions here, and argued that they would have been resolved if Harrington had made his bourgeois assumptions explicit. Mr New admits the contradictions (euphemistically) and argues that they followed from Harrington's desire to maintain the Agrarian intact. The arguments rest on a false premise: that Harrington thought any constitutional measures were needed to safeguard the Agrarian. He did not; he held that the Agrarian, once established, was impregnable because neither the few nor the many would have both the interest and the physical power to overthrow it.

[4] *Oceana*, p. 125 (135). [5] *Ibid.*, p. 133 (143).
[6] *Prerogative*, pp. 244, 247 (261, 265).

Thus the bicameral legislature with veto power in the representatives of 'the meaner sort' was not offered as a safeguard of the Agrarian. Hence it cannot have been 'to maintain the Agrarian Law intact' that he allowed himself the contradiction of recommending a bicameral superstructure which would not, in a commonwealth of 5,000 owners (though it would in the England of 1656 for which he was in the first place recommending it), 'reflect the overbalance of property faithfully'.

Again, Harrington did *not* think that in a commonwealth of 5,000 owners, 'their interests might still collide with the People's at large'. He admitted that some of the 5,000 might wish to overthrow the Agrarian, but at the expense of the rest of the 5,000, not of the people at large; and he relied on the self-interest of the rest of the 5,000, not on the people, to prevent it. Harrington did not 'envisage the possibility of a class clash'; he argued, against those who did envisage it, that such a clash was impossible (for reasons having nothing to do with the political structure).

(4) Returning to the Agrarian, Mr New writes: 'Such a scheme for limitation and dispersal of property can hardly be called bourgeois, for in principle it involved a negation of market relations, and an interference with private ownership'. It involved neither. Abolition of primogeniture in estates above £2,000 a year not only is consistent with, but by 1656 might well be considered an encouragement to, market relations, and this for the very reason given in the passage Mr New quotes (at his note 11) and in the next paragraph of *Oceana*, namely, that it multiplies the fertility of capital. Harrington's scheme does not involve 'a negation of market relations', it brings more land into market relations. Nor is its net effect 'an interference with private ownership'. Capitalist relations require freedom of disposal of property. In so far as primogeniture had any legal or customary force by 1656, it interfered with that free disposal: the Agrarian removed the interference. True, an opposite compulsion was set up: the owner of a very large landed estate was no longer free to leave that whole estate to one son. But this is a lesser interference with capitalist private ownership than is primogeniture. Mr New has shown nothing in the Agrarian inconsistent with Harrington having had bourgeois assumptions.[7] Nor does he challenge any of

[7] For the consistency of bourgeois society with state interference, see my

the evidence I presented for Harrington having had those assumptions.

(5) Mr New suggests finally that Harrington cannot 'be called a realist, for he believed that the Agrarian would work to obviate class divisions, guarantee political stability, achieve true liberty, justice, security, vast empire and national renown for ever'. Harrington did *not* believe that the Agrarian would work to obviate class divisions, nor did he want the existing class differences obviated. The gentry and the people were different, but necessary to each other.[8] The Agrarian was simply to prevent a new and dangerous class division from arising. Nor was it on the Agrarian that he relied to guarantee political stability, achieve true liberty, and the rest; it was on his ingenious fitting, to the *present* balance of property, a superstructure so arranged that it would not only match the present balance but would allow both the classes (nobility-gentry and the people) the freedom of enterprise which would make England great. It was a perfectly realistic proposal, given the assumption I found in Harrington—namely, that the gentry were sufficiently bourgeois not to use their co-ordinate legislative power to hinder market relations. Even the extremely high maximum set by the Agrarian was not too high on that assumption.

Political Theory of Possessive Individualism: Hobbes to Locke (Oxford, 1962), chap. 2, sec. 3 (iv), esp. p. 58.
[8] *Oceana*, p. 53 (56–7).

V

THE MEANING OF
HARRINGTON'S AGRARIAN*

John F. H. New

In the exchange over Harrington in the last issue of *Past and Present* (pp. 54–66) Professor Macpherson saw that the crux of the case against him was the meaning of the Agrarian Law. Yet though he quoted the inheritance provision, his gloss upon it distorted the plain sense of the passage. Its intention was not to divide large estates 'as unequally as possible, i.e., as unequally as is consistent with the £2,000 a year upper limit'. Rather, equality was to be absolute among the sons when the individual inheritances amounted to more than £2,000 per annum; and equality was to be at least approximate when the inheritances fell below the limit. In both categories primogeniture was abolished. It is true that, in theory, in the second instance, favouritism could be shown towards the first-born. But Harrington expected that in practice this concession would be negated.[1]

> A Man has five Sons; let them be call'd: Would they enjoy their Father's Estate? It is divided among them: for we have four Votes for one in the same Family, and therefore this must be the Interest of the Family, or the Family knows not its own Interest.

And further on, speaking generally, Harrington described primogeniture as 'a flinty Custom' and scorned those who 'think ill of

---

* From no. 25 (July 1963).
[1] *Oceana*, p. 107. References are to James Harrington, *The Oceana and Other Works*, ed. J. Toland *et al.* (London, 1737).

a Government that will not indure it'.[2] These provisions applied to smaller properties as well as to the larger holdings. (It should be said that Harrington rejected the *reductio ad absurdum* of his cause, levelling, as impossible.[3]) Certainly, it is naive to imagine that Harrington wanted merely the break-up of a few large estates. He hoped to be both more effective and more gradual than the Gracchus brothers, and, like them, aimed to develop a numerous landed citizenry in order to strengthen the army and to stabilize the Republic.[4] 'The true cause whence *England* has bin an over-match in Arms for *France*', he recalled, 'lay in the communication or distribution of Property to the lower sort'.[5] His equal Agrarian intended land to be 'diffus'd thro the whole People'.[6] Yet Professor Macpherson categorically denied what I had affirmed along with Harrington, that an Agrarian exists 'when the Law commands an equal or near distribution of a Man's Estate in Land among his Children'.[7]

Notwithstanding its equalizing tendency, the Agrarian would lead to prosperity. Since money was not confined the Agrarian did not constrain trade.[8] The nobility-gentry, however, were not expected to make their 'increase' from trade, but from 'an Industry less greasy, or more noble',[9] in the public service, and military endeavour.[10]

> For such an Agrarian makes a Commonwealth for increase: the Trade of a Commonwealth for increase, is Arms; Arms are not born by Merchants, but by Noblemen and Gentlemen. The Nobility therfore having these Arms in their hands, by which Provinces are to be acquir'd, new Provinces yield new Estates.[11]

[2] *Oceana*, p. 108.
[3] Families would not press distribution beyond a point of no return. See *Oceana*, p. 166; *Prerogative of Popular Government*, pp. 264–5.
[4] *Oceana*, pp. 57, 61; *Art of Lawgiving*, p. 458.
[5] *Art of L.*, p. 457.   [6] *Prerogative*, p. 290.   [7] *Oceana*, p. 105.
[8] It would, indeed, stimulate it. 'A populous Country makes a populous City by weaning; for when the People increase so much, that the dug of Earth can do no more, the overplus must seek som other way of Livelihood: which is either Arms . . . or Merchandize and Manufacture.' *Prerogative*, p. 301.
[9] *Oceana*, p. 108.
[10] Pay scales are set out in *Oceana*, pp. 162, 224.   [11] *Prerogative*, p. 301.

The Agrarian would set the nobility-gentry upon the path of Empire by a combination of lure and limitation. New lands, apportioned by an Agrarian, would be the spoils of conquest and colonization. 'Who knows how far the Arms of our Agrarian may extend themselves?'[12] he mused; and the question should cause the reader to wonder whether Harrington was primarily bourgeois-minded or a social and political idealist, entranced by former civilizations (especially by 'the Paragon', Rome[13]), who believed that land distribution would lead to untold expansion and riches for all.

[12] *Oceana*, p. 108.   [13] *Ibid.*, p.196.

VI

THE LEVELLERS AND DEMOCRACY*

J. C. Davis

Professor C. B. Macpherson's thesis that the Levellers were never democrats, in the modern sense,[1] is rapidly becoming the new orthodoxy. His view of them as consistent proponents of a limited franchise has been basically accepted, although there has been some quarrel with his statistics, particularly in regard to the size of the servant class.[2] I believe that Macpherson's thesis is not proven and that, before more theorizing is done on the basis of the Levellers' assumed moderation, a re-examination of the evidence is necessary.

Macpherson's case centres around the Putney debates and the following resolution, passed by the General Council of the Army on 4 or 5 November 1647:[3]

> That all soldiers and others, *if they be not servants or beggars*, ought to have voices in electing those which shall represent them in Parliament, although they have not forty shillings per annum in freehold land.

* From no. 40 (July 1968).
[1] C. B. Macpherson, *The Political Theory of Possessive Individualism: Hobbes to Locke* (Oxford, 1962), chap. 3, 'The Levellers: franchise and freedom'.
[2] See, for example, Christopher Hill's enthusiastic review, 'Possessive Individualism', *Past and Present*, no. 24 (April 1963), pp. 86–9; Maurice Ashley, 'Oliver Cromwell and the Levellers', *History Today*, vol. xvii, no. 8 (August 1967), pp. 539–44; Peter Laslett, 'Market Society and Political Theory', *The Historical Jl*, vii (1964), pp. 150–4.
[3] *A Letter sent from Several Agitators of the Army to their Respective Regiments* (1647) in A. S. P. Woodhouse (ed.), *Puritanism and Liberty* (London, 1950), p. 452.

Clearly this proposes an exclusive franchise; according to Macpherson, exclusive of two-thirds of the adult male population.[4] Since copyholders would be enfranchised on this basis, the resolution was a defeat for Cromwell and Ireton who wanted to restrict the franchise to the freeholder. If one sees the Levellers as unflinching democrats,[5] one also has to see it as a defeat for them since it did not incorporate manhood suffrage.

This is rejected by Macpherson.[6] The resolution represented what the Levellers had always wanted. The Putney debates were not about manhood suffrage at all but were a contest between the freehold franchise, represented by Cromwell and Ireton, and a franchise inclusive of copyholders but exclusive of servants and paupers, represented by the Levellers. The latter triumphed. His evidence for this consists of two statements made by Maximilian Petty, one of the two civilians present. The first of these came early on the second day of the debate: 'We judge that all inhabitants that have not lost their birthright should have an equal voice in elections'.[7] This looks democratic but, according to Macpherson, the Levellers included in those who had lost their birthright criminals, delinquents, servants and alms-takers. His proof of this comes in Petty's second statement:[8]

> I conceive the reason why we would exclude apprentices, or servants, or those that take alms, is because they depend upon the will of other men and should be afraid to displease [them]. For servants and apprentices, they are included in their masters, and so for those that receive alms from door to door. . . .

From this Macpherson infers that all other Levellers must identify the birthright of freemen in the same way, that is, as exclusive of

---

[4] Macpherson, *op. cit.*, pp. 112–15, 279–92. According to his calculations, the franchise for all men except servants and alms-takers would comprise 417,000 men. Manhood franchise would comprise about 1,170,000, less any allowance for criminals and delinquents. See Laslett, *op. cit.*, pp. 151–2, for a criticism of his view of the servant class.

[5] Cf. H. N. Brailsford, *The Levellers and the English Revolution*, ed. Christopher Hill (London, 1961), p. 554.

[6] See Macpherson, *op. cit.*, pp. 117–36.

[7] A. S. P. Woodhouse, *op. cit.*, p. 53, quoted by Macpherson, *op. cit.*, p. 122.

[8] Woodhouse, *op. cit.*, p. 83; quoted by Macpherson, *op. cit.*, p. 123.

servants and paupers. Consequently all Leveller statements at, before or after Putney which refer to 'freemen' or 'birthright' must be similarly interpreted. Further, vaguer assertions of apparent democracy can be dismissed because the unspoken assumption is that servants and paupers are excluded. Finally, Macpherson concludes that the Levellers were always consistent advocates of a franchise exclusive of servants and paupers but inclusive of copyholders, that they triumphed at Putney but not in the name of manhood suffrage because they were never democrats.[9]

Assuming that Macpherson was correct in interpreting Petty as wanting the limited or exclusive franchise, let us look at the inferences from this. These are, first, that Petty's views were those of the Levellers at Putney; in other words, in this he was *the* Leveller spokesman. However, apart from this appearance at Putney and the fact that he sat on some Leveller/Independent committees, we know nothing at all about him. Through the Thomason collection we have the tract material of the day in great abundance, but nothing appears by Maximilian Petty to elucidate his views for us. He was not one of the ideological leaders of the Levellers. At the similarly constituted Whitehall debates in December 1648 Petty was withdrawn and Lilburne took his place. On the first and third days of the Putney debate Petty said nothing; Wildman and Colonel Thomas Rainsborough acted as spokesmen for the Levellers. Similarly, on the second day, when Petty made the statements Macpherson has used, it is Wildman and Rainsborough (particularly the latter) who do the talking for the Levellers. Can we rely, as Macpherson has done, on two reported sentences from Petty, one of which is incomplete, for a wholesale reinterpretation of the very extensive writings of the Levellers?

The second inference that Macpherson makes is that one can ascribe the views that Petty holds to all Levellers at all times. This assumes too high a degree of consistency amongst the Levellers both in personnel and time. To take the first—Henry Denne in a pamphlet of his, *The Levellers Designe Discovered*, published in 1649, wrote, 'We were an Heterogenial Body, consisting of parts very diverse one from another, setled upon principles inconsistent one with another'.[10]

Why should we assume that no other Leveller could be a

9 Macpherson, *op. cit.*, p. 136.
10 Henry Denne, *The Levellers Designe Discovered* (1649), p. 8.

72

democrat if Maximilian Petty was not? Why should we have to believe that the Levellers could *never* be democrats if they were not advocating democracy at Putney? Macpherson says because, 'The Levellers were zealots for principle, and had they ever embraced the full principle of universal suffrage they could scarcely have withdrawn it from all the agricultural labourers on such wholly expedient grounds'.[11] Such uncompromising zeal for principle is not, however, a feature of the Levellers' record on, for example, tithes. The Levellers felt that tithes were a matter of principle[12] and Richard Overton, in 1645, devoted a whole pamphlet to the issue.[13] In the March Petition of 1647[14] and the July Appeal of 1647[15] they demanded the abolition of tithes apparently without compensation. In the First Agreement, which was being debated at Putney, tithes did not figure in the Leveller programme. In 1648, in the January Petition, they deliberately left tithes out as an issue so as not to 'disingage any considerable partie, and so continue our distractions'.[16] Later in 1648, in the Humble Petition[17] and the Second Agreement,[18] the abolition of tithes

---

[11] Macpherson, *op. cit.*, p. 295.

[12] See, for example, William Walwyn, *A Whisper in the Eare of Mr. Thomas Edwards Minister* (1646), p. 6. Walwyn says: 'the Scripture manifesting to my understanding, tythes to be ceremoniall and Jewish, and so to cease at the comming of Christ: and that to enforce or enjoyn a maintenance though under any other notion, is as I apprehend contrary to the rule and practice of the Apostles . . .'.

[13] *The Ordinance for Tithes Dismounted* (December 1645).

[14] *To the right Honourable and supreme Authority of this Nation, the Commons in Parliament Assembled*, pp. 3, 6, in W. Haller (ed.), *Tracts on Liberty in the Puritan Revolution* (New York, 1965), iii, pp. 397–405; also in D. M. Wolfe, *Leveller Manifestoes of the Puritan Revolution* (New York, 1944), pp. 135–41. The argument used here was that there was no 'ground' for tithes 'under the Gospel'.

[15] *An Appeale from the Degenerate Representative Body of the Commons of England Assembled at Westminster* (1647) in Wolfe, *op. cit.*, pp. 156–95, see p. 193.

[16] *To the Supream Authority of* ENGLAND, *the Commons Assembled in Parliament. The earnest Petition of many Free-born People of this Nation* (1648) in Wolfe, *op. cit.*, pp. 263–72; John Wildman, *Truths triumph, or Treachery anatomized* (1647), p. 4.

[17] *The humble Petition* (September 1648), p. 6, in W. Haller and G. Davies (eds), *The Leveller Tracts 1647–1653* (New York, 1944), pp. 148–55.

[18] *Foundations of Freedom; or An Agreement of the People* (December 1648) in Wolfe, *op. cit.*, pp. 293–303, see p. 302. See also *An Agreement of the Free People of England* (May 1649), p. 6, in Haller and Davies, *op. cit.*, pp. 318–28.

is back in the programme—now with the proviso 'satisfying all Impropriators'.

Evidently, on tithes at least, the Levellers were capable of compromise when they thought they were being taken seriously. A similar type of development could be traced in the Levellers' attitude to the questions of local self-government, the position of the House of Lords and the king, or to parliamentary reform in general.

So that, even if we accepted Macpherson's interpretation of the Putney debate, we might feel that he was straining his material into something of a straitjacket. Still, we might decide that the balance of credibility was on his side. Closer examination of the Putney debate, however, casts Macpherson's interpretation of it and his whole theory into doubt.

Let us take Macpherson's idea that the Levellers were proposing a franchise exclusive of servants and paupers and see how well it fits the actual debates. On the second day of the debate the General Council got down to discussing the soldiers' proposals clause by clause. The first clause in their proposals reads:[19]

That the People of England being at this day very unequally distributed by Counties, Cities, & Burroughs, for the election of their Deputies in Parliament, ought to be more indifferently proportioned, according to the number of the inhabitants: the circumstances whereof, for number, place, and manner, are to be set down before the end of this present Parliament.

Ireton began by arguing that this proposal had democratic implications and as such he was against it. Surely, if the Levellers had been in favour of an exclusive franchise, they would now have made this clear in order to dissociate their proposal from a democracy they did not espouse. On the contrary, Colonel Thomas Rainsborough, who replied to Ireton, merely reinforced Ireton's inference:[20]

[19] *An Agreement of the People for a firme and present Peace, upon grounds of common-right and freedome* (November 1647) in Wolfe, *op. cit.*, pp. 223–35; see p. 226.
[20] In analysing the debate I have used the edition of the Clarke MSS. in Woodhouse, *op. cit.*, pp. 1–125. This quotation is on p. 53.

I think that the poorest he that is in England hath a life to live, as the greatest he; and therefore truly, sir, I think its clear, that every man that is to live under a government ought first by his own consent to put himself under that government; and I do think that the poorest man in England is not at all bound in a strict sense to that government that he hath not had a voice to put himself under.

Macpherson, of course, interprets this as excluding two-thirds of all adult males. Yet, if this is the case, Rainsborough failed to make it clear and Ireton immediately came back to press what he conceived of as his advantage. Taking Rainsborough to mean that every man born has political rights (that is, manhood suffrage) he says, 'by a man's being born here he shall have a share in that power that shall dispose of the lands here, and of all things here, I do not think it a sufficient ground',[21] and argued, in familiar vein, that manhood suffrage would mean communism:[22]

> Those that chose the representers for the making of laws by which this state and kingdom are to be governed, are the persons who, taken together do comprehend the local interest of this kingdom; that is, the persons in whom all land lies, and those in corporations in whom all trading lies. And if we shall go to take away this, we shall plainly go to take away all property and interest that any man hath either in land by inheritance, or in estate by possession, or anything else—if you take away this fundamental part of the civil constitution.

Again, surely if the Levellers believed in a limited franchise they would have been at some pains to escape these damaging implications by denying the grounds on which they were based, by making clear that they were not democrats but for a limited franchise.[23] Far from this, however, Rainsborough, who again

---

[21] *Ibid.*, p. 54.   [22] *Ibid.*, pp. 54–5.

[23] Similarly, just as the Levellers sought to establish that they were against 'levelling' in the economic sense by proposing a fundamental and unalterable law against 'levelling' (see e.g. *Foundations of Freedom*, in Wolfe, *op. cit.*, p. 301), might one not expect the same kind of provision against manhood suffrage, if, as Macpherson suggests, this was only a smear used against them by their opponents.

replied, confirmed Ireton's premise that he was dealing with democrats. God, he argued, had given reason to all men equally:[24]

> I do not find anything in the Law of God, that a lord shall choose twenty burgesses, and a gentleman but two, or a poor man shall choose none; I find no such thing in the Law of Nature, nor in the Law of Nations.

Are the people who fought for Parliament or contributed to the Parliamentary cause, and are now impoverished—are they to go without the vote?

Ireton, caught somewhat on the defensive by this appeal to military sentiment, but still able to play the red scare against Rainsborough, said:[25]

> All the main thing that I speak for, is because I would have an eye to property . . . the most fundamental part of the constitution.
> For thus: by the same right of nature (whatever it be) that you pretend, by which you can say, one man hath an equal right with another to the choosing of him that shall govern him—by the same right of nature, he hath the same right in any goods he sees—meat, drink, clothes—to take and use them for his sustenance.

Rainsborough in answer did not deny the inference of his democratic position but did deny the communist smear. To imply that the law of nature can repudiate property, he argued, is to forget the law of God. 'Thou shalt not steal' implies property. At this point Cromwell puts the crucial question to the Levellers, 'Where is there any bound or limit set?'[26]

Here, if anywhere, we would expect a party advocating an exclusive franchise to set forth the limits of their franchise. But Rainsborough in turn posed two questions. How does the property of the franchise come to be the right of some and not others? Is it the law of England that they should be bound by laws in which they have no voice?[27] Petty, the supposed advocate of limited franchise, then joined in, *not* to suggest a limited franchise but to argue that, although government was instituted

[24] Woodhouse, *op. cit.*, p. 56. [25] *Ibid.*, pp. 57–8.
[26] *Ibid.*, p. 59. [27] *Ibid.*, pp. 60–1.

to preserve property, this does not mean that those without property should have no consent in government.[28]

As if this were not enough to show that the Leveller position was redolent of manhood suffrage rather than limited franchise, Ireton, speaking after Petty, renewed Cromwell's question, 'Show me what you will stop at; wherein you will fence any man in property by this rule'.[29] To which John Wildman replied, not by proposing to exclude servants and paupers, but by sticking to apparent democracy of an unlimited form:[30]

> Every person in England hath as clear a right to elect his representative as the greatest person in England. I conceive that's an undeniable maxim of government: that all government is in the free consent of the people.

Finally it was Cromwell himself, and not one of the Levellers, who proposed a franchise based on the exclusion of servants and paupers,[31] and Petty's remarks after this could be interpreted as an examination of the proposal rather than an endorsement of it:[32]

> I conceive the reason why we would exclude apprentices, or servants, or those that take alms, is because they depend upon the will of other men and should be afraid to displease them. For servants and apprentices, they are included in their masters, and so for those that receive alms from door to door.

The resolution passed by the General Council of the Army could then be seen as a compromise between two positions rather than as a victory for either side; but with the Levellers giving more away than Cromwell and Ireton. Rainsborough himself seems to have been dissatisfied with the compromise motion and proposed a general rendezvous of the army, itself a democratic device. Thomas Rainsborough indeed provides problems for Macpherson's analysis which cannot be got round by dismissing him as 'a somewhat eccentric figure who was more or less out on a limb',[33] or his speeches as 'rhetorical flourishes'.[34]

The trouble with both those who see the Levellers as democrats,

[28] *Ibid.*, pp. 61–2.   [29] *Ibid.*, p. 63.   [30] *Ibid.*, p. 66.
[31] *Ibid.*, p. 82.   [32] *Ibid.*, p. 83.   [33] Ashley, *op. cit.*, p. 540.
[34] C. Hill, *The Century of Revolution, 1603–1714* (London, 1961), pp. 130–1.

and Macpherson, is that they are too insistent on consistency. Brailsford, for example, wants the Levellers to be 'unflinching democrats'. Macpherson sees them as such zealots for principle that they must have been unflinching non-democrats. This, it seems to me, is to miss the whole point about the Levellers. They were interested in political and constitutional arrangements as means and not as ends in themselves. They were not democrats for the sake of democracy—nor, if you will excuse the phrase, were they non-democrats for the sake of non-democracy. They adopted a democratic stance when they believed it was indispensable to their purposes, and equally they abandoned it when it was a hindrance to their achievement.

Macpherson does valuable service in reminding us of context. 'The people', in the seventeenth century, did not mean what it does today. What I hope to have suggested here is that it is still possible to conceive of the Levellers as having, at times, a radical concept of 'the people' akin to our own.

VII

RECONSIDERING
THE LEVELLERS: THE EVIDENCE
OF THE *MODERATE**

Roger Howell Jr and David E. Brewster

The Leveller movement has been one of the most extensively analysed aspects of the English Revolution.[1] The writings of Lilburne, Overton and Walwyn have been searched, scrutinized and examined, and many of the basic Leveller texts have been made available in modern editions. Scholars of note from Gardiner to Christopher Hill, from Firth to C. B. Macpherson have sought to unravel the strands of Leveller thought and to make clear what their programme consisted of.[2] In recent years, as a result mainly of the work of Professor Macpherson, many scholars have dramatically revised their views on the Leveller programme.

* From no. 46 (February 1970).
[1] Portions of this paper were delivered by R. Howell as a public lecture at the University of Oxford and at the University of Lancaster in November 1967. Much of the research was made possible through a grant from the Faculty Research Fund, Bowdoin College.

[2] See especially C. H. Firth (ed.), *The Clarke Papers*, i (Camden Soc., new ser. xlix, London, 1891); C. B. Macpherson, *The Political Theory of Possessive Individualism: Hobbes to Locke* (Oxford, 1962); S. R. Gardiner, *History of the Great Civil War, 1642–1649*, 4 vols (London, 1893); [J. E.] C. Hill, *Puritanism and Revolution: Studies in the Interpretation of the English Revolution of the Seventeenth Century* (London, 1958); [J. E.] C. Hill, 'The Many-Headed Monster in Late Tudor and Early Stuart Political Thinking', in C. H. Carter (ed.), *From the Renaissance to the Counter-Reformation: Essays in Honour of Garrett Mattingly* (London, 1966), pp. 296–324; A. S. P. Woodhouse (ed.), *Puritanism and Liberty* (London, 1951); D. M. Wolfe (ed.), *Leveller Manifestoes of the Puritan Revolution* (New York, 1944); W. Haller and G. Davies (eds), *The Leveller Tracts 1647–1653* (New York, 1944).

Gone are Firth's democrats with their demands for universal manhood suffrage; in their place are prototype Whigs. 'They ought rather to be considered radical liberals than radical democrats. . . . The Levellers paved the way, unwittingly, for Locke and the Whig tradition, for their whole doctrine of natural rights as property, and natural right to property, could be converted as readily to Locke's purposes as to any more radical ends.'[3]

Professor Macpherson has performed a valuable service in bringing to the fore some of the underlying assumptions of the Levellers and his book is a healthy corrective to enthusiastic accounts of the movement as one composed of full-blown democratic theorists. But historians might well exercise care before they take up the new orthodoxy completely. While it has apparently demolished the older view with great success, there are some very troublesome points that still remain. One such point is common to both old and new orthodoxies. This is the view that the Levellers, as a group, presented a coherent and unified programme.[4] All old-style Levellers stood for manhood suffrage (except in the Officers' *Agreement* of January 1649); all post-Macpherson Levellers stand with equal solidity behind a non-servant franchise. Is this a realistic view? Professor Macpherson raises, only to dismiss as unwarranted, the possibility that Leveller thought changed at about the time of the Putney debates.[5] This is not, however, the only, nor perhaps even the major question that should be raised. More to the point is the suggestion that Leveller thought may not have been monolithic, that the various writers associated with the movement held diverse opinions about political, social and economic problems even when they were drawn together as a political pressure group by the force of shared grievances. The Leveller Henry Denne com-

[3] Macpherson, *Possessive Individualism*, p. 158.
[4] Christopher Hill pointed out to R. Howell in Oxford in November 1967 an exception to this prevailing tendency: M. A. Barg, *Narodniye Nizy v Angliyskoy Revolyutsii 17v.* [The Lower Orders in the English Revolution of the 17th Century] (Moscow, 1967). See also Hill's note on this in *Past and Present*, no. 41 (Dec. 1968), p. 213. Another exception, which appeared after the text of this article was complete and which anticipates some of its arguments, is J. C. Davis, 'The Levellers and Democracy', *Past and Present*, no. 40 (July 1968), pp. 174–80 (pp. 70–8 in this volume).
[5] Macpherson, *Possessive Individualism*, pp. 118 ff.

mented: 'We were an Heterogenial Body, consisting of parts very diverse one from another, setled upon principles inconsistent one with another'.[6] It is possible that there may be more truth in this than historians have been willing to allow. It seems at least as plausible to read the Putney debates, for example, with the assumption that the Leveller spokesmen differed in their demands as it is to read them with the assumption that all shared whole-heartedly the views of Maximilian Petty. There can be no doubt that Petty advocated at Putney a franchise narrower than universal manhood suffrage. It is not so clear that others such as Rains-borough did. Arguing from inference (as Macpherson does) it can be suggested that Rainsborough's famous comments about 'the poorest man in England' and 'the poorest hee that is in England'[7] really meant the same thing as Petty's 'all inhabitants that have nott lost their birthright'.[8] On the other hand, they *could* mean simply what they say, provided one is willing to think that the Levellers may have differed among themselves over the exact degree of reform. The assertion that Rainsborough explicitly denied at Putney that he intended to include servants in the franchise is based on the interpretation of a somewhat garbled passage in Clarke's notes.[9] It is a passage which does not seem to point clearly either towards or away from a non-servant franchise, even in the emended version of Woodhouse.[10] In any case, Rainsborough's next speech, in which he refers back to this particular point, lends itself most easily to the interpretation that he took a very broad view of the suffrage, for he asserts that if the poor, who constitute four-fifths of the nation, were to be dis-franchised, then the numerically fewer rich would make them their slaves. 'I say the one parte shall make hewers of wood and drawers of water of the other five, and soe the greatest parte of the Nation bee enslav'd.'[11] There is little basis here for the suggestion that Rainsborough preferred 'to retain the present property qualification rather than risk that "the poor" should outvote "the people" '.[12]

Even in the standard Leveller tracts, there is some evidence

[6] H. Denne, *The Levellers Designe Discovered* (London, 1649), p. 8.
[7] *Clarke Papers*, i, p. 301.   [8] *Ibid.*, i, p. 300.
[9] *Ibid.*, i, pp. 315–16.   [10] Woodhouse, *op. cit.*, p. 64.
[11] *Clarke Papers*, i, p. 320.
[12] Macpherson, *Possessive Individualism*, p. 128.

that such differences did exist, and that Levellers, far from being
a unified party with an agreed programme, were a complex and,
in many ways, unhappy alliance of malcontents, not wholly
certain either in aim or in leadership. Generally speaking the
Levellers defended vigorously the institution of private property,
yet Walwyn at least was alleged to have spoken in favour of
common ownership, and it is difficult to find in his writings an
explicit defence of the institution of private property in the
manner of the other Levellers.[13] It is with this consideration in
mind—that the Levellers may not have had a unified outlook on
key issues—that we should examine the treatment of two important problems by the *Moderate*. The *Moderate*, the newspaper
edited by Gilbert Mabbott and published between July 1648 and
September 1649, has long been recognized as an important source
for the history of the Leveller movement.[14] It is surprising, in view
of this, how little attempt has been made to use it as a source for
Leveller ideas. Macpherson, for example, basing his case on what
he calls 'the standard Leveller documents',[15] makes no reference
to the editorial comments of the paper. Brailsford, who devoted
a chapter of his study to the *Moderate* and used it extensively in
other parts of his account, made no serious attempt to analyse its
contents as a contribution to Leveller thinking.[16] Only Frank has
made such an attempt and it is very sketchy.[17]

There are, of course, dangers in attempting to make such an
analysis. It is difficult to make precise attributions of authorship

[13] See W. Schenk, *The Concern for Social Justice in the Puritan Revolution*
(London, 1948), p. 49.
[14] It is generally assumed that Gilbert Mabbott, one of the official
licensers of the press, was editor for most of the paper's existence: J. B.
Williams, *A History of English Journalism to the Foundation of the Gazette*
(London, 1908), pp. 104 ff. But a denial of his editorship appears in *The
Moderate*, no. 12: 'As for one *Mabbot* that thou barkest at so violently,
I professe I know him not, nor to my knowledge ever saw him, which
will satisfie the Moderate Reader', *Moderate*, no. 12, 26 Sept.–3 Oct. 1648,
p. 96. The *Moderate*'s pagination is erratic. Citations are calculated from
the nearest previous numbered page.
[15] Macpherson, *Possessive Individualism*, p. 118 n. 1.
[16] H. N. Brailsford, *The Levellers and the English Revolution*, ed. C. Hill
(London, 1961), pp. 401–16.
[17] J. Frank, *The Levellers* (Cambridge, Mass., 1955), pp. 169–70 and *passim*;
J. Frank, *The Beginnings of the English Newspaper 1620–1660* (Cambridge,
Mass., 1961), pp. 154–60, 178–82.

for the *Moderate*'s contents, though it is possible to suspect that Overton had a hand in some of the better writing.[18] Because of its appearance as a weekly news-sheet, it did not have the space or the inclination to develop at any length a coherent political theory or an extended theoretical discussion of the basis for proposed reforms. One should be cautious about asserting how representative the paper was. These limiting factors are real, but they still do not destroy the utility which the paper can have for assessing the Leveller programme. If one surveys in the *Moderate* the treatment of the franchise issue and of the issue of religious toleration, some further light is cast on the Leveller programme—and that light seems to reinforce the interpretation that Leveller thought was not entirely a platform of agreed principles.

The political thought of the *Moderate* is neither startling nor original in many of its aspects. Much of what the paper had to say about government, the people, God, and their mutual relations was built on political commonplaces. The *Moderate* clearly believed that governments had their origins in the people and were established for the people's good. 'All Governments', said the editorial in number 20, 'come originally from the People, and are mutable at their pleasure, for their further good and wel-being. . .'.[19] But governments did not have human sanction alone. So long as they worked in the interests of the governed they were also approved by divine law. The editorial in number 14 of the *Moderate* proclaimed that 'All lawfull powers are ordained of God. . . .'.[20]

Properly exercised civil authority is considered to have a divine sanction and all governments are divinely approved, no matter what their form, so long as they are lawful—that is, so long as they function in the interests of the governed. God has no concern with the particular form of government a country might choose to adopt. If one form of government had special holy approval, then that form would be '*all one* in *all Nations*,

---

[18] Brailsford, *The Levellers*, pp. 408, 416 n. 4.
[19] *Moderate*, no. 20, 21–28 Nov. 1648, p. 165. The *Moderate* made a similar comment that 'All Powers are ordained by the supream Authority of the people, for their good and wel-being' in no. 60, 28 Aug.–4 Sept. 1649, p. 689. The statements are obviously very similar to comments by John Lilburne in *Londons Liberty in Chains Discovered* (London, 1646), p. 2, and *Regall Tyrannie Discovered* (London, 1647), p. 99.
[20] *Moderate*, no. 14, 10–17 Oct. 1648, p. 113.

seeing *God and Nature are one to all*'.[21] Since this was not the case, the *Moderate* concluded that the diversity of governments throughout the world and throughout history indicated that the selection of a particular form of civil authority was left to the people. Consequently, any given system of government required popular endorsement in order to be legal: 'these particular formes [of government] are left unto every Nation or Countrey, to chuse as they shall think best, and most fit for their Natures and conditions'.[22]

All governments, then, derive their ultimate authority from God, but their immediate authority comes from the governed. Without both sanctions, civil government becomes tyranny. In number 23, the *Moderate* stressed the emphasis it placed on divine and popular endorsement. By divine law 'God approves that form of Government which every Common wealth doth choose unto it self, as also the Conditions, Statutes, and Limitations which it self shall appoint unto her Princes'.[23] Human law taught that:[24]

> Princes are subject to Law and Order, and that the Commonwealth which gave them that authority for the common good of all, may also restrain, or take the same away again, if they abuse it, to the common evill, and may punish their Princes for such evill doings, he being not absolute. . . .

The *Moderate* maintained that governments held their power from the people by virtue of a trust which embodied the civil authority's responsibility to rule in the interests of the governed. Violation of this trust by the ruler, whether it be king or parliament, justified the people in resisting the established government. In fact, the *Moderate*'s position was even stronger than this. Not only were the people justified in their resistance under such conditions, they were under an obligation to refuse obedience. In an early number, the *Moderate* affirmed that civil authority came from God, 'but when misused, abused or unjustly executed, the duty of obedience is discharged, because the good intended thereby to man is diverted to mans utter ruine'.[25] Later, the *Moderate* stated that since civil authority is ordained by the people for the people's well-being, when governments act contrary to that pur-

21 *Moderate*, nos 20, 21–28 Nov. 1648, p. 165.
22 *Ibid.*   23 *Ibid.*, no. 23, 12–19 Dec. 1648, p. 202.
24 *Ibid.*   25 *Ibid.*, no. 14, 10–17 Oct. 1648, p. 113.

pose they 'not onely cease to be any longer obeyed, but ought to be questioned for all that evil and misery which they have brought the Nation into, by their breach of Trust, Corruption, Self-Interest, etc. . . .'[26] Because God's divine sanction had ordained government for the good of the people, misuse of civil power was a sin. Furthermore, obedience to a government that did not work in the people's interests was also a sin, since it was compliance with actions taken against God's will. As the editorial in number 14 put it, when the king falsifies his trust:[27]

> then his Commands being unlawfull, and destructive, it is lawfull for the people to disobey them, and on the contrary, it is no lesse then sin, and the forfeiture of all the Liberties, Freedoms, and Birth-rights of the people to give obedience thereunto.

These general outlines of the *Moderate*'s political thinking are not difficult to establish. The difficulty in interpreting them lies in determining what the *Moderate* meant by the use of the term 'the people'. This is, of course, precisely the problem raised by Macpherson in *The Political Theory of Possessive Individualism*. He has rightly cautioned the historian not to make the assumption that the use of the term 'the people' necessarily indicates an advocacy of manhood suffrage. He has shown how Leveller theorists such as John Harris could combine in a single sentence the assertion that 'all persons . . . should have a voyce in the electing their Representatives, or Members of Parliament' with the apparently contradictory assertion that the franchise was to extend to 'all men that are not servants or Beggers'.[28] His explanation of the Levellers is useful in revealing some of the complexities of their thinking. It is weakened, however, by its assumption of a considerable degree of consistency in the thinking of the Leveller movement. It is also suspect because of the extent to which it depends on inference from statements made mainly by one man in the Putney debates. Macpherson establishes his case by analysing the statements made at Putney, concluding that whenever the Levellers spoke of 'the people' they had in mind only members of the non-

26 *Ibid.*, no. 60, 28 Aug.–4 Sept. 1649, p. 689.
27 *Ibid.*, no. 14, 10–17 Oct. 1648, p. 114.
28 Macpherson, *Possessive Individualism*, p. 125, quoting J. Harris, *The Grand Designe* (London, 1647).

servant class—those who did not work for wages or receive charity.[29] With this for a basis he then expands his conclusions to include the entire Leveller movement, both before and after the Putney debates.

Macpherson is on unsafe ground when he assumes this kind of consistency. He himself has to admit that practically none of the pre-Putney statements on the franchise explicitly excludes servants or alms-takers.[30] And there is at least one post-Putney Leveller franchise demand that explicitly included servants. This is *A Charge of High Treason exhibited against Oliver Cromwell, Esq., for several Treasons by him committed*, published late in the summer of 1653:[31]

> all the people of *England* would as one man, as well Masters, Sons, as Servants, repair unto every Country-Town, or some other convenient place within *England*, and *Wales*, and appear Armed with such weapons of war as with conveniencie they can, then and there to Elect, and Chuse such and so many persons as the people of the respective Counties, Cities, and Boroughs wont to chuse for to represent them in Parliament.

Too much should not be made of *A Charge of High Treason*. It is, of course, a product of the dying moments of the Leveller movement, and it would be rash to assume that it represented a typical expression of their views. Macpherson is certainly correct in his assertion that some of the Levellers desired a non-servant franchise at all times. It would also appear to be well documented that most Levellers advocated a non-servant franchise during and

[29] It is not at all certain that the words 'servant' and 'free-born' had the precise meaning that Macpherson attributes to them. Particularly the term 'free-born' seems to have been a piece of political oratory rather than a precise legal term. K. V. Thomas is considering this problem further in a forthcoming study. This point is also discussed in A. L. Morton, *Leveller Democracy: Fact or Myth?* (London, 1968), *Our History*, Pamphlet no. 51, pp. 16–20. Morton's study raises a number of useful questions about Macpherson's views. The authors are indebted to K. V. Thomas for bringing this reference to their notice.

[30] Macpherson, *Possessive Individualism*, p. 118.

[31] Brit. Mus., 669, f. 17 (52): *A Charge of High Treason Exhibited Against Oliver Cromwell, Esq.*, (London, 1653). This is noted by Macpherson, *Possessive Individualism*, p. 118 n. 2.

after the Putney debates. But what of the *Moderate*, whose publishing career falls in the post-Putney period?

Early in its history, the *Moderate* showed that it equated 'the people' with those who had voting rights. The editorial in number 19 asked the question: 'But who are the People of this Nation?' The answer was:[32]

> Such as have never engaged for the King, against the Kingdom, and such as shall sign to an Ageeement [sic], to be drawn up by a Representative of the People, which is to be above Law, and the rest to be disfranchised, at least wise for some time, till the Kingdom be settled.

But, who was included in the people who would be asked to sign the Agreement? This is a central question.

It is important to note that the *Moderate* placed practically no qualification on the term 'the people' in any of its numbers. In this respect, it is closer to the spirit of the pre-Putney Leveller documents than to the Putney and post-Putney statements. Nowhere were servants explicitly excluded. It is clear that the *Moderate* believed that all men possessed the same birthright and that a crucial component of the birthright was freedom. This freedom was God-given. 'No man lives happily if he want the freedom of liberty', said the editorial in number 19, 'because slavery's the greatest misery, which all the people under the sun (though free born) have been subjected unto by the sword. . . .'[33] And the editorial in number 14 maintained:[34]

> There is a naturall discord between Tyrannie and Freedom, Slavish Popery, and Christian Liberty: *Ambrose* renders the reason thus, Because Christ the King of Kings, by his Rigtheousnesse [sic] hath made his people free therefore the Kings of the earth, by Tyrannie, Injustice, or Popish Interest, cannot make them slaves. . . .

Finally, the editorial in number 51 stated:[35]

> For the Lord will break the Rod of the Oppressor, and make his people free indeed, not onely in Christ, as to a spiritual,

---

[32] *Moderate*, no. 9, 14–21 Nov. 1648, p. 154.
[33] *Ibid.*, p. 153.
[34] *Ibid.*, no. 14, 10–17 Oct. 1648, p. 113.
[35] *Ibid.*, no. 51, 26 June–3 July 1649, p. 579.

but also the world, a temporal condition; so shall they submit to no power upon earth, but such as they shall choose
for their good and wel being. All [c]reatures being in sub-
j[e]ction to them, and they to none, but God, or such as they
themselves shall please to appoint, for the end aforesaid.

The editorial in number 61 was the closest the *Moderate* came to
summing up its attitudes towards the birthright, freedom and
government. Wars, claimed the editorial, had generally proved
destructive to the people and harmful to the nation, no matter
what justification was given for them. They had made 'the Sword
(and not the People) the original of all Authorities . . .'. In so
doing, wars had '[taken] away each mans Birth-right, and [settled]
upon a few, a cursed propriety (the ground of all Civil Offences
between party and party) and the greatest cause of most Sins
against the Heavenly Deity'. This tyranny had continued so long
that 'the vulgar' had come to look upon it as a natural state, and
this was 'the onely reason why the people at this time are so
ignorant of *their equal Birth-right, their onely Freedom*'.[36]

However, with God's approval, the people had at last managed
to cast off corrupt royal authority, thus making themselves free
'(as they fancied) from their former Oppressions, Burdens, and
Slaveries, and happy in what they could imagine, the greatest
good, both for their Soul and Body'. But the overthrow of
monarchy had not been enough, and the people, having discovered
their birthright—and their authority—cried out for 'a lawful
Representative, and such other wholesom Laws as will make them
truly happy'.[37]

This editorial, together with the *Moderate*'s other treatments of
the birthright, indicates that those connected with the paper
believed that the freedom to determine the type of civil authority
was an essential characteristic of the birthright given by God to
all men. This is, of course, similar to the position Macpherson
attributes to the Levellers. He would add, however, that the
political aspects of the birthright are alienable and that such
alienation occurs when the individual gives up his status of economic independence.[38] The position of the *Moderate* on this is not

[36] *Moderate*, no. 61, 4–11 Sept. 1649, p. 701. Italics ours.
[37] *Ibid.*, pp. 701–2.
[38] Macpherson, *Possessive Individualism*, esp. pp. 148 ff.

completely clear, but there is some indication that it approached this issue from a slightly different standpoint. It is true that the *Moderate* admitted that men could give up this freedom to choose their rulers, but it stressed that they did so at the risk of their souls. Citizens were under a divine obligation to authorize the form of government they thought would best serve their interests. If they failed to do this, or if they acquiesced in a government that had become tyrannical, they opposed God's will which declared that civil authority was instituted for the people's benefit. Thus, a government created by the people seemed to be 'the greatest good, both for . . . Soul and Body'.[39]

Some further light may be cast on the *Moderate*'s attitudes towards the franchise by looking at the way the newspaper used the phrase 'the people' in other, more non-political contexts. In many cases the *Moderate* tended to link 'the people' with those who made some kind of contribution to society, or at least in normal circumstances would have done so. These were the individuals who supported the government through taxes, billeted troops in their homes when necessary, or who were engaged in some gainful occupation.

Numerous examples could be cited that indicate plainly enough that the *Moderate* considered 'the people' to include those who paid taxes (especially assessments) and those who provided billeting.[40] This group obviously included all the freeholders and also all of those involved in the ratepayer franchise. It would in addition include all (or the vast majority) of the non-servant class. But potentially, it reached out even further than this. Among those who were servants by reason of being dependent on wages were some who occupied property which could be utilized to provide free quarter for troops. Gregory King's analysis of the population includes some 364,000 families of 'labouring people and out-servants'. Some at least of these could have been included in the terms which the *Moderate* chose to use.[41]

There is at least one very suggestive sign that the *Moderate* did

[39] *Moderate*, no. 61, 4–11 Sept. 1649, p. 701.
[40] See for example *ibid.*, no. 24, 19–26 Dec. 1648, p. 221; no. 29, 23–30 Jan. 1649, p. 283; no. 36, 13–20 March 1649, p. 361; no. 41, 17–24 April 1649, p. 425.
[41] See the summaries of King in Macpherson, *Possessive Individualism*, p. 281. That such properties were utilized for free-quarter seems to be confirmed by the case of Newcastle mentioned below.

not feel wage-earners should necessarily be disfranchised or exempted from inclusion among the people. The paper's last issue, number 63, mentioned the problems that could be created by billeting in Newcastle. The *Moderate*'s reporter felt there was a danger that 'the people will be opprest with Free-quarter; which if once laid, they are not longer able to subsist, many of them being poor day-laboring men, and can hardly get bread to feed their Wives, and Children'.[42] As labourers, the Newcastle workers would be included in Macpherson's servant class; and they would have depended virtually exclusively on wages for their livelihood. Yet when the *Moderate* spoke of 'the people' it drew no distinction between these labourers and the non-servants.

These statements from the *Moderate* may make the paper's attitude towards the franchise somewhat clearer. The editorial in number 19 equated 'the people' with those who had voting rights. The editorial comments in other issues lead to the conclusion that the *Moderate* did not believe 'the people' were restricted to those who paid taxes, provided billeting, owned property, or were non-servants—though all these groups were included in the term. It is important to note in this respect that the *Moderate* did not give its support to proposals that clearly demanded a restricted franchise. The *Agreement* of 20 January 1649, that asked for a rate-payer franchise, was not printed or referred to by the paper, nor was the *Agreement* of 1 May, drawn up by Lilburne, Overton, Prince and Walwyn, which called for a non-servant voting body. The neglect of the *Agreement* of 1 May is especially significant in the light of the active concern the *Moderate* showed for the *Agreement*'s authors during their imprisonment.

A group that also presents difficulties in regard to the *Moderate*'s views on the franchise is the alms-takers. The *Moderate* made references to the poor who were forced to beg in order to survive, and these references were frequently made in terms of 'the people'. There was the unmistakable implication throughout all these accounts that alms-takers had been thrown out of their rightful, productive place in society by governmental mismanagement or by the general hard times that the Civil Wars created. These men might be forced to live on charity, but if order were restored they would soon be in better condition. There are indications that the *Moderate* would have considered giving alms-

[42] *Moderate*, no. 63, 18–25 Sept. 1649, p. 735.

takers the franchise, especially since the paper seemed to believe this group had suffered the most from a government that did not rule in the people's interests.

The conclusion that the *Moderate* would have allowed alms-takers to exercise the franchise admittedly sounds somewhat unlikely, but it is certainly not impossible. Doubtless in practice there would have been attempts to differentiate between the various groups that were dependent on charity. The sturdy vagrant beggars were almost certain not to be included in this and we can agree with Macpherson that they were probably left out of the Levellers' calculations entirely, on the grounds that they had put themselves outside society by their refusal to labour usefully.[43] But the partially dependent poor and the impotent poor may well represent another case. If so, this would serve to make some sense of the account of Leveller suffrage demands contained in the parliamentary diary of John Boys. On 23 November 1647, Boys reported Oliver Cromwell's speaking in the following terms:[44]

> And for a more equall representative, because he saw many honest officers were possest with it, he gave waye to dispute about it at the Counsell of war, partly to perswade them out of the unreasonablenes of that representation these London Agents would have, but when he saw, that they would exclude children and servants, yet such as received almes they insisted on as persons competent for electors etc. he saw such a dangerous consequence of that, they which had no interest in estate at all should choose a representation (and they being the most, were likely to choose those of their own condition) that this drive at a levelling and paritye etc. he could not but disclayme and discountenance such endeavours.

Cromwell's comments seem to bear little relation to what was demanded at Putney, but they do open up the possibility that some of the Levellers were willing to extend the franchise beyond the non-servant category. The *Moderate* appears to have continued to think in this way at a later date when the rest of the Leveller

---

[43] Macpherson, *Possessive Individualism*, pp. 146 ff.
[44] D. Underdown, 'The Parliamentary Diary of John Boys, 1647-8', *Bull. Inst. Hist. Res.*, xxxix (1966), pp. 152-3.

movement had decided on the exclusion of alms-takers from the franchise.

The *Moderate*'s political theory centred around citizens who, by virtue of their productive employments, made a contribution to society and had a direct interest in the nation's welfare. This sounds whiggish, but it did not necessarily exclude wage-earners as a class. Alms-takers were included in this group as well because their condition was thought to be due to peculiar circumstances. Previous to the Civil Wars, their difficulties had been the result of a tyrannical monarchy. During the 1640s, their condition was perpetuated by poor economic conditions and by Parliamentary misrule.

In the end, the *Moderate* maintained that government was instituted for the benefit of these productive individuals, and that it required their endorsement. The franchise, as a part of their birthright, could not be alienated so long as they themselves did not betray the country and their own souls. Many Levellers would have objected to such a broad definition of 'the people', and to such an extension of the franchise. On the franchise issue, the Levellers do not appear to have been united to a man. The *Moderate*'s position should be considered as one element in the theory of the Leveller movement, and it points to the fact that the movement itself was not always consistent or unified in its attitudes or its objectives.

If a discussion of the franchise reveals what appear to be differences between individual Levellers, so does a review of the question of religious toleration. It is normally stated that the Levellers' position on religious toleration (with the exception of the compromise Officers' *Agreement* of January 1649) was a consistent demand for complete religious toleration coupled with a willingness and indeed enthusiasm for a non-compulsory public profession of faith.[45] The situation was rather more complex than this and again an analysis of the *Moderate* may help to clarify the issue. If one were to follow the account of Brailsford, it would be easy to believe that such an analysis would be fruitless. Discussing the paper's attitude towards religion, Brailsford comments in part:[46]

[45] See, for example, D. M. Wolfe, *Milton in the Puritan Revolution* (London, 1963), chap. 2.　　　[46] Brailsford, *The Levellers*, p. 409.

The policy of a newspaper is disclosed as much by what it omits as by what it includes. It is a remarkable fact that during the weeks when the Agreement of the People and the difficult issue of toleration were under discussion in the Whitehall Debates, the *Moderate* published no account of these proceedings. . . . For a time, while negotiations were going on, silence may have been praiseworthy, but only for a time. It may be significant that the *Moderate* never discussed toleration in a leading article, and never on this issue sided with the Levellers against Ireton and Cromwell.

This is oversimplified, for it seems clear that the *Moderate* had a policy on toleration and that in some respects it was even more consistent in its advocacy than were the other Leveller publications.

Until January 1649, the Levellers did consistently favour religious toleration. The *Remonstrance of Many Thousand Citizens*, published in July 1646, and probably written by Richard Overton, reminded Parliament that 'Yee may propose what Forme [of worship] yee conceive best, and most available for Information and well-being of the Nation, and may perswade and invite thereunto'. But, Overton went on to add:[47]

> compell, yee cannot justly; for ye have no Power from Us
> [the people] so to doe, nor could you have; for we could not
> conferre a Power that was not in our selves, there being none
> of us, that can without wilfull sinne binde our selves to
> worship God after any other way, then what (to a tittle,)
> in our owne particular understandings, wee approve to be
> just.

Parliament's most important obligation regarding religion was 'to protect and defend all that live peaceably in the Commonwealth, of what judgement or way of Worship whatsoever . . .'.[48]

The Levellers' attitudes towards religion began to grow more complicated in 1649. In January of that year, an *Agreement* which some of the Levellers supported appeared providing that some form of Christianity—so long as it was not Catholicism or

---

[47] [R. Overton], *A Remonstrance of Many Thousand Citizens* (London, 1646) in Wolfe, *Leveller Manifestoes*, p. 122.
[48] *Ibid.*

Anglicanism—should be the public religion. The *Agreement* went on to stipulate that those Christians who did not subscribe to the public form of worship should not be penalized or persecuted.[49] But this article was seriously compromised by a clause which said: 'it is not intended to bee hereby provided, That this liberty shall necessarily extend to Popery or Prelacy'.[50] This *Agreement*, which admittedly reflects more accurately the views of the officers than those of the Levellers, indicates that by January 1649, the argument that toleration should not be extended to Catholics and Anglicans was gaining force. Moreover, the restriction of provisions to Christians meant that the Jews were also being excluded.

Yet it is dangerous to conclude that the Leveller leadership had changed its position. The implication of the *Agreement*'s statement on religion was fairly clear, but its wording was vague; and in *Englands New Chains Discovered*, published the following February, John Lilburne attacked it as such, saying there was much dissatisfaction 'with what is exprest as a reserve from the Representative, in matters of Religion, as being very obscure, and full of perplexity, that ought to be most plain and clear; there having occurred no greater trouble to the Nation about any thing than by the intermedling of Parliaments in matters of Religion'.[51] In a later section of *Englands New Chains*, Lilburne complained that Parliament had censured a member of the House 'for declaring his judgement in a point of Religion, which is directly opposite to the Reserve in the Agreement concerning Religion'.[52] In this case, Lilburne was almost certainly not thinking of the recent *Agreement* that did not deal with the religious qualifications of office holders, but rather of the *Foundations of Freedom*, published in December 1648, which held that Parliament 'shall not disable any person from bearing any Office in the Common-wealth for any opinion or practice in Religion, though contrary to the public way'.[53] Despite the January *Agreement*, Lilburne himself still

---

[49] *An Agreement of the People* (London, 1649), in Wolfe, *Leveller Manifestoes*, pp. 348–9.   [50] *Ibid.*, p. 349.
[51] J. Lilburne, *Englands New Chains Discovered* (London, 1649) in Haller and Davies, *Leveller Tracts*, p. 159.
[52] *Ibid.*, p. 162.
[53] *Foundations of Freedom; or An Agreement of the People* (London, 1648) in Wolfe, *Leveller Manifestoes*, p. 302. Lilburne was not the only Leveller to feel this way. See W. Walwyn, *The Vanitie of the Present Churches* [London, 1649] in Haller and Davies, *Leveller Tracts*, p. 274 and [W.

apparently favoured general toleration in both public and private affairs.

The toleration issue was, however, considerably confused by the appearance on 1 May 1649 of *An Agreement of the Free People of England.* Signed by Overton, Lilburne, Walwyn and Thomas Prince, this pamphlet purported to set out 'the ultimate end and full scope of all our desires and intentions concerning the Government of this Nation, and wherein we shall absolutely rest satisfied and acquiesce. . .'.[54] The tenth article was a restatement of one of of the Levellers' common religious demands:[55]

> we do not inpower or entrust our said representatives to con-
> tinue in force, or to make any Lawes, Oaths, or Covenants,
> whereby to compell by penalties or otherwise any person to
> any thing in or about matters of faith, Religion or Gods
> worship or to restrain any person from the profession of his
> faith, or exercise of Religion according to his Conscience. . . .

But the twenty-sixth point of the *Agreement* seriously qualified this article by holding that Parliament 'shall not disable any person from bearing any office in the Common-wealth, for any opinion or practice in Religion, excepting such as maintain the Popes (or other forraign) Supremacy'.[56] Thus Catholics were clearly penalized for their religion by being excluded from public office. And there is the implication that the intention was to exclude Anglicans also, since it could be argued that the Church of England was under 'forraign Supremacy' because of the support it gave to Charles II.

At best, Leveller policy on toleration was imprecise from the *Agreement* of January 1649, to the one of May. Possibly Lilburne, Walwyn, Overton and their followers changed their views on the matter, but it seems more likely that they were compromising their demands for full toleration somewhat in order to gain at least partial acceptance of the Leveller programme. The vague article on religion in the January *Agreement*, the subsequent state-ments of Lilburne, Overton, Walwyn and Wildman, and the

---

Walwyn] *A Manifestation* [London, 1649] in Wolfe, *Leveller Manifestoes*, p. 393 for similar comments.
[54] *An Agreement of the Free People of England* (London, 1649) in Wolfe, *Leveller Manifestoes*, p. 401.
[55] *Ibid.*, p. 405.   [56] *Ibid.*, p. 408.

strange juxtaposition of the two articles on religion in the May *Agreement* suggest that the compromise was not an easy one, nor one with which all the Levellers could have been pleased.

The *Moderate*, like the Levellers generally, regarded religion as only a part, and perhaps not in every case the most important part, of a wide programme of social revision. But unlike the Leveller leaders who did insert restrictions on Catholics and Anglicans, the *Moderate* appears to have been consistent in its advocacy of religious toleration. The paper showed its attitude not only towards the Levellers, but towards toleration as well by the support it gave to the petition of 11 September 1648, which it printed complete—'because of [its] great importance, and to undeceive the People'.[57] This petition, like many other Leveller documents of 1648, asked for a general toleration.

Religion did not, however, draw a great deal of the paper's attention until the spring of 1649. This is admittedly surprising. Not only were the Whitehall debates ignored, but during the last month of 1648 and the beginning of 1649 several important Leveller documents were issued that dealt in whole or in part with religion, among them *No Papist nor Presbyterian*, *The Vanitie of the Present Churches*, and the January 1649 *Agreement*. The *Moderate* did not discuss these publications, although it did print several petitions that included demands for toleration, together with the text of Lilburne's *Englands New Chains* which contained many of its author's objections to the January *Agreement*.

The *Moderate* began to display a more active concern with the toleration question two months after the appearance of the January *Agreement* when, on 17 March, the Commons debated the qualifications of its members. The paper spoke out strongly against religious qualifications, demanding liberty of conscience for all or none, and adding that 'To sequester a Roman Catholike, because so, without any matter of Fact against him, though he hath alwayes adhered to the Parliament, or never engaged against them, is a new Law, and an old error.'[58]

Parliamentary discussion over the possible establishment of Presbyterianism as the official profession of faith caused another outburst from the *Moderate* in April. In that month, Cromwell made overtures to the English Presbyterians. He assured them

[57] *Moderate*, no. 9, 5–12 Sept. 1648, p. 68.
[58] *Ibid.*, no. 36, 13–20 March 1649, p. 370.

that he was prepared to consent to the establishment of the Presbyterian system (though he doubtless envisaged this without a coercive jurisdiction) and to the readmission to Parliament of the members who had been excluded at Pride's Purge.[59] The proposals came to nothing; the gap between Cromwell and the Presbyterians was too wide to be bridged in this manner. But the attempt brought a sharp protest from the *Moderate*. The paper declared that it thought the question had been disposed of long since:[60]

> must we again begin to dispute it *de Novo*, though all these accounted nothing more base, or mis-beseeming a Christian, then to question, vex, or reproach any man for his Iudgment, or practise, touching matters of Religion, and inciting all men to peace, unity, love and true friendship, though of never so many several opinions, or different wayes in Religion.

It is perhaps significant that the May *Agreement*, which contained limitations on Catholics and Anglicans, elicited no comment from the *Moderate*, though under the news for 1 May (the day the *Agreement* appeared) the *Moderate* printed a petition in behalf of Walwyn, Overton, Lilburne and Prince, the authors of the *Agreement*.

Throughout the summer of 1649, the *Moderate* continued to report in favour of toleration, and this policy appears to have established the paper as something of a champion of religious liberty among the weekly sheets. In June, the parishioners of St Alkmans in Shropshire wrote to Mabbott, though they knew him only through the *Moderate*, complaining that the justices of the peace in their county were attempting to force religious conformity upon them. They asked Mabbott to print a warrant issued against their churchwardens by the justices in order 'that all the people may take notice of their [the justices'] impudency, and presumptuous dealings with the honest party, if the power lay in their hands'.[61] Mabbott acknowledged the parishioners' request by printing both their letter and the warrant.

[59] S. R. Gardiner, *History of the Commonwealth and Protectorate* (New York, 1965 edn), i, p. 64.
[60] *Moderate*, no. 39, 3–9 April 1649, p. 398.
[61] *Ibid.*, no. 49, 12–19 June 1649, pp. 557–8.

In early September, the *Moderate*'s correspondent in Bristol noted that the Levellers were gaining influence among the people of that area, especially among those who had risked all they had 'to maintain that which we called *The publike Cause of the whole Nation*, which we understood was for *liberty of Conscience* . . .'. The correspondent also commented rather dejectedly that at one time Anglicans had labelled a Puritan as 'an *Hiretick*, *Schismatick*, an *enemy to God*, and the worst of *Creatures*', and that the Presbyterians, under the guise of championing toleration, had risen against the established church. But the Presbyterians, once in power, turned upon the Independents calling them '*Anabaptists*, *Schismaticks*, *Libertines*, *Atheists*, and what not . . .'. There was bitterness and thinly-veiled anti-Parliament feeling in the correspondent's closing remarks:[62]

> And that we now should so much exercise the power of the Sword, for taking in, gaining, or feeding the fancy of another repugnant Interest, which hath so often appeared in Arms against us, and would cut our throats if it lay in their power, and thereby so much displease tender or other *Consciences*, persecuting and imprisoning them for exercising a formal *Worship*, which their Consciences are bound up unto, and which can neither of it self prejudice, or advantage the soul, being but the shadow of a substance (as all other Church-Governments are) is to honest people in these parts most strange. And likewise, that those who have faithfully served the Republike, and been as (if not more) instrumental in the removal of all our burthens and Grievances, laid upon us by the late King, Bishops, High Commission Court, Star Chamber, House of Peers. . . .

The *Moderate*'s correspondent in Ipswich summed up the attitude of the paper briefly in the *Moderate*'s last number when he wrote: 'let us commit all judgment to God, who will avenge all disobedience to his Gospel, and the folly, and madness of all opposers shall be made manifest. . .'[63]

The *Moderate*, then, appears to have been more consistent in its endorsement of religious toleration than many of the Levellers. The paper was primarily concerned with the secular aspects of

[62] *Moderate*, no. 62, 11–18 Sept. 1649, p. 722.
[63] *Ibid.*, no. 63, 18–25 Sept. 1649, p. 732.

society, and while it hoped England would exist and prosper as a Christian nation, it does not seem to have thought it either just or necessary for the country to enforce a national religion. God, the *Moderate* seemed to think, could manage religion quite well without assistance from the government.

Unfortunately, the *Moderate* did not contain much in the way of justification for its position on the toleration question. There is enough, however, to rescue it from the accusation that its piety was dictated by its circulation. Those connected with the *Moderate* seemed to realize that a country torn by religious disputes could not progress rapidly in the areas of secular reform that were so important to the paper. Civil war or serious internal unrest of any kind provided a stumbling block to social progress; and the paper knew this, much as it might clamour for Charles's execution and the popular cause. Religion was one of several things that could lead to civil disruption. 'Wars have been ever clothed with the most specious of all pretences', recorded the *Moderate*:[64]

> *viz.* Reformation of Religion, The Laws of the Land,
> Liberty of the Subject, etc. though the effects thereof have
> proved most destructive to them, and ruinous to every
> Nation; making the Sword (and not the People) the original
> of all Authorities, for many hundred yeers together; taking
> away each mans Birth-right, and setling upon a few, a cursed
> propriety (the ground of all Civil Offences between party
> and party) and the greatest cause of most Sins against the
> Heavenly Deity.

The position of the *Moderate* was similar to that of the *Politiques:* it was better to have toleration and peace than to have a country bedevilled by Christian warriors.

But it is not entirely adequate to explain the *Moderate*'s advocacy of toleration simply in terms of expediency, for this would ignore an important element of idealism and sincere belief which is apparent in the paper's religious position. The paper was moving beyond tolerance to genuine toleration. The Bristol correspondent, for example, had considered toleration to be a crucial—if not the crucial—matter at stake in the Civil Wars, and his bitterness at having the prize withheld after the victory had been won is

[64] *Ibid.*, no. 61, 4–11 Sept. 1649, p. 701.

patent. The Ipswich reporter seems to have voiced the *Moderate*'s general opinion as well as his own when he remarked that religious truth would triumph, irrespective of men's actions. This is not to deny that the *Moderate*'s consistent advocacy of toleration was strongly buttressed by practical and expedient considerations. But it rested as well on what appears to have been a firmly held theoretical foundation which considered religion to be one area in which all men were liable to error and where only God could claim infallibility.

Consideration of two major areas of concern—the franchise and religious toleration—does not exhaust the utility which an analysis of the *Moderate* can have for the interpretation of the Leveller movement. It would be useful to analyse fully the secular reforms proposed by the paper, to see, for example what its attitude towards agrarian legislation was. A preliminary survey indicates that the *Moderate* attempted, particularly in 1649, to present the Levellers as having an agrarian, nationwide programme. Though the defence of property was firmly maintained, it appears that the paper was trying to alter the impression that the Levellers were an urban (and particularly a London) group. But even the consideration of only two issues suggests that some re-thinking of our view of the Levellers is required. It suggests that the Leveller programme was not so unified as most seem to think, that there were significant differences over basic issues of political philosophy and of practical reform. It also suggests that further use could be made of the paper. Besides being simply a source of information on the history of the Leveller movement, the *Moderate* should also be used to analyse the content of Leveller thought.

VIII

GENTLEMEN LEVELLERS?*

G. E. Aylmer

When there has been so much controversy about the social and economic implications of Leveller political ideas, possible information about the social origins of leading individual Levellers may be of interest. The foremost army Agitator (or rank-and-file delegate) who took part in the Putney debates was Edward Sexby, while the most articulate civilian Leveller present was Maximilian Petty *alias* Pettus. It is, to say the least, a striking coincidence that two young men of these names had been apprenticed in the same London Company within two years of each other.

 1 Maximilian, son of John Petty of Tetsworth, Oxon., Esquire, was apprenticed to John Randall of the Grocers' Company, for eight years, in May 1634.[1] We know from the Oxford antiquary, Anthony Wood, who was an in-law of one branch of the Pettys, that a Maximilian was the second son of John of Stoke Talmage, near Tetsworth, and of Anne daughter of one Johnson of Witney, and widow of a Witney clothier called Webley. Since she died in 1622, and there were additional younger children, a date of birth around 1618 appears reasonable, making him sixteen, or the normal age for being apprenticed, in 1634.[2]

* From no. 49 (November 1970).
 [1] Guildhall, MS. 11593/1, Grocers' Company Register of Apprentices, vol. i, fo. 46v.
 [2] A. Wood, *Life and Times*, ed. A. Clark (Oxford Hist. Soc., xix, 1891), i, p. 34. I am grateful to Mr Keith Thomas for this reference and for other help.

2 Edward, son of Marcus Sexby *alias* Saxbie of London, Gentleman, was apprenticed to Edward Price of the Grocers' Company, in 1632.[3] If the identification is correct, this would make him two years older than Petty, and about thirty-one at the time of his confrontation with the Generals. The established view, that Sexby was a 'Suffolk man', having served as a trooper first in Cromwell's own regiment and subsequently in Fairfax's, rests on his own reported testimony when he was cross-examined for presenting the soldiers' letter to Major-General Skippon in April 1647.[4] But a Suffolk origin, or some other tie with that county, seems quite compatible with his father having been a Londoner when Edward was about sixteen.

In view of the prominent part played by apprentices—and journeymen—in the London demonstrations and riots of 1640–2, it is tempting to wonder whether Sexby and Petty might not already have served their apprenticeship in popular agitation before they emerged as Leveller spokesmen. It is of course paradoxical that it was Petty who first and most specifically of any Leveller, stated the case for excluding apprentices from the parliamentary franchise,[5] a point crucial to Professor Macpherson's argument on this issue.[6] Men of gentry social background might also perhaps have been both readier, and educationally better equipped to cross dialectical swords with the redoubtable Henry Ireton and to withstand interjections from Oliver Crom-

---

[3] Guildhall, MS. 11593/1, fo. 32v.

[4] *The Clarke Papers*, ed. C. H. Firth, i (Camden Soc., new ser., xlix, 1891), p. 431, from Bodl. Lib., MS. Tanner lviii, fo. 84; see also *Dict. Nat. Biog.* article by Firth; *Clarke Papers*, i, pp. 82–3, note c; Firth and G. Davies, *The Regimental History of Cromwell's Army*, 2 vols (Oxford, 1940), i, pp. 61–2, 64–6; ii, pp. 561–3; H. N. Brailsford, *The Levellers and the English Revolution*, ed. C. Hill (London, 1961), pp. 183–4. The references to Petty *alias* Pettus by Firth (*Clarke Papers*, i, *passim*) and Brailsford (*Levellers*, pp. 270, 372) do not provide any hint for or against the Oxfordshire connection. Aubrey describes him as Oliver Cromwell's 'kinsman' ('*Brief Lives*', *chiefly of Contemporaries, set down by John Aubrey, between the Years 1669 & 1696*, ed. A. Clark, 2 vols (Oxford, 1898), i, p. 290), in his account of Harrington's 'Rota Club' during 1659. I have not been able to verify this.

[5] *Clarke Papers*, i, p. 342; also available in A. S. P. Woodhouse (ed.), *Puritanism and Liberty* . . . (London, 1938 and 1950), p. 83.

[6] C. B. Macpherson, *The Political Theory of Possessive Individualism: Hobbes to Locke* (Oxford, 1962), pp. 108, 122–3, 127, 146.

well himself. Moreover, this might also help to explain Sexby's rapid promotion from the ranks, to Captain and then Lieutenant-Colonel in 1649–50.

It is far beyond the scope of this short note to offer a detailed analysis of the social origins of all the Leveller leaders. Nor, even if it could be shown that they came predominantly from one kind of social background rather than another, should this be taken as the cause of their holding the ideas which they did, still less as explaining the worth or significance of these ideas. But, in order to put what has been suggested above about Sexby and Petty into some kind of context, the following brief notes will remind the reader of the present state of our knowledge about some of the others. John Lilburne was the second son of a gentleman from county Durham (himself a second son); his maternal grandfather was the Yeoman of the King's Standing Wardrobe at Greenwich, a minor official of the royal household; John was apprenticed to a London clothier.[7] William Walwyn was the second son of a Worcestershire gentleman (though his elder brother was entered at the university as an esquire); he was apprenticed to a London silkman; his maternal grandfather was bishop of Hereford.[8] Richard Overton was not of armigerous gentry origin but his family's precise social standing is unknown; he may perhaps have been born at the end of the sixteenth century, and have been in Holland as a member of an exiled religious sect by 1615, and may have completed his education or had some training there; he may well have been a parson's son from the midlands. The Reverend Valentine Overton of Bedworth, Warwickshire (d. 1647) had a son Richard, a son William (who was himself a puritan clergyman), and another younger son Henry (this is the printer and stationer Henry Overton, who is often said to have been a relative of Richard the Leveller); he also had a daughter Katherine, who was married to the Reverend Samuel Clarke (a leading Presbyterian and writer of puritan 'lives', and an opponent of religious toleration). Whatever the truth about

[7] *Dict. Nat. Biog.*; Pauline Gregg, *Freeborn John. A biography of John Lilburne* (London, 1961), chaps 1–2.

[8] *Dict. Nat. Biog.*; J. Frank, *The Levellers. A History of the Writings of Three 17th-century Social Democrats: John Lilburne, Richard Overton, William Walwyn* (Cambridge, Mass. 1955), p. 29; Brailsford, *Levellers*, p. 59; see also *Visitation of Worcs. 1634* (Harleian Soc., vol. xc), p. 30.

his early years and family connections, by 1641 Richard Overton was back in England, working as an unlicensed printer in London; from his writings, Brailsford believed that, 'Evidently he had a good grammar school education'.[9] Although he lived to be knighted as a well-to-do alderman of the City, John Wildman (1621 or 1623–93) remains mysterious and elusive; according to Clarendon's account he was 'bred a scholar in the University of Cambridge'. Certainly he must have been a law clerk, conceivably at one of the lesser Chancery Inns, perhaps articled or apprenticed straight off, for he was practising as a solicitor or attorney by the late 1640s. It was his forensic skill which made him so valuable an ally, in debate and on paper; and it was his legal expertise which helped him to become a successful land speculator in the 1650s. Wildman did not belong to an armigerous gentry family, but again no more than this can safely be said.[10] Of the four leaders, Overton and Wildman seem the likeliest candidates for non-gentry origins.

Of those in the second rank, or among the fellow-travelling

[9] Prerogative Court of Canterbury, Wills, 172 Fines (will of Valentine Overton, clerk, proved by his sons Richard and William); A. G. Matthews (ed.), *Calamy Revised* (Oxford, 1934), no. 376 (William, son of Valentine Overton); D. F. McKenzie (ed.), *Stationers' Company Apprentices 1605–1640* (Bibliog. Soc. of Univ. of Virginia, Charlottesville, 1961), no. 2355 (Henry Overton, son of Valentine of Bedworth, clerk, apprenticed 1622, free of the Co. 1629); *Dict. Nat. Biog*, 'Samuel Clarke (1599–1683)', 'Richard Overton'; Samuel Clarke, *The Lives of sundry Eminent Persons in this later Age. . . .*(in two parts, bound as one, small folio, London, 1683), ii, pp. 152–65, 'The Life and Death of Mrs. Katherine Clark [née Overton] who Died, Anno Domini 1675'. Frank, *Levellers*, pp. 39–40, 298 n.; Brailsford, *Levellers*, pp. 49–50. There is a conceivable armigerous Richard Overton, *alias* Orton from Leicestershire, but he seems very, very unlikely: *Visitation of Leics. 1619* (Harl. Soc., ii), p. 193. It is of course tempting to connect him with the strongly republican Colonel, later Major-General Robert Overton from east Yorkshire, but no Richard in that family fits at all: *Dict. Nat. Biog.*; *Yorks Pedigrees G-S*, ed. J. W. Walker (Harl. Soc., xcv), pp. 303–5. Whether he went to Holland as a religious refugee himself, or became a General Baptist and joined the exiled congregation after he had got there, remains unknown.

[10] *Dict. Nat. Biog.*; *Clarke Papers*, i, pp. xlvii–liii; Maurice Ashley, *John Wildman Plotter and Postmaster* (London, 1947), p. 9; J. and J. A. Venn, *Alumni Cantabrigienses*, part 1, vol. iv (Cambridge, 1927), p. 408, corrects J. Foster, *Alumni Oxonienses*, i (Oxford, 1891–2), p. 1632; Brailsford, *Levellers*, p. 270.

army officers, Agitators and other sympathizers, some are easy to place, others totally obscure. Colonel Thomas Rainsborough, *alias* Rainborow(e), was the grandson of a 'mariner' (a generic name for any seafaring man from common seaman to master), but the son of a captain in the Royal Navy who ended his days as a vice-admiral and an MP; Thomas was trained as a sea officer, but is remembered of course as the most radical of all the speakers in the Putney debates, although he is not known to have had any prior connection with the Levellers.[11] Thomas Prince, the co-treasurer of the party, who was arrested with Lilburne, Overton and Walwyn in 1649, was by trade a cheesemonger, actually a wholesale dealer in both cheese and butter; presumably he had been apprenticed in this trade; his origins are unknown but he does not seem to have come from an armigerous family.[12] His colleague as treasurer, Samuel Chidley, was the son of a formidable female puritan pamphleteer; he and his mother are said to have conducted a 'Brownist' (that is, Independent) church at Bury St Edmunds; he wrote mainly in favour of reforming the laws for debt and against the death penalty for theft; his father was a citizen and haberdasher of London.[13] Of the other leading

[11] *Dict. Nat. Biog.*; H. R. Williamson, *Four Stuart Portraits* (London, 1949), pp. 109–42, 151–3, 'Colonel Thomas Rainsborough'. Both rely heavily on E. Peacock, 'Notes on the life of Thomas Rainborowe . . .', *Archaeologia*, xlvi (1877), pp. 9–64; see also Firth and Davies, *Regimental History*, and for his father, M. F. Keeler, *The Long Parliament* (Philadelphia, 1954) and D. Brunton and D. H. Pennington, *Members of the Long Parliament* (London, 1954).

[12] Brailsford, *Levellers*, p. 482. I have also found Prince as a party to a case before the parliamentary Indemnity Committee, as a trader in butter: Pub. Rec. Off., SP 24, Indemnity Papers. He had helped to supply the Army in Ireland in the early 1640s, and also kept his own shop: see W. Haller and G. Davies (eds), *The Leveller Tracts 1647–1653* (New York, 1944), 'The Picture of the Councel of State', [April] 1649, p. 234 *et seq.*, 'The Narrative of the Proceedings against Mr. Thomas Prince . . .'.

[13] Brailsford, *Levellers*, p. 38; see also G. K. Fortescue (ed.), *Catalogue of the Thomason Tracts*, ii (London, 1908), index, 'Chidley'. Haberdashers' Company of London MSS., 'Bindings' 1630–55, and 'Freedom Books', ii, Index 1642–1715. I am grateful to the officers of the Company for allowing me to consult their records, and to Mrs C. E. Price, the Records Clerk, for her help. A hostile pamphlet of December 1647 described him as a stocking-seller: (anon.), *A Bloody Independent Plot Discovered. Prosecuted by the open Malice and Fury of divers Agitators, Levellers, Anabaptists, Brownists and other Sectaries and London Agents* (Brit. Mus., E.419/2).

Agitators, William Allen who—like Sexby—rose from the ranks to become Adjutant-General and a thorn in the flesh of Henry Cromwell in Ireland during the later 1650s, came from Warwickshire and was then apparently trained as a felt-maker in Southwark—another apprentice in all probability.[14] Robert Everard, who was initially described by William Clarke (the scribe of the Putney debates) simply as 'Buffcoat', described himself as a poor man unacquainted with the affairs of the kingdom, and we may perhaps assume in that a genuine working-class (peasant or labourer) background.[15] William Thompson—the only one of the 1649 mutineers to fight it out to the death—was not, strictly speaking, a mutineer at all because he had been cashiered for misconduct, and at the time of the mutinies seems to have been out on bail after further criminal offences committed in Essex earlier in 1649; he had originally been a corporal in Whalley's regiment. William's brother James who was one of the three men executed after the suppression of the Leveller mutiny at Burford, had even risen to be a cornet before then.[16] Is there a kind of half-parallel here with the famous Richard Parker of the 1797 naval mutiny at the Nore?[17] Lieutenant-Colonel William Eyres or

[14] *Clarke Papers*, i, pp. 430–3. There is an ambiguity because the text as printed by Firth, makes Allen say that he was a feltmaker by trade in 'Southw', which Brailsford reads as Southwark; it could conceivably mean 'in south Warwick(shire)', since he had already said that he was a Warwick man; Brailsford, *Levellers*, p. 183; Firth and Davies, *Regimental History*, adds little to the original Firth note in the *Clarke Papers*. See also P. H. Hardacre, 'William Allen, Cromwellian ag itator and "fanatic" ', *Baptist Quarterly*, xix (1962), pp. 292–308.

[15] *Clarke Papers*, i, pp. 285 n. and 286. He is normally distinguished from William Everard, who was cashiered from the Army and then became Winstanley's chief ally as the leader of the Diggers in 1649. But as Mr Thomas has pointed out to me (and as is noted in D. W. Petegorsky, *Left-Wing Democracy in the English Civil War*, London, 1940, p. 134 n.), it is William, not Robert who is credited with having signed *Englands Freedom, Souldiers Rights* (B.M., E.419/23), on behalf of William Thompson, in December 1647.

[16] *Clarke Papers*, ii (Camden Soc., new ser., liv, 1894), pp. 199–200, and n. 'b'; again Firth and Davies, *Regimental History* and Brailsford, *Levellers*, add nothing on the brothers' origins.

[17] See G. E. Manwaring and Bonamy Dobrée, *The Floating Republic: an account of the mutinies at Spithead and the Nore in 1797* (London, 1935), App. iv (Penguin edn, 1937, pp. 262–5), 'Notes for the Life of Richard Parker'.

Ayre(s) spent over a year in prison 1649–50 for his support of the mutiny but was never brought to trial and was eventually released on parole; he may have been the Captain Ayres who commanded the 6th troop in Oliver Cromwell's horse regiment and this would seem to argue a kind of rural middle-class background.[18] Lieutenant-Colonel William Wetton, *alias* Witton did not take as active a part on the Leveller side as Rainsborough or Ayres (in their different ways); when the Independents refused to admit Walwyn as one of the Leveller negotiators in the winter of 1648–9 (because of his alleged freethinking and crypto-communism), Lilburne and the others brought Wetton along instead; it is not clear whether his commission was in the field army or the London militia; he appears to have come of a London family and some of his forbears may indeed have been of armigerous status. Unlike the New Model, the colonels of the London militia forces were almost all men of some commercial substance.[19]

This is not an exhaustive roll-call, either of the writers or the men of action connected with the Leveller movement.[20] More than anything else it underlines the case for fuller investigation of the Cromwellian officer corps and the social background of the New Model. It may also serve as a reminder of the extreme difficulty, except for rare lucky breaks, in tracing the family and

[18] Firth and Davies, *Regimental History*, i, pp. 9, 179, 300; ii, pp. 528–9; Brailsford, *Levellers*, pp. 342, 512. For his later imprisonment and release, see in addition *Cal. State Papers Domestic, 1649–50*, p. 442; *ibid., 1650*, p. 263. He was not the William Eyre, recruiter MP for Chippenham (Brunton and Pennington, *Members*, pp. 223, 231; *Commons Jls*, vi, p. 117), who also sat in Richard Cromwell's 1659 parliament and was then described as a colonel (see T. Burton, *Parliamentary Diary*, ed. J. T. Rutt, 4 vols, London, 1828, iv, index; *Commons Jls*, vi, p. 606).

[19] W. Haller and G. Davies (eds), *Leveller Tracts* (New York, 1944), pp. 416 ff., Lilburne 'Legal Fundamental Liberties'; Firth and Davies, *Regimental History*, ii, p. 641; in addition *Cal. State Papers Domestic, 1651*, p. 540; there was a London family of Witton entitled to bear arms in 1568 (*Visitation of London 1568*, Harl. Soc., i, p. 53, and *ibid.*, cix–x, pp. 55–6), but it does not appear in the subsequent visitations of 1633–5 and 1664 (*ibid.*, xv, xvii, xcii).

[20] Amongst others of interest should be noted Captain William Bray, Giles Calvert and William Larner the publishers, Cornet Christopher Cheeseman, Lieutenant Edmund Chillenden (who later changed sides), Major John Cobbett, Lieutenant-Colonel John Jubbes, Major Thomas Scott, MP, and Major (later Lieutenant-Colonel) Francis White.

connections of anyone in the seventeenth century below the ranks of the gentry and outside the upper civic and professional élites.[21]

[21] Historians have more to learn from genealogists than most of us care to admit. For a short-cut to see whether a family was armigerous, consult G. W. Marshall, *The Genealogist's Guide* (last edn Guildford, 1903) and J. B. Whitmore, *Genealogical Guide* (London, 1955; also printed in four parts as Harl. Soc., xcix, ci, cii, civ); if none of the pedigree refs. are to heralds' visitations, then except for one or two counties (visited by the heralds too infrequently) the answer is likely to be negative. This does not mean that no members of such families called themselves gentlemen or were recognized as such by their contemporaries; for several counties we know that the numbers of gentry, especially by *c.* 1640, vastly exceeded the numbers whose pedigrees appeared in the visitations: e.g. Alan Everitt, *The Community of Kent and the Great Rebellion* (Leicester, 1966), chap. 2; J. T. Cliffe, *The Yorkshire Gentry From the Reformation to the Civil War* (London, 1969), chap. 1; the same is certainly true of Dorset and Herefordshire.

IX

ENGLANDS SPIRIT UNFOULDED, OR AN INCOURAGEMENT TO TAKE THE *ENGAGEMENT*

A NEWLY DISCOVERED PAMPHLET BY GERRARD WINSTANLEY*

G. E. Aylmer

INTRODUCTION

The Clarke papers are familiar to students of the seventeenth century. It is perhaps less well known that William Clarke's collection of interregnum and other documents, bequeathed to Worcester College, Oxford, by his son George, contains a great deal more besides the famous Putney and Whitehall debates, printed by Firth and later by Woodhouse. Still less does it appear to be widely known that William Clarke also collected contemporary pamphlets and newspapers. Fortunately, successive Librarians of Worcester College in this century have kept an interleaved and annotated copy of the *Catalogue of the Thomason Tracts*, from which it can be seen that there are numerous items in the Clarke collection which are not in the British Museum. Among the items so entered is a hitherto unknown work, by the leader of the Diggers, Gerrard Winstanley, *Englands Spirit Unfoulded* (1650).[1]

---

* From no. 40 (July 1968).

[1] For the lack of any previous reference to this work, see (in chronological order of publication) *D.N.B.*, 'Gerrard Winstanley', article by Charles William Sutton; G. K. Fortescue (ed.), *Catalogue of the Pamphlets . . . collected by George Thomason, 1640–1661* (London, 1908), ii, p. 762 (index entry for Winstanley); G. H. Sabine (ed.), *Works of Gerrard Winstanley* (Ithaca, N.Y., 1941); D. G. Wing, *Short-Title Catalogue . . . 1641–1700*, 3 vols (New York, 1945); The Institute of Historical Research, London, *Corrections and Additions to the D.N.B. 1923–1963* (Boston, 1966),

The pamphlet's sub-title, *An Incouragement To take the Engagement*, helps us to place it in its historical context. In February 1648/9 the new republican regime had introduced an oath or 'Engagement', to be taken by those elected to the first Council of State. This at once had to be modified as a result of objections by several of the councillors themselves; any explicit approval of the recent regicide was removed from the version which was finally adopted.[2] Then, in the following autumn of 1649, a shortened version of this test, sometimes also known as the 'New Engagement' to distinguish it from earlier such tests (for example the Solemn League and Covenant), was ordered to be taken by all present and future MPs, all office-holders under the Commonwealth, beneficed ministers, university staff, state pensioners, etc.[3] Later in the winter of 1649–50 the Engagement (as it soon came to be called) was extended to the entire adult male population.[4] Its enforcement proved difficult,[5] and there was an extensive, if on the whole intellectually mediocre debate in print, for and against subscription. Those involved included such well-known figures as John Dury, John Goodwin, John Lilburne, and William Prynne.[6] So, in a sense, it may not seem remarkable that

---

which substantially revises the biographical but not the bibliographical part of the earlier entry; D. G. Wing, *A Gallery of Ghosts: books published between 1641 and 1700 not found in the S.T.C.* (for the Modern Language Association of America, Index committee, Baltimore, 1967). *Englands Spirit* is not recorded in any other library catalogue to which I have had access; while it would be quite wrong to assert, on this limited basis, that the Worcester College copy is unique, the evidence so far suggests that it well may be.

[2] See S. R. Gardiner, *History of the Commonwealth and Protectorate*, 3 vols (London, 1894–1901), i, pp. 5–8.

[3] *Ibid.*, i, pp. 196–7.

[4] *Ibid.*, i, pp. 215–16. For the text as finally shortened, see S. R. Gardiner (ed.), *The Constitutional Documents of the Puritan Revolution 1625–1660*, 3rd edn (Oxford, 1906), no. 92, p. 391, or C. H. Firth and R. S. Rait (eds), *Acts and Ordinances of the Interregnum 1642–1660*, 3 vols (London, 1911), ii, p. 325.

[5] Gardiner, *Commonwealth and Protectorate*, i, p. 275. See also Firth and Rait, *Acts and Ordinances*, ii, p. 348.

[6] J. D. [John Dury], *Considerations concerning the present Engagement, whether it may lawfully be entered into* (Dec. 1649); John Dury, *Just Re-Proposals to Humble Proposals* (Jan. 1649–50); J. D., *Objections against the taking of the Engagement answered* (Aug. 1650); anon. [John Goodwin],

Winstanley too joined in, although the main argument lay between the Independents, or supporters of the Commonwealth, and the Presbyterians, or ex-parliamentarians of 1642–8.

The pamphlet which is printed below[7] does not add anything of substance to what is already known about the development and structure of Winstanley's social and economic ideas as an agrarian communist, nor of his religious tenets as a mystical and humanistic Christian pantheist. Its interest lies rather in what it tells us about the Digger leader's attitude towards the government of the Commonwealth, after the Council of State had twice, if not three times, ordered Fairfax, as commander-in-chief, to suppress the

---

Englands Apologie, for Its late Change: or, A Sober Persuasive, ... to a Seasonable Engagement ... (1651, before September); *The Engagement Vindicated and Explained, or the Reasons Upon which Lieut. Col. John Lilburne tooke the Engagement* (Jan. 1649–50); anon. [William Prynne], *A Brief Apologie for all Non-Subscribers, and Looking-Glasse For All Apostate perjured Prescribers and Subscribers of the New Engagement* (Feb. 1649–50). There are also numerous other anonymous pamphlets, wholly or in part devoted to this topic: e.g. *The Engagement Vindicated* (Jan. 1649–50); *The Grand Case of Conscience concerning the Engagement Stated and Resolved* (Jan. 1649–50); N. W., a friend to the Commonwealth, *A Discourse concerning the Engagement* (Jan. 1649–50); anon., *A Logical Demonstration of the Lawfulness of Subscribing the New Engagement* (Jan. 1649–50); *A Disingagd Survey of the Engagement In relation to publike Obligations* (Feb. 1649–50); *The English Presbyterian and Independent Reconciled. Setting forth the small ground of Difference between them Both* ... (July 1651), pp. 110, 127–8. See also J. M. Wallace, 'The Engagement controversy 1649–1652: an annotated list of pamphlets', *Bull. New York Pub. Library*, lxviii (1964), pp. 384–405. Professor Wallace lists seventy-two items, excluding one or two of those mentioned in this note—and *Englands Spirit*. P. Zagorin, *A History of Political Thought in the English Revolution* (London, 1954), chap. 5, 'Theorists of the Commonwealth: I', section 2, pp. 67–70, contains easily the best short exposition of the theoretical grounds on which the Commonwealth was supported, but does not deal specifically with the Engagement. J. M. Wallace, *Destiny His Choice: The Loyalism of Andrew Marvell* (Cambridge, 1968), chap. 1, pp. 43–68, 'The Engagement Controversy', and Q. Skinner, 'Conquest and consent ...' in *The Interregnum: the Quest for Settlement 1646–1660*, ed. G. E. Aylmer (London, 1972), pp. 79–98, 208–9, 222–4, are now the fullest discussions available.

[7] By kind permission of the Provost and Fellows of Worcester College. I am particularly grateful for their help to the Librarian, Dr R. Sayce, and to the Assistant Librarian, Miss L. Montgomery. I also wish to thank Mr Webster, of the Bodleian Library, for his help in having a copy made at short notice.

Digger experiment (in April and October 1649).[8] David Caute's perception, in his brilliant historical novel *Comrade Jacob* (London, 1961), that Fairfax was most reluctant to take decisive military action against the Diggers, and had to be pushed into it by an alliance of the civilian authorities and local property interests, may in fact have an even stronger documentary basis than he realized. Caute seems to have exaggerated somewhat the soldiers' role in the November 1649 attack on the Digger colony.[9] It may likewise be suggested that his emphasis on the sadism of Captain Gladman and the troopers is an historical as well as an aesthetic error. None the less, his novel is remarkable alike for its evocation of the atmosphere during the 'digging' experiment, and for its attempt to recreate the working of Winstanley's mind, also— no mean achievement—that of Fairfax.

Englands Spirit makes it clear beyond any shadow of doubt that Winstanley still regarded the republican regime as a possible, perhaps indeed the only possible, basis for further social advance. There are passages which bear some relation to this argument in two of his other works,[10] while the postscript's sharp attack on the Ranters can be paralleled in another,[11] all three dating from January 1649–50 to March 1650. But none of his other writings is so strictly political, in the sense of being directly related to a current political problem, other of course than to the government's attitude towards the Digger experiment itself—the attempt at communal cultivation of the commons on St George's Hill and near Cobham in Surrey from April 1649 to April 1650.

It is hardly for the historian to say whether, in some absolute sense, Winstanley was right to support subscription, but granted

[8] See *Cal. State Papers Domestic, 1649–1650*, p. 95; *The Clarke Papers*, ed. C. H. Firth, 4 vols (Camden Soc., new ser., xlix, liv, lxi, lxii, 1891–1901), ii, pp. 209–10, for the first directive of 16 April; and *Cal. State Papers Domestic, 1649–50*, pp. 335–6, for the second of 10 October 1649. But on 2 October Bradshaw, the Lord President of the Council of State, had apparently already written to Fairfax, urging renewed and more effective action against the Diggers: Worcester College, MS. clxxxi (loose Clarke MSS.), Box 1.

[9] See Sabine, *Works*, pp. 16–17, 19, 362, 395–6.

[10] *A New-Yeers Gift for the Parliament and Armie* (Jan. 1649–50), and *An Appeale to all Englishmen, to judge between Bondage and Freedome* (March 1650); see Sabine, *Works*, pp. 353–96 and 407–15.

[11] *A Vindication of those . . . called Diggers* (Feb.–Mar. 1949–50); see Sabine, *Works*, pp. 399–403.

his premises (eccentric as these seemed and still seem to many) the argument is a cogent one. He cannot have been so naïve, certainly not by the winter of 1649–50, still less by later in 1650[12] as to believe that the establishment of the Commonwealth was in itself going to be sufficient to bring about the kind of social order which he wanted. Yet he was surely correct to suppose that the maintenance of republican rule was a necessary precondition for further economic and social change. In this sense his diagnosis was conceivably more realistic, if the term is not too paradoxical, than that of the Levellers, whose attitude towards the Commonwealth was more equivocal. His consistency may be contrasted with Lilburne's tongue-in-cheek subscription, simply so that he could become a common councilman of the city of London—a post from which in any case he was immediately ejected.[13]

Another of Winstanley's works might be thought to help us to date *Englands Spirit* more exactly. If other historians are correct in dating his *Fire in the Bush*[14] to the summer of 1650, after, but not long after the final collapse of the Digger experiment, then *Englands Spirit* must surely be earlier than that. *Fire in the Bush* is altogether more apocalyptic in tone; it looks forward to the overthrow of all government which upholds the present distribution of landed property, including those who 'sit downe in that Chaire of Government, out of which the former Tyrants are gone', although even here Winstanley is careful to deny that he is an anarchist.[15] Despite the weighty arguments adduced by Petegorsky, Sabine and Hudson,[16] it is still possible to argue on internal

[12] Unlike Thomason, Clarke did not usually put a date on the items of which he obtained copies. Logically, publication could have been anywhere from 1 January 1649–50 to 24 March 1650–1, according to whether his printer dated the new year from 1 Jan. or 25 Mar. But in view of the controversy about the Engagement, the early months of 1650 (that is, by modern dating from 1 Jan.) seem the likeliest.
[13] See P. Gregg, *Freeborn John* (London, 1961), pp. 303–4.
[14] Sabine, *Works*, pp. 445–97. See now Mr Keith Thomas's argument in 'The date of Gerrard Winstanley's *Fire in the Bush*', *Past and Present*, no. 42 (Feb. 1969), pp. 160–2 (pp. 138–41 in this volume), which invalidates my argument in this paragraph, but still leaves unsolved the exact date of *Englands Spirit*.
[15] See especially, Sabine, *Works*, pp. 463–4, 471–2.
[16] D. Petegorsky, *Left-Wing Democracy in the English Civil War* (London, 1940), p. 148 n. 2, and p. 176 n. 1; Sabine, *Works*, pp. 443–4; W. S. Hudson, 'Economic and social thought of Gerrard Winstanley: was he a

evidence that Berens[17] was correct, and that the imprint '1650' on the title page of *Fire in the Bush* may be an error for 1649. If that were so, then this pamphlet antedates and does not follow the Digger experiment; its references to the Levellers and to divisions in the Army would seem to fit 1649 better than 1650.[18] Or, perhaps most likely of all, it may have been written early in 1649, laid aside, then taken up again and published—as dated— in 1650.[19] Moreover, by the autumn of 1651 when he returned to the composition of his longest work, published in February 1651-2 as *The Law of Freedom in a Platform or True Magistracy Restored*,[20] he had reverted to at least some hope of reform by and through the arm of the magistrate, in the person of Oliver Cromwell as Lord General. His disillusionment with the Army and the Independent leaders was hardly permanent or universal. He had reverted too, to what can fairly be called a greater emphasis on limited piecemeal reform, as a means of moving even haltingly towards a better, more just society. When he wrote 'For surely the disorderly actings of Officers[21] break the peace of the Commonwealth more, then any men whatsoever',[22] he was as far from the gloomy brooding fundamentalism of *Fire in the Bush*, as from the mystical, 'Utopian' fervour of *The New Law of Righteousnes*,[23] the main exposition of his social and economic ideas before the period of actual Digger activity. Be this as it may, if *Fire in the Bush* does not belong to the summer of 1650, and so set a date later than which *Englands Spirit* cannot have been written, then the terminal dates within which that work can be placed become wider not narrower.[24]

---

seventeenth-century Marxist?', *Jl of Mod. Hist.*, xviii (1946), pp. 1-21, esp. pp. 15-16.

[17] L. H. Berens, *The Digger Movement in the days of the Commonwealth as revealed in the writings of Gerrard Winstanley, the Digger Mystic and Rationalist, Communist and Social Reformer* (London, 1906). Sabine (*loc. cit.*) also allows the possibility of the earlier date.

[18] Sabine, *Works*, pp. 467, 471, 492 (also cited in Hudson, *op. cit.*).

[19] I am grateful to Christopher Hill for this suggestion. For Winstanley's activities during the latter part of 1650, see Paul H. Hardacre, 'Gerrard Winstanley in 1650', *Huntington Library Quarterly*, xxii (1958-9), pp. 345-9.

[20] Sabine, *Works*, pp. 501-602.

[21] This clearly refers to officials of the civil government (in the widest sense), not to army officers.   [22] Sabine, *Works*, p. 538.

[23] *Ibid.*, pp. 149-244, (?) Feb. 1648/9.   [24] Above, n. 12.

Near the end of the dialogue, in the form of which the pamphlet is cast, Winstanley appears to concede that social and economic inequalities are bound up with profound defects in human nature, that personal regeneration is necessary as well as institutional reform.[25] Perhaps this passage alone touches the fundamental structure of his beliefs. And it reminds us that his thought has a moral, and in its own way a theological dimension, which is inseparable from his communist principles and programme.[26] The main interest of *Englands Spirit* remains political or ideological, according to definition. It deals with one of the great and universal issues of obligation and allegiance: what support should the man of principle give to a regime which contains some of the pre-requisites for bringing about the juster social order which he desires, but which at the same time is characterized by backsliding and human frailty? It is a question which is as relevant today as it was in 1650.

The genuineness of the pamphlet's authorship is scarcely in question. That is, unless one is to imagine someone, presumably on behalf of the Commonwealth government, deliberately imitating Winstanley's style and his views, in order to win support for the Engagement among—of all people—the Diggers and their well-wishers; or, alternatively, someone from a royalist or presbyterian standpoint seeking to discredit the Commonwealth, by identifying the Engagement with Digger ideas. Stranger than fiction as fact so often is, neither of these possibilities is easily credible. As for 'W.L.', the publisher, he seems likely to have been William Larner, who put out a good deal of Leveller material, although Giles Calvert was Winstanley's normal publisher; there

[25] Below, pp. 121–2.
[26] Again, Zagorin, *Hist. of Political Thought*, chap. 4, 'Utopian Communism', pp. 43–58, seems to me the best short account of Winstanley's ideas. For longer accounts, see Petegorsky, *Left-Wing Democracy* and the Introduction to Sabine, *Works*. (N.B. For those without access to Sabine, there is L. D. Hamilton (ed.), *Selected Works of Gerrard Winstanley*, London, 1944, with Introduction by Christopher Hill.) For interpretations with a stronger religious emphasis, see W. S. Hudson, 'Gerrard Winstanley and the early Quakers', *Church Hist.*, xii (1943), pp. 177–94, and Hudson, 'Economic and social thought of G. Winstanley . . .', cited above, n. 16, and W. Schenk, *The Concern for Social Justice in the Puritan Revolution* (London, 1948), chap. 4, pp. 97–113.

may or may not be any significance in this.[27] The text given here is not a facsimile reprint, but it follows the original exactly as to use of capitals, italic type, spelling[28] and punctuation. The pamphlet consists of the title page, eleven pages of the main text, and two of the postscript; its size is duodecimo ($5\frac{1}{2}$ by $3\frac{1}{2}$ inches). Its shelf mark is Worcester College Library, L.R.4, 12 (15).

ENGLANDS SPIRIT Unfoulded.
OR *AN* INCOURAGEMENT TO TAKE THE *ENGAGE-MENT*. SHEWING

The end of that Cause that was first declared for, in the beginning of the Warres against the *King*, by a salutary *Discourse* between two Friends.

Written by Jerrard Winstanley.

Freedom is the mark, at which all men should aime
But what true freedom is, few men doth know by name,
But now a light is rise, and nere shall fall
How every man by name, shall freedom call.
LONDON, Printed for *W.L.* 1650.

[1][29] A. *Well met my dear friend, Where hast thou been this long time?*
O. I have been travelling through *England*, to see and observe the frame of the spirit in the people.
A. *And how dost thou find it?*
O. Why truly the spirit of the Land, is under a threefold bondage in some, and is rising out of bondage in others; But for the present, the great dispute is about the *Engagement*.
[3] A. *And how stands the people affected to it?*
O. The generality of people like it well, and their Reasons are these. First say they, If we must maintain the present Government, without King or House of Lords, then we

[27] See P. G. Morrison, *Index of Printers, Publishers and Booksellers in D. Wing's Short-Title Catalogue 1641-1700* (Charlottesville, Va, 1955).
[28] For those unfamiliar with seventeenth-century English, the use of 'then' where we should write 'than' can be confusing, but the context normally makes it clear enough which is meant.
[29] Page numbers are in square brackets; the pagination goes straight from 1 to 3.

must enjoy successive Parliaments: and so we shall be freed from the corruption of particular men to be perpetuall Governours; for if one sort of men should constantly sit in that governing chaire, they would prove as bad, or worse then Kings or House of Lords.

Secondly, Those two Acts or Lawes which this present State Government hath made, since it cast out Kingly power and House of Lords; declares plainly what this State Government aimes at, and that is, that all *English* men may have their freedom in and to the Land; and be freed from the slavery of the *Norman* Conquest.

A.   *What are those two Acts or Lawes?*

O.   The one is to free the people from obedience to the King, and from all that hold claiming under him. The other is, to make *England* a free *Common-wealth*.[30] Now these two Acts of State Government, takes away the Tirany of conquests, which is Kingly and Lordly power; and restores *England* to their Creation right, as it was before any Conquest by sword came in. The meaning is this: That the Land of *England* shall be a common Treasury to all *English* men without respect [4] of persons: even as the severall portions of *Canaan* were the proper Birth-right and livelihood of such and such a Tribe: neither hedging in the elder, nor hedging out the younger brother.

A.   *What other reason doth move the people to affect the Engagement?*

O.   As it doth establish successive Parliaments, by taking away King and House of Lords:[31] so it gives a full liberty to all sort of people that are *English* men, and who are called upon by the State to subscribe the taking of it: to have their freedom in the choosing of their Representatives.

For now those Letters and Messengers formerly used to be sent from the House of Lords, nor the over-awing lookes of Kingly power, to make the people choose men by favour of

[30] The Acts are those of 17 Mar. 1648–9, abolishing the office of king, and of 19 May 1649, declaring the people of England to be a commonwealth and free state (see Gardiner, *Const. Docs*, nos 88 and 90, pp. 384–7, 388; Firth and Rait, *Acts and Ordinances*, ii, pp. 18, 122).

[31] In fact the House of Lords was abolished by a third Act, of 19 Mar. 1648/9 (see Gardiner, *Const. Docs*, no. 89, pp. 387–8; Firth and Rait, *Acts and Ordinances*, ii, p. 24).

them, shall never heareafter fright them; but everyone shall have his full liberty in the Land for his livelihood, and likewise in the choice of the representing power, according as *England* is called a free people, or *Common-wealth*, without King, conquering power, or House of Tyrant Lords to rule over them as formerly.

A. *But may not the House of Parliament prove as Tyrannicall as House of Lords or King, and what remedy have the people against them?*

O. No, they cannot, for no one Representative, shall expect to sit alwayes, unless the people [4][32] will choose them again, but shall willingly arise and give their seats to another;[33] for a *Common-wealth* Government, implies a Government by our equalls, chosen out freely for a time. And if any should assume a power to abide constantly in that Parliamentary Seate, and so to rule as if they were Conquerours over the people, as *King* and House of *Lords* did; then they do thereby, endeavour to bring in *Kingly* power, and themselves to be the house of *Lords* again: and so they corrupt *Common-wealth* Government; and breaks the *Common-wealths* Engagement, and declares themselves Traytors to *Englands* freedom, because they strive to bring in Tyrany againe.

A. *But is this the joynt approbation of all the people?*

O. Yes, of all unbyassed men, that loves *Englands* freedom; but there are some that stormes extreamly at the *Engagement*, and refuse to take it.

A. *Who are they?*

O. They are Lords of Manours, Tithing Priests, who preach up *Kingly* and *Lordly* conquering interests, Impropriators, Lawyers, Covetous Usurers, and oppressing Land-Lords.

A. *And why should these be offended at the Engagement?*

---

[32] There are two pages 4 in the original.

[33] The so-called Rump, or purged House of Commons of the Long Parliament, had begun to discuss electoral reform and a future representative in the summer of 1649. A comprehensive scheme for the redistribution of seats had been reported to the House from a select committee 9 Jan. 1649–50 (*Journals of the House of Commons*, vi, pp. 344–5). The question of sitting members, in relation to the election of the next parliament, was to prove more of a stumbling block, and indeed helped to bring about Cromwell's dissolution of the Rump in April 1653.

O. Because the *Kingly* or *Lordly* power is the [5] foundation
of their standing, and they are the men that uphold the power
of Conquest, and so are enemies to publick freedom; for
if that Power be taken away, then they must be equall to
other *English* men their brethren; and must suffer them to
live as comfortably in the Land as themselves; and this their
covetousnesse and pride, will not suffer them quietly as yet
to submit unto.

*A. But what warrant hath the Common people to demand this
Nationall freedom, as well as Lords of Manours and the other.*

O. Because the Parliament declared what they did, they did
it not for themselves, but for publick freedom; the Army
declared what they did, they did it for publick freedom; and
thereupon both Parliament and Army calls upon the Common
people to bring in their Monies, give Free-quarter, and adventure their lives with them, to cast out the Conquer or
Tyrant Power: and they would make *England* a free *Commonwealth*, as they have now declared it to be by Act of Parliament.

Therefore the people may boldly, and lawfully claime their
freedom in the possession of the Land; and those that hinder
this freedom, do begin to set themselves down in that *Kingly*
and *Lordly* conquering chaire, out of which they have cast
King *Charles* and House of *Lords*; And so they [6] prove
themselves, tenne times greater hypocrites then *Judas*, and
worse Tyrants then either *King* or house of *Lords*. For they
ruled by their sword as Conquerours over us, but these that
endeavour to Rule, by the same Power as *Kings* did over us,
Rules by treachery and hypocrisie; and therefore they that
endeavour to uphold themselves in such a Power, will loose
themselves, and be cast out with greater distast, then either
King or House of *Lords* were.

*A. But do these men that are so offended at the Engagement, lose
any of their Creation right by the fall of the Kingly and Lordly
power?*

O. No they shall injoy their Creation right as much as
any, for *England* is their Birth-right as well as any ones. But
they lose only the power of Conquest, which bred all Tyrany;
And this is all the power which is taken from them.

A. Why then it is plaine, that all their trouble is, because they

cannot Rule as Tyrants over their Brethren, as they did formerly
when Kingly and Lordly power ruled in strength?
O.   Very true, that is the bottome of all their trouble; for
they would be free-men themselves, but they would have all
others bond-men. And so, though they professe the Scriptures, and keep Fasting-dayes, and Thanksgiving-dayes, yet
they [7] do not do as they would be done unto; and so they
deny the Scriptures, and declare themselves hypocrites.
A.   *But will the Parliament do, act, and suffer others to do*
according to this Engagement?
O.   Yes, doubtlesse they cannot deny it.
First, because they have declared *Englands* freedom.
Secondly, because the people now do generally understand
their freedom.
And therefore thirdly, if the Parliament should be contrary to
their words, Acts, and Engagements, wherein *Englands* freedom is concerned, the people may freely plead against them;
and every Towne and County, may call those treacherous
Parliament men off their Seats and choose new men into
their place: for now the eyes of all men will be much upon
their Representatives, and will narrowly observe, whether
their care be to cast out *Kingly* and *Lordly*, and Conquest
power; and to endeavour to make *England* a free *Common-*
wealth, yea, or no?[34]
A.   *Well, for this let us stand still, and waite to see the workings*
of every thing, for Time, Love, and Patience brings all things to
perfection. But thou wast saying, that there was a threefold [8]
bondage lay upon the spirit of the Land. What are they?
O.   Why, truly I'le tell thee, that some are troubled how to
live, their poverty is so great, and this is a great burden
among our friends, who have lost all in the time of the
Warres: some by their free hearts in furthering the *Parliaments*
cause, and by being plundered, are brought to mighty straits.
A.[35]   *But though it be so hard with them, yet those two Acts of*

---

[34] Again, this assumes that there are shortly to be elections for a new
representative.
[35] In relation to the dialogue down to this point, in which 'A.' is the
questioner and 'O.' the expositor, it would make better sense if this
passage were to be ascribed to O., as a continuation of his answer to A.'s
previous question.

Parliament aforesaid, and the true intent of this Engagement will
relieve them, for thereby they have freedom given them, to go build
and plant upon the Common Land, and so to recruite themselves
with a comfortable livelihood: And likewise thereby, they are protected
from the Power of Lords of Mannours, who holds claiming or Title
under the King, who ruled over England *as a Conqueror. And this*
is the benefit, that this present Common-wealth Government, which
the people have Engaged to maintaine, against King and House of
Lords:[36] *For now the Ancient Lawes of the Conquerour are thereby*
broake, and the Common Land now, is the true propriety and
right of every poor man, as it was formerly the rights of King
Charles, *while he stood Conquerour.*

[9] A. *But do we not see, that great men, who uphold the Law of*
Conquests, do make their wills a Law, as if the Conquering Power
ruled still?

O. It is true, their will hath been a Law, but they cannot
now, rule by will, for he or they that endeavour to rule by
their will, brings in the Kingly power again, and sets up
tyrany still; and so breakes the *Engagement*, and proves
himself a traytor to the *Common-wealth* of *England*; And assure
yourself, the people are now so sensible of freedom, that they
will have no mercy upon such a one.

A. *Shall the conquered Cavaleere party, have any benefit by the*
Engagement?

O. Yes, if they take it, and keep it, they are to have equall
freedom with others, for they are *Englishmen.*

A. *But doth none uphold, The power of Conquests, and Kingly*
power, but Lords of Mannours, Tything-Priests, Impropriators,
and Lawyers.

O. Yes, that enslaving covetous Kingly power, is corrupt
bloud, that runs in every man, and womans vaines, more or
lesse, till reason the spirit of burning cast him out.[37] And

---

[36] This sentence lacks a verb in the main clause; perhaps understand
'gives' or 'provides' after 'Government'.

[37] Unless 'reason the spirit of burning' is a misprint, or a wrong word
order, this implies some kind of intellectual or metaphorical purging
by fire. The general idea is fully consonant with Winstanley's thought as a
whole; he also used 'Reason' as a synonym for God (e.g. Sabine, *Works*,
p. 251). I find it hard to agree with Hudson (articles cited above) that
this was usual among the religious radicals of the 1640s and 1650s.

as this Kingly power is cast out from within, so it falls from without likewise.

[10] A. *Well, what is the second trouble, that lies upon the Peoples spirits?*

O. Why truly those that would be Tyrants, are afraid and mighty troubled, lest the enslaved people, should fall off from them, and neither fight for them, nor work for them.

A.[38] *Alas poor men, these that would enslave others, are slaves themselves, to the Kingly Power within themselves. But if these would give the poor their freedom, and remove the heavy yoke of Norman Conquest, which they hold in their hands over the people, they would win the peoples hearts, and free themselves from that trouble. And if this they do not do quickly, that which they fear will come upon them, for they will be left naked.*

A.[39] Well, what is the third trouble?

O. *The third is this, People would faine know, what the creating spirit is, called the Lord God Almighty: And what shall become of them after they are dead, and what the Resurrection is; And their Ministers confounds them more and more, and instead of healers, they prove destroyers, and the people are much troubled about these things.*

A. I am mighty glad I have met with thee, come, unfold freely to me, what the creating, preserving, and governing spirit is, for I perceive thou canst.

[11] O. *I will answer thy request freely, upon our next meeting; but now time, and many businesses abridges me, therefore for this present we must bid farewell.*

A WATCH-WORD.[40]

BEware you Women of the ranting crew
And call not freedom those things that are vaine,
For if a child you get, by ranting deeds
The man is gone and leaves the child your gaine,
Then you and yours are left by such free-men,
For other women are as free for them.

---

[38] Again, it makes better sense to treat this as a continuation of O.'s answer to A.'s previous question.

[39] The kind of type used to distinguish the two spokesmen is reversed from here to the end of the dialogue.

[40] The postscript is unpaginated. A new page begins here.

IT is reported, that the Digging practises, leads to the *Ranting* principles; but this is to certifie, that if any of the Diggers fall into the practise of Ranting, they fall off from their principles, as some in all Churches does.

Let this be a *Watch-word* to all, to beware of this *Ranting* practise; for it is that Golden, pleasing, and deceitfull baite whereby the foolish young man is taken, ensnared, and wrapped up into many bondages. It is a nursery of idlenesse, hardness of heart and hipocrisie, making men to speak one thing and do another, that they may injoy their destroying delights; it fills the body with diseases, rottennesse, sicknesse and pox; it fills the mind with anger, distempers and vexation; it is the[41] Kingdom of Satan without, which lies in objects which may be taken away, and which moth and rust may corrupt: it is an enemy to the Kingdom of Christ within, which lies in the enjoyment of a meek, patient, sincere, moderate and chast spirit within the man, which moth and rust cannot corrupt, and which theeves cannot break through and steale: It is the resurection of the unclean, boggish[42] darke power, which is called the wicked man, or the Devill, that is to appear to shew himself a perfect man of darknesse, and the great troubler and murderer of the Creation; that being rise up to his hight, and come to his full growth of a man of darknesse, he may be cast out of mankind by the resurection of the man of righteousnesse, or restoring power, who is coming to reconcile all to himself, and so to make peace.

FINIS

[41] New page here.
[42] Elsewhere (as printed in Sabine, *Works*, p. 402), Winstanley writes of 'the unclean doggish, beastly nature . . .' of Ranting. Printers' readings apart, 'boggish' seems to me the more expressive of the two. Whether the doctrine and practice of sexual promiscuity were correctly ascribed to the Ranters is hard to know; according to N. Cohn (*Pursuit of the Millennium*, London, 1957, Appendix) they partook of certain characteristics of the Free Spirit, but for a more cautious and detailed view of the Free Spirit itself, see G. Leff, *Heresy in the Later Middle Ages*, 2 vols (Manchester, 1967), chap. 4.

X

ANOTHER DIGGER BROADSIDE*

Keith Thomas

Readers of *Past and Present* who were interested by Professor Aylmer's recent discovery of Gerrard Winstanley's *Englands Spirit Unfoulded* may care to know of the existence of another previously unnoticed Digger tract. This is *A Declaration of the grounds and Reasons, why we the poor Inhabitants of the Parrish of Iver in Buckinghamshire, have begun to digge and manure the common and wast Land belonging to the aforesaid Inhabitants, and there are many more that gives consent*. It is a single-sheet broadside, closely printed in double column and dated 1 May 1650. An apparently unique copy is to be found in the Guildhall Library, London, and is listed (along with many other previously unrecorded items) in Miss K. I. Garrett's recent catalogue of books in the Guildhall Library published before 1701.[1]

In style and format this Iver declaration belongs to a recognizable genre of Digger publication, inaugurated in April 1649 by *A Declaration to all the Powers of England, and to all the Powers of the World, shewing the cause why the common people of England have begun, and gives consent to digge up, manure, and sowe corn upon George-Hill in Surrey; by those that have subscribed, and thousands more that gives consent*. This statement by the Surrey Diggers was signed by

* From no. 42 (February 1969).

[1] *Guildhall Library. A List of Books printed in the British Isles and of English Books printed abroad before 1701 in Guildhall Library* (London, 1966–7), item no. GL 1638. I am indebted to the Guildhall Library staff for their help and to the Librarian for his kind permission to reprint the broadside.

Winstanley and others and formed the text of *The True Levellers Standard Advanced*.[2] During the next twelve months it was followed by similar manifestoes which set out in numbered paragraphs and rhetorical questions the reasons which had led their signatories to embark upon the work of cultivating the commons. Of those now extant the nearest in style to the Iver broadside seem to be Robert Coster's *A Mite cast into the Common Treasury* (18 December 1649), *An Appeale to all Englishmen* by Winstanley and others at St George's Hill (26 March 1650), and *A Declaration of the Grounds and Reasons why we the Poor Inhabitants of the Town of Wellinborrow, in the County of Northampton, have begun and give consent to Dig up, Manure and Sow Corn upon the Common, and Waste Ground, called Bareshanke, Belonging to the Inhabitants of Wellinborrow, by those that have Subscribed, and Hundreds more that give Consent* (12 March 1650).[3] This latter Wellingborough broadside bears a particularly close resemblance to the Iver manifesto. The wording of the title is very similar, and the argument of the first three paragraphs (obviously derived from Winstanley's writings) is the same in both tracts. The Iver broadside, however, was published not by Giles Calvert, but by Thomas Brewster and Gregory Moule, a well-known partnership who put out many radical writings at this time.[4] They are not known to have published any other Digger works, although it was from the same address of the Three Bibles in St Paul's churchyard that Winstanley's *An Humble Request* had been issued on 9 April 1650, three weeks earlier.[5]

The Iver broadside does not throw much new light upon the evolution of Digger thought. In attacking the inequalities produced by private property and the manorial system the authors seem to have drawn heavily upon Winstanley, though they add some vivid touches of their own and their tone is unusually bitter and defiant. Like the Digger leader, they urge the rights of

[2] Printed in *The Works of Gerrard Winstanley*, ed. G. H. Sabine (Ithaca, New York, 1941), pp. 245–66.

[3] *Ibid.*, pp. 653–61, 405–15, 649–51. The Guildhall Library also holds an unnoticed copy of the Wellingborough *Declaration* (item no. GL 1639).

[4] H. R. Plomer, *A Dictionary of the Booksellers and Printers who were at work in England, Scotland and Ireland from 1641 to 1667* (London, 1907); P. G. Morrison, *Index of Printers, Publishers and Booksellers in Donald Wing's Short-title Catalogue* (Charlottesville, Va, 1955).

[5] *Works*, ed. Sabine, p. 73.

the inhabitants to the common land and stress that it is only its communal cultivation which can relieve the plight of the poor. This is a much-needed reminder that the aims of the Diggers were practical as well as symbolic. Winstanley frequently pointed out that a large area of the country (which he variously estimated at between a third and two thirds) was waste land awaiting cultivation. He saw communal digging and manuring as an urgently needed way of increasing the food supply.[6] Indeed the whole Digger movement can be plausibly regarded as the culmination of a century of unauthorized encroachment upon the forests and wastes by squatters and local commoners, pushed on by land shortage and the pressure of population.[7] In the Iver broadside the emphasis upon food scarcity and high prices is particularly marked.

But the main interest of the tract lies in the new information it provides about the extent of the Digger movement. The Diggers have hitherto been assumed to have set up colonies in Surrey (St George's Hill and Cobham), Northamptonshire (Wellingborough), Kent (Cox Hall)[8] and, possibly, in Buckinghamshire[9] and Gloucestershire.[10] The Iver *Declaration* confirms the existence of all of these settlements and adds five more to the list: Barnet, Enfield, Dunstable, Bosworth, and an unspecified location in Nottinghamshire. This suggests that the fund-raising and

[6] *Works*, ed. Sabine, pp. 200, 304, 356, 408, 414.
[7] For some account of the squatters see *The Agrarian History of England and Wales*, iv, *1500–1640*, ed. J. Thirsk (Cambridge, 1967), pp. 95–7, 107–8, 224–5, 409–12, 445–6.
[8] *Works*, ed. Sabine, p. 411. Sabine takes this to be Cox Hill, a hamlet five miles north-west of Dover, but the identification seems doubtful. For other possibilities see C. Hill, *The World Turned Upside Down* (London, 1972), p. 99 n. 79.
[9] *Works*, ed. Sabine, pp. 646–7.
[10] The enclosure riots of June 1650 at Slimbridge and Frampton (*Cal. State Papers Domestic, 1650*, p. 218) are cited in this connection by D. W. Petegorsky, *Left-Wing Democracy in the English Civil War* (London, 1940), p. 174. There had been periodical demonstrations in this area since the early seventeenth century: see W. B. Willcox, *Gloucestershire. A study in local government, 1590–1640* (New Haven, 1940), p. 280, and D. G. C. Allan, 'The Rising in the West, 1628–1631', *Econ. Hist. Rev.*, 2nd ser., v (1952–3), pp. 81–2, 84. Digger influence in Staffordshire and Cumberland was suggested by M. James, *Social Problems and Policy during the Puritan Revolution, 1640–1660* (London, 1930), p. 101, but the evidence seems slight.

evangelizing Digger agents who were apprehended in April 1650 after an itinerary through Berkshire, Buckinghamshire, Hertfordshire, Huntingdonshire, Middlesex, Northamptonshire and Surrey[11] may have had more success than is usually realized. At any rate it is clear that the Digger movement did not end abruptly in April 1650 as has been previously assumed.

In addition the Iver broadside tidies up a number of other loose ends in Digger history. It shows that the Surrey Diggers left their children behind to be maintained by the parish after their experiment collapsed in April 1650. It also reveals that the Wellingborough Diggers were acquitted (though not released) by the Northamptonshire Quarter Sessions of 16–17 April 1650, despite the prior attempt by the Council of State to arrange for their conviction on charges of riot and intrusion upon property.[12] The Iver manifesto may even throw some indirect light upon the obscure question of Winstanley's movements between the Surrey Quarter Sessions of Easter 1650 and his reappearance at Pirton, Hertfordshire, in the following August. It seems worth reviving the suggestion[13] that the Digger leader moved north across the river to Colnbrook, Buckinghamshire, less than ten miles from St George's Hill. Colnbrook was the point where the Digger agents started their journey and it is a mere three miles from Iver. Indeed the possibility that Winstanley had a hand in the compilation of the Iver manifesto cannot be ruled out.

The broadside also raises the old question of the relationship between the Diggers and the Levellers. The two tracts, *Light Shining in Buckinghamshire* (December 1648) and *More Light Shining in Buckingham-shire* (March 1649), advocated agrarian egalitarianism rather than communism.[14] They are usually assumed to have been the work of a group of advanced rural Levellers and they

---

[11] *Works*, ed. Sabine, pp. 440–1. William Everard said in April 1649 that the Diggers planned to extend their activities to Newmarket, Hounslow and Hampstead: Petegorsky, *Left-Wing Democracy*, p. 163.

[12] *Cal. State Papers Domestic, 1650*, p. 106. The records of the Sessions do not survive.

[13] Made by L. H. Berens, *The Digger Movement in the days of the Commonwealth* (London, 1906), p. 79. For Winstanley's presence at Pirton see P. H. Hardacre, 'Gerrard Winstanley in 1650', *Huntington Library Qtly*, xxii (1958–9), pp. 345–9.

[14] *Works*, ed. Sabine, pp. 609–40; Petegorsky, *Left-Wing Democracy*, pp. 138–42.

bear only passing points of similarity to the Iver *Declaration*. But the fact that Iver is in Stoke Hundred must re-focus attention upon *A Declaration of the Wel-Affected in the County of Buckinghamshire: being a representation of the middle sort of men within the three Chilterne Hundreds of Disbrough, Burnum, and Stoke, and part of Alisbury Hundred* (10 May 1649).[15] This had begun by setting out a number of typical Leveller demands, but had ended by affirming solidarity with the poor in their attempt to regain the commons for communal cultivation. The same juxtaposition of Leveller and Digger programmes is to be found a year later in the Iver *Declaration*. For the most part it is a typical Digger manifesto, but its demands for the reform of the prisons and the law relating to debt, and its references to the arrears of pay owing to ex-soldiers, suggest a link with earlier Leveller agitation.

Such speculation must be left to the further research which the Digger movement can still repay. In the meantime it is worth noting that the ten signatories of the Iver broadside bring up the total of identifiable Diggers to ninety. Although the difficulties are not to be underrated, patient research could reveal a good deal about these remarkable men. Iver, for example, was a large parish in the seventeenth century, with 420 communicants in 1603 and some 700 residents a century later.[16] The ten signatories to the Digger manifesto do not have very idiosyncratic names and the spelling is uncertain. Yet a preliminary search reveals that every one of them can be traced in the records of the locality. The majority were copyholders, well versed in the ways of the manorial courts against which they protested. At least three could not sign their names. The identifications offered in the ensuing footnotes are necessarily tentative, but it is certain that the Iver Diggers were genuine inhabitants rather than itinerant agitators, and that most of them continued to reside in the parish long after the short-lived Digger movement had subsided.

In the text that follows I have preserved the erratic spelling, capitalization, italicization and punctuation of the original.

A Declaration of the grounds and Reasons, why we the poor Inhabitants of the Parrish of *Iver* in *Buckinghamshire*, have begun

[15] *Works*, ed. Sabine, pp. 641–7.
[16] W. H. Ward and K. S. Block, *A History of the Manor and Parish of Iver* (London, 1933), p. 193.

to digge and mannure the common and wast Land belonging to
the aforesaid Inhabitants, and there are many more that gives
consent.

1. The word of God hath witnessed unto us, that the Lord
created the earth with all that is therein for whole Mankind,
equall to one as to another, and for every one to live free upon to
get an ample Livelihood therein, and therefore those who have
by an unrighteous power made merchandize of the earth, giving
all to some, and none to others, declares themselves tyranicall and
usurping Lords over Gods heritage, and we affirm that they have
no righteous power to sell or give away the earth, unlesse they
could make the earth likewise, which none can do but God the
eternall Spirit.

2. We are very sensible that although Mankind was by the
will of his Maker, constituted in all his branches, a supream Lord
over all Creatures of other kinds, yet we see that no creature is so
much deprived of a Being and subsistance as mankind is; and
though those who are become Lords and Masters over their
fellow Creatures, do challenge a larger circuit of earth to be given
of God, more particularly to them then to others; we say that this
is false, unlesse they mean their God covetousnesse, the God of
this world, who hath blinded their eyes, and hardned their
hearts, and this God is an unequall and impartial divider, and
therefore he must be destroyed.

We know that *Cain* is still alive in all the great Landlords, and
such like Earthmongers who are continally crucifying their
poor Brethren by oppression, cheating and robbery: therefore
you Lords of Mannors especially, the Lord hath set *Cains* mark
upon you, because he will surely find you out, if you do not
repent and give over, lye down therefore and submit (and why
not) that your Iniquities may be no more in remembrance, and
that the cry of your cruelty may be heard no more in the Land.

3. Then thirdly, there is a promise in Scripture (which God
hath made) to free us from that bondage wherein you have involved us, and that pride and oppression shall be heard of no
more in the Land, and that the Lord will restore the whole
Creation into the glorious liberty of the Sonnes of God, which is
no other liberty then that which Christ himself by his spirit hath

invested us withall, and that is equality, community and fellow-ship with our own kind; for the first shall be last, and the last shall be first, and he that sitteth, as he that serveth.

4. We are urged to go forth and Act in this righteous work, because of our present necessity, and want of the comfort which belongs to our Creation, that the earth being inclosed into the hands of a few, whereby time, custome and usurping Lawes have made particular Interests for some, and not for all: so that these great Taskmasters will allow us none of the earth whilst we are alive, but onely when we are dead, they will afford us just as much as will make the length of our graves, because they cannot then keep it from us, and that then we should be equall with them; but why may we not whilst we are alive with them, have as much of the earth as themselves: yes truly, remove but covetousnesse, and kill that cursed power, and then those men would not keep all to themselves, but would willingly suffer their fellow Creatures to enjoy the Birthright of their creation; for whiles the great ones like Ratts and Mice drawe all the treasures and fruits of the earth into their nests and holes after them, resolving rather to spoile these good things, then to suffer the common sort to have part with: and therefore they have now got a custome to dyet the Markets, and make a dearth in time of plenty, and though the Lord be pleased to give us joyfull and fruitfull seasons, yet we see that this helpeth us nothing: we must be starved neverthelesse, and why? because the rich will have it so, no other reason can be rendred: Therefore you of the poorer sort, understand this, that nothing but the manuring of the common Land, will reduce you into a comfortable condition; and likewise we declare, that though we keep our selves close to our hard labours, breaking our due and necessary rest which should refresh us, whereby our lives are become a burthen to us, and yet our carefull and diligent labour, will afford us no other then a distracted, languishing and miserable life, for how can it be otherwise? seeing we cannot enjoy the benefit of our labors ourselves, but for the maintenance of idle persons, slow bellies who raigne and ride over the common people in every Parrish, as Gods and Kings: And therefore this be that freedom which we have for these nine yeares striven for: then we pray you to exchange this freedom for our old bondage, and to set us down in that kennel where you did first lift us out.

5. And further we declare before God and the whole World, that the inhumane cruelty of our Taskmasters is, and hath ever been the just cause of all our miseries, and of the whole Nation into this sad condition, and that we see no hope, comfort, or redresse to be had from any that are in Authority in our Parrish, who say they will do nothing but what they are forc'd to do: therefore from their own words we may gather, that their full intent is to make us absolute slaves and vassalls to their wills.

6. We have great encouragement from this present *Parliament*, by making of those two excellent Lawes, the one to cast out *Kingly Power*, and the other to make us all a free people,[17] which we understand, is to break the neck of the *Norman Power* which was brought in upon us by the *Norman Bastard*, continued and encreased ever since within this Nation, by every King who was his Successour.

7. This act of ours endeavouring to make the wast Land fruit-full, is an Act full of Honour, Righteousnesse, Justice and Peace, and consequently agreeing with the Law of God and the Law of reason; for the Scripture saith, *The meek shall inherite the earth:* this work therefore of ours is not to be carried on by force of Armes, it is a thing which we much abhorre, but in love onely and meeknesse, and this power onely shall at last conquer, and bring in the *Kings* and *Princes* of the earth: therefore all you that are prepared to act freedom and love, come forth and break your Swords into Plough shares, and leavie Warre no more.[18]

8. There is a principle of Reason that teacheth every man to do as he would be done by, that is to live in love, and be at peace with all men, and to do as we would be done by, is to allow the same

---

[17] The two Acts, abolishing the office of king (17 Mar. 1649), and declaring England to be a commonwealth and free state (19 May 1649), are printed in *Acts and Ordinances of the Interregnum, 1642-1660*, ed. C. H. Firth and R. S. Rait (London, 1911), ii, pp. 18-20, 122. They were repeatedly cited by Winstanley in justification of the Digger argument that the abolition of the monarchy implied the automatic restoration of the commons to the people: see *Works*, ed. Sabine, pp. 324-5, 330, 353, 358, 364-5, 366, 372-3, 411-13, 429-31, 507, and *Englands Spirit Unfoulded*, ed. Aylmer, *Past and Present*, no. 40 (July 1968), pp. 9-10 (pp. 109-23 in this volume).

[18] This pacifism was characteristic of the Digger experiment. Cf. *Works*, ed. Sabine, pp. 182-3, 247, 256, 266, 272, 286, 346, 364, 378-90, 434, and Berens, *The Digger Movement*, p. 37.

liberty to others, that we our selves are willing to enjoy,[19] which is food and rayment, freely without being a slave to any of our fellow Creatures: We desire all those that are free to act with us in this work, that they would come forth and set their hands to remove this bondage which we have lain under this 600. yeares: And further we desire, that those who cannot come forth as yet in person, that they would lend us their assistance and encouragement to supply our necessities whilst our labours lies buried in the earth untill the fruit comes up; our condition being but poor at the beginning, that so this righteous work may not fall off and perish, to give the Adversarie cause to perceive that we are again brought back into bondage.

10.   And lastly, we do not intend to proceed upon this work in any other power, but that which is before exprest, which is the Lords own way, even peace and love, stedfastly resolving not to meddle with any mans propriety, but what is known to be common Land,[20] and these are the essentiall grounds and reasons of us the poor Inhabitants of *Iver* in *Buckinghamshire*, whose names are hereunder written.

And we much desire the fishing Trade may presently be set up,[21] for then we might have more fish for one shilling, then now we have for 4 *s.* which would be great comfort to us the poor, and no hurt to you therefore; and likewise that Potters List[22] might be paid, which so long from them have been stayed.

[19] For similar emphasis upon the golden rule see *Works*, ed. Sabine, pp. 361, 365, 408, 509, 537, 596, 611, 615, 658, and Petegorsky, *Left-Wing Democracy*, p. 134.

[20] The Diggers consistently refused to invade private property, although they looked forward to the day when it would be voluntarily surrendered: *Works*, ed. Sabine, pp. 182-3, 272, 283; Berens, *The Digger Movement*, p. 37. Their threat to pay no more rent (below, p. 133) seems a departure from this policy.

[21] A demand which does not occur in other Digger writings, but was often made by contemporary social reformers. See, e.g. [J. Wetwang, *et al.*], *To his excellency Thomas Lord Fairfax . . . The Humble Representation of the desires of the Officers and Souldiers in the Regiment of Horse, for the County of Northumberland* (1648) (Brit. Mus., E 475(13)), p. 3, and *Provision for the Poore: or, a brief representative to make known the way, by a Fishing Trade, to imploy many thousands of poore people* (1649) (Brit. Mus., 669 f. 14(16)).

[22] A list of some 2,500 persons to whom arrears of pay for service in the Parliamentary army had been outstanding since at least June 1647. Despite several complaints of hardship, a sum of £14,750 was still owing in

And that Ingrosers and buyers of Corn might be lookt to, that we might have it at some reasonabler rate. And that there may be Commissioners granted, to call the Church-wardens and Overseers of the poor for the Countrey as well as for the City to an account.[23] [They are at work at *Barnet*, and at *Enfield*,[24] and there they are resolved if they will not let them plant and build, they will leave them in *Barnet* 7. Children, and at *Enfield* nine Children. They were better leave them then starve them, and themselves too; and they are at work at *Dunstable*, in *Buckinghamshire* also,[25] and we hear they are going to build in many Countries,[26] and are resolved to pay no more Rent, things are so deare they cannot.][27] We hear that they have begun mannuring the Commons in *Kent*, at *Willingborough*, and *Bosworth* old in *Northamptonshire*[28] & in *Gloucestershire*,[29] & in *Nottinghamshire*, and they intend to sowe roots till *July*, & then follow[30] for winter corne, and then to build for the poorest in the Parishes, and if the rich will not let them

---

November 1649. On 17 May 1650, i.e. a fortnight after the Iver *Declaration*, the matter was referred to a special committee, but I have not managed to trace the outcome. See *Cal. of the Proceedings of the Committee for Compounding, 1643–1660*, i, pp. 97, 143, 147, 158, 163, 167, 226, and *Commons Journals*, v, p. 484; vi, p. 323. (I am much indebted to Professor Aylmer for helping me to identify this allusion.)

[23] Cf. *Light Shining in Buckinghamshire* (*Works*, ed. Sabine, p. 620).

[24] The scene in June 1649 of riots (*Cal. State Papers Domestic, 1649–50*, p. 192) and in 1659 of violent disturbances provoked by the partial sale and enclosure of Enfield Chase. It was this latter episode which led William Covell, obviously much influenced by Winstanley, to publish his scheme for setting up collectivist communities on the Chase: see J. M. Patrick, 'William Covell and the troubles at Enfield in 1659. A sequel of the Digger movement', *Univ. of Toronto Qtly*, xiv (1944–5), pp. 45–57.

[25] Dunstable is actually in Bedfordshire. It had been on the route of the Digger agents arrested in April 1650. *Works*, ed. Sabine, p. 441.

[26] I.e. counties.

[27] This passage in square brackets is a marginal note to the original broadside.

[28] Probably not Market Bosworth, which is deep in Leicestershire, but Husbands Bosworth, which, though also in Leicestershire, is at least on the border of Northamptonshire.

[29] Apart from Slimbridge and Frampton (above, p. 126 n. 10), the most likely area is the Forest of Dean, where there was to be trouble with squatters in 1656: D. G. C. Allan, 'The Rising in the West, 1628–1631', *Econ. Hist. Rev.*, 2nd ser., v (1952–3), p. 84.

[30] I.e. fallow.

alone, the poor will leave them their Children to keep, as they have done in *Surrey*.

And we pray release all Prisoners for debt, that cannot pay their debt,[31] and let the Prisons be for work-houses for the poor to make things for the fishing Trade,[32] what will poor mens bones do you good?

Some QUERIES.

1. *Whether there be any Statute or Law against breaking up, or manuring of the Common which was left out for us ever since the Conquest, onely for the poor by all old records, and now we intend to make use of our own, and if the rich will not let us provide for our Wives and Children truly, then they must, for we will not be such slaves as we have been formerly.* 2. *Whether there be any Statute or Law extant, or can be produest or showen to us by any Lord of Manner, to take honest poor men from their true and righteous labour, and put them into a Norman strong hold, and there to lye as long as corrupt Law, and unjust Justices wils please.*[33] 3. *Whether the Parliament, Councell of State, High Court of Justice, and Council of Warre, will uphold such Norman Lawes, seeing that the Successors head is cut of, we hope you will not maintain the same still, if you will, we fear you may want poor mens help when you stand in need of them.* 4. *Whether those words in your Acts against Kingly Power, and all that hold claiming under the King, do not take away all Lords of Mannors,*[34] *and Tything Priest Power too likewise, seeing they came in all by the Normand Conqueror, and those words in the other Act, that you made England a free Commonwealth, doth not mean all the poor as well as you rich, and if it mean but onely the rich,*

31 Winstanley was naturally against imprisonment for debt (*Works*, ed. Sabine, p. 197), but the closest parallel to this demand comes in *More Light Shining in Buckingham-shire* (*ibid.*, p. 638).

32 Cf. above, p. 132 n. 21.

33 Earlier statements of this legal argument occur in *Works*, ed. Sabine, pp. 431–2, 656. It was the Diggers' only defence against prosecution by manorial lords.

34 The dependence of manorial authority upon that of the Crown is repeatedly emphasized in *Works*, ed. Sabine, pp. 287, 311, 343, 347, 359, 429. Cf. above, p. 131 n. 17. Winstanley's position varied, however, between asserting that the abolition of the monarchy meant that the commons had automatically reverted to the people (*ibid.*, pp. 287, 411–13, 430) and urging Parliament to take steps to put this restoration into effect (*ibid.*, pp. 305–6, 373–4).

then let the rich fight all the battels that are to be fought, for we will
have some assurance of our true freedom, and what you mean by your
words, and how we shall have our pay and our debentors; for we cannot
live for or by fair words any longer, and they not performed neither.

5. Whether it be not fellony in or by any man to set fire on his
house and burn it down, the Law saith it is;[35] and if so, what will
it be in any man to get some 30. or 40. or more together, and go
and set fire on 6 or 7 very poor mens houses that had set them up
in some wast places, and these People before mencioned, came
and burned them down, and some of their goods too: now no
question, and if the first be fellony, this is in a higher nature,
more fellonies then the first: we desire it may be taken notice of
by all rationall men in this whole free Common-wealth of *England*
for ever hereafter, that no such fellony be committed again by
any man whatsoever.

We wright this, because we have 9 especiall friends[36] that were
at work in their own ground as they conceived, and were taken
from their righteous Labour, and carried from *Wellingborough* to
Northampton Goale, and at Sessions last, being the 16. & 17. of
April last; they could prove nothing against them, and yet would
not set them free by Proclamation according to Law; but we hope
our honest Army will not passe by there, till they have freed
them: the Generalls own Cornet *Spinege*[37] was on the bench, and

[35] This was not so. It was no felony at this time to burn one's own house
unless one succeeded in burning that of one's neighbour in the process.
But it does seem to have been felony for a landlord to burn down a house
occupied by his tenant. See *The Third Part of the Reports of Sir George
Croke*, ed. Sir H. Grimston, 2nd edn (London, 1669), pp. 376–8, and L.
Radzinowicz, *A History of English Criminal Law and its Administration
from 1750* (London, 1948), i, pp. 688–91.
[36] Presumably the nine signatories of the Wellingborough broadside:
Works, ed. Sabine, p. 651.
[37] In Feb. 1658 Anthony Spinage, then a Captain, was (along with
Captain Gladman, who had been sent to investigate the Surrey Diggers in
April 1649) one of six Baptist officers dismissed by Cromwell for their
republican sympathies. In 1672 his house was licensed as a Baptist
meeting-place: Sir C. Firth and G. Davies, *The Regimental History of
Cromwell's Army* (Oxford, 1940), i, pp. 73, 75, 78–9, 160; *The Clarke
Papers*, ed. C. H. Firth (Camden Soc., new ser., xlix, liv, lxi, lxii, 1891–
1901), iii, p. 141; G. L. Turner (ed.), *Original Records of Early Nonconformity
under Persecution and Indulgence*, 3 vols (London, 1911–14), ii, p. 883.

saw that they could prove nothing against them, we hope he will help release them.

Henry Norman.[38] *Edw: Dun.*[39] *Rob: Dun.*[40] *Benj: Dunt.*[41] *Tho. Taylor.*[42] *Wil. Saunders.*[43] *Henry Slave.*[44] *Tho. Beedle*, younger.[45] *Rich: Moseley.*[46] *John Currant.*[47]

London, *Printed for* T. Brewster, *and* G. Moule, *at the three Bibles in* Pauls *Church-yard, near the West end of* Pauls, *the 1. of May,* 1650.

[38] An ironical exception to Dr Christopher Hill's observation that the names of the signatories of the Digger manifestoes, like those of Shakespeare's lower-class characters, are all 'pure Saxon': *Puritanism and Revolution* (London, 1958), p. 69. This may, however, have been the Henry Niman living in Iver in 1694. (*N.B.* For this and the ensuing identifications I have drawn upon the following sources, several of which are unfortunately incomplete: Iver Parish Registers (in the custody of the Vicar, the Revd T. E. F. Coulson, to whom I am most grateful for making it possible for me to consult them in Oxford); *Buckinghamshire Parish Registers*, viii, ed. W. P. W. Phillimore and T. Gurney (London, 1912); Archdeaconry visitations, wills, and 1694 Poll Tax assessment (in Bucks. County Record Office, Aylesbury; I owe the staff thanks for their help); Monthly assessments for Bucks., *c.* 1644–6, and Hearth Tax assessment for Stoke Hundred, *c.* 1662 (in the Public Record Office, SP 28/150, part 6, and E 179/80/34); Manor of Iver, court rolls, 1644–5, court book, 1665–6 and miscellaneous court papers, 1666–78; Manor of West Drayton, court rolls and miscellaneous papers, 1648–72; Middlesex Hearth Tax assessment, 1664 (all in Greater London Record Office [Middlesex Records], whose staff have been exceptionally helpful); *County of Buckingham. Calendar to the Sessions Records*, i (1678–1694), ed. W. le Hardy (Aylesbury, 1933); *The Minute Book of the Monthly Meeting of the Society of Friends for the Upperside of Buckinghamshire, 1669–1690*, ed. B. S. Snell (Bucks. Archaeol. Soc., Records Branch, 1937).)

[39] *Alias* Edmund Dun or Donne. Born 1613, son of Robert Dun. Had a daughter born in 1650. Possibly the Edw. Dunt assessed at one hearth in 1662. Defaulter at Iver manorial court 1665. Held office of headborough, 1671. Father and son of the same name were presented for nonconformity in 1683–4. (The younger man was a Quaker in 1687.) His will, signed with a mark, gives his occupation as husbandman and was proved in 1693.

[40] Married 1612. Father of the above. Juror at Iver manorial court, 1644–5, and held the manorial office of sigillator in the latter year.

[41] Married 1643. Two sons born 1644 and 1647. He (or his son of the same name) defaulted at Iver manorial court in 1665, was presented for nonconformity in 1683–4, and was still resident in Iver in 1694. The other died in 1682.

[42] Born 1624. Married 1665. Constable of Iver, 1671. Died 1697. His will (proved 1699), though signed with a mark, reveals him to have been a yeoman and property-owner. A man of the same name was a copyhold

tenant in the neighbouring manor of West Drayton, 1648–72, and assessed at two hearths in 1664.

[43] A grandfather, father (born 1620) and son (born 1647) bore this name. This could have been either of the former as the grandfather was still alive in 1646. His wife had been prosecuted for absence from church in 1635 and he was excluded from communion for drunkenness in 1636. A William Sander signed *The Husbandmans Plea against Tithes* (1647), a petition emanating from 5,000 inhabitants of Hertfordshire and adjacent parts of Beds. and Bucks. William Saunders, the younger, is mentioned in Iver manorial court proceedings, 1645.

[44] Probably Henry Slane or Slann. He was a copyholder of Iver manor between at least 1644 and 1678. He married for a second time in 1657 and was assessed at three hearths in 1662. He signed his name with a mark in 1666. A man of the same name was assessed at one hearth in the adjacent parish of Harmondsworth in 1664.

[45] A common Iver surname. This was probably the yeoman who re-married in 1657 and was assessed at two hearths in 1662. He was a juror at Iver manorial court in 1665. His father was tax-collector in 1644 and 1646.

[46] Married 1635. Accused in the same year of spreading malicious rumours about a neighbour's adultery, in the George Inn, Aylesbury. A son (also called Richard) was born in 1636. Another was born in 1648. Assessed at one hearth in 1662. Died 1689. A labourer of the same name, presumably a descendant, was living in the parish in 1707.

[47] Made essoin (i.e. excuses for absence) at Iver manorial court, 1644. Perhaps the John Carron mentioned in the same court in 1665. The surname Currant appears among the early eighteenth-century Iver burials.

XI

THE DATE OF GERRARD WINSTANLEY'S *FIRE IN THE BUSH**

Keith Thomas

Until the recent discovery of *Englands Spirit Unfoulded*,[1] *Fire in the Bush* was the only one of Gerrard Winstanley's writings which could not be fairly precisely dated. Most of the others were known to bear an exact date, either printed by the publisher or inserted in manuscript by the contemporary bookseller, George Thomason. But no copy of *Fire in the Bush* was to be found among the Thomason Tracts in the British Museum, and the printer's imprint '1650' might have been consistent with publication at any time between 1 January 1649/50 and 24 March 1650/1, according to when the beginning of the new year was dated. The problem has given rise to a good deal of discussion, since *Fire in the Bush* is the most apocalyptic of Winstanley's writings and has normally been regarded as the product of a distinct phase in the development of his thought. In particular, it has always been assumed that the pamphlet could not have appeared during the period of the Digger experiment, but must have been issued either after the movement's collapse in the summer of 1650 or before its beginning in April 1649; in the latter case the date of '1650' must have been a printer's error for 1649. A third suggestion is that the tract was written early in 1649, but not published until the summer of 1650. All these possibilities were recently canvassed by Professor Aylmer, in the hope that by dating *Fire in the Bush*

* From no. 42 (February 1969).
[1] By G. E. Aylmer. *Past and Present*, no. 40 (July 1968), pp. 3–15 (pp. 109–23 in this volume). I am grateful to Prof. Aylmer for helpful discussions.

it would then be possible to set a terminal date for the publication of *Englands Spirit Unfoulded*.[2]

It is now possible to put a close to these speculations. *Fire in the Bush* is one of the items contained in a missing volume of Thomason Tracts which was returned to the British Museum in 1963, after over a century's absence in the United States.[3] Thomason dated it 'Mar. 19. 1649', i.e. 19 March 1650 (he always used the Old Style dating). If this was the date of the pamphlet's publication then its composition must have been around the beginning of March 1650, since Winstanley says in his preface that he delayed publishing his revelation for a fortnight.[4]

This new date may be thought to create more problems than it solves. For in *Fire in the Bush* Winstanley looks forward to the overthrow of all government which upholds private property, the newly erected Commonwealth included. How then could he issue it, perhaps only a few weeks after *Englands Spirit Unfoulded*, in which he urged his readers to take the Engagement to uphold the Commonwealth, and certainly only a few days before *An Appeale to All Englishmen* (26 March 1650), in which he justified the Digger experiment by reference to the Engagement and to the two Acts abolishing the monarchy and declaring England to be a free commonwealth?[5] Did he really oscillate between widely opposed attitudes to established authority? For if the message of *Fire in the Bush* was as incompatible with that of the other two tracts as it is usually taken to be, then Winstanley is revealed as a capricious and unstable thinker, in whose writings it would be hopeless to seek any consistency or clear development.

A brief reconsideration of *Fire in the Bush* will rule out this unsatisfying conclusion. For there is nothing in its argument which is inconsistent with the policy of political conformity which Winstanley was simultaneously advocating in his other tracts. It is true that *Fire in the Bush* looks forward to the coming of Christ,

---

[2] Aylmer, *op. cit.*, pp. 6–7 (pp. 112–14).

[3] The circumstances are described by F. B. Williams, Jr, 'Five lost Thomason Tracts come home', *The Library*, 5th ser., xix (1964), pp. 230–4. The pamphlet has been entered in the card catalogue of accessions since 1956, but not in the main catalogue. The shelf-mark is C.124 h. 1(1).

[4] *The Works of Gerrard Winstanley*, ed. G. H. Sabine (Ithaca, New York, 1941), p. 445.

[5] *Works*, ed. Sabine, pp. 407–15, esp. pp. 411–13.

who will deliver the Creation from bondage by destroying the
power of the 'four beasts', namely 'kingly power', the Church,
the Law, and private property. This triumph of universal love
will undoubtedly involve the overthrow of the existing Commonwealth.[6] But Winstanley is not urging violent revolution. On the
contrary, he tells his readers: 'whatsoever your condition is,
murmur not at it, but waite'.[7] The revolution will not come by the
sword, but by internal regeneration: 'your Saviour must be a
power within you, to deliver you from that bondage within'.[8]
Indeed the Redeemer has appeared for 'some of your brethren
already, who are witnesses, that he is rising and spreading himselfe
in the Earth, casting out death, hell, and bondage, and establishing life, peace, and liberty in mankinde, and in the whole creation'.[9] This is surely a reference to the Diggers themselves, the
true Levellers, in whom the spirit of Christ fights 'by the sword
of Love, patience and truth'.[10]

For, as Winstanley never tired of urging, the Diggers did not
plan to invade private property. They confined their digging to
the commons and wastes, which on their leader's interpretation
of the Acts establishing the Commonwealth had legally reverted
to the people.[11] Hence the importance for the time being of upholding these Acts and the authority of the Commonwealth itself.
But Winstanley's long-term expectation was that the example of
the Diggers would lead to the voluntary surrender of private
property itself and the consequent withering away of the political
authority necessary to uphold it.

The new dating of *Fire in the Bush* should therefore cause us no
perplexity, for the tract itself is perfectly consistent with Winstanley's other writings at this period. The latter were largely
concerned to show the legality of the Digger occupation of the

---

[6] *Works*, ed. Sabine, pp. 463–4, 471–2.
[7] *Ibid.*, p. 488.
[8] *Ibid.*, p. 496. Cf. Aylmer, '*Englands Spirit Unfoulded* ...', pp. 115, 121–2.
[9] *Works*, ed. Sabine, p. 487.
[10] *Ibid.*, p. 471. Sabine, by contrast, assumed that there was no reference in
Fire in the Bush to the Digger movement (p. 443). The allusion to the
'Levellers' has usually been taken to refer to the Leveller party rather than
to the Diggers themselves and hence to suggest a date in 1649 for *Fire in
the Bush*. Aylmer, *op. cit.*, p. 7 (p. 114 in this volume).
[11] See the references cited in Keith Thomas, 'Another Digger broadside'
(p. 131 n. 17, and p. 132 n. 20 in this volume).

commons. But in *Fire in the Bush* Winstanley permitted himself to look forward to the reign of universal love and the abolition of private property which he believed the Digger movement by its example would ultimately engender.

XII

THE *CIVIL POLITY* OF
PETER PAXTON*

J. A. W. Gunn

In 1703 John Locke set out the reading suitable for a gentleman interested in politics, and thereby created an unusual situation. Here was one of the more modest giants of political speculation pausing at the end of his life to assess the voluminous literature of a brilliant century. From Hobbes one would have expected a list with one name; Locke had the candour to recommend his own contribution, but included as well those of Algernon Sydney (whom he confessed never to have read), Hooker, and Pufendorf. Only two English contemporaries warranted inclusion; James Tyrrell, and the author of a book described as 'a Treatise of *Civil Polity*, printed this year'.[1]

The author of this latter book was Peter Paxton, a London doctor scarcely less versatile than Locke himself. There are no constitutions to Paxton's credit and his genius flared only briefly, all of his works falling in the years 1701–7. In fact, his was prob-

---

* From no. 40 (July 1968).

[1] 'Some Thoughts Concerning Reading and Study for a Gentleman' in *A Collection of Several Pieces of Mr John Locke* (London, 1720), p. 237. Although Locke was unaware of the author's identity, Paxton admitted authorship in later writings and this fact is recorded by the editor of the edition of Locke cited here. The author of the brief *Dict. Nat. Biog.* article on Paxton credited him with his minor works, and while generously acknowledging his radical economic views, remained unaware of his major literary effort. One of the few modern authors who has cited the work has also failed to attribute it to its author. See S. Kliger, *The Goths in England. A Study in Seventeenth and Eighteenth Century Thought* (Cambridge, Mass., 1952), p. 201.

ably a comparatively short life, for he graduated from Cambridge in 1687 and died in 1711. In his productive period he wrote on medicine, trade and the union with Scotland, and in addition produced the major work cited by Locke, a six-hundred-page treatise on history, anthropology, philosophy and politics.[2] As an attempt at integrated social investigation it bears comparison with Montesquieu; among Englishmen of the age, only Sir William Temple could boast a remotely comparable enterprise—and, be it said, an inferior one. Oddly enough, in recommending Paxton's book, Locke placed it in the same category as his own, that of literature directed to the explanation of social and governmental origins, not in the other category containing writings on 'the Art of Governing Men in Society'.[3] Locke's self-estimation strikes one as a fair one and a useful corrective to those who despair at his frustrating generality; but applied to Paxton this description leaves one wondering whether Locke had read him, either.

Writing in a terse, unadorned style, Paxton made no mystery of his main theoretical objectives. The book was subtitled:

> Wherein the Reasons of that Great Diversity to be observed
> in the Customs, Manners, and Usages of Nations, are
> Historically Explained.

This in itself suggested something more than the unstrung collection of marvels then passing in amateur universal history. Pressing ahead, Paxton declared—somewhat breathlessly—that it was not climate, topography or any other 'natural cause' that governed the manner and degree in which trade and the arts would flourish, rather they would be found to 'proceed from, or at least relate to Society or Government'.[4] Social and political arrangements being traced as fundamental for understanding variations in civilization, they were themselves in need of explanation, and so he stated his chief purpose as that of examining governments to discover:[5]

> the Basis upon which they stand; and what it is that cements
> and holds Men together, in the Same Community; And
> then by what Methods *Civil Polities* are continued; why they

---

[2] *Civil Polity. A Treatise Concerning the Nature of Government* (London, 1703), hereafter cited as *CP*.

[3] Locke, *loc. cit.*, p. 236.   [4] *CP*, sig. a3v.   [5] *Ibid.*, sig. [a5].

flourish, and why after a time some are necessarily ruined; from what Reasons some are naturally peaceable, and Others always Turbulent and Unquiet; why in some the general and common good of the whole People is pursued, and why only a part of them in Others; why some are incident to sudden and violent Revolutions, and why all naturally decline from their first and Original Institutions.

Although properly called a follower of Harrington,[6] Paxton was a critical follower; no immortal commonwealths for him.

METHOD

The virtues and weaknesses of eighteenth-century history are well known. Scorning the facts in favour of sociological conjecture, *histoire raisonnée* was consciously different from its academic and popular predecessors.[7] In the spirit of a tradition not yet established, Paxton insisted that it was not his purpose to write the history of his times, or indeed, history at all.[8] Conventional historians erred in quibbling about details as to 'Time, Place, Numbers, or Names' and even the admired ancients emphasized battles at the expense of 'Political Remarks'.[9] Historians often deserted their province by being didactic, and frequently they invoked divine intervention by way of explanation.[10] His disenchantment with the methods of historical writing throws light on several aspects of Paxton's mind.

He was, for one thing, a confirmed 'modern', critical of all attempts to dictate style and cultural norms from 'mouldy' (a favourite epithet) rules derived from the past. Since these rules were not antecedent to usage, he felt that they had to remain as

[6] Kliger, *op. cit.*, p. 201.
[7] On this tradition as displayed by the great Scots of the century, see Gladys Bryson, *Man and Society: The Scottish Inquiry of the Eighteenth Century* (Princeton, 1945). For patterns in seventeenth-century historical writing, see F. Smith Fussner, *The Historical Revolution* (London, 1962), and for discussion of comparative studies, such as they were, see M. T. Hodgen, *Early Anthropology in the Sixteenth and Seventeenth Centuries* (Philadelphia, 1964).
[8] *CP*, pp. 195, 593.   [9] *Ibid.*, sig. [a8v], p. 151.
[10] *Ibid.*, sig. [a8v].

responsive to change as usage itself.[11] Applied to the materials of history, this meant that while one might consult the political forms of the past, there was little point in feeling obliged to copy them. Contemporaries, with capacities equal to their forefathers', should no more bind themselves to earlier ways than future generations would be compelled to ape the present.[12] Complementing this attitude was an uncompromising legal positivism which dismissed queries about the respective natures of *de jure* and *de facto* kingship as irrelevant. Similarly, claims for rights, so often sustained by suppositious history, were described as having no other firm basis than the municipal laws enforced by the supreme power.[13] Power might certainly be gained unjustly, but Paxton felt assured that such aberrations were healed by the passage of time. Should men attempt to define political legality in terms of precedents, they would remain eternally in doubt.[14]

True to the English empirical tradition, the abstract, universal quality of Paxton's premises, so at odds with the antiquarianism then prevalent in academic circles, was joined to a tough-minded adherence to some positions based on the variable and specific aspects of society. A nominalist, he eschewed any effort to find in words 'something real'. All too often contemporaries, trying to discover the nature of things, argued from 'uncertain and equivocal Terms'.[15] More consistently than a nominalist such as Hobbes, Paxton felt the need of proceeding behind formal categories in order to reveal multitudes of particulars. In this spirit, he commented frequently on the difficulty of finding English equivalents for foreign political vocabulary and of describing a profusion of different arrangements with a limited number of terms. Words were 'but the arbitrary signs of men's thoughts'—an insistence that constantly drove Paxton back to facts of some sort, even if they were not the ones that figure in historical chronicles.

The chief factor serving to qualify Paxton's *a priori* method was his commitment to cultural diversity of a sort that dignified a wider range of behaviour than was normally contemplated by eighteenth-century rationalists. If history failed through an excessive concern for minute investigation of the past, it was no

[11] *Ibid.*, pp. 122, 125.   [12] *Ibid.*, p. 62.   [13] *Ibid.*, pp. 158, 165.
[14] *Ibid.*, p. 385.   [15] *Ibid.*, sig. a4.

less guilty of ethnocentrism. Europeans shared in the general human tendency of thinking those institutions valuable:[16]

> that we know, teach, or practise; imagining, as it were . . .
> as if all the rest of Mankind, whose Conditions or
> Circumstances are in most respects extreamly unlike ours,
> should notwithstanding stand in need of what we do. . . .

Europeans always exaggerated their 'small advantages' over others, unmindful that at all times there had been peoples who excelled in some aspect of civilization. Turning to the politics of contemporary Europe, Paxton noted how all people were fond of their own institutions and:[17]

> are ordinarily prone to ridicule and dispise what they have
> not tried: As is most evident by the Opinions of People under
> different Forms; for the *French* scoff at the *British* Model,
> and the *English* deride that of *Holland*, and so on.

This implied relativism applied not only between cultures but within them. It was characteristic of man to make his own opinions the 'Standard and touchstone' for measuring all others. Serene in his partial perspective, he accepted his own opinions as planted 'by the hand of Nature'; all who differed were simply held to lack 'what is Common to all Men'.[18] In a manner popularized by Hobbes and Joseph Glanvill, Paxton expounded at length the doctrine that moral judgments were based upon the universal desire for advantage, not the 'intrinsick excellency' of actions or intentions. Human wants were, in the main, subjective, for apart from some 'Natural' or 'Real' pleasures such as rest and food, people chiefly valued 'Relative' or 'Imaginary' goods varying with time, place, temperament and circumstances.[19]

Curiously enough, this blend of positivism, cultural relativism and subjectivism did not lead Paxton to forego the comforts of a natural-law doctrine, a fact that will not greatly surprise students of English empiricism. However, he did, in fact, make comparatively little use of natural-law conventions. Such laws as existed were, apparently, deduced from reason and were common to all mankind. But just because of their universality, Paxton deemed

[16] *CP*, sig. a4.   [17] *Ibid.*, p. 421.
[18] *Ibid.*, p. 141.   [19] *Ibid.*, p. 47.

them incapable of conferring civil rights, which, of necessity, varied with the system of government.[20] Explicit appeals to natural law played no further role in his writings, presumably because self-interest served quite as well to support Paxton's political ethics.

Thus Paxton's method of enquiry emerged as a compromise between the two major approaches that he rejected. History as chronicle was jettisoned, but so too was any uncritical reliance upon universal and timeless categories. Forced back upon history, he remained convinced that it was least helpful when it entailed looking at 'remote countries' or 'distant ages'. His own description of the method was that it was 'plain and Historical', with proofs 'deduced . . . either from the certain and undeniable Nature of Men, or from evident Fact'.[21] At the same time Paxton suggested mildly that he had no doubt assigned causes in history 'somewhat different' from the usual. Since this comment was the culmination of a long catalogue of errors by historians, it can confidently be assumed he did not feel that a 'plain and historical method' had normally been employed. 'Historical' certainly meant something closer to what we might call 'empirical', for he chose to describe his approach to the study of anatomy in precisely the same terms—'a plain and historical Method'.[22]

In choosing to combine the cultural relativist's catholicity with assumptions about the nature of man, Paxton enmeshed himself in the difficulties characteristic of much eighteenth-century social thought. How might one reconcile a natural law and human constants with a relativist position? Without actually addressing himself to the question, Paxton handled it more successfully than most. Man's irremediable self-interest was expressed in terms of his capacity to endow his own opinions with an aura of truth. Self-interest thus served both to give content to a common human nature and to explain mankind's passionate attachment to different sets of institutions. Paxton could thus begin his major book

---

[20] *Ibid.*, pp. 159–60.
[21] *Ibid.*, sig. [a5]. For an illuminating discussion of the failure of seventeenth-century philosophers to distinguish between rationalism and empiricism, see L. Krieger, *The Politics of Discretion. Pufendorf and the Acceptance of Natural Law* (Chicago, 1965), p. 43.
[22] *An Essay Concerning the Body of Man* (London, 1701), sig. A2v. A similar expression was sometimes used by Locke.

with chapters on the nature of man and lead progressively into a discussion of the factors sustaining political and cultural differences. Far from being a conventional rationalist treatment of man and the commonwealth, it was a venture in comparative institutions, bent on describing and explaining the 'marvellous Differences in the several *European* Governments'.[23]

Such an attempt was rare indeed; for most writers on politics chose either to describe political institutions or to analyse the logic of obedience. The first was generally fact without analysis; the second, analysis largely abstracted from particular facts. So complete was the adherence to these approaches that Sir William Temple, with his method of 'indolent induction', has been called a political scientist just because he essayed a body of political generalizations freed from the restricting categories of natural law and social contract.[24] It has already been suggested that Paxton's commitment to a similar task was explicit, methodologically sophisticated and far from indolent. To document this further one need only turn to the substance of his work.

THE PROBLEM OF ORIGINS

True to his concern to avoid false history, Paxton refused to recreate the origins of government. It was apparent, he felt, that all peoples produced it naturally. Marks of 'Order or Oeconomy' came early and no savage peoples (*pace* Locke) had ever been found 'singly to wander in the unfrequented Woods'.[25] Interestingly, Paxton simply ignored the social contract, neither employing it nor attacking it; while the judicious Temple had relied upon a curious sort of patriarchal theory.[26]

The logic of social contract had been deemed necessary to bridge the gap between self-interested beings and social control. In this respect Paxton found himself with the same problem that had confronted Hobbes, Locke or Pufendorf. If all men desired

---

[23] *CP*, sig. [a8].
[24] C. B. Macpherson, 'Sir William Temple, political scientist?', *Canadian Journal of Economics and Political Science*, ix (1943), p. 46.
[25] *CP*, p. 3.
[26] 'An Essay Upon the Original and Nature of Government', 1672, in *The Works of Sir William Temple, Bart. Complete. In Four Volumes* (London, 1814), i, pp. 1–30.

their own welfare, how came some to be subordinated to others? As Rousseau was later to ask, 'why had they not run away from oppressors?' In seeking some 'cement or bond' that served to hold communities together, Paxton was led to consider topics much more demanding on our attention than suppositious contracts.[27] Government in its rudimentary forms he found, without difficulty, in septs and hoards, but in order to explain 'more elaborate and refined' forms he looked to the 'Cement of political Power'—landed property.[28] In simple communities without private property in land there would be no incentive to obey, beyond the immediate promptings of personal security. Having rejected any state-of-nature atomism, Paxton did not have to worry about how an onerous government could arise before property. Government came as a matter of course, and as soon as property was recognized, 'inequalities' were protected by the law. Some men through greater 'Cunning' or 'Industry' would accumulate a surplus of wealth beyond their immediate needs and use it to 'cement' the poor 'to their Interest'.[29] Hungry men, requiring satisfaction of their natural wants, would not worry much about sovereignty or dominion.[30]

In a manner more uncompromising than some modern Marxists, Paxton insisted that differences in wealth and power might originate wholly from factors within a social structure. At the same time, he noted the effect of war, and the subjection of neighbours, on stratification. Conquest greatly increased community wealth through tribute and, this tribute being unequally distributed, even the bulk of the victorious population would be

---

[27] Most writers who dispensed with contract were believers in divine right. English thought of the mid-eighteenth century has been characterized as involving a revolt against state-of-nature primitivism, but this has not led to close consideration of the early part of the century. See H. V. S. Ogden, 'The state of nature and the decline of Lockian political theory in England', *American Historical Review*, xlvi (1940), pp. 21–44. After Paxton, others managed to avoid both whiggish contracts and the alternatives of Jacobite theory. See, for instance, Sir Richard Blackmore, 'An Essay Upon the Origin of Civil Power' in *Essays Upon Several Subjects*, 1st edn, 2 vols (London, 1716–17), i, p. 432; and Thomas Chubb, 'Some Short Reflections on the Grounds and Extent of *Authority* and *Liberty*, with Respect to *Civil Government*' in *A Collection of Tracts on Various Subjects* (London, 1730), p. 456.

[28] *CP*, pp. 33, 284–5.   [29] *Ibid.*, pp. 50–51.   [30] *Ibid.*, p. 43.

found to have drawn upon themselves the slavery to which they subjected their neighbours.[31] The trend could be circumvented only if communities remained very poor with few opportunities for class distinction, or if they progressed right through the economic cycle to replace expenditure on luxury and retainers by the bourgeois virtue of quietly amassing wealth.[32]

Having linked government and stratification in the manner of modern anthropology, Paxton had to try to explain stratification. His general proposition was that 'the disproportions in the Qualities or fortunes of Men, must be in some Measure as [their] Numbers are . . .'.[33] This was based, in part, on the assumption that in small social units there was less need for those 'Marks, Signs, or Characters, by which Persons may be known and distinguished'.[34] While the most primitive societies gave some scope for differentiation of ranks, only the more complex ones with large numbers of people had the resources to support such ostentation—an observation that Paxton used to relate the state of the arts and 'inwardly acquired' distinctions, such as learning, to social structure.[35] Through all of this ran another assumption —that wealth and numbers of people might in some measure be seen as equivalents. This he supported by citing the function of numbers in increasing consumption, raising rents, inciting people to industry and, in general, serving as the wealth of a nation.[36] That population growth was a good index of political health was already widely accepted, but Paxton seems to have been alone in his further inferences regarding social structure. He might usefully have spelled out the idea in somewhat more detail than he did, since his ideas about the origin of ranks seemed to require some explanation as to why people, however dependent on the bounty of the rich, did not leave the community to find their own land. The assumption of a populous country seemed to answer

[31] CP, pp. 288–9. This formulation has more radical implications than, and seems quite as plausible as, some twentieth-century refinements of Engels's theory of state origins. See Franz Oppenheimer, The State, trans. J. M. Gitterman (Indianapolis, 1914), chaps 2 and 5.
[32] On the contrast between luxury and the frugal prosperity of a trading people, see CP, p. 230.
[33] Ibid., p. 199.   [34] Ibid., sig. [a6].   [35] Ibid., sig. [a6v].
[36] P. Paxton, M.D., A Discourse Concerning the Nature, Advantage, and Improvement of Trade: With Some Considerations Why the Charges of the Poor do and will Increase (London, 1704), p. 90.

this classic problem by ensuring that all the land would already
be taken up.

Another consideration arising here was Paxton's own preference as to the size of polities. Since he adhered to the popular
stereotype of oriental despotism as consisting in large, centralized
units, Paxton was partial to states either small, such as Holland
and England, or decentralized as in Germany.[37] He recognized
too that states that were too small were simply not viable in a
continent such as Europe.[38] The chief difficulty in his position
arose from his desire to increase population because of the
economic advantages, while avoiding the differences in power
and dignity which, on his own showing, would follow. His
reconciliation of these desires was made possible by certain
refinements in the original generalization about population,
wealth and stratification.

POLITY AND ECONOMY

The complicating factor in his analysis was the interaction between government and economic processes. Paxton was conventionally Harringtonian in allowing that either wealth would
command political power or those controlling the means of
violence would seize wealth. In one major respect he went well
beyond Harrington, to take cognizance of wealth arising from
trade and, in fact, to insist that in any community power would
tend to be divided in proportion to the relative profits of land
and trade.[39] Here government appeared to be the creature of
economic interests; elsewhere, Paxton attempted to describe the
relationship, not by the relative power of land and trade, but in
terms of the sort of economic activity conducive to serving the
needs of the government. In this instance he argued that government, bringing with it the need to symbolize status differences,
stimulated the arts and trade in order to produce luxuries.[40]

A problem arose because of the nature of despotic governments,

---

[37] *Discourse . . . of Trade*, p. 70, and *CP*, p. 632.
[38] P. Paxton, M.D., *A Scheme of Union Between England and Scotland, With
Advantages to Both Kingdoms* (London, 1705), pp. 6–7.
[39] *CP*, p. 56.
[40] *Ibid.*, sig. [a6v], p. 242.

which were obviously in need of luxuries to mirror class distinctions while notably lacking in that foreign trade which would best provide them. Paxton had two answers to this puzzle. The first, an implied one, lay in his general observation that the money required by all governments would be raised from land, trade or tribute, depending on which was most advantageous to the rulers.[41] This suggests that the absence of trade in despotisms was due to its being ill-suited to the interests of those in power. Whether or not he assumed this, Paxton chose instead to stress the fact that certain forms of government just failed to afford the proper environment to encourage trade, for:[42]

> a Legal, and lasting property, can never be ascertained in any community, unless each particular Member, or at least each *Classe* of Men, have either *by themselves or proxy, some Share in the Legislature*; because whosoever is not someway concerned in that, can have no sure defence, against the oppression of those that are.

Despotism, for all its need of 'marks of distinctions', was 'inconsistent with the ascertaining a private property', which was only possible 'where the People have a Share in the Legislature'.[43]

Of the European states with which Paxton dealt, only England and Holland passed the crucial test of serving the general good by protecting private property. The scope of this vital property right was made clear in the economic writings where Paxton showed himself most concerned, not with total national wealth (despite a few suspiciously bullionist sentiments), but with benefit from trade that was diffused 'to the Mass of People'.[44] The point was most important for Paxton's argument, for this concern for maximizing the gainers from trade explained how he hoped to combine prosperity and popular government. His assumption

[41] *CP*, p. 80.
[42] *Ibid.*, p. 226. This remarkable intrusion of the spectre of class was paralleled by other references to the term in the sense of stratification, especially in the writings of Defoe, but these did not serve to describe basic political relations in quite the manner of Paxton. For Defoe's use of the term, see Asa Briggs, 'The language of "class" in early nineteenth-century England' in A. Briggs and J. Saville (eds), *Essays in Labour History. In Memory of G. D. H. Cole* (London, 1960), p. 43 n. 3.
[43] *CP*, pp. 225–9.
[44] *Discourse . . . of Trade*, p. 27; see, too, the similar remarks, p. 51.

that, even without sumptuary laws, a trading people might avoid pomp and great social differences, was similarly based. The eighteenth century was prone to a romantic alliance between political freedom and poverty—and few ideas could serve better to underline the gap now separating us from pre-industrial society. Paxton's view of the political impact of commerce was not presented in detail, but it was unclouded, precisely because he did not allow himself to be drawn away from the point through concern for avoiding the evils of luxury. With the help of trade, societies could spread wealth widely, thus allowing them to be both rich and free of the great disparities of economic power that would prove incompatible with liberty.[45]

Of course, even among trading nations, some managed such matters better than others. The success of the Dutch economy was judged greater than that of England because it better performed the role of maintaining low prices, general prosperity and the sort of stratification most compatible with a free state. Since the Dutch constitution did not permit 'any marvellous Differences in the *Qualities and Conditions* of Men', it forbade hereditary titles, and by a combination of inheritance laws and the small size of the country effectively prevented the accumulation of vast estates.[46] By contrast, the weaknesses of the English constitution were that it required 'such marvellous Differences in the Qualities and Fortunes of Men',[47] while the laws leaned too much in favour of land. This does not mean that Paxton saw economic life as readily responsive to all political demands made upon it; like his famous contemporary, Charles Davenant, he noted the extraordinary complexity of social causation. While 'natural' effects might be traceable to a single cause, 'political' effects were frequently produced by a complex of factors, both diverse and remote.[48] Recognizing the impotence of legislation over certain aspects of trade, he still adhered to the position that the general nature and level of economic activity was responsive to government. Since Paxton was both an exceptionally frank free trader

[45] *CP*, pp. 230–2. Ernest Gellner has commented on the archaic quality of a later figure such as Gibbon in treating the supposed possibility of separating freedom and prosperity; see his *Thought and Change* (London, 1964), p. 36 n. Paxton defended luxury in *A Directory Physico-Medical* (London, 1707), pp. 7–8.
[46] *Discourse ... of Trade*, p. 69.   [47] *Ibid.*, p. 46.   [48] *Ibid.*, p. 21.

and a critic of English political arrangements, he could be expected to stress the impact of government on commerce (and its attendant dangers) rather than the reverse. But undoubtedly he saw the relationship as reciprocal.

Like Harrington, Paxton avoided any rigorous economic determinism. The virtue of his treatment lay in the very wide range of factors deemed relevant to causation. He managed both to cover a much greater range of economic activity than Harrington and to contemplate a greater variety of factors conditioning economic life. Thus where his famous predecessor had been content to dwell on the role of Tudor acts of state in producing economic change, Paxton found room as well for social expectations and the 'ways of living', as in Holland.[49] Of earlier observations on the subject, those of Sir William Temple were certainly known by Paxton, but he surpassed Temple's casual suggestion about an affinity between constitutional government and commerce.[50] Indeed, modern scholars, seeking insights into the connection of polity and economy prior to Adam Smith, have tended to fly to Montesquieu as the major contributor.[51] Paxton was, in turn, surpassed in detail and cogency of analysis before the time of Smith—a brilliant essay competition at Cambridge elicited a much more thorough exploration[52]—but his contribution for all that was a striking one, coming at a time when informed opinion was confined to the function of trade as the sinews of war, with occasional references to its civilizing influence.

A REPUBLICAN THEORY OF OPINION

While Paxton's discontent with the *status quo* was apparent in his treatment of trade, it was much more evident in the discussion of opinion and its role in government. The place of non-political

[49] *Discourse . . .of Trade*, p. 69.
[50] See Temple, 'Observations Upon the United provinces of the Netherlands' in *Works*, i, p. 175. Paxton quoted Temple on trade in *Discourse . . . of Trade*, p. 47.
[51] See L. M. Levin, *The Political Doctrine of Montesquieu's Esprit des Lois: Its Classical Background* (New York, 1936), p. 171.
[52] The best effort (which also won the competition) was by one William Hazeland: see *A View of the Manner in Which Trade and Civil Liberty Support Each Other* (London, 1756).

institutions in supporting a political system was little examined at this time, presumably because most people still tried to derive the rightness of political arrangements as well as religious ones from a common superior standard—divine will, even after 1689, or natural reason. Here Paxton again differed from the age in scorning revelation as a source of political truth but still (unlike some contemporaries) retaining an interest in the way in which organized religion might sustain the polity. To have a church as a 'Body Distinct', independent of political control was a political 'Solecism'.[53] However great his dislike of persecution, he seemed to fear disintegration from religious conflict even more. His own preferences may have been expressed when he commended the failure of the Chinese publicly to acknowledge any revealed religion, and in the perhaps too-casual comment that he would not deal with natural religion since it had little influence upon government.[54]

At a time when some of the most astute defenders of toleration stressed how society might prosper through a fruitful tension between religious parties, Paxton preferred to nip the problem in the bud by discouraging religious sects, suppressing polemical literature and allowing freedom of religious opinion only if the latter remained unorganized. Dutch practice, combining effective freedom with a state church and careful scrutiny of religious bodies was probably his inspiration here, but was milder than what he contemplated. Ideally he favoured a government with such a congruence of interest between governors and governed that subjects could interpret scripture for themselves without benefit of constraint, while still posing no challenge to the state.[55] His suspicion of institutionalized religious diversity can best be explained by his conviction that absolutism in France and Spain had employed the threat of heresy as a pretext by which to hold both church and army loyal to the crown. Cynical rulers were not above encouraging religious faction to this end.[56] Furthermore, in poor countries, and among the poor in all countries, appeals to religious fervour were very likely to be effective means of reducing political freedom, and the rights of property: 'for having little of their own to lose, they are not so very solicitous about the Defence of what doth not appertain to them'.[57]

[53] CP, p. 106.   [54] Ibid., p. 92.   [55] Ibid., p. 89.
[56] Ibid., pp. 620-9, 614.   [57] Ibid., p. 616.

Paxton was thus very conscious of the adaptability of religious doctrine to secular needs and the related need for a 'Hierarchy ... befitted to the Civil Constitutions'.[58] Religion was responsive to interest not only on a national but also on an individual scale. This led him to examine the basis of religious commitment and its political significance. Now nothing had been more common in the previous fifty years than for observers to attribute certain political views to Catholics or Presbyterians. Many sources even from the early seventeenth century associated puritanism with the 'industrious sort of people', and there were references to the sectarian leanings of some 'mean' persons, but Paxton went farther:[59]

> we so often observe that People of the meanest fortunes, usually disprove [sic] an *Hierarchy* in the Church, which makes a disparity in the Orders, or degrees of its Ministers, in that it so nearly Resembles the Civil Constitution which Ordains so vast an Inequality between its Members.

In a similar vein he sketched the common pattern of those 'born to estate' both in terms of their initial loyalties, and likely destination in the event of their deserting the Church of England. While Anglicans not uncommonly discovered seditious levellers among the sects and might even be aware that religious loyalties varied with rank, it was most unusual to find anyone who sought to derive both civil and religious opinions from social status. Paxton did nothing less. To emphasize the novelty of the opinion one need only observe that Locke at this time could find no indication that the poor were sufficiently rational to frame coherent interests at all.

The place of ideas in political weaponry might also be illustrated in other social contexts. Paxton's disenchantment with the England of his time was nowhere better displayed than in his survey of how opinion was moulded in the interests of the regime. In this connection, he remarked on the manner in which the universities were the creatures of 'such, who ... have a dependance upon the Court'. Nor could he expect anything else,

[58] *CP*, p. 58.
[59] *Ibid.*, p. 98. Indications of contemporary awareness of the socio-economic correlates of religious affiliation are provided in [J. E.] C. Hill, *Society and Puritanism in Pre-Revolutionary England* (London, 1964), chap. 4.

it being 'miraculous if some out of that August Body, will not Believe and Teach what will most certainly advance them'.[60] Tied to the world by their opinions, men could do no other. One might wish to claim for the universities somewhat more independence of spirit than Paxton would allow, but without doubt the charge was substantially just. Again the point was a broadening and deepening of current notions. The latter half of the seventeenth century was well supplied with cynical books on the art of self-promotion; it was generally assumed that people sought their own best interests with a fierce necessity.[61] But this was a far cry from explaining national institutions and their political functions in the same manner. However bold men's thoughts, they hesitated to commit such ideas to print.

The basic insight was amplified in a discussion of the arts, as again at every turn Paxton spied the presence of the power structure. Style was normally valued according to the quality of the writer or speaker.[62] Cultural products were naturally fashioned so as not to give offence to potential consumers and so writers were well aware that the theatre audience 'appears to be composed of what we may call a gentile [sic] sort of People, who are not destined to Laborious Employments'.[63] Significantly, the theatre was very kind to 'men in power' and, since the Restoration, had systematically ridiculed 'that party of Men that have been supposed to be in an Interest contrary to that of the court'.[64] Presumably some concessions were made to the pit, as Paxton noted that 'the Inferior Bench will Clap, or Hiss, as the Superior Frown, or Smile'.[65] The stage had to reflect social interests and so those who sought to reform a lewd age by attacking the stage began at the wrong end; the original, not the copy, had to be changed.[66] Students of literature have commended John Dennis, the contemporary critic, for unusual perception in relating literature to its social environment, for no other reason than that he noted the

---

[60] *CP*, pp. 180–1.

[61] The *genre* of literature purporting to advise ambitious men on how to rise in society frequently involved quite perceptive observations on social structure and processes. See B.B., *The Young Gentlemans Way to Honour. In Three Parts* (London, 1678); A.B. [William de Britaine], *Humane Prudence* (London, 1680) and anon., *The Way to Promotion* . . . (London, 1682).

[62] *CP*, pp. 113–14.

[63] *Ibid.*, p. 134.　　　　　　　[64] *Ibid.*, pp. 137–40.

[65] *Ibid.*, p. 136.　　　　　　　[66] *Ibid.*, p. 143.

connections between letters and other branches of learning.[67] Paxton's sociology betrayed no sensitivity to this sort of erudition, but cut very much closer to the bone.

Paxton's treatment of opinion and its political relevance was quite the most original aspect of his enquiry, but it was not without antecedents. Temple's unsubstantiated judgment that government was based 'on opinion as to interest' has been called 'remarkably original',[68] but even this had numerous anticipations from the time of Harrington. Few men familiar with seventeenth-century public life doubted that 'interest' moved all political actors, and opinion as to one's interest came to nothing more than interest subjectively defined.[69] There was nothing striking then about Paxton's general principle, except his applications illustrating the ideological content of supposedly apolitical opinion. But these must surely have been unique.

THE PRICE OF REPUBLICANISM

Widely advertised in the press from January 1703, *Civil Polity* should have been a popular book. A work of genuine erudition, it offered examples from a great fund of information about most governments of Europe—Austria, Denmark, Sweden and Hungary. As an attempt at comparative government, a pursuit even now notoriously prone to disintegrate into parallel accounts, it was impressive, despite the preponderance of English material.[70] The total system was readily intelligible, even when one considers the contributions of the specialized minor writings; and individual judgments were perceptive, whether they involved the causes and merits of unions and confederations[71] or passing

[67] See Emerson R. Marks, *Relativist and Absolutist. The Early Neoclassical Debate in England* (New Brunswick, N.J., 1955), pp. 80–90.

[68] Macpherson, *op. cit.*, p. 49.

[69] I have treated one aspect of this all-pervasive sentiment in 'Interest will not lie. A seventeenth-century political maxim', *Jour. Hist. Ideas*, xxix (1969), pp. 551–64.

[70] One of the rare such attempts which, whatever its limitations, was a careful effort to compare political institutions, was anon., *An Historical and Political Essay, Discussing the Affinity or Resemblance of the Ancient and Modern Governments* (London, 1706). In point of fact, it dealt with the current position of estates in the nations of Europe.

[71] *Scheme for Union*, pp. 3–9.

references to the striking novelty of seventeenth-century theories of divine right.[72] Still, while respectfully reviewed at great length, the reviewer was judiciously vague on all of the most significant passages and left the reader with the impression that *Civil Polity* was primarily a chronicle of English history.[73]

Surely a major cause of subsequent obscurity was the republicanism that lurked behind every argument. Despite professed admiration for Queen Anne, Paxton was quite forthright in asserting the functionless character of a feudal monarchy.[74] His constant recourse to Dutch practice allowed him not only to regret the power of the landed interest (not in itself a rare complaint) but also to criticize the '*swelling Honours and large Estates*, which our Constitution not only admits, but requires'.[75] In analyzing the state of the poor, he implied pointedly that purely economic barriers to reform might prove resistant to rapid change, while defects in the laws and their manner of execution might more quickly be set right, given the will.[76] The opinion most shocking to contemporaries may well have been his unconcealed disrespect for the Gothic constitution of England, even as improved by the Revolution. Fear of the factious instability and eventual despotism inherent in such systems informed all of his writings and found particularly pungent expression in his identification of Poland as the purest surviving example of this form of government.[77] Frequently this was deemed an honour, and one accorded to England. For monarchy, nobility and parties he had no use.

Thus at a time when both Whigs and Tories, in and out of office, embraced the balanced constitution, disagreeing only about what constituted disequilibrium, Paxton alone sought the higher path of a modified republican virtue. It need not however be seen as a dead end for a Harringtonian *epigone*; Paine and others would pass the same way.

---

[72] *CP*, p. 312. The novelty of divine-right claims at this time has often been missed even by some modern students of political ideas.
[73] *The History of the Works of the Learned*, v (Jan. 1703), pp. 47–53; (Feb. 1703), pp. 102–10.
[74] *CP*, p. 421.
[75] *Discourse . . . of Trade*, p. 72.
[76] *Ibid.*, p. 71.
[77] *CP*, p. 599. See, too, *Scheme for Union*, p. 10 and *Discourse . . . of Trade*, pp. 69–70.

XIII

WILLIAM HARVEY AND THE
IDEA OF MONARCHY*

Christopher Hill

I

When William Harvey published his *De motu cordis* in 1628 it was
dedicated to Charles I.[1] The dedication included the following
passage: 'The *Heart* of creatures is the foundation of life, the
Prince of all, the Sun of their Microcosm, on which all vegetation
does depend, from whence all vigor and strength does flow.
Likewise the King is the foundation of his Kingdoms, and the
Sun of his Microcosm, the *Heart* of his Commonwealth, from
whence all power and mercy proceeds'. It was useful for a prince
to study the heart, 'as being a divine resemblance of his actions'.
The heart is 'the Principle of Man's Body, and the Image of your
Kingly power'.[2]

This passage has often been quoted by historians of ideas to

* From no. 27 (April 1964).

[1] I have no medical knowledge, and in this article I am concerned only
with the 'ideological' aspects of Harvey's theories: not with their truth or
falsehood.

[2] W. Harvey, *De motu cordis*, in *The Anatomical Exercises of Dr. William
Harvey*, ed. G. Keynes (London, 1928), pp. vii–viii; cf. references to the
sovereignty of the heart at pp. 59, 114, and the various analogies quoted
in *De motu locali animalium* of 1627: the heart is a general or ruler, a
musician or architect, a captain, maker, owner, prime mover (ed. G.
Whitteridge, Cambridge, 1959, pp. 150–1). I quote from Keynes's reprint
of the 1653 English translations because they were published in Harvey's
lifetime, probably authorized, certainly never repudiated by him. They
seem to me in some ways more accurate than those made by Robert
Willis for the Sydenham Society in 1847 (see p. 172 below).

illustrate parallel movements of thought in different spheres. The Reformation abolished the medieval hierarchy in the church and in heaven, substituting a direct relationship between God and believers who were equal in his sight. Simultaneously the helio-centric theory in astronomy abolished the seven heavens and established an equality of the earth with other planets under the sun. Harvey, who referred to the Copernican theory in the passage quoted above,[3] abolished the hierarchy of heart, liver and brain within the human body. He later abolished those vital spirits which had previously been held responsible for the motion of the blood.[4] All these new ways of looking at man and the universe can, if we wish, be seen as parallel to the establishment of absolute monarchies over much of western Europe, with the accompanying downfall of the secular feudal hierarchy. Harvey's friend Thomas Hobbes in political theory summed up the doctrine of absolute sovereignty over a community of equal individual atoms. So it was as natural for Harvey, personal physician successively to James I and Charles I, to compare the king to the heart as it was for Louis XIV's flatterers to call him *le roi soleil*.[5]

So far so good. But we must not exaggerate Harvey's original-ity simply because historians of ideas read him and do not read his lesser predecessors. The sovereignty of the heart was a medieval commonplace, deriving ultimately from Aristotle: it was repeated (for instance) by John Halle in 1565: 'Let us call the heart of man a king, the brain and the liver the chief governors under him . . .'.[6] Harvey's parallel between the heart and the sun may have been more original, though Copernicus had spoken of the sun as a ruler, 'sitting on the royal throne'.[7] But Harvey had a much more striking contribution to make. In 1649, the year in which Charles I had been executed, Harvey explicitly and precisely renounced his earlier opinion: he dethroned the heart. 'I do not think', he wrote, that the heart is 'the framer of the blood'; nor that the latter has 'force, vertue, motion, or heat, as the gift of

---

[3] See also Keynes, *op. cit.*, p. 59; cf. R. O[verton], *Mans Mortalitie*, 2nd edn (Amsterdam, 1644), p.33.

[4] Keynes, *op. cit.*, pp. 155–6; cf. Harvey, *Anatomical Exercitations concerning the Generation of Living Creatures* (London, 1653), pp. 447–62, and Whitteridge, *op. cit.*, pp. 94–5.

[5] S. F. Mason, *A History of the Sciences* (London, 1952), p. 145.

[6] J. Halle, *An Historiall Expostulation*, Percy Soc. (London, 1844), p. xxii.

[7] Copernicus, *De Revolutionibus* (1543), Book i, chap. 10.

the heart . . . the blood delivers that heat which it has receiv'd to the heart, as likewise to all the rest of the parts [of the body], as being the hottest of all'. (In the *De motu cordis* Harvey had written 'all . . . things do depend upon the motional pulsation of the heart'.)[8] '[The] *blood*', Harvey added in 1651, 'is the *prime genital Part*, whence the *soul* primarily results . . . the *blood* lives and is nourished of it selfe, no way depending upon any other part of the *body*, as elder or worthier then it self'. 'Being therefore ascertained out of those things which I have observed in an *Egge*, and the *dissection* of *Animals* while they were alive, I conclude (against *Aristotle*) that the *blood* is the first *Genital particle*, and that the *Heart* is its Instrument designed for its *Circulation*. For the *Hearts* business or function is the propulsation or driving forth of the *blood*'. Harvey spoke no longer of 'the sovereignty of the heart' but of 'the prerogative and antiquity of the *blood*'. 'The Heart himselfe, I say, doth by the *Coronary Arteries* receive the Blood, its influent *heat* and *life*, both which it enjoyes upon no other account, than the meer bounty of the *Blood* . . . the *Heart* is erected for this end and purpose onely, that it may by continual *pulsation* (to which the *Veins* and *Arteries* are ministerial and subservient) entertain this *blood*, and spout it out again up and down through the whole *body*. All which is the clearer discovered by this, that the *Heart* hath not a *pulsation* in all *Animals*, nor yet at all times; when yet the *blood*, or something proportionable to *blood* is never wanting in any'.[9] (Contrast the *De motu cordis*: 'the heart is the beginning of life', 'the heart is the first subsistent'.)[10]

If the *De motu cordis* of 1628 used anatomical analogies to support theories of absolute monarchy, what shall we say of Harvey's *De circulatione sanguinis* of 1649 and of the *De generatione animalium* of 1651? Their implication can only be described as republican— or at best they suggest a monarchy based on popular consent. In 1649 moreover, Harvey went out of his way to repudiate the astronomical analogy which he had used in 1628. 'The knowledge we have of the heavenly bodies' is 'uncertain and conjectural'; its example 'is not here to be followed'.[11] An astronomical allusion in the *De generatione* confirms this point, since Harvey no longer

[8] Keynes, *op. cit.*, pp. 187, 59.
[9] Harvey, *Generation of Living Creatures*, pp. 275, 279–82.
[10] Keynes, *op. cit.*, pp. 59, 114.   [11] *Ibid.*, pp. 179, 168.

draws a parallel between the heart and the sun but between the blood and 'the superiour Orbes, (but especially the *Sun* and *Moon)*', which 'do, by their *continual motions*, quicken and preserve the *inferiour* world'.[12] (That inveterate obscurantist, Alexander Ross, was quick to spot the dangers of Harvey's new position. In a book published in 1651, which also attacked Bacon and Comenius, he particularly insisted on the sovereignty, the prerogative, of the heart, and on the hierarchical order in the human body: the testicles are 'ignobler than the heart and brain'.)[13]

Harvey's somersault is surely remarkable. So is the coincidence between the change in his way of expressing himself and the political changes of the two decades which followed 1628. Harvey dethroned the heart in the same year as the English Republic was proclaimed. Three possible explanations suggest themselves. (i) Harvey may have changed his mind on this subject after 1628, as he is known to have done on the subject of spontaneous generation;[14] (ii) he may have deliberately suppressed his true views in 1628; or (iii) he may have been muddled in 1628 and have clarified his views later. Either (ii) or (iii) is suggested by the fact that in lectures attributed to 1618 he spoke of the blood as the origin of both heart and liver:[15] (iii) is suggested by the fact that in 1627 he still attributed a great deal to 'spirits' in the blood, though in a confused way. 'Spirit is the organ of movement. . . . Blood and spirit are one thing. . . . Spirit is set in motion by the heart'.[16] I am not sure which of the above possible explanations of Harvey's change of expression is the true one, but whichever of them we adopt, interesting reflections suggest themselves about the relationship between Harvey's thought and the society in which he lived.[17]

[12] Harvey, *Generation of Living Creatures*, p. 459.
[13] A. R[oss], *Arcana microcosmi* (2nd edn, London, 1652), pp. 2, 30, 11.
[14] C. D. O'Malley, F. N. L. Poynter and K. F. Russell (eds), *William Harvey—Lectures on the Whole of Anatomy* (Berkeley, Los Angeles, 1961), p. 126. [15] *Ibid.*, p. 180.
[16] Whitteridge, *op. cit.*, pp. 102–3; see also pp. 94–5.
[17] Attention was drawn to Harvey's dethroning of the heart by J. G. Curtis in 1915 (*Harvey's Views on the Use of the Circulation of the Blood*, New York). But this book was published posthumously, and the full significance of the contrast between Harvey's earlier and later views was not drawn out by the editor. L. Chauvois in his *William Harvey* (London, 1957) is more explicit (see esp. pp. 151, 206, 258).

II

First of all, we must note Harvey's attitude to Aristotle. It was always one of extreme deference, especially in the *De motu cordis*. The passage in which Harvey in 1628 announced his theory that the blood might have a circular motion is introduced in a way which shows how great was his own 'venerable reverence of antiquity', and how nervous he was about challenging traditional views.[18] The first seven chapters of the *De motu locali animalium*, attributed to 1627, take the wholly conventional form of recapitulating and commenting upon Aristotle's views.[19] When in 1651 Harvey finally declared his disagreement with Aristotle, he started by recalling how highly he had always prized Aristotle's judgment, and appealed to his own great accumulation of experimental evidence. And he still tried to spare Aristotle as much as possible: 'If by the *Heart* he [Aristotle] understand that particle which is first seen in the *Egge*; namely, the *Blood*, together with its receptacles (the *Vesiculae pulsantes*, and the Veins) as one and the same *Organ*; I then conceive he speaks most true'. But in fact, Harvey goes on to say, 'the substance of the *Heart*, being considered without the *Blood* . . . is generated long after'.[20] Yet even in 1651 Harvey advised Aubrey to 'goe to the fountain head and read Aristotle'.[21] In his early lectures Harvey had been equally deferential to Galen, suggesting that the failure of anatomical findings in dissection to confirm Galen might be explained by men's physical degeneration since his time![22]

In his practical work Harvey was true to the modern principle which he proclaimed so nobly: 'I do not profess to learn and teach Anatomy from the axioms of Philosophers, but from Dissections and from the fabrick of Nature'.[23] But his theories clearly lagged behind his practice. It was only in 1651 that he could smile at 'those, who perswade themselves, that all things

---

[18] Keynes, *op. cit.*, pp. 57–8.
[19] G. Whitteridge, 'De motu locali animalium', in *Circulation: Proceedings of the Harvey Tercentenary Congress*, ed. J. McMichael (Oxford, 1958), p. 61.
[20] Harvey, *Generation of Living Creatures*, pp. 52, 275, 291.
[21] J. Aubrey, *Brief Lives*, ed. A. Clark (Oxford, 1898), i, p. 300.
[22] O'Malley, Poynter and Russell, *op. cit.*, p. 61.
[23] Keynes, *op. cit.*, p. xiii.

were so consummatly and absolutely delivered by *Aristotle*, *Galen* or some other great Name, as that nothing was left to the superaddition of any, that succeeded.'[24] It was with real sympathy that Harvey wrote of his critic Riolan: 'As Dean of the College of Paris he was bound to see the physic of Galen kept in good repair, and to admit no novelty into the school, without the most careful winnowing, lest, as he says, the precepts and dogmata of physic should be disturbed'.[25] The Censor of the College of Physicians in London may have had similar scruples.

III

This leads us on to consider the reception of Harvey's views. In 1628 Harvey himself was very anxious to emphasize that they had the approval of his colleagues at the College of Physicians;[26] but we need not take this too literally. Thomas Winston, who was probably present at Harvey's lectures in 1616, made no mention of the circulation of the blood in his *Anatomy Lectures at Gresham College*, published over forty years later. Aubrey tells us, on Harvey's own authority, that the latter's practice fell off after he had published the *De motu cordis*, and that he was thought to be mad. All the physicians were against him: it took twenty or thirty years for his opinions to become established.[27] Aubrey's story is confirmed by another remark of Harvey's which Ent quoted: 'You are not ignorant, how great troubles my *Lucubrations*, formerly published, have raised'.[28] When Ent proclaimed his acceptance of Harvey's doctrine in 1641, he was the first Englishman to do so in print in England, though there had by that date been many attacks.[29] Robert Fludd, another Fellow of the College

[24] Harvey, *Generation of Living Creatures*, sig. A 3v—A 4.
[25] Harvey to Slegel, 1651, in *Works*, translated by R. Willis (London, 1847), p. 598.
[26] Keynes, *op. cit.*, pp. ix–xiii.
[27] Aubrey, *op. cit.*, i, p. 300; J. H. Aveling, *Memorials of Harvey* (London, 1875), pp. 16–20; H. P. Bayon, 'William Harvey, physician and biologist: Part I', *Annals of Science*, iii (1938), pp. 85–95.
[28] Harvey, *Generation of Living Creatures*, sig. A 5v.
[29] G. Ent, *Apologia pro circulatione sanguinis* (London, 1641); cf. Harvey, *Works* (1847), pp. xli–xliv.

of Physicians who may have attended Harvey's lectures and who was one of his earliest converts, published almost all his works abroad. At the Oxford Act of July 1633 Edward Dawson defended for the degree of M.D. the affirmative response to the question 'An circulatio sanguinis sit probabilis?'[30] This is an early and apparently isolated recognition by Oxford of the existence of Harvey. Dawson, originally of Sidney Sussex College, Cambridge, incorporated at Lincoln College, Oxford, in 1620. He became a Fellow of the College of Physicians in 1634, but is otherwise unknown to medical history. He died in 1635. The Regius Professor of Physic at Cambridge, Francis Glisson (appointed 1636: later Fellow of the Royal Society) and his more famous pupil John Wallis maintained the circulation of the blood in the late 1630s; but the latter had no intention of practising physic. The first text-book of anatomy in English to accept Harvey's doctrine was that of Nathaniel Highmore, which appeared in 1651. Two years later Boyle and Petty were conducting experiments in Ireland to test the theory. None of the editions of Alexander Read's *Manuall of the Anatomy* recognizes the circulation of the blood. It was still ignored in a text-book published in 1659.[31]

Significantly enough, Harvey's discovery was at first much more favourably received in the Dutch Republic than (in public, at least) in England. Descartes (living in Holland) mentioned it in 1637, after his attention had been drawn to it by Mersenne. Roger Drake, the son of a wealthy London mercer, defended it in a doctoral dissertation at Leyden in 1639. Like Wallis, Drake was not to practise as a doctor: he became a presbyterian minister. Harvey's discovery was much discussed in the Netherlands from this time onwards. Franciscus Sylvius at Leyden and Regius at Utrecht proclaimed their adherence in public lectures. In 1640 Walaeus of Leyden accepted the circulation of the blood in his *De*

---

[30] I am indebted to my friend and former pupil Mr Nicholas Tyacke for kindly allowing me to use this information, which he discovered in the University Archives, Bodleian Library, Reg. P. 15, fo. 277b. He also supplied the details of Dawson's career.

[31] Sir W. Osler, *The Growth of Truth*, Harveian Oration (London, 1906), pp. 30–3; cf. E. Weil, 'The echo of Harvey's *De motu cordis* (1628), 1628 to 1657', *Jour. Hist. Med.*, xii (1957), pp. 167–74; C. Newman, 'The influence of medical education', in *The Evolution of Medical Practice in Britain*, ed. F. N. L. Poynter (London, 1961), p. 26.

motu chyli et sanguinis.[32] As with Bacon, Hakewill and Hobbes, Harvey's reputation in his own country became established only after 1640. Harvey's most enthusiastic supporter was George Ent, whom I described above as the first Englishman to accept the circulation of the blood in print. But Ent was only just an Englishman: his father was a merchant refugee from the Netherlands, and Ent himself was at school in Rotterdam before going to puritan Sidney Sussex, Dawson's college: from there he went to Padua for five years. With Wallis and Glisson, Ent was a member of the group which met at Gresham College in 1645 and formed the nucleus of the later Royal Society.

In the early sixteen-fifties the circulation of the blood was being demonstrated at Cambridge: and at least one student noted that its opponents relied on authority rather than on Harvey's own weapons of reason and experiment.[33] Marchamont Nedham, writing in 1665, agreed with Aubrey that it was after about the mid-forties that Harvey's doctrine began to be accepted.[34] Hobbes, rather enviously, said his friend Harvey was the only man he knew who had lived to see his new doctrines victorious over opposition.[35] Thus Harvey came into his own only in republican Holland and republican England. The coincidence was noted in the Preface to the first English translation of the *De motu cordis*. 'O disturber of the quiet of Physicians! O seditious Citizen of the Physical Common Wealth! Who first of all durst oppose an opinion confirm'd for so many ages by the consent of all'.[36] In France the University of Paris opposed the circulation of the

---

[32] Sir Humphrey Rolleston, 'The reception of Harvey's doctrine of the circulation of the blood in England', in *Essays on the History of Medicine presented to Karl Sudhoff*, ed. C. Singer and H. E. Sigerist (London, 1924), pp. 248–54; K. J. Franklin, *William Harvey, Englishman* (London, 1961), p. 82; Willis, *op. cit.*, p. xliv.

[33] J. E. B. Mayor (ed.), *Autobiography of Matthew Robinson* (Cambridge, 1856), p. 31; F. J. Cole, 'Henry Power on the circulation of the blood', *Jour. Hist. Med.*, xii (1957), p. 294.

[34] M. N[edham], *Medela Medicinae* (London, 1665), pp. 16–17, 215.

[35] T. Hobbes, *The Elements of Philosophy*, in *English Works*, ed. Sir W. Molesworth (London, 1839–45), i, p. viii: first published 1655 (in Latin) and 1656 (in English).

[36] *The Anatomical Exercises of Doctor William Harvey . . . Concerning the motion of the Heart and Blood*, translated by Zachariah Wood, English physician at Rotterdam (London, 1673), sig. A 2: first printed 1653.

blood for nearly half a century after Harvey had announced its discovery. Molière was quicker to appreciate the significance of Harvey's discovery than most French doctors.[37] Opposition in the universities of Italy and Spain also lasted much longer than in the Netherlands and England.[38]

Nor was it only that Harvey had to wait until after 1640 for public support in England. His early admirers were also in many cases dangerously radical persons. Robert Fludd was a Rosicrucian, a heretic, and a medical man who had many brushes with the College of Physicians.[39] John Webster, one of those would-be reformers of the universities whom Harvey so much disliked, was nevertheless one of his admirers.[40] James Harrington, the republican theorist, quoted Harvey as a model.[41] Gerrard Winstanley the Digger seems to have echoed Harvey.[42]

[37] Osler, The Growth of Truth, pp. 34–7; cf. Osler, The Evolution of Modern Medicine (New Haven, 1921), p. 172. Le Malade Imaginaire appeared in 1673. Boileau, La Fontaine and Racine also accepted the circulation of the blood (Chauvois, op. cit., pp. 232–40).

[38] Bayon, Annals of Science, iii, pp. 97–101.

[39] D. Saurat, Milton, Man and Thinker (London, 1944), pp. 248–67.

[40] J. Webster, Academiarum Examen (London, 1654), p. 74. In The Display of Supposed Witchcraft (1677), Webster noted that it took a long time for Harvey's views to win acceptance. For Harvey's objections to radical reformers of the universities, see L. M. Payne, 'Sir Charles Scarburgh's Harveian Oration, 1662', Jour. Hist. Med., xii (1957), p. 163. The royalist Scarburgh, speaking in the panic year 1662, is perhaps not the most reliable of witnesses.

[41] J. Harrington, The Oceana and other Works, ed. J. Toland et al. (London, 1737), p. 38; cf. pp. 242, 249, 429, 514, 593. I owe these references and an appreciation of Harrington's debt to Harvey to the late Dr Felix Raab. See his The English Face of Machiavelli, a Changing Interpretation, 1500–1700 (London, 1964), pp. 198–201.

[42] Cf. G. Winstanley, The Law of Freedom (1652), in The Works of Gerrard Winstanley, ed. G. H. Sabine (Ithaca, N.Y., 1941), p. 565, with Harvey, Generation of Living Creatures, pp. 456–7. Harvey's treatise was not published in English until 1653. Winstanley could read Latin, and he had plenty of leisure after the dissolution of the Digger colony in 1650; he knew something of anatomy (The Breaking of the Day of God (London, 1648), pp. 17–18). He may have heard of Harvey's argument at second hand; or they may both derive from a common source. One possible common source is a denunciation of Servetus, such as is to be found in T. Rogers, The Faith, Doctrine and Religion professed and protected in the Realm of England (Cambridge, 1681), p. 13: first published (in this revised form) in 1607.

IV

More important for our purposes, the doctrine of the circulation of the blood, as expressed by Harvey in 1651 (but not, in print at least,[43] in 1628), has heretical overtones of a very dangerous kind. The soul has its dwelling-place in the blood. The blood is the soul (*anima*).[44] It was from Harvey that Dr John Collop derived the view which he versified in 1656, clearly rejecting the sun-heart analogy:[45]

> Thus blood, Sun-like, gives motion, life and sense . . . .
> Distinct from Blood, who can the Soul aught call?

That the soul was in the blood, and died with it, had been argued in the mid-sixteenth century by Michael Servetus, one of the earliest persons to mention a pulmonary circulation in theoretical terms, though he did nothing to establish it experimentally. Servetus was an anti-Trinitarian, and so radical a heretic that he was burnt in person by Calvin at Geneva, and in effigy by the Roman Catholic authorities at Vienne. With Servetus the view that the blood was the soul was associated with the heresy of mortalism: the doctrine that the soul sleeps from the moment of death until the time when the body is resurrected. It is indeed difficult, if the soul is the blood, to conceive of its having any existence between these two events, though for all I know theologians may have an answer to this.[46] (Hence, incidentally, the fierce resistance put up by seventeenth-century defenders of

---

[43] The doctrine seems to be hinted at in Harvey's lectures of 1618 (O'Malley, Poynter and Russell, *op. cit.*, pp. 90, 180; but cf. p. 174).

[44] Harvey, *Generation of Living Creatures*, pp. 276–7, 281–4, 296, 454–5. Alexander Ross chose this point for special attack (*Arcana Microcosmi*, pp. 230–2).

[45] F. N. L. Poynter, 'An unnoticed contemporary English poem in praise of Harvey, and its author, John Collop, M.D.', *Jour. Hist. Med.*, xi (1956), pp. 380–1.

[46] Luther and some English Lutherans believed in the sleep of the soul, including probably William Tyndale (*An Answer to Sir Thomas More*, Parker Soc., Cambridge, 1850, pp. 180–1; *Doctrinal Treatises*, Parker Soc., Cambridge, 1848, p. lxiii). The doctrine arose in part by reaction against the papal doctrine of Purgatory, a point which Overton stressed in *Mans Mortallitie*. Cf. also A. Pirnat, *Die Ideologie der Siebenbürger Antitrinitarier in den 1570er Jahren* (Budapest, 1961), p. 151.

Christianity like Henry More[47] to Hobbes's mockery of the concept of 'incorporeal substances': if the soul was a corporeal substance its separate existence was more difficult to imagine.) Servetus's prosecutors at Geneva emphasized especially the socially dangerous nature of his doctrine.[48]

Throughout the sixteenth and early seventeenth centuries the mortalist heresy was associated with lower-class Anabaptism, Familism and Socinianism; but it was also a heresy to which medical men were especially prone. The doctrine flourished notably in Padua, where Harvey and Ent studied medicine. Calvin, in attacking mortalism, alluded particularly to its association with medical teaching.[49] Many English Mortalists, including Milton, were probably disciples of the Hermeticist Dr Robert Fludd, for whom the blood was the life.[50] Sir Thomas Browne at some date before 1635 believed that 'the souls of men perished with their bodies'.[51] He may well have been influenced by Harvey, whom he admired.

Another heretic who speculated about the circulation of the blood was Giordano Bruno, who was in England in 1582-3, and was burnt at Rome in 1600. He may have influenced Walter Warner, who claimed to have given Harvey the idea of the circulation of the blood.[52] Certainly there was much rather risky discussion in Sir Walter Ralegh's circle, to which Warner

[47] H. More, 'Antipsychopannychia; or the third Book of the Song of the Soul: containing a Confutation of the sleep of the Soul after death', in *Philosophicall Poems* (Cambridge, 1647).
[48] R. Willis, *Servetus and Calvin* (London, 1877), p. 352. Willis had translated Harvey's *Works* for the Sydenham Society in 1847. Cf. R. H. Bainton, *Hunted Heretic* (Boston, 1960) and S. F. Mason, 'Science and religion in seventeenth-century England', *Past and Present*, no. 3 (Feb. 1953), p. 35 (p. 208 in this volume).
[49] G. H. Williams, *The Radical Reformation* (Philadelphia, 1962), pp. 20-2, 105, 199, 400, 556, 562, 568-9, 584-9, 622, 698-9, 716, 723, 752, 779-80.
[50] R. Fludd, *Anatomiae amphiteatrum effigie triplici* (Frankfurt, 1623), quoted by J. B. Craven, *Dr. Robert Fludd* (Kirkwall, 1902), p. 219.
[51] Sir T. Browne, *Religio Medici*, in *Works* (Bohn edn, London, 1852), ii, p. 329.
[52] Aubrey, *Brief Lives*, ii, p. 291; cf. W. Pagel, 'Giordano Bruno: the philosophy of circles and the circular movement of the blood', *Jour. Hist. Med.*, vi (1951), pp. 116-24; ——, 'The philosophy of circles—Cesalpino —Harvey', *ibid.*, xii (1957), p. 140; G. Rolleston, *The Harveian Oration* (Oxford, 1873), pp. 50-62; J. W. Shirley, 'The scientific experiments of Sir Walter Ralegh, the Wizard Earl, and the Three Magi in the Tower, 1603-1617', *Ambix*, iv (1949), p. 55.

belonged, about the nature of the soul. In an enquiry held in 1594 into Ralegh's alleged atheism, one question asked was whether anyone had spoken against the immortality of the soul, or had said that 'a man's soul should die and become like the soul of a beast or such-like'.[53] Edward Wightman, a draper of Burton-on-Trent who was the last Englishman to be burnt for heresy (in 1612), held that 'the soul doth sleep in the sleep of the first death as well as the body, and is mortal . . . as the body is'.[54] In New England the heretical Mrs Ann Hutchinson in 1638 defended mortalism among a number of other enormities.[55] After the outbreak of civil war soul-sleeping achieved new notoriety with the publication of *Mans Mortallitie* (Amsterdam, 1643) by Richard Overton, later the Leveller leader. Overton used medical arguments, but derived them from Ambrose Paré, whose *Works* had been translated into English in 1634.[56] Harvey's *De motu cordis* was not translated until 1653. Mortalism was being preached in the Parliamentary army in 1645, and was worrying the Westminster Assembly of Divines.[57] The heresy was adopted by the Muggletonian sect as well as by Milton.[58] In 1648 two royalist

[53] Aubrey, *Brief Lives*, i, p. 287; N. L. Williams, *Sir Walter Ralegh* (London, 1962), pp. 118–21; G. B. Harrison (ed.), *Willobie His Avisa (1594)* (London, 1926), p. 256. Alexander Ross, who in 1645 published a full-dress attack on mortalism (*The Philosophicall Touch-Stone*, London, Part ii and Conclusion, *passim*; cf. *Medicus, Medicatus*, London, 1645, pp. 50–1) thought Ralegh's views on the soul needed special refutation (A. Ross, *Some Animadversions and Observations upon Sir Walter Raleighs Historie of the World, wherein his mistakes are noted*, London, n.d., pp. 4–5, 51).

[54] C. Burrage, *The Early English Dissenters* (Cambridge, 1912), i, p. 219.

[55] 'A report of the trial of Mrs. Ann Hutchinson before the Church in Boston, March, 1638', *Publications of the Prince Soc.*, xxi (1894), p. 292, quoted by L. Ziff, *The Career of John Cotton* (Princeton, 1962), p. 143.

[56] R. O[verton], *Mans Mortalitie* (1644), pp. 11, 13, 18. Overton also quoted Copernicus and Tycho Brahe.

[57] *Hist. MSS. Commission, Fourth Report*, p. 273; cf. *The Oxinden Letters, 1642–70*, ed. D. Gardiner (London, 1937), pp. 76–7; J. Lightfoot, *Works* (London, 1823–4), xiii, pp. 335–6; A. F. Mitchell and J. Struthers (eds), *Minutes of the Sessions of the Westminster Assembly of Divines* (London, 1874), p. 275.

[58] D. Masson, *Life of Milton* (London, 1871–80), vi, p. 833; Saurat, *op. cit.*, pp. 268–87; Lodowick Muggleton, *A Transcendent Spiritual Treatise* (London, 1711), pp. 71–2, 75–9 (first printed 1651); *The Acts of the Witnesses of the Spirit* (London, 1764), pp. 25, 79, 102, 122–3 (first printed 1699).

newspapers denounced the mortalist heresy, and said that it had been partly responsible for the revolutionary nature of the Civil War.[59] Even in 1847 the translator of the Sydenham Society's edition of Harvey's *Works* tried wherever possible to avoid the word 'soul' for Harvey's '*anima*':[60] though any schoolboy could have told him it was the right translation.

Now there is no evidence that Harvey knew of the radical associations of the doctrine that the soul is the blood. Like his friend Hobbes, he prided himself on not reading many books. But it would be foolish to assume that he was not aware of these associations. The burning of Wightman, four years before Harvey's Lumleian lectures, could hardly have escaped his notice. Harvey had studied at Padua, and had no doubt read of the mortalist doctrines of his favourite Aristotle. Harvey quoted Fludd's writings, and almost certainly knew him personally: Fludd refers to Harvey as 'my most dear countryman and colleague', and a Richard Fludd witnessed Harvey's will.[61] In this will Harvey left £10 to Hobbes, who was attacked as a mortalist.[62] Harvey was not unaware of contemporary ideas. He accepted the Copernican theory. He seems not to have believed in witches, helping to get four old ladies pardoned in 1634, and dissecting a witch's 'familiar' in order to demonstrate that it was just a toad.[63] He was no recluse, but a man of affairs, the son of the mayor of Folkestone and the brother of five Turkey merchants. His comparison of the heart to a waterbellows or pump, propelling the

---

[59] *Mercurius Bellicus*, 8–14 Feb. 1648; *Mercurius Melancholicus*, 20–27 March, 1648: both quoted by J. Frank, *The Levellers* (Cambridge, Mass., 1955), p. 299.

[60] Harvey, *Works* (London, 1847), pp. 379, 391: 'the vital principle', 'the living principle'. Dr Pagel also wants to think that Harvey did not really wish to identify the soul with the blood (W. Pagel, 'William Harvey and the Purpose of Circulation', *Isis*, xlii, 1951, pp. 29–31). But the translator of *De generatione* identified them clearly enough in 1653, unrebuked by Harvey.

[61] Whitteridge, *op. cit.*, pp. 94–5; O'Malley, Poynter and Russell, *op. cit.*, p. 104; R. Fludd, *Medicina Catholica* (Frankfurt, 1629); W. Pagel, *William Harvey's Biological Ideas* (Basel, 1967), pp. 113–16.

[62] [Luke Fawn], *A Beacon Set on Fire* (London, 1652), pp. 14–15; Joseph Glanvill, *Lux Orientalis* (London, 1682), both quoted by S. I. Mintz, *The Hunting of Leviathan* (Cambridge, 1962), pp. 60, 70; Harvey, *Works* (1847), p. xciv.

[63] G. Keynes, *The Personality of William Harvey* (Cambridge, 1949), p. 30, quoting *The Gentleman's Magazine* (1832), Part i, pp. 405–10.

blood along the veins and arteries as along a system of pipes, shows his acquaintance with the crafts of his day.[64] His own emphasis on anatomy, unusual in his profession, shows a leaning to the practical, the craft side of medicine: anatomy was usually left to the despised barber-surgeons.

All this suggests some further questions. Why did Harvey not publish the De motu cordis for twelve years after his discovery had been announced in lectures? Why did he then publish it abroad? It has been suggested that Fludd recommended his own Frankfurt publisher to Harvey as offering better terms than could be got in England.[65] All Fludd's writings were indeed published abroad: but a sufficient reason for that is their heretical nature. Harvey's delay in publishing is usually explained by reference to his natural diffidence: the parallel cases of Copernicus, Bacon, Napier, Newton and Darwin are cited.[66] This is a possible explanation, though in most of the examples suggested there might also have been prudential reasons for delaying publication. But we may observe that, despite the discouraging early reception of the De motu cordis in England, Harvey showed no reluctance to publish, and to publish in England, and in English, in the freer years 1649-53.

V

Let us suppose, just for the sake of argument, that Harvey *was* aware of the dangers lurking in his argument. He delayed publication for twelve years, during which time he did his best to get his colleagues at the College of Physicians to accept his discovery. When he did publish, it was abroad, in Latin, with a title which concealed rather than advertised the contents of his book; and to make doubly sure he persuaded Charles I, no anatomical expert, to accept a fulsome dedication. By 1628 Charles had been long enough on the throne for his protection of men like Richard Montague to convince Harvey that the King would stick blindly

[64] S. F. Mason, *A History of the Sciences*, p. 177; S. Lilley, 'The nature of the physical world', in *The Making of Modern Science*, ed. A. R. Hall (Leicester, 1960), p. 41.
[65] Bayon, 'William Gilbert (1544-1603), Robert Fludd (1574-1637) and William Harvey (1578-1653) as Medical Exponents of Baconian Doctrines', *Proc. Roy. Soc. Med.*, xxxii (1938-9), p. 36.
[66] Osler, *The Growth of Truth*, pp. 26-8.

by his favourites, right or wrong; as the more politic James I, whose personal physician Harvey had also been, did not. (We recall Cowell, Bacon, Cranfield.) In the text of the *De motu cordis* Harvey made great play with his agreement with Aristotle, though by 1649 he had rejected him. By this latter date the Independents, more favourable to science and less attached to Aristotle than Bishops or Presbyterians, were firmly established in power; and Harvey's reply to Riolan was published simultaneously in Cambridge and Rotterdam in 1649. The *De generatione* was published in London in 1651. English translations of this and of the *De motu cordis* followed in 1653.

Despite the very sharp difference between the opinions which Harvey expressed in 1628 and in 1649-51, there is no evidence that he deliberately suppressed his true views at the earlier date. His thought may well have developed or clarified itself later. But even if this was the case, it is difficult to believe that Harvey's development was not assisted by the political events of the 1640s. If the dedication to Charles and the references to Aristotle were not camouflage, as they almost certainly were not, a sharp jolt was needed to get Harvey to contemplate the possibility of dethroning the heart. What greater jolt than the dethroning of a king, the equivalent in the commonwealth of the heart in the body? The more we emphasize the genuineness of Harvey's beliefs in 1628, the more need there is to posit external influences which shattered those beliefs. The jolt may have come from the republican Netherlands. In 1648 Jacob de Back, physician-in-ordinary to Rotterdam, published his *Dissertatio de corde*, in which he argued that the heart was not the chief organ in the motion of the blood. 'It performeth the office of a steward. The heart in the body of an animal has no rule or principality.' De Back rightly regarded this as a correction of the *De motu cordis*, which he had read about 1633.[67] Harvey might well have read de Back's book before writing his letters to Riolan, in which he uses very similar words. Whether Harvey got the idea of dethroning the heart from a Dutchman, or arrived at it independently himself, the idea may in either case have been stimulated by the experience of living in a republic. This is of course impossible to prove: but the dates are

[67] Jacob de Back, *Discourse of the Heart*, pp. 88-93 and sig. 1-2, printed with *The Anatomical Exercises of Doctor William Harvey. . . . Concerning the motion of the Heart and Blood* (1673); cf. Weil, *op. cit.*, p. 172.

significant. And the obverse is certainly true—that Harvey was for long prevented from drawing the full consequences of his own discovery by his preconceived Aristotelian ideas about the heart's supremacy.

In considering Harvey's position in the history of ideas, then, we should not restrict ourselves to quoting the dedication of the *De motu cordis*. The Copernican parallel is striking, as is Harvey's later rejection of vital spirits in the blood, which compares with Copernicus's rejection of the angelic beings which moved the planets. The discoveries of both Copernicus and Harvey can be seen as ideological counterparts to the denial of the hierarchical principle; in this sense Copernicus 'democratized the universe' and 'dethroned the earth'.[68] In 1628 Harvey seemed to have abolished hierarchy in the human body only to establish the sovereignty of the heart. But he went further. The supremacy of the blood cannot be fitted into the categories of absolute monarchy. The heart receives life and being from and ministers to the blood, as a constitutional monarch draws his being from the electorate and ministers to it. If Newton's physics is the ideological analogue of monarchy limited by law, Harvey's anatomy is the analogue of monarchy limited by representative assemblies. The heart too was dethroned—a point made in the title of a book by one of Harvey's earliest French admirers.[69] Such analogies do not lead men to create limited monarchies: but they make them seem more reasonable, less shocking, in a world still dominated by analogy, and a world in which such traditional analogies were among the strongest supports of monarchy. To be able to conceive of the possibility of something new was the first step towards introducing it. The case of Harvey shows how difficult was the intellectual first step.

A consideration of Harvey thus rams home the familiar point that we should never consider ideas in abstraction from the social environment of the thinker. The tyranny of traditional concepts was such that Harvey had great difficulty in escaping from the

[68] S. F. Mason, article cited above (note 48), pp. 31–42, pp. 201–17 in this volume; W. P. D. Wightman, *The Growth of Scientific Ideas* (London, 1951), p. 44.
[69] P. Vattier, *Le Cœur Déthroné* (Paris, 1660). For Vattier see Chauvois, 'Le Docteur Pierre Vattier (1623–70) . . .', *La Presse Médicale*, 31 December 1955, p. 1887.

notion of hierarchy, and could do so in the first instance only with the help of equally traditional notions of the sovereignty of the heart and of the circle of perfection, even though Harvey knew perfectly well that blood from a severed head did not spurt out with a circular motion. He found it even more difficult to conceive that the blood might move itself. Here Hobbes's doctrine of the self-motion of matter may have helped him, a doctrine derived both from Galileo and from observation of society.[70] It is difficult for us to appreciate the intellectual revolution involved in assuming that matter—the planets, the blood—might move of itself without being pushed around by an angel or a spirit. No wonder Hobbes got so excited about it and thought that motion was life, just as Harvey came to think of the self-moving blood as the soul. So we see interconnections between thought about astronomy, about mechanics, about the human body and about society. In all these spheres, however apparently self-contained and 'pure', old ideological concepts delayed the discovery of scientific truth, and its discovery was aided by new ideological concepts which themselves derived ultimately from the replacement of a society based on serf labour by one in which the free labour of craftsmen and independent peasants predominated.

VI

Harvey the Royalist is often quoted against those who suggest a connection between scientific ideas and the Parliamentary cause in the English Civil War.[71] Since the argument is that there is a trend of thought which works in a particular direction, it is not disproved by finding one or two individual thinkers who are exceptions to the general trend. But it may be worth looking again at Harvey's 'royalism' in the light of the argument of this article. As personal physician to two kings from 1618 onwards, Harvey, like Bacon, was a royal employee: like Harrington he was also a personal friend of Charles I. Harvey was moreover a

[70] C. B. Macpherson, *The Political Theory of Possessive Individualism: Hobbes to Locke* (Oxford, 1962), pp. 76–8. Galileo was teaching in Padua when Harvey was a student there.
[71] I have tried to argue the case for this connection in my *Intellectual Origins of the English Revolution* (Oxford, 1965).

Fellow of the College of Physicians, and in 1613, 1625 and 1629 he was one of the four Censors of the College. That is to say, he was responsible for enforcing the College's monopoly by prosecuting any unlicensed person who ventured to practise physic within seven miles of London.[72] Like all monopolies, that of the College of Physicians was dependent on royal charter and royal favour: during the interregnum it came under attack.[73] It would have been difficult, in these circumstances, for Harvey not to have had royalist predilections. In 1645, by an act as arbitrary as those of the later Parliamentary Commissioners, Charles I deposed Sir Nathaniel Brent, the Warden of Merton College, Oxford, and intruded Harvey in his place.

Yet Harvey seems to have wished to remain as neutral as possible between the two sides in the Civil War. He took great pains in 1642 to get not only Parliament's permission to attend Charles I as his personal physician, but even their command.[74] In 1644 a motion to have Harvey dismissed from his post as physician to St Bartholomew's Hospital, on the ground that he had 'withdrawn himself from his charge and is retired to the party in arms against the Parliament', was apparently unsuccessful.[75] When Oxford surrendered to Parliament, he quietly abandoned the Wardenship of Merton to Brent, and went back to London. His estates were never sequestrated, and there is no evidence that he was ever in trouble with the Parliamentary, Commonwealth or Protectorate authorities.[76] Harvey mentions Charles I two or three times in the *De generatione*, but with no particular affection or regret.

About Harvey's political opinions, if any, we know very little, and again the evidence is ambiguous. In the notes of his anatomy

---

[72] Franklin, *op. cit.*, p. 56; cf. Charles Goodall, *The Royal College of Physicians of London* (London, 1684), pp. 289–472; R. S. Roberts, 'The personnel and practice of medicine in Tudor and Stuart England. Part I. The provinces', *Medical History*, vi (1962), pp. 364, 378.
[73] Adrian Huyberts, *A Corner-Stone Laid towards the Building of a New College* (London, 1675), p. 7; Goodall, *The College of Physicians Vindicated* (London, 1676), p. 11.
[74] Harvey, *Generation of Living Creatures*, p. 418.
[75] *Commons Journals*, 12 Feb. 1643–4. The motion was made on behalf of Dr Micklethwayte. But Micklethwayte did not succeed Harvey until May 1653 (Chauvois, *op. cit.*, p. 146).
[76] Franklin, *op. cit.*, p. 99.

lectures (*c.* 1618?) there is an irreverent passage comparing a belch
to a motion sent up from the House of Commons to the Lords.
Another derisive reference to saints on their knees is taken by the
editors to be a hit at Puritans; but it might equally well be aimed
at Catholics.[77] Harvey was an undoubted Protestant, and a friend
of the puritan divine Samuel Ward, though he was critical of
'Anabaptists and fanatics' who, he thought, threatened the
property of the universities.[78] Aubrey's story that Harvey read a
book during the battle of Edgehill, whether true or not, would
hardly have been told about a man who had very strong partisan
feelings. Compare too the invitation to Dr Charles Scarburgh to
desert the royal army and come to London: 'Prithee leave off thy
gunning, and stay here; I will bring thee into practice'. Aubrey's
other records of Harvey's conversation suggest that the great
physician had considerable contempt for those of his aristocratic
patients who married for blue blood, rather than for more eugenic
reasons; and that Harvey, with Bacon, thought that 'From the
meanest person, in some way or other, the learnedst man may
learn something',[79] as Harvey himself had done from the water
pump. We might suspect that Harvey respected learning more
than rank from the fact that he never received a knighthood, as
other personal physicians of the Stuart kings had done. Conveniently, he left on record, in one of his marginalia, the view that
titles were mere 'wooden leggs'.[80]

VII

Finally, a comment upon the relationship between protestantism
and the rise of science. This is now so well established[81] that it is

[77] O'Malley, Poynter and Russell, *op. cit.*, p. 15.
[78] S. W. Mitchell, *Some Recently Discovered Letters of William Harvey*
(Philadelphia, 1912), p. 15; L. M. Payne, 'Sir Charles Scarburgh's
Harveian Oration, 1662', *Jour. Hist. Med.*, xii (1957), p. 163; *Two
Elizabethan Puritan Diaries*, ed. M. M. Knappen (Chicago, 1933), p. 46.
Cf. note 40 above.
[79] Aubrey, *Brief Lives*, i, pp. 297–304.
[80] J. J. Keevil, *The Stranger's Son* (London, 1953), p. 130. The book
annotated, Galen's *Exhortatio ad medicinam et artes*, is now in the British
Museum.
[81] See especially Alphonse de Candolle, *Histoire des Sciences et des Savants
depuis deux Siècles* (Geneva, 1873); R. K. Merton, 'Science, technology and

becoming rather smart to try to deny it: though no attempt to do so has yet met with any success. But the way in which the relationship is stated needs care. Professor Trevor-Roper has plausibly argued that the Counter-Reformation brought a change in the Catholic attitude towards science as well as towards capitalism;[82] and in Spain at least—the country least troubled by heresy in the sixteenth century—the hardening of attitudes towards science did not come until the seventeenth century. The Copernican revolution was accepted without difficulty, and Copernicus was a recommended text at Salamanca in 1594. Philip III invited Galileo to Madrid.[83] But by 1671 it was regarded as 'wonderful that a Spaniard should write a mathematical book'.[84] On the other hand the burning of Servetus reminds us of protestant intolerance. But the heresies for which Servetus was burnt had little direct connection with science: his execution led to an outcry. There is no protestant parallel to Galileo's enforced recantation, under a Pope who believed in magic. There was no protestant Index like that on which all books advocating the Copernican theory remained until 1757, and on which the works of Descartes stayed still longer. On the contrary: Bodley's first Librarian used to scan the Index carefully so as to know which books and which editions to buy for his Library.

Many protestant ministers would have wished to be as intolerant as their Catholic counterparts: protestantism was a liberating force mainly in so far as it ended or diminished the power of priests. The least tolerant protestant creed, presbyterianism, was the most priest-ridden: Geneva began to make important contributions to science only after the authority of strict Calvinism had weakened. Yet even an intolerant protestant clergy like that of New England was open to receive the new astronomy and other

society in seventeenth-century England', *Osiris*, iv (1938), pp. 360–632; J. Pelseneer, 'L'Origine protestante de la science moderne', *Lychnos* (Uppsala, 1946–7), pp. 246–8; S. F. Mason, 'The Scientific Revolution and the Protestant Reformation', *Annals of Science*, ix (1953), pp. 64–87, 154–75.
[82] H. R. Trevor-Roper, 'Religion, the Reformation and social change', *Historical Studies*, iv (1963), pp. 43–4.
[83] I owe this information to the kindness of Mr John Elliott.
[84] John Bertit to John Collins, *Correspondence of Scientific Men of the Seventeenth Century*, ed. S. J. Rigaud (Oxford, 1841), i, p. 158.

scientific discoveries.[85] With the circulation of the blood in mind, we can see a sort of spectrum: Harvey's discovery was easily accepted in the republican Netherlands and republican England; it had to be approached very cautiously in monarchical but protestant England; it was received only much later and with difficulty in monarchical but Catholic France; later still in Italy (outside Venice) and Spain. But republican Venice, Catholic but with strong trading links with protestant Germany, protected Paolo Sarpi, whom Rome would gladly have burnt if it could (and who is another early claimant to the discovery of the circulation of the blood). Galileo fell into the hands of the Inquisition only after he had left the territory of the tolerant Venetian Republic. Robert Hooke thought that Bacon might have suffered the same fate in a Roman Catholic country, 'for being too prying into the then receiv'd philosophy'.[86]

How much earlier would the circulation of the blood have been discovered if Vesalius had not been hounded down by the Inquisition, if Servetus and Bruno had not been burnt?[87] Would Harvey ever have fully developed his ideas if it had not been for the intellectual stimulus of life in the Dutch and English republics? What mattered for the development of science was not so much protestant doctrine (though this might contribute something) as the breaking of clerical monopoly control—in Venice, last of the Italian bourgeois republics, no less than in republican Holland and England. Then an educated lay opinion could prevail over the privileged monopoly corporations, whether clerical or professional. The prejudices of a professional monopoly could be almost as stultifying as, if less vicious than, clerical suppression and persecution. A monarchy, even a protestant monarchy, was more likely to foster those professional corporations which would (in Harvey's words) 'admit no novelty into the school'.[88] The English Revolution was directed against monopoly in church and

[85] S. E. Morison, 'The Harvard School of Astronomy in the seventeenth century', *New England Quarterly*, vii (1934), pp. 5–6, 13; Candolle, *op. cit.*, p. 127; J. N. L. Myres, 'Thomas James and the Painted Frieze', *Bodleian Library Record*, iv (1952), p. 44.
[86] Quoted by C. D. Bowen, *Francis Bacon: the Temper of a Man* (London, 1963), pp. 182–3.
[87] Osler, *The Evolution of Modern Medicine*, pp. 157–60; Franklin, *op. cit.*, pp. 31–2.
[88] Harvey, *Works* (1847), p. 598.

state: the radicals impartially attacked the monopolies of lawyers, priests and physicians.[89]

The progress of Harvey's thought may suggest how arduous and hard-won were the great breakthroughs in science. Not only was an external stimulus required (for Harvey perhaps the pump, so much used in mine-drainage) but also a liberated intellectual climate and freedom to publish. It is instructive that in France it was the men of letters, Molière, La Fontaine, Boileau, with the backing of Louis XIV, who ultimately laughed the doctors out of court. In seventeenth-century France there was no Inquisition, just as in sixteenth-century Spain the Inquisition had been subordinated to the royal government. The monarchy of Louis XIV ultimately saw that medicine was too serious a matter to be left to monopoly corporations of physicians: saw the advantages of modern science as well as of the modern commercial practices which Colbert imitated from the Dutch and English republics.

[89] Nicholas Culpeper, *A Physicall Directory or A Translation of the London Dispensatory* (London, 1649), sig. A—Av.

XIV

WILLIAM HARVEY: A ROYALIST AND NO PARLIAMENTARIAN*

Gweneth Whitteridge

Mr Christopher Hill in his article on 'William Harvey and the idea of monarchy', *Past and Present*, no. 27, April 1964, has expressed the opinion that William Harvey before his death was no longer a Royalist but a supporter of the Commonwealth and that he was moreover a believer in the heresy of mortalism. Mr Hill supports both parts of this hypothesis by a series of quotations taken from Harvey's writings.

With regard to Harvey's political views, Mr Hill claims that in 1628, in *De motu cordis*, Harvey 'used anatomical analogies to support theories of absolute monarchy'. He bases this claim on the fact that in the text Harvey compares the heart to a prince in the commonwealth, and in the elaborate dedication of that work to Charles I compares the King with the heart ('the Principle of Man's Body, and the Image of your Kingly power'). From the Second Letter to Riolan, written in 1649, and from the *De generatione*, published in 1651, Mr Hill quotes passages in which Harvey clearly states that the blood is generated before the heart is formed in the body. On the basis of these quotations Mr Hill claims that 'In 1649, the year in which Charles I had been executed, Harvey explicitly and precisely renounced his earlier opinion: he dethroned the heart', and thereafter 'spoke no longer of "the sovereignty of the heart" but of the "prerogative and antiquity of the blood".' In Mr Hill's opinion this dethroning of the heart constitutes a 'somersault' in Harvey's political ideas, particularly

* From no. 30 (April 1965).

as it occurred 'in the same year as the English Republic was proclaimed'.

At the outset this argument seems to be based on a time series linked causally where no cause can be shown to exist and to incorporate a logical error in the shape of a *post ergo propter* assumption. It is, moreover, by no means certain that the notions of the sovereignty of the heart and the antiquity of the blood had for Harvey the political significance which Mr Hill would attribute to them, for both are concepts intimately connected with anatomical and physiological theories current not only in the seventeenth but also in the preceding centuries. If, however, for the sake of argument, this political significance be conceded, then a further examination of what Harvey does in fact say on these two points seems to show that Mr Hill is mistaken and has based his argument on a false premise. Harvey did not dethrone the heart in favour of the blood after 1649.

The notion of the antiquity of the blood belongs to the debate on the order of the formation of the parts in the embryo, a debate which continued from classical times down to the seventeenth century and beyond. As no conclusive proof could be had until the microscope provided the necessary evidence, it was a subject of much controversy among physicians, physiologists and anatomists, and philosophers. On the order of the formation of the parts depended, in the estimation of certain of these writers, their dignity and consequent hierarchy.[1] When, in 1616, Harvey first delivered his *Prelectiones anatomie universalis*, he discussed the question as to which part was the first to be formed and explained that in his view it was the blood which was the first engendered part and that from which all the others took their shape. 'WH If I could show what I have seen, it were at an end between physicians and philosophers. For blood is rather the author of the viscera than they of it, because blood is in being before the

[1] This is only one of the several possible methods used from classical times onwards to determine the dignity and hierarchy of the parts. Mr Hill quotes from Alexander Ross the statement that 'the testicles are "ignobler than the heart and brain",' a statement which is a contradiction of an opinion expressed by Galen in *De semine*, i. 15, where he is using teleological argument: '[cor] quidem vivendi solum, testes vero bene vivendi fuerint principium. Quanto autem melius est bene vivere, quam simpliciter et solum vivere, tanto sunt in animalibus testes corde praestantiores'.

viscera. . . .'² 'WH . . . it is blood which is the primary source of both the liver and the heart as I have seen.'³ Turning to *De motu cordis*, chapter 4, it will be seen that Harvey there repeats his belief that the blood is formed before the heart. When discussing the order of the formation of the parts in a hen's egg he writes: 'first of all there is in it a drop of blood, which moves [inest primum ante omnia gutta sanguinis, quae palpitat], as *Aristotle* likewise observ'd, which receiving encrease, and the Chicken being form'd in part, the ears of the heart are fashioned. . . .'⁴ It is, therefore, obvious that when in 1651, in *De generatione*, he wrote: 'I conclude (against Aristotle) that blood is the first genital particle', he was saying precisely the same thing about the antiquity of the blood that he had already said in 1616 and in print in 1628. Mr Hill's claim that Harvey dethroned the heart in favour of the blood in the year of the execution of Charles I cannot be taken seriously.

The notion of the sovereignty of the heart is a concept of a different kind from that of the antiquity of the blood. They are not contradictory ideas but complementary and Harvey held both in mind simultaneously when writing *De motu cordis*. The idea of the sovereignty of the heart is not associated with the order of the formation of the parts in the embryo, but with the role played by the heart in the completed animal. As in *De motu cordis* Harvey is primarily concerned to prove that the blood circulates throughout the whole body, the importance of the heart in this process is naturally stressed. This does not prevent him from being aware at the same time of the antiquity of the blood in the sense that it was formed before the heart in the embryo, but this topic is not here under discussion. In his *Prelectiones* of 1616, written before he had discovered the circulation of the blood throughout the whole body,⁵ Harvey uses the well-known Aristotelian analogies

² *The Anatomical Lectures of William Harvey*, ed. Gweneth Whitteridge (Edinburgh, 1964), p. 127.
³ *Ibid.*, p. 257.
⁴ From the first English text of 1653 reprinted in *The Anatomical Exercises of Dr. William Harvey*, ed. Geoffrey Keynes (London, 1928), p. 31. The full title of the work is *Exercitatio anatomica de motu cordis et sanguinis in animalibus*. It would seem that its most usual abbreviation to *De motu cordis* has misled Mr Hill into believing that it was published 'with a title which concealed rather than advertised the contents' (pp. 65–6: p. 173 in this volume).   ⁵ *Anatomical Lectures*, pp. xxxvii–li.

to describe the importance of the heart: 'Wherefore, seeing that the heart imparts heat to all the parts and receives it from none, it is the citadel and abode of heat, the presiding god of this edifice, the fountain and conduit-head'.[6] His original remarks on this subject, preceded as is characteristic of him in these notes by the letters WH, make it plain that the reason why he believes the heart important is that the blood which it contains is the source of the innate natural heat of the body: 'WH it [sc. the heart] is the chiefest of all the parts of the body not on its own account . . . , but on account of the abundance of blood and spirit which exists in its ventricles, for which reason it is the source of all the heat in the body'.[7] These same ideas occur in the Second Letter to Riolan:[8]

> Yet in the mean time I will say and propound it without demonstration (with the leave of most learned men, and reverence to antiquity), that the heart, as it is the beginning of all things in the body, the spring, fountain, and first causer of life, is so to be taken, as being joyn'd together with the veins, and all the arteries, and the blood which is contained in them . . . . But if you understand by this word heart, the body of the heart, with the ventricles and ears, I do not think it to be the framer of the blood, and that it has not force, vertue, motion, or heat, as the gift of the heart.

At the same time this quotation reveals the fact that part of the difficulty for us in understanding Harvey's thought on this topic lies in his use of the word 'heart'. Obviously, too, his contemporaries experienced the same trouble. Hence the explanation here and the further explanation in De generatione, Ex. lii where he is at pains to make clear what he means by 'heart' and 'blood'.

> Now if by the Heart he understand that particle which is first seen in the Egge; namely, the Blood, together with its receptacles (the Vesiculae pulsantes and the Veins) as one and the same Organ; I then conceive he speaks most true.[9]

[6] Ibid., p. 251.　　　　　　　[7] Ibid., p. 249.
[8] From text printed by Keynes, op. cit. above, pp. 186–7.
[9] De generatione, Ex. lii: Anatomical Exercitations concerning the Generation of Living Creatures (London, 1653), p. 291.

Blood . . . as it is a *living part* of the Body, . . . falls under
a two-fold consideration. And therefore *materialiter and per se*,
it is called nutriment; but *formaliter*, as it is endued with *heat*,
and *spirits*, (which are the immediate *instruments* of the *Soul*)
and with the *Soul* itself: it is to be counted the Bodies *Genius*,
and *Conserver*, the *Principal*, *Primogenit*, and *Genital part*.[10]

These are the notions which underlie Harvey's statements on the
supremacy of the heart in *De motu cordis*:[11]

seeing all creatures live by nourishment inwardly concocted,
it is necessary that the concoction and distribution be perfect,
and for that cause the place and receptacle where the nourishment is perfected, and from whence it is deriv'd to every
member. But this place is the heart, since it alone of all the
parts (though it has for its private use the coronal vein and
arterie) does contain in its concavities, as in cisterns, or a
celler (to wit ears or ventricles), blood for the publick use
of the body; but the rest of the parts have it only in vessels
for their own behoof, and for private use. Besides, the heart
only is so plac'd and appointed, that from thence by its
pulse it may equally distribute and dispence (and that according to measure and the concavities of the arteries, which are
to supply every part) to those which want, and deal it after
this manner, as out of a treasure and fountain. Moreover to
this distribution and motion of the blood, violence, and an
impulsor is requir'd, such as the heart is.

When, therefore, Harvey writes in *De generatione*: 'all *Natural
Motions* proceed from the power of the *Heart*, and are as his
Retinue',[12] he is merely reiterating some part of the ideas which
he published in 1628 and is neither contradicting them nor his
own statement elsewhere in *De generatione*:[13]

I conclude . . . that the *blood* is the first *Genital particle*, and
that the *Heart* is its Instrument designed for its *Circulation*. For
the *Hearts* business or function is the propulsation or driving
forth of the *blood*, as appears in all *Animals* that have *blood*.

[10] *De generatione*, Ex. lii: *Anatomical Exercitations concerning . . . Generation*,
p. 295.   [11] Keynes, *op. cit.*, pp. 94-5.
[12] *De generatione*, Ex. lvii: *Anatomical Exercitations concerning . . .
Generation*, p. 352.   [13] *Ibid.*, Ex. li, p. 275.

With regard to the heresy of mortalism with which Harvey is also charged, Mr Hill is more guarded for he does say that 'there is no evidence that Harvey knew of the radical associations of the doctrine that the soul is the blood'. There is indeed not one shred of evidence to show that Harvey subscribed to the belief that the soul of man dies with the blood or sleeps with the body until it and the body are recreated at the general resurrection. Mr Hill's accusation rests on the fact that Harvey says, not that the soul is the blood, but that the soul is in the blood. This belief will be found in Leviticus, chapter 17, verses 11 and 14: 'For the life of the flesh is in the *blood*' and 'For it is the life of all flesh; the blood of it is the life thereof'. In both verses the Vulgate uses the word *anima*, which by the Jacobean translators was rendered 'life'. To these verses Harvey alludes in *De generatione* when he says: '*Life* therefore consists in the *blood*, (as we read in *Holy Scripture*) because in it the *Life* and *Soule* do first dawn, and last set'.[14] It is plain, therefore, that in this belief there is no heresy. Nor does Harvey express this opinion only in the latter part of his life. It will be found in the *Prelectiones* of 1616: 'The soul is in the blood',[15] and also in *De motu cordis*. For any Christian physician of Harvey's time the notion conveyed by the word *anima* was immensely complicated. Though 'any schoolboy' may know that the right translation of the word is 'soul', he may not be aware of the fact that in its Latin significance it comprised also the three aspects of the soul found in Greek philosophy and was therefore applicable not only to man, but also to animals and plants. All these connotations of *anima* will be found in Harvey's works, but to discuss this, as also the meaning attached by Harvey to the word *spiritus* and the connection of *spiritus* with *anima*, is not to the present purpose. Mr Hill's irresponsible accusation of heresy has no substance, and cannot overset the testimony of Harvey's friends, John Aubrey, Sir Charles Scarburgh and the Catholic earl of Arundel.

As a grain of evidence is worth a ton of conjecture on Harvey's political views, it may be as well to remember that on 25 April 1650 the Council of State and Admiralty gave Harvey a pass allowing him to come to London for fourteen days to attend his former patient, the Dowager Lady Thynne, in her sickness. The pass was granted 'on her engagement that he shall do nothing

[14] *Ibid.*, Ex. li, p. 277.   [15] *Anatomical Lectures, op. cit.*, p. 127.

prejudicial to the commonwealth'. When the fourteen days were up, on 6 May 1650, a further licence was given to Harvey to remain in London for four more weeks, if the Lady Thynne were to live so long.[16] Had Harvey been known as a supporter of the Commonwealth it seems unlikely that such permission would have been required or so specific an undertaking demanded on his behalf.

We know, furthermore, on the authority of Sir Charles Scarburgh, that Harvey had intended to endow a professorship of experimental philosophy at Cambridge and to provide that University with a laboratory and herb garden, but was deterred from so doing by the thought that he might be supporting views and doctrines reflecting the religious and political opinions of the Commonwealth which was so distasteful to him:[17]

The University lost, as we have said, this most splendid Institute, projected by our Harvey, robbed by the inequity of those most wicked times [sceleratissimorum temporum injuria interceptum]. I see, he said (for he often spoke to me of this matter and not without tears in his eyes and mine), I see plainly that, were I to dedicate my fortune, as I had intended, to the promoting of the knowledge of truth and to the public weal, I should do nothing other than make Anabaptists, Fanatics and all manner of thieves and parricides my heirs.

Finally, Harvey clearly expresses his own state of mind in 1651 in his reply to George Ent's question 'Are all Affaires well, and right?'[18]

How can they, He gravely answered, when the Commonwealth is surrounded with intestine troubles; and I my self as yet far from land, tost in that tempestuous Ocean? And, unfeignedly (added He) if the comfort of my Studies, and the remembrance of many things, long since fallen under my observation, were not some refreshment to my Mind; I know not what could prevaile upon me, to desire to survive the present.

[16] *Cal. State Papers Domestic, 1650,* pp. 537, 540.
[17] Translated from Bodleian Lib., MS. Rawlinson D 815, fo. 6v.
[18] From the Epistle Dedicatory to Harvey's *Anatomical Exercitations concerning . . . Generation,* sig. A.3v.

XV

WILLIAM HARVEY (NO PARLIAMENTARIAN, NO HERETIC) AND THE IDEA OF MONARCHY*

Christopher Hill

In her comment on my article, 'William Harvey and the idea of monarchy',[1] Mrs Whitteridge accuses me of saying 'that William Harvey before his death was no longer a Royalist but a supporter of the Commonwealth and that he was moreover a believer in the heresy of mortalism' (*W.*, p. 104; p. 182 in this volume). I have re-read my article very carefully and can find nothing in it to justify either of these assertions. On the first, I said 'it would have been difficult . . . for Harvey not to have had royalist predilections'. The most I suggested was that he 'seems to have wished to remain as neutral as possible between the two sides in the Civil War' (*H.*, p. 69; p. 177 in this volume). That is hardly claiming him as a Parliamentarian. On this point there is no dispute between Mrs Whitteridge and myself. I would however see less significance than she does in the passage from Sir Charles Scarburgh which we both quote (*H.*, p. 69, p. 178; *W.*, p. 109, p. 188). Scarburgh was writing after the Restoration; he was a violent partisan, whose enthusiastic royalism I contrasted with Harvey's scepticism (*H.*, p. 70; p. 178); yet even Scarburgh attributes to Harvey no more than a dislike and a fear of radical sectaries, which were shared by many staunch Parliamentarians. This fear

---

* From no. 31 (July 1965).
[1] *Past and Present*, no. 27 (April 1964); pp. 160–81 in this volume. The abbreviation *H.* followed by a page number refers to this article; *W.* to Mrs Whitteridge's 'William Harvey: A Royalist and No Parliamentarian', *Past and Present*, no. 30 (December 1964), pp. 104–9; pp. 182–8 in this volume.

is no evidence for Harvey's views about the Commonwealth government, which was *not* composed of 'Anabaptists and fanatics'; unless indeed the conversation took place during the Barebones Parliament, in which case it can be used as evidence only of disapproval of that short-lived experiment. If this makes Harvey a partisan Royalist, then Oliver Cromwell was one of Charles I's warmest supporters.

Nor did I claim Harvey as a believer in mortalism. The only direct quotation which Mrs Whitteridge gives to support either of her attributions to me runs: 'there is no evidence that Harvey knew of the radical associations of the doctrine that the soul is the blood' (*W*., p. 108, p. 187; *H*., p. 64, p. 172). I added indeed that 'it would be foolish to assume that he was not aware of those associations', but that is hardly an 'irresponsible accusation of heresy'. But if I have given any other reader the impression that I thought Harvey was either a Parliamentarian or a Mortalist, I am glad to have this opportunity of correcting it. I did not and do not.

What then are the points in dispute? If Mrs Whitteridge's argument is that Harvey did not change his views significantly between 1616 and 1651, this can easily be refuted. In 1616 and 1628 Harvey still thought the heart heated the blood; in 1649 he thought the blood heated the heart.[2] In 1616 he thought the heart drove the blood;[3] in 1649 he denied this, and asserted that the pulse was derived from the blood.[4] In 1628 'the fountain . . . of blood' is 'in the *lungs* and in the *heart*';[5] in 1649 this 'doctrine as old as Aristotle' was specifically rejected.[6] In 1616 Harvey thought the heart 'the chiefest of all the parts of the body', 'the presiding god of this edifice, the fountain and conduit head'. The heart was the noblest part of the body.[7] In 1651 Harvey wrote that '*blood*

[2] G. Whitteridge (ed.), *The Anatomical Lectures of William Harvey* Edinburgh, 1964), p. li; cf. a letter from Harvey to Robert Morison, 28 April 1652, in *The Circulation of the Blood*, ed. K. J. Franklin (Oxford, 1958), pp. 85–6.

[3] Whitteridge, *op. cit.*, p. 271; *The Anatomical Exercises of Doctor William Harvey. . . . Concerning the motion of the Heart and Blood* (London, 1673), pp. 84–5. Translation first published 1653.

[4] Harvey, *Works* (London, 1847), p. 136; *Anatomical Exercitations Concerning the Generation of Living Creatures* (London, 1653), p. 276.

[5] *Concerning the motion of the Heart and Blood*, p. 107.

[6] Harvey, *Works* (1847), p. 136.

[7] Whitteridge, *op. cit.*, pp. 249, 251, 297; cf. *H*., p. 54 n. 2 (p. 160 n. 2 in this volume) and references there cited.

lives and is nourished of it selfe, no way depending upon any other part of the *body*, as elder or worthier than it self'. 'Nor is the *Blood* therefore onely to be called the *Primigenial* and *principal part*, because that in, and from it the fountain of *motion* and *pulsation* is derived; but also, because the *Animal heat*, or *vital spirit* is first radicated and implanted, and the *soul* takes up her first mansion in it'. '*Blood . . .* is to be counted the Bodies *Genius*, and *Conserver*, the *Principal*, *Primogenit* and *Genital part*.'[8]

In the light of these passages I do not think we can accept Mrs Whitteridge's interesting suggestion that Harvey consistently held to a theory that the blood was prior in time (but only in time) to the heart, and that he never 'dethroned' the heart from the traditional sovereign position which he had accorded it in 1628 (*W.*, pp. 106–8, 184–6; see p. 193 below). In 1616 Harvey clearly stated in lectures that the blood was the primary source of the heart (*W.*, p. 105; pp. 183–4). But in his printed *De motu cordis* of 1628 he did not express even the temporal primacy of the blood with the same clarity as in these lectures or as he was to state it in print, and in English, in 1649–53.[9] Nor did he (as Mrs Whitteridge lucidly explains) define his most unusual use of the word 'heart' clearly in print until 1651 (*W.*, p. 107; p. 185). Alexander Ross, in whose opinion the heart is 'the noblest and chiefest of all our members' *because* it is 'the first member that lives and is formed in our bodies', thought Harvey worth refuting only after the publication of the *De generatione*.[10]

My suggestion was that Harvey expressed his views with less than full clarity in 1628, taking careful refuge behind the authority of Aristotle (*H.*, p. 57; p. 164), just as Vesalius seventy years earlier had tried—in print—to accommodate his views to those of Galen.[11] In the freer intellectual climate of the Republic Harvey expressed specifically and without ambiguity what he had only hinted at

[8] *Generation of Living Creatures*, pp. 282, 276, 295, and pp. 273–95 *passim*.
[9] Contrast the passages quoted *H.*, p. 55 (pp. 161–2 in this volume) with the one obscure sentence which Mrs Whitteridge cites from the *De motu cordis* (*W.*, p. 106; p. 184 in this volume).
[10] See especially Ross's *Arcana Microcosmi* (second edn, London, 1652), pp. 230–2. The chapters on Harvey were not in the 1651 edition.
[11] W. Pagel and P. Rattansi, 'Vesalius and Paracelsus', *Medical History*, viii (1964), p. 318. The same two authors suggest another possible influence on Harvey between 1628 and 1649—Marcus Marci of Bohemia, whom the English radical John Webster admired: *ibid.*, pp. 79–80.

before. Two points may be added to the evidence given on *H.*, pp. 57–8, 64–5 (pp. 164–5, 172–3), which suggest that Harvey was aware both of the existence of a censorship and of the potential riskiness of his own views. In his lectures of 1616 he said '*If I could show what I have seen,* it were at an end between physicians and philosophers. For blood is rather the author of the viscera than they of it'.[12] Since Harvey was at that very moment 'showing what he had seen', his difficulty was clearly one of publication, not of expression. Again in a letter of 1649, referring to those who believed the heart was the primary cause of pulsation and of life, Harvey said '*did I speak openly,* I should say that I do not agree with the common opinion'. He promised soon to lay even more wonderful things before the world.[13] This would at least be compatible with the explanation that in the *De motu cordis* he did not 'speak openly', but that he did so in the *De generatione* of 1651.

Mrs Whitteridge and I are in fact asking different questions. For the biographer of Harvey, if it can be established that he held certain views in 1616, and that he stated those views clearly in print in 1649–51, then the fact that he did not state them clearly in 1628 is of minor significance. Provided he did not contradict them, they can be read into his 1628 text. But for the historian of ideas what matters is what Harvey stated unequivocally in print, and what his contemporaries believed him to think; not what he himself may have privately thought. It still seems to me that there is an important contradiction either between what Harvey thought in 1628 and 1649–51 or (if Mrs Whitteridge is right) between what he thought all along and what the printed record declared him to think. The object of my article was not to clear up a biographical point. Nor did I wish to claim that after 1649 Harvey gave the same political significance to the supremacy of the blood as he gave in the *De motu cordis* to the sovereignty of the heart. I did want to draw attention to the fact that so many of Harvey's earliest admirers were religious and political radicals, and to ask whether it might not have been easier in a republic to state, perhaps even to think, some of the things which de Back stated in 1648 and Harvey in 1649–51, than it had been in England under the monarchy. My answer may be wrong, though Mrs

12 Whitteridge, *op. cit.*, p. 127. My italics.
13 Harvey, *Works* (1847), pp. 136–7. My italics again.

Whitteridge has not convinced me of this; but I still think that my question was worth asking.

Mrs Whitteridge objects to the phrase 'dethrone the heart'. It was, however, not mine but that of Vattier, a contemporary of Harvey's (*H.*, p. 67; p. 175). The point was also made by Alexander Ross, who rejected Harvey's discovery,[14] and by Jacob de Back, who thought Harvey had not gone far enough, referring in 1648 to the 'subserviency' of the heart, 'the instrument dispersing the blood'.[15] Descartes in the late sixteen-thirties thought he was correcting Harvey when he described the heart as a passive organ, worked by the blood.[16] If I have misinterpreted Harvey, a great many of his contemporaries misinterpreted him in the same way. Mrs Whitteridge says nothing about Harvey's later deliberate rejection of the heart-sun-king analogy which he had so confidently used in 1628 (*H.*, p. 56; pp. 162–3).[17]

Mrs Whitteridge is however quite right to rebuke me for missing the Biblical sources of the doctrine that the soul is in the blood. Many friends had already pointed this out to me,[18] and my failure to notice it was inexcusable. The matter is, however, perhaps not quite so simple as Mrs Whitteridge makes out. The Vulgate version of Leviticus xvii. 14 is 'anima omnis carnis in sanguine est'. The Lollard Bibles sometimes translated 'anima' as 'soul'.[19] Coverdale, Lutheran-influenced,[20] translated Genesis

[14] Ross, *Arcana microcosmi* (1652), pp. 230–2; cf. *H.*, p. 56 (pp. 162–3 in this volume).

[15] J. de Back, *The Discourse of the Heart* (London, 1673), p. 47. To the references given at *H.*, p. 66 n. 67 (p. 174 n. 67), add sig. I 4, pp. 4–5, 82.

[16] R. Descartes, *Discours de la Méthode* (1637), cinquième partie; *Correspondance*, eds C. Adam et G. Milhaud (Paris, 1936–63), iii, p. 177 (to Mersenne, 9 Feb. 1639).

[17] When I said that Harvey's 1628 title, *Exercitatio anatomica de motu cordis et sanguinis in animalibus* 'concealed rather than advertised the contents' (*H.*, pp. 65–6, p. 173; *W.*, p. 106, p. 184), I meant what I said. Surely none of Harvey's contemporaries would have thought there was anything novel in the *motion* of the blood? The novelty lay in the nature of the motion.

[18] I am particularly grateful to Miss Beryl Smalley, who also pointed out that Aristotle referred to the doctrine in *De anima*, i. 2, attributing it to Critias and other philosophers.

[19] J. Forshall and Sir F. Madden (eds), *Wycliffe's Bible* (Oxford, 1850), 4 vols (Leviticus xvii. 14); C. Lindberg (ed.), *MS. Bodley 959* (Stockholm, 1959–63), 3 vols (Leviticus xvii. 14, Deuteronomy xii. 23).

[20] Alexander Ross described the mortalist doctrines of some 'sects sprung

ix. 4: 'the blood of you wherein your soul is'; and Leviticus xvii. 11: 'the soul of the body is in the blood'. These unorthodoxies were hastily corrected four years later in the Great Bible of 1539, and in all subsequent English Bibles 'anima' becomes 'life'. But Servetus cited the texts from Genesis, Leviticus and Deuteronomy xii. 23 in support of his mortalism.[21] Descartes, who quoted these texts to prove his own orthodoxy, had to argue that they applied exclusively to animals, not to human beings.[22] Harvey's friend Thomas Hobbes in 1651 translated Deuteronomy xii. 23 as 'Eat not the blood, for the blood is the soul, that is the life'; and went on to use the passage to support his view that the soul could not be an incorporeal substance.[23] So contemporaries were not unaware of the unorthodox possibilities of these texts.

In his 1616 lectures Harvey declared 'the soul is in the blood'. So far as I know he did not express this so clearly in print until 1651. (Mrs Whitteridge refers to the presence of the doctrine in the *De motu cordis*, but gives no reference—*W*., p. 108; p. 187). Does Harvey always observe as clearly as Mrs Whitteridge suggests a distinction between the two propositions—'the soul is in the blood' (orthodox) and 'the soul is the blood' (heretical)? Servetus himself failed to distinguish: Mrs Whitteridge translates him as saying 'the soul is in the blood and the blood itself the very soul'.[24] The passages from Harvey which Mrs Whitteridge and I quote (*W*., p. 107; pp. 185–6; *H*., pp. 55–6, 61–2; pp. 161–3, 169–70) do not all seem to me unambiguously on her side, though some clearly are. But John Collop, who *did* believe that the blood was the soul, certainly learnt the doctrine from Harvey (*H*., p. 62; p. 169).

Collop is relevant to my main point about the new and stimulating intellectual atmosphere of the interregnum. In the 1590s the defeat of the Spanish Armada and the victories of the Dutch made some protestant Englishmen feel secure enough to re-evaluate the heritage of popery, with fewer inhibitions than when

---

out of Lutheranism' (*A View of all the Religions in the World*, London, 1655, p. 231). Cf. *H*., p. 62 n. 46, p. 169 n. 46.

[21] C. D. O'Malley, *Michael Servetus* (Philadelphia, 1953), pp. 202–6.

[22] Descartes, *Correspondance*, ii, p. 7.

[23] T. Hobbes, *Leviathan* (Everyman edn), p. 337.

[24] Whitteridge, *op. cit.*, pp. xxxix–xl.

England had been in mortal peril.[25] Similarly in the 1650s former Royalists had to accept that their opponents' doctrines had been justified by the God of Battles, and they too began to approach these doctrines with more open and receptive minds. Collop had been a far stauncher royalist than Harvey, and a far more Laudian enemy of the sectaries; yet in 1656 he described himself as a 'heretic in divinity, a heretic in philosophy, and in physic'.[26] Collop in fact modified his royalism very substantially in the 1650s, and advocated something like an ideological surrender by the Royalists.[27] Walter Charleton was another former royalist physician who wrote a treatise urging ideological disarmament on the intransigent exiles.[28] He too was a keen Harveian, who—unlike Hobbes— used Harvey's *De generatione* to demonstrate the incorporeality of the soul.[29]

A final point, only tangential to Mrs Whitteridge's contribution. Professor N. O. Brown, whose exciting psychoanalytical interpretation of history, *Life against Death*, will be well known to readers of *Past and Present*, reminds me that Hobbes compared the circulation of money in the artificial body of the commonwealth to the circulation of blood in the human body.[30] Now Hobbes went as far as the Harvey of 1628 in his emphasis on the supremacy of the heart, 'the fountain of all sense', 'the original of life'.[31] But he had read the *De generatione*, and he believed that the Bible said the blood was the soul.[32] For Hobbes the blood, 'circulating, nourisheth by the way every member of the body of man'.[33] Was the circulating currency the soul of the body politic? This would fit neatly the view that Hobbes thought of his commonwealth as an essentially bourgeois affair, an extrapolation from the

[25] See my *Society and Puritanism in Pre-Revolutionary England* (London, 1964), pp. 501–6.
[26] *The Poems of John Collop*, ed. C. Hilberry (Madison, 1962), pp. 5–6, 9–10, 8.
[27] *Ibid.*, p. 75.
[28] W. Charleton, *The Immortality of the Human Soul* (London, 1657), *passim*.
[29] *Ibid.*, pp. 183–5. I owe this point to Mr P. Rattansi.
[30] Hobbes, *Leviathan*, pp. 133–4.
[31] Hobbes, *English Works*, ed. Sir W. Molesworth (London, 1839), i, pp. 392, 406.
[32] *Ibid.*, p. viii; cf. n. 23 above.
[33] *Leviathan*, p. 133.

capitalist society which he saw growing up around him.[34] What then would be the relation of the sovereign to this soul? For Hobbes described the sovereign as the 'public soul, giving life and motion to the commonwealth', and jeered at the idea that there might be more than one soul in a body.[35] With anyone less exemplary in his consistency than Hobbes, it would be fanciful to press the argument from analogy. But with Hobbes one never knows.

[34] C. B. Macpherson, *The Political Theory of Possessive Individualism: Hobbes to Locke* (Oxford, 1962), chap, 2, *passim*; see also my essay on Hobbes in *Puritanism and Revolution* (London, 1958), pp. 278–83. Harrington thought that 'Trades and Mysterys' fed the veins of Oceana, and that the Council of Trade was 'the *Vena Porta* of this Nation'. Parliament was the heart which 'sucks in, and spouts forth the vital Blood of *Oceana* by a perpetual circulation' (J. Harrington, *The Oceana and Other Works* (London, 1737), pp. 127–8, 161).
[35] *Leviathan*, pp. 1, 174, 178.

XVI

SCIENCE AND RELIGION IN SEVENTEENTH-CENTURY ENGLAND*

S. F. Mason

The growth of a scientific movement in early modern England has been ascribed to a variety of factors.[1] The most important of these, susceptible to historical analysis, were the economic stimulus afforded by new technical problems encountered in the fields of industry, navigation, and war,[2] and the religious drive of the Puritans towards the performance of 'good works', amongst which were included the useful applications of science.[3] However, such factors, being essentially of a practical character, account satisfactorily only for the particular sciences opened up during the sixteenth and seventeenth centuries, notably magnetism, mechanics and astronomy, but not for the structure and the pattern of the new theories, such as the heliocentric system of the world, or the theory of the circulation of the blood. Different forces were at work shaping the new theories of the early modern sciences, namely the ideological movements of the sixteenth and seventeenth centuries, of which the theology of Calvin and his followers was perhaps the most important in England. The elements common to the new theology and the new science were not perceived for some time. The medieval view of the world had been composed of a theology and a natural philosophy that were closely integrated.

* From no. 3 (Feb. 1953).
[1] G. N. Clark, *Science and Social Welfare in the Age of Newton* (Oxford, 1937), pp. 60–91.
[2] B. Hessen, 'The social and economic roots of Newton's *Principia*', in N. Bukharin (ed.), *Science at the Crossroads* (London, 1931), pp. 149–92.
[3] R. K. Merton, 'Science, technology and society in seventeenth century England', *Osiris*, iv (1938), p. 360.

It was overthrown only in a piecemeal fashion, on the one hand by the protestant reformers who attacked the theological aspects, and on the other by the scientists who controverted the cosmological features. However it is possible to discern that the criticisms of the Calvinists and of the scientists proceeded along lines which bore some similarity one to the other, and the congruence between them was recognized in England during the second quarter of the seventeenth century. Such an eventuality is perhaps to be expected, since both Calvinism and early modern science, separately, have been connected with that single, but many-sided, social movement, the rise of capitalism.

At first scientific activity in England centred largely round the new navigational problems met by the geographical explorers, and the traditional problems of keeping accounts, calendar making, surveying, and military engineering which had come down from the civilizations of antiquity. Science, in fact, was closely connected with mercantile enterprise throughout the sixteenth century. The mathematicians, Robert Recorde (c. 1510–58) and John Dee (1527–1608), for example, were technical advisers to the Muscovy Company and the Cathay Voyagers, whilst merchants promoted science through the sponsoring of mathematical lecture ships and the translation of scientific works.[4] Most important in this connection was Gresham College, set up in 1597 by the Company of Mercers and the Mayor and Aldermen of London with money and property bequeathed by the Elizabethan financier, Sir Thomas Gresham (1519–79). In his will Gresham had specified that three of the seven chairs at the College should be devoted to scientific subjects, and he had laid it down that the astronomy professor in particular should devote a considerable proportion of his time to the teaching of navigational science.[5]

Gresham College was the main centre of scientific activity in England during the first half of the seventeenth century, English science still being connected primarily with navigational and other mercantile problems. The first Gresham professor of geometry, Henry Briggs (1561–1630), was himself a member of the Virginia

---

[4] E. G. R. Taylor, *Tudor Geography 1485–1583* (London, 1930), pp. 24–7; —, *Late Tudor and Early Stuart Geography 1583–1650* (London, 1943), pp. 29–30.
[5] J. Ward, *The Lives of the Professors of Gresham College* (London, 1740), p. 19 ff.

Company, and he and his colleagues, and their immediate successors, were associated with a group of ship-wrights and navigators
who met at the house of John Wells and his son, the Keepers of
H.M. Naval Stores at Deptford during the first half of the seventeenth century.[6] However, during this period industrial and ideological problems came to interest English scientists more and
more, a trend which became conspicuous first in the *De magnete*
(1600) of William Gilbert of Colchester, physician to Elizabeth I.
Gilbert devoted one tenth of his work to cosmological theory,
and another tenth to the mining, smelting, and fashioning of iron,
whilst a quarter of the book was taken up with navigation and
nautical instruments, and just over a half with his work on magnetism.[7] After Gilbert, Francis Bacon stressed even more the value
of science for the advancement of industry and the building up of
a new world-view,[8] notably in his *Novum Organum* (1620).

During the same period English science became associated to
an increasing degree with the puritan movement.[9] The Gresham
professor of astronomy, Henry Gellibrand (1597–1636) was
arrested in 1631 for bringing out an almanac which omitted the
list of Catholic saints and martyrs usually included in such works,
and his successor, Samuel Foster (d. 1652) was ejected from his
chair for refusing to kneel at the communion table.[10] With the
events leading to the outbreak of the Civil War, Foster was reinstated, and Gresham College became the meeting place of a
group of scientists terming themselves the 'Philosophical College',
an organization which was the immediate precursor of the Royal
Society. Besides Foster, the 'College' included the Gresham professor of medicine, Jonathan Goddard (1617–75) who was Cromwell's physician, and a mathematician, John Wallis (1616–1703),
who decoded royalist ciphers during the Civil War, whilst the
leader of the group was the puritan divine, John Wilkins (1614–72)
who later became Cromwell's brother-in-law, and who at the:

[6] F. R. Johnson, 'Gresham College: precursor of the Royal Society',
Jour. Hist. Ideas, i (1940), pp. 413–38.
[7] E. Zilsel, 'The origins of William Gilbert's scientific method', *ibid.*, ii
(1941), pp. 1–32.
[8] B. Farrington, *Francis Bacon: Philosopher of Industrial Science* (London,
1951).
[9] D. Stimson, 'Puritanism and the new philosophy in seventeenth
century England', *Bull. Inst. Hist. Med.*, iii (1935), pp. 321–34.
[10] J. Ward, *op. cit.*, pp. 82–3, and *Dict. Nat. Biog.*

time was chaplain to the Prince Elector of the Palatinate, then the candidate of the Parliamentary party for the English throne. Wilkins did much to promote the application, dissemination, and organization of science in mid-seventeenth-century England, advocating in 1648 the study of mechanics 'for such gentlemen as employ their estates in those chargeable adventures of Drayning, Mines, Cole-pits, etc.'[11] He gathered round him an important group of science students when he was intruded into Oxford by the Commonwealth in 1649, and became the first secretary to the Royal Society at its foundation in 1660.[12] Wilkins was also one of the first to perceive the congruity between Calvinist theology and the new theories of modern science, a relationship which he endeavoured to consolidate and make explicit.

The *leit-motif* of the medieval view of the world, to which both the Reformers and the early modern scientists had taken exception, was the concept of hierarchy. This concept was rooted in the idea that the world was peopled by a graded chain of beings, stretching down from the Deity in the Empyrean heaven at the periphery of the universe, through the hierarchies of angelic beings inhabiting the nine heavenly spheres concentric with the earth, to the ranks of men, animals, and plants, of the base terrestrial sphere at the centre of the cosmic system.[13] A sharp qualitative distinction was drawn between the entities of the terrestrial and celestial domains of the universe. In particular, the natural motions of bodies composed of the four terrestrial elements were rectilinear, such motions having a beginning and an end like all terrestrial phenomena, whilst the natural motions of the heavenly bodies, which were composed of a more perfect fifth element, were circular, as motion in a circle was noble and eternal. According to the ancient mechanics, the constant action of a moving force was required to keep a body in motion, and an important integration of ancient natural philosophy with early Christian theology had taken place through the identification of the movers of the heavenly bodies with the angelic beings mentioned in the Scriptures. Pseudo-

11 J. Wilkins, *Mathematicall Magick* (London, 1648), sig. A4v.
12 M. Ornstein, *The Role of Scientific Societies in the Seventeenth Century* (Chicago, 1928), pp. 96–106.
13 See A. O. Lovejoy, *The Great Chain of Being* (Cambridge, Mass., 1936), for the history of the idea, and E. M. W. Tillyard, *The Elizabethan World Picture* (London, 1943) for the late medieval version.

Dionysius in the fifth century had arranged these angelic beings into a hierarchy of nine orders,[14] and it was generally accepted by the medieval schoolmen that these orders were the motors of the nine heavenly spheres.[15] In such a view of the world, the government of the universe was thought to be such that a given creature had dominion over the others below it in the scale of beings, whilst it served those above it in the scale.[16]

The Calvinists in theology and the astronomers in science reacted against this conception that the universe was hierarchically ordered. Pseudo-Dionysius, by means of his celestial hierarchy of angelic beings, had justified the existence of the ecclesiastical hierarchy of Church government on earth, an organization to which Calvin took the strongest exception.[17]

> To the government thus constituted some gave the name of Hierarchy—a name, in my opinion, improper, certainly one not used by Scripture. For the Holy Spirit designed to provide that no one should dream of primacy or domination in regard to the government of the Church.

To the justifications offered by Pseudo-Dionysius Calvin replied that there was no 'ground for subtle philosophical comparisons between the celestial and earthly hierarchy',[18] and he averred that man could not know whether the angelic beings were ordered by rank or not.[19] In formulating a positive point of view on these matters, Calvin tended to minimize the role of the angelic beings in the government of the universe and to assign to the Deity a more absolute and direct control over His creatures. Speaking of the relation between God and the angelic beings, Calvin affirmed:[20]

> Whenever he pleases, he passes them by, and performs his own work by a single nod: so far are they from relieving him of any difficulty.

[14] Dionysius, *Works*, trans. J. Parker (Oxford and London, 1897–9), ii, p. 22.
[15] P. Duhem, *Le Système du Monde*, 10 vols (Paris, 1913–59), v, chaps 10–12, pp. 404–559.
[16] St Thomas Aquinas, *Summa contra gentiles*, trans. by members of the Dominican Order, 4 vols (London, 1923–9), iii, pt 1, chaps 78–82, pp. 195–207.
[17] J. Calvin, *The Institutes of the Christian Religion*, trans. H. Beveridge (Edinburgh, 1863), ii, p. 330.
[18] *Ibid.*, ii, p. 360. [19] *Ibid.*, i, p. 144. [20] *Ibid.*, i, p. 149.

Not only did the Deity govern the universe more directly, but also, according to Calvin, He had predetermined all events from the beginning.[21]

> we hold that God is the disposer and ruler of all things,— that from the remotest eternity, according to his own wisdom, he decreed what he was to do, and now by his power executes what he has decreed. Hence we maintain that, by his providence, not heaven and earth and inanimate creatures only, but also the counsels and wills of men are so governed as to move exactly in the course which he has destined.

Thus the workings of the Calvinist universe were orderly and fully predeterminate. As the puritan theologian, John Preston (1587–1628) put it: 'God alters no Law of nature'.[22] Miraculous happenings contravening the laws of nature were no longer to be expected, whilst the angelic beings lost their power, and ultimately their place, in the cosmic scheme. Such a development was regretted by some Protestants, but they admitted that it was the case. The Presbyterian, Richard Baxter (1615–91) remarked in a work published during the last year of his life:[23]

> It is a doleful Instance, of the effect of a perverse kind of opposition to Popery, and a running from one Extream to another, to note how little Sence most Protestants shew of the great Benefits that we receive by Angels: How seldom we hear them in publick or private, give thanks to God for their Ministry and Helps? And more seldom pray for it?

Baxter himself confessed that he had not come across many instances of the ministry of angelic beings; most of the stories he related were concerned with the activities of evil spirits. However, it seems that even the evil spiritual beings had disappeared from educated English opinion by this time, for John Aubrey (1626–97) tells us:[24]

> When I was a child, and so before the civill warres, the fashion was for old women and maydes to tell fabulous stories,

---

21 J. Calvin, The Institutes of the Christian Religion, i, p. 179.
22 J. Preston, The New Covenant, 5th edn (London, 1630), p. 46.
23 R. Baxter, The Certainty of the Worlds of Spirits (London, 1691), pp. 222–3.
24 J. Aubrey, Brief Lives, ed. A. Clark (Oxford, 1898), ii, p. 318.

night-times, and of sprights and walking of ghosts, etc. This was derived downe from mother to daughter, etc, from the monkish ballance, which upheld holy Church: for the divines say 'Deny spirits, and you are an atheist.' When the warres came, and with them liberty of conscience and liberty of inquisition, the phantomes vanish.

Some doubts concerning the existence of spiritual beings appear to have been raised before the Civil Wars, for Thomas Browne (1605–82) writing about 1635, remarked that it was a riddle to him 'how so many learned heads should so far forget their Metaphysicks, and destroy the ladder and scale of creatures, as to question the existence of Spirits'.[25]

The removal of the angelic beings from the government of the universe in Calvinist theology was indeed a criticism of the idea that the universe was peopled by a graded scale of creatures, or rather it was a criticism of the concept of hierarchy which was the kernel of the idea. The Deity no longer ruled the universe by delegating His powers to a hierarchy of spiritual beings, each with a degree of authority which decreased as the scale was descended, but now He governed directly as an Absolute Power by means of decrees decided upon at the beginning. These decrees were nothing other than the laws of nature, the theological doctrine of predestination thus preparing the way for the philosophy of mechanical determinism. It is of interest to note that both the concept and the term, 'the laws of nature', were first used consistently by Descartes, who also generalized the notion that all material entities were mechanical contrivances, and thus were of the same qualitative nature. For Descartes, the Deity in the beginning had created matter and motion, and thereafter the universe was governed by the 'laws established in Nature by God', namely the laws of mechanics.[26] According to the historian of the idea of 'laws of nature', the use of the concept derived from the hypostatization into the cosmic realm of the earthly rule through statute law developed by the absolute monarchs of the

[25] Thomas Browne, *The Religio Medici and other writings*, Everyman edn (London, 1947), p. 34.
[26] R. Descartes, *A Discourse on Method*, Everyman edn (London, 1946), p. 33.

sixteenth and seventeenth centuries.[27] 'It is not a mere chance', wrote Zilsel, 'that the Cartesian idea of God, the legislator of the universe, developed forty years after Bodin's theory of sovereignty.' Perhaps it is also not a matter of chance that, some forty years before Bodin, Calvin was working towards a conception of God as the lawgiver of the universe, an Absolute Ruler who exercised His power directly, not through the mediacy of subordinate spiritual beings.

Whilst the Calvinists in theology were moving away from the hierarchical conception of the government of the universe towards an absolutist theory of cosmic rule, the early modern scientists were effecting a not dissimilar transformation in natural philosophy. Copernicus (1473–1543) whose heliocentric system of the world was published in 1543, rejected, implicitly at least, the gradation of the elements, for he assigned to the earth and its four elements that circularity of motion which hitherto had been the prerogative of celestial matter. He further emphasized the similarity of the earth to the other planets by investing the heavenly bodies with the property of gravity which previously had been considered to be peculiar to the earth. Again, according to his pupil Rheticus, Copernicus rejected the hierarchical conception that the higher celestial spheres influenced the motions of the lower:[28]

in the hypotheses of my teacher, . . . the sphere of each planet advances uniformly with the motion assigned to it by nature and completes its period without being forced into any inequality by the power of a higher sphere.

In the stead of the medieval view Copernicus advanced the conception that the sun had an absolute rule over the solar system:[29]

In the middle of all sits Sun enthroned. In this most beautiful temple could we place this luminary in any better position

---

[27] E. Zilsel, 'The genesis of the concept of physical law', *Philosophical Review*, li (1942), p. 278.

[28] Rheticus, *Narratio Prima*, trans. E. Rosen, in *Three Copernican Treatises* (New York, 1939), p. 146.

[29] Copernicus, *De Revolutionibus*, Bk I, chap. 10, trans. J. F. Dobson and S. Brodetsky, *Occasional Notes*, Roy. Astronomical Society, vol. ii, no. 10 (London, 1947), p. 19.

from which he can illuminate the whole at once? He is rightly called the Lamp, the Mind, the Ruler of the Universe ... So the Sun sits as upon a royal throne ruling his children the planets which circle round him.

In all the important new systems of the world put forward during the sixteenth and seventeenth centuries the sun assumed a position of particular importance in the cosmic order. Such was the case even in the conservative system of Tycho Brahe (1546–1601) which supposed the earth to be immobile at the centre of the universe, as in the medieval scheme. Brahe wrote in 1582:[30]

> I think, that the celestial motions are disposed in such a manner that only the moon, and the sun, with the eighth sphere, the most distant of all, have the centre of their motions in the earth: the five other planets turn about the sun as round their Chief and King. ... Thus the Sun is the Rule and the End of all the rotations, and, like Apollo in the midst of the Muses, he rules alone the entire celestial harmony of the motions which surround him.

William Gilbert of Colchester adopted yet another system of the world, which was similar to Brahe's scheme save that the earth performed a diurnal spin upon its axis and was not immobile, but his cosmic values were identical with those of Copernicus. The sun, Gilbert thought, was the noblest body in the universe, 'as he causes the planets to advance in their courses', and served as the 'chief inciter of action in nature'.[31] The status of the earth was equal to that of the other heavenly bodies, for 'The earth's motion is performed with as little labor as the motions of the other heavenly bodies', wrote Gilbert, 'neither is it inferior in dignity to some of these.'[32] In rejecting the concept of hierarchy, Gilbert seems to have sensed some connection between theology and natural philosophy.[33]

> The sun is not swept round by Mars' sphere (if sphere he have) and its motion, nor Mars by Jupiter's sphere, nor Jupiter by Saturn's: ... The higher do not tyrannize over

[30] Tycho Brahe, *Opera Omnia* (Frankfurt, 1648), Lib. II, pp. 95–6.
[31] William Gilbert, *De Magnete*, trans. P. Fleury Mottelay (London, 1893), p. 333.   [32] *Ibid.*, p. 339.   [33] *Ibid.*, p. 325.

the lower, for the heaven both of the philosopher and of the divine must be gentle, happy, tranquil, and not subject to changes.

With Johannes Kepler (1571–1630) who finally showed in 1609 that the earth and the planets moved in elliptical orbits round the sun, the connection became more explicit, for he located the domicile of the theological Ruler of the universe in the central power of the world of the natural philosophers:[34]

> The sun ... alone appears, by virtue of his dignity and power, suited for this motive duty [of propelling the planets] and worthy to become the home of God himself. ... For if the Germans elect him as Caesar who has most power in the whole empire, who would hesitate to confer the votes of the celestial motions on him who already has been administering all other movements and changes by the benefit of the light which is entirely his possession?

Such a change in cosmic evaluations from the hierarchical to the absolute was effected not only in the philosophy of the larger world, the macrocosm, but also in theory of the lesser world, the microcosm of the human frame. Here the Scientific Revolution and the Protestant Reformation found their most intimate and direct connection, for it was the Reformer, Michael Servetus (1509–53) who first put forward the theory of the lesser circulation of the blood in a small section of his theological work, *The Restoration of Christianity* (1553). The main intellectual obstacles in the medieval world view to the development of the theory of the circulation of the blood were the notion that only celestial matter could move naturally with a circular motion, all terrestrial motions, including that of the blood, being rectilinear, and the conception that the human body was governed by a hierarchy of three distinct organ systems, each with its own separate function. The vegetative life of man—nourishment and growth —had its seat in the liver, and was mediated by the dark red venous blood which ebbed to and fro in the veins under the impulse of a natural spirit. The animal function of muscular activity had its seat in the heart, and it was served by the bright red

[34] Quoted by E. A. Burtt, *The Metaphysical Foundations of Modern Physical Science* (London, 1949), p. 48.

arterial blood which ebbed and flowed in the arteries, driven by a vital spirit. Finally the nervous function of irritability and sensitivity had its seat in the brain, and it functioned through a fluid in the nerves which was impelled by an animal spirit (from the Latin *anima*, soul). Such a scheme was a particular manifestation of the general medieval view that the hierarchy of natural things was ordered triadically at every level—classes, orders, genera, species, and individuals within those species. All of the beings of the universe fell into one or other of three general classes—those that were wholly material, such as minerals, plants, and animals, those that were wholly spiritual, such as the angelic beings, and those that were mixed, namely human beings. Each group and sub-group divided triadically. Thus there were animals of the land, the sea, and the air, men of labour, men of prayer, and men of war, according to early medieval versions, or labourers, burghers, and nobles, with a separate ecclesiastical triadic hierarchy, according to late medieval versions,[35] whilst above mankind were three triadic orders of angelic beings, and at the head of the scale of all beings in the universe was the supreme Trinity.

In theology Servetus was a Unitarian, rejecting the doctrine of the Trinity. He denied that the Son was co-eternal with the Father, and he was of the view that the Holy Spirit was the breath of the Deity, a pneuma pervading the atmosphere and the whole world.[36] Just as he denied the supreme Trinity, so Servetus denied the general concept of triadic hierarchy. In particular, having had a medical training, Servetus criticized the application of the concept to physiological theory, claiming that the natural, vital, and animal spirits in a human body were one and the same, as 'In all of these there is the energy of the one spirit and of the light of God'.[37] Thus there were not two kinds of blood, the venous and the arterial, differentiated by the natural and the vital spirits, but only one blood containing a single spirit, since 'The vital is that which is communicated by the joins from the arteries to the veins in which it is called the natural'.[38] This single spirit of the blood was

---

[35] *La Théologie naturelle de Raymond Sebon*, trans. Montaigne (Paris, 1581), chap. 220, p. 262.
[36] R. Willis, *Servetus and Calvin* (London, 1877), p. 200.
[37] Michael Servetus, *Christianismi Restitutio* [Nuremburg, 1790], p. 169.
[38] *Ibid.*, p. 169.

the soul, or rather 'The soul itself is the blood', a view which
Servetus supported with texts from the Old Testament.[39]
Such a view implied that man was wholly mortal, the soul perishing with the body, and this heretical implication of his system was
charged against Servetus at his trial by Calvin. The medieval
doctrine of the three physiological fluids, the two bloods and the
nervous fluid, had been a great obstacle to the development of
the circulation theory, for any large scale movement of the blood
from the veins to the arteries and the arteries to the veins, which
the circulation theory required, would have involved the complete
mixing of what were regarded as quite different fluids, each with
their own separate function. The ideological innovations of
Servetus enabled him to suggest that the blood circulated from
the right to the left chamber of the heart through the lungs. In
the lungs the blood encountered the inspired air and was purified,
for 'by air God makes ruddy the blood', and the soul in the blood
participated in the Divine, as 'the Divine breath is in the air'.[40]

For Servetus the blood as vector of the soul had primacy of
place in the human body, and with the blood was associated the
heart as the prime organ: 'The heart is the first to live, the source
of heat in the middle of the body'.[41] Such a conception was
developed by William Harvey (1578–1657) physician to Charles I,
who generalized and proved experimentally the theory of the
circulation of the blood. Harvey wrote in 1628:[42]

> The heart . . . is the beginning of life; the sun of the
> microcosm, even as the sun in his turn might well be desig-
> nated the heart of the world; for it is the heart by whose
> virtue and pulse the blood is moved, perfected, made apt to
> nourish, and is preserved from corruption and coagulation
> . . . the heart, like the prince in a kingdom, in whose hands
> lie the chief and highest authority, rules over all; it is the
> original and foundation from which all power is derived, on
> which all power depends in the animal body.

Harvey constantly searched for examples of circular motion in
terrestrial bodies, of which the circulation of the blood was the
first, in order to give them parity of status with the presumed

[39] Michael Servetus, *Christianismi Restitutio* p. 170.
[40] *Ibid.*, pp. 169, 182.   [41] *Ibid.*, p. 169.
[42] William Harvey, *Works*, trans. R. Willis (London, 1847), pp. 47, 83.

superior celestial bodies. In his later work on generation (1651), Harvey suggested that the embryological development of the chick was circular, and that the succession of individuals constituting a species was a form of circular motion emulating the movements of the heavenly bodies:[43]

> And this is the round that makes the race of the common fowl eternal; now pullet, now egg, the series is continued in perpetuity; from frail and perishing individuals an immortal species is engendered. By these, and means like to these, do we see many inferior or terrestrial things brought to emulate the perpetuity of superior or celestial things.

Such re-evaluations in the theories of the microcosm of the human body and of the macrocosm of the world at large appear to have had an influence upon the metaphors and similes of majesty used at the period. It had been customary to compare a monarch in his realm to the mind in the body, or to the Primum Mobile governing the universe from above, but now the sun at the centre of the world, and the heart at the centre of the body, came in as the images and analogies of majesty. John Norden (1548–1626), in his *Christian Familiar Comfort* (1600) described Elizabeth I as the Primum Mobile of England,[44] and Francis Bacon too used the same analogy in his essay *On Sedition*.[45] But William Harvey dedicated his *De motu cordis* (1628) to Charles I as 'the sun of the world around him, the heart of the republic'[46] and when Louis XIV came of age in 1660 he was hailed, not as the Primum Mobile of France, but as *le roi soleil*.

The new cosmic evaluations also had an influence upon the theology of one of the protestant movements of the English Civil War period, the Mortalists, so termed because they held that the soul of man perished with his body. The most notable member of the sect was John Milton,[47] whilst the chief exponent of the mortalist theology was Richard Overton, a prominent figure in the Leveller movement. Overton held that the Deity must reside in the sun, since the scientists considered that the sun was the

[43] *Ibid.*, p. 285.
[44] J. Norden, *A Christian Familiar Comfort* (London, 1596), p. 59.
[45] F. Bacon, *Essays*, Everyman edn (London, 1939), p. 43.
[46] W. Harvey, *Works* (1847), p. 3.
[47] D. Saurat, *Milton: Man and Thinker* (London, 1946), p. 268 ff.

most exalted and powerful of the heavenly bodies. The Deity, Overton argued, 'ascended upward from the Earth into some part of the coelestiall bodies above ... therefore, without doubt he must be in the most excellent, glorious, and heavenly part thereof, which is the SUN, the most excellent peece of the whole Creation, the Epitome of Gods power, ... and according to the famous *Copernicus* and *Tycho Braheus*, it is highest in station to the whole Creation'.[48] The Mortalists' central doctrine that the soul of man perished with his body was supported by the view of Servetus, Harvey, and others, that the soul was itself the blood, a view which Overton quoted but did not draw upon extensively, discussing at greater length the idea that the soul was the sum total of man's faculties, those faculties perishing with the body. The doctrine that the soul of man perished with his body served to carry further the attack upon the concept of hierarchy which had been initiated by the Calvinists and the scientists. Calvin and the astronomers had questioned the existence of the celestial hierarchies but the Mortalists now came to doubt the reality of the terrestrial hierarchies of men, animals, and plants. If man were wholly mortal, then he did not differ essentially from the animals, Overton argued, for animals as well as man would ultimately rise again:[49]

> For all other *Creatures* as well as man shall be raised and delivered from Death at the Resurrection. . . . That which befalleth the sonnes of men, befalleth Beasts . . . as the one dyeth, so dyeth the other; yea they have all one breath, so that man hath no preheminence above a beast.

Thus Overton accorded the same status to all beings, though they were all subject to a single Absolute Power. Such a conception also pervaded Overton's political philosophy, the radical democratic individualism of the Leveller movement. Over and above individual men, though acting with their consent, was the power of parliament, 'chosen to work our deliverance, and to estate us in natural and just liberty agreeable to reason and common equity.'[50] Basing himself on the new mechanical philosophy, rather than the new reformed religion, and placing a greater emphasis

[48] R[ichard] O[verton], *Mans Mortallitie* (Amsterdam, 1643), p. 33.
[49] *Ibid.*, p. 50 and title page.
[50] Quoted by G. H. Sabine, *A History of Political Theory* (London, 1937), p. 484.

upon the sovereignty of the state power, Hobbes advanced the similar conception that human society consisted of atomic, self-moving individuals, by birth equal in their capacities, who had contracted to relinquish their autonomy in return for the protection of an absolute sovereign—a monarch or an assembly of governors—who controlled the great Leviathan of the state, 'that Mortal God, to which we owe under the Immortal God, our peace and defence'.[51] More radical political thinkers, such as the Diggers and the early Quakers, placed a greater emphasis upon the equality of all men and all beings, carrying the criticism of the concept of hierarchy to its ultimate conclusion within the framework of theology—pantheism. The Divine Absolute was merged into His creatures, to provide the communal sovereignty of egalitarian human society and the rational integument of the universe as a whole. 'The whole Creation of fire, water, Earth and Aire', wrote Gerrard Winstanley, 'and all the varieties of bodies made up thereof, is the cloathing of God'.[52] The Deity was a moving spirit, present in all things and in all men; 'He is the incomprehensible spirit, Reason'.[53] There was no distinction between Man and God,—'he that hath the same Spirit that raised up Jesus Christ, is equal with God',[54] as George Fox put it—and a fortiori there should be no gradations between man and man: 'None ought to be lords or landlords over another,' wrote Winstanley, 'but the earth is free for every son and daughter of mankind to live free upon.'[55]

Generally speaking, criticism of the medieval concept of hierarchy amongst men who were influential in politics, religion, or science, did not proceed during the seventeenth century beyond the idea of cosmic absolutism. Pantheism and the mechanical philosophy were integrated by Spinoza (1632–77) who was associated with the Dutch Collegiants, a sect similar to the English Quakers, but his system did not exert much influence until the nineteenth century. Even within the limitations of the idea of cosmic absolutism, the mortalist synthesis of theology with natural philosophy did not command an extensive following,

[51] Sabine, *Political Theory*, p. 468.
[52] G. Winstanley, *Works*, ed. G. H. Sabine (Ithaca, New York, 1941), p. 451.   [53] *Ibid.*, p. 107.
[54] G. Fox, *Saul's Errand to Damascus* (London, 1653), p. 8.
[55] Sabine, *Political Theory*, p. 491.

though some of the mortalist doctrines enjoyed a certain vogue during the seventeenth century,[56] and they were perpetuated, with minor modifications, by the Christadelphian sect.[57] The early modern astronomers and the Mortalists adhered to the view, which had been generally accepted during the middle ages, that there was but one world, our own solar system, which was bounded by the fixed stars. However, it came to be accepted, notably through Giordano Bruno (1548–1600), that each star was a sun surrounded by planets, which were inhabited by creatures similar to those on earth, and it was this doctrine of the plurality of worlds which helped to bring together the theories of early modern science and Calvinist theology as developed by the Puritans in England. The doctrine, even in its most restricted form wherein it was supposed that the planets of our solar system or the moon alone were inhabited, carried implications which ran counter to the concept of hierarchy, for it gave weight to the notion that the earth and the heavenly bodies were of the same qualitative nature, and were not graded in status, since they supported the same creatures. Through arrogance, wrote Montaigne, man 'dareth imaginarily place himselfe above the circle of the Moone, and reduce heaven under his feet. It is through the vanity of the same imagination that he dare equall himselfe to God, that he ascribeth divine conditions unto himselfe, that he selecteth and separateth himselfe from out the ranke of other creatures.'[58] In its extended form, wherein it was supposed that there was an infinity of inhabited worlds in the universe, the doctrine tended to assign the same status to all finite existents. This was one of the aspects of the infinite which led to Pascal's inquietude:[59]

> In comparison with all these Infinites all finites are equal, and I see no reason for fixing our imagination on one more than on another. The only comparison which we make of ourselves to the finite is painful to us.

In England during the 1630s John Wilkins attempted to overcome the greatest single obstacle to the union of science and

[56] R. Fludd, *Mosaicall Philosophy* (London, 1659), p. 66. J. B. van Helmont, *Oriatrike*, trans. J. Chandler (London, 1662), p. 796.
[57] Saurat, *op. cit.*, p. 268 ff.
[58] Montaigne, *Essays*, Everyman edn, 3 vols (London, 1938), ii, p. 142.
[59] Pascal, *Pensées*, Everyman edn (London, 1931), p. 20.

Calvinist theology—the early protestant practice of interpreting the Scriptures literally—and to integrate his science with his theology by means of the doctrine of the plurality of worlds. In 1638 he published his *Discovery of a New World*, a work endeavouring to prove that there was another world of animate and rational creatures on the moon. Here he had no texts from Scripture against him, indeed some were in his favour, but even these he rejected.[60] Wilkins did not defend the new Copernican theory in this work, but he attempted to establish the doctrines which had derived from that theory, or which had become ancillary to it. Quoting the work of the astronomers, who had shown that there were spots on the face of the sun, and mountains and apparently seas on the moon, Wilkins affirmed, 'That the Heavens do not consist of any such Pure matter, which can Priviledg them from the like Change and Corruption, as these Inferiour Bodies are Liable unto'.[61] Since the moon in particular resembled the earth, 'we may Guess in the General that there are some Inhabitants in that Plannet: for why else did Providence Furnish that place with all such Conveaniences of Habitation'.[62] A similar consequence followed, Wilkins noted, from the theory adopted by the followers of Copernicus: 'Now if our Earth were one of the Plannets, (as it is according to them) then why may not another of the Plannets be an Earth'.[63]

Wilkins' next work, *A Discourse Concerning a New Plannet* (1640), was a full defence of the Copernican theory. Much of the book, about half of it in fact, attempted to reconcile the Copernican theory with the Biblical texts which seemed to favour the idea of the diurnal motion of the heavens, or to oppose the theory of the motion of the earth. Here again Wilkins rejected the practice of interpreting the Scriptures literally, declaring that the Bible was not a philosophical treatise but a work intended for the capacity of the popular mind. In bringing together his science and his theology, Wilkins applied Calvin's thesis that the angelic beings were superfluous in the government of the universe, to the particular case of the motions of the heavenly bodies. It was unreasonable of the schoolmen, wrote Wilkins, 'who make the Faculty, whereby the Angels move the Orbs, to be the very same

[60] J. Wilkins, *A Discovery of a New World*, 4th edn (London, 1684), Bk I, p. 145.
[61] *Ibid.*, Bk I, p. 31.   [62] *Ibid*, Bk I, p. 144.   [63] *Ibid.*, Bk I, p. 70.

with their Understandings and Will ... Since it were then a needless thing for Providence to have appointed Angels unto this business, which might have been done as well by the only Will of God.'[64] Wilkins' argument here exemplified his general contention that nature was essentially economical and frugal in her operations. It was 'agreeable to the Wisdom of Providence,' Wilkins felt, that Nature 'does never use any tedious difficult means, to perform that which may as well be accomplished by shorter and easier ways.'[65] Such a notion, with its Calvinist flavour, was of particular importance in modern science, providing the root concept of the various 'minimum', and 'conservation' principles governing motion and change in nature, which were developed, often with theological justifications, by the scientists of the seventeenth and eighteenth centuries.[66] There had been approaches towards the idea during the middle ages, notably in the case of Occam's razor principle, but such approaches for the most part had remained comparatively fruitless. While change took place by routes of minimum effort in nature, according to Wilkins, the world was peopled by a large, if not a maximum diversity of beings. 'There may be many other Species of Creatures beside those that are already known in the World,' he wrote, '. . . 'Tis not Improbable that God might Create some of all Kinds, that so He might more Compleatly Glorifie himself in the Works of his Power and Wisdom.'[67] Such an idea was not specifically modern, for similar notions had been current in antiquity and the middle ages. The translator of a medieval theology, in arguing for the existence of a multiplicity of angelic beings, had expressed the idea in the following way: 'We must believe that the angels are there in marvellous and inconceivable numbers, because the honour of a king consists in the great crowd of his vassals, while his disgrace or shame consists in their paucity.'[68] However the Deity of the seventeenth century was a more powerful being than the God of the middle ages, for He had created a plurality, or

[64] J. Wilkins, *A Discovery of a New World*, Bk II, *A Discourse Concerning a New Planet*, p. 159.
[65] *Ibid.*, Bk II, pp. 150–1.
[66] P. E. B. Jourdain, 'The principle of least action', *Monist*, xxii (1912), pp. 285–304, 414–59, and xxiii (1913), pp. 277–93.
[67] Wilkins, *Discovery*, Bk I, p. 146.
[68] *La Théologie naturelle de Dom. Raymon Sebon . . . mise premièrement de Latin en François par Ian Martin* (Paris, 1566), Bk VI, p. 155b.

even an infinity of similar worlds, not just one, and the maximum possible diversity of creatures, not merely a large number.[69] These creatures were no longer connected by relations of domination and servitude, for under the Divine Absolute they had some degree of autonomy, deriving their self-government from an inner source. In the motions of bodies, and in her operations generally, wrote Wilkins, 'Nature does commonly make use of some inward Principle'.[70] Such a world, stocked to the maximum capacity with thrifty, self-moving beings, whose actions were predetermined by the cosmic laws laid down by the Deity in the beginning, came to be considered the best and most perfect of all possible worlds. 'The most sagacious man', wrote Wilkins after the Restoration, when he became bishop of Chester, 'is not able to find out any blot or error in this great Volume of the World, as if any thing in it had been an imperfect essay at the first, such as afterwards stood in need of mending: But *all things continue as they were from the beginning of the Creation*'.[71] Such a notion, which was very popular in the late seventeenth and early eighteenth centuries, implied, as Pope put it, that 'Whatever is, is right', and that any possible change must be, of necessity, for the worse.[72] Thus it was that the new world view constructed by the puritan scientists of the mid-seventeenth century served as a basis for the cosmic toryism of the literary theologians of the later Stuart period.

The early works of Wilkins, the *Discovery* (1638) and the *Discourse* (1640) were directed in particular against the Anglican, Alexander Ross (1591–1654), one of Charles I's chaplains, who with Biblical texts, had attacked the new science and defended the medieval cosmology in his *Commentum de terrae motu* (1634). In this work Ross had attacked not only scientific, but also theological criticism of the medieval cosmology, objecting in particular to a book published in 1625 by Nathanael Carpenter (1589–1628), who had made light of the idea that hierarchies of angelic beings propelled the heavenly bodies round their courses, but who had

[69] Lovejoy, *op. cit.*, chaps 4–6, pp. 99–208.
[70] Wilkins, *Discovery*, Bk II, p. 158.
[71] J. Wilkins, *Of the Principles and Duties of Natural Religion*, 4th edn (London, 1699), p. 78.
[72] B. Willey, *The Eighteenth Century Background* (London, 1946), chap. 3, pp. 43–56.

refused to accept the Copernican theory, mainly on the grounds that it conflicted with the Scriptures.[73] After the publication of Wilkins's books, Ross returned to the attack in *The New Planet No Planet* (1646), taking his stand again on the ground of Scriptural literalism. Ross, in fact, conducted a last-line defence against many criticisms of the medieval world-view in mid-seventeenth-century England, and counter-attacked against the new concept of cosmic absolutism. He assailed Hobbes in the *Leviathan drawne out with a Hooke* (1653), quarrelled with the mechanical philosophy of Ralegh's historiography in *Raleighs errors corrected* (n. d.), and in two further works (1645 and 1651) Ross even took the conservative Thomas Browne to task for criticizing the 'Vulgar Errors' of the ancients.

After the period of the Civil Wars and the Commonwealth, the Bible and the works of the ancient and medieval philosophers were no longer, in England, taken as authoritative upon matters relating to the structure of the world. Even the makers of popular almanacs generally adopted the Copernican system of the world[74] and critics of science took pains to deny, for fear of ridicule, that they believed in the medieval world system.[75] When Newton's *Principia* appeared in 1687, it encountered little religious opposition in England, for Wilkins and the men of his generation had borne the brunt of the Anglican resistance to science, and had made apparent the elements common to the new science and the new religion. The physicotheological system of Newton, like its immediate predecessors, enshrined the concept of cosmic absolutism, although, in the Newtonian system, the Deity was more of a privileged observer of the universe than a privileged ruler. If the universe were governed entirely by laws laid down in the beginning, then there was no need for Divine intervention in the day-to-day running of the world. Calvin had not discussed such an implication, and he had supposed the Deity to be both the legislator and active ruler of the universe. However, the English Puritans of the mid-seventeenth century developed the idea latent in Calvin's teachings that the Deity was bound by his own ordi-

[73] G. McColley, 'The Ross-Wilkins controversy', *Annals of Science*, iii (1938), pp. 153–89; p. 180.
[74] M. Nicolson, 'English Almanacks and the "New Astronomy" ', *ibid.*, iv (1939), pp. 1–33.
[75] R. F. Jones, *Ancients and Moderns* (St Louis, 1936), chap. 9.

nances, so that God could not do 'that which is contrary to the Rule of Nature'.[76] Thus the Deity came to be considered as the constitutional Head of the cosmic system rather than the absolute Ruler of the universe. As the Independent theologian, Thomas Goodwin (1600–80), put it: 'Men do with God as the Venetians do with their duke. They set him up in all matters of state-attendance as a sovereign prince, but level his power so low that he is no more than an ordinary senator'.[77] In the systems of the natural philosophers the role of the Deity was changed similarly from that of the Ruler of the universe to that of the Observer of cosmic events. Descartes had presumed that the *concours ordinaire* of the Deity was necessary to the preservation of the universe as it is from instant to instant, but Newton found only a few defects in the machine of the universe which required the constant attention of an omnipresent cosmic engineer, and soon it was demonstrated that the Newtonian world was entirely self-running and self-repairing. However, the idea that there was, or could be, a single privileged observer in the universe, an idea which was part of the early protestant-scientific theory of cosmic absolutism, lived on until the twentieth century when the cosmological principle that all observers in the universe are equivalent was found to be a more satisfactory basis for physical theory.

[76] Quoted by Perry Miller, *The New England Mind* (New York, 1939), p. 226.
[77] Thomas Goodwin, *Works*, 11 vols (Edinburgh, 1861–65), vi, p. 507.

XVII

PURITANISM, CAPITALISM AND THE SCIENTIFIC REVOLUTION*

H. F. Kearney

The study of the Scientific Revolution of the seventeenth century reached some time ago the stage of sophistication when the historian was required to deal not with the 'facts' of Copernicus or Galileo but a variety of interpretations. For those seeking an explanation why the acceleration of scientific advance took place between 1540 and 1700, the choice is threefold. In the work of some historians, the role of individual genius is stressed as the decisive factor; with others, the evolutionary character of scientific development; or among the sociologically minded, the significance of the immediate social environment against which the discoveries took place. It would be easy to illustrate the differences between these interpretations by means of specially chosen examples, but it would be less misleading to suggest that among the leading historians of science, the distinction is mainly one of emphasis. All agree, for example, in recognizing the importance of the unique insight which is called genius; where they differ is in the varying significance which they attach to it. Butterfield, while stressing that the lightning of genius strikes unpredictably, would admit that some atmospheric conditions are more favourable to electrical disturbance than others. Marxist historians, on the other hand, find it difficult to ignore the personal role of Copernicus, Galileo and Newton, though they may argue that social forces would have filled any gap in the ranks. For the moment, however, it will be convenient to stress the differences between these various historical points of view.

* From no. 28 (July 1964).

Of those who emphasize the role of men of genius, the most outstanding are Butterfield, Koestler and Koyré.[1] Butterfield, for example, uses phrases like 'an epic adventure', 'a certain dynamic quality', 'a creative product of the west', 'a great episode in human experience', all of which hint at indefinable entities. He continually emphasizes the difficulty of putting on 'a new thinking cap', of breaking the bonds of education, habit and practical experience. Clearly, from this point of view, the Scientific Revolution is ultimately inexplicable; it could not have been predicted. Butterfield refers to the existence of a complicated set of conditions which existed only in Western Europe, such as the rise of the middle class or the influence of technology, but this background is only hinted at and barely sketched in. He also devotes considerable space to the medieval 'forerunners' of Galileo. But the main weight falls on the great men in the foreground. In Arthur Koestler's book *The Sleepwalkers*, to which Butterfield wrote an introduction, similar assumptions are made. Although it is written from a very personal point of view, it is essentially a sketch of three great individual thinkers, whose achievement was based upon an admixture of genius, insight, delusion and error and who were right for the wrong reasons. Alexander Koyré, the third member of this trio, regards the Scientific Revolution as almost the personal creation of a single man, Galileo. In their different ways, these three historians of ideas ultimately come down on the side of the great man in history, an interpretation for which there is a great deal to be said. As Lord Acton remarked in a somewhat different context, 'better one great man than a dozen immaculate historians'. The unique insight is the really decisive factor.

The first main alternative to this point of view is to be found in the work of historians such as Crombie and Clagett.[2] Both of them in a sense derive their inspiration from the work of Duhem, who, writing in the early part of this century, regarded the achievement of the faculty of arts at medieval Paris as an

---

[1] H. Butterfield, *The Origins of Modern Science 1300–1800* (London, 1950). A. Koestler, *The Sleepwalkers* (London, 1959). A. Koyré, *Études Galiléennes* (Paris, 1939).

[2] A. C. Crombie, *Augustine to Galileo* (London, 1952). M. Clagett, *The Science of Mechanics in the Middle Ages* (Madison, Wisconsin, 1959). See also the works of A. Maier cited in Clagett.

essential part of the story of modern science. Looked at in this way, the history of science takes on an evolutionary character. Galileo and company were not the absolute pioneers they believed themselves to be. They took off from a springboard, which their despised predecessors had erected. The dive into novelty was much less striking than it appeared to be at first glance, or, to use Butterfield's phrase, the task of putting on a new thinking cap was not quite so formidable. This interpretation has never lacked support in recent years, and in England it received striking reinforcement with the publication of Dijksterhuis's *The Mechanization of the World Picture*, and Randall's *The Career of Philosophy*.[3] These books, though very different in character, have one thing in common. They each adopt a much more sympathetic attitude towards Aristotelianism than is common in the general run of textbooks. In their view, the work of Aristotle, far from being an obstacle to the advance of science, was an essential ingredient in the recipe for success. Randall, whose work on Renaissance Italy is well known, puts forward this thesis most forcibly. He singles out the work of sixteenth-century Aristotelians such as Zabarella as of the highest importance. Galileo's work marked the take-off stage in the Scientific Revolution, but only because much intellectual capital had been already created by the patient under-rewarded labour of others.

In contrast to all this, the influence of sociological considerations indicated alternative theories, based upon the nature of seventeenth-century society. For some, such as R. K. Merton, the work of Weber suggested the existence of a close link between puritanism and scientific study.[4] This is a thesis which has recently come under heavy fire.[5] Merton also noted the importance of

---

[3] E. J. Dijksterhuis, *The Mechanization of the World Picture* (Oxford, 1961). J. H. Randall, *The Career of Philosophy* (New York, 1962).

[4] R. K. Merton, 'Puritanism, Pietism and science' in *Social Theory and Social Structure* (Chicago, 1957); see also ——, *Science, Technology and Society in Seventeenth Century England* (repr. New York, 1970). For a full discussion of the literature on this point, see T. K. Rabb, 'Puritanism and the rise of experimental science in England', *Jl of World History*, vii (1962), pp. 46–67. There is a good bibliography in the facsimile edition of Sprat, *History of the Royal Society*, ed. J. I. Cope and H. W. Jones (St Louis/London, 1958), p. xii.

[5] See especially L. S. Feuer, *The Scientific Intellectual* New York/London, 1963), as well as M. M. Knappen, *Tudor Puritanism* (Chicago, 1939);

technology, from the influence of which even so abstract a work as Newton's *Principia* was not immune. Others, such as Zilsel, sought the key to the rise of science in the alliance between the intellectual and the artisan, which took place only towards the end of the sixteenth century.[6] According to this view, scientific advance took place when the Renaissance studio and the workshop were brought together in fruitful conjunction. Marxist historians also considered that the rise of modern science must be explained by considering contemporary social changes. They have tended to follow the lead given by Engels in his letter to Starkenburg, written in 1894.[7] Engels wrote:

> If society has a technical need, that helps science forward more than ten universities. The whole of hydrostatics (Torricelli, etc.) was called forth by the necessity for regulating the mountain streams of Italy in the sixteenth and seventeenth centuries. We have only known anything reasonable about electricity since its technical applicability was discovered. But unfortunately it has become the custom in Germany to write the history of the sciences as if it had fallen from the skies.

Engels also goes on to make the point that there is no place for unique genius in the materialist interpretation of history. Great men such as Napoleon have their part to play but they are not unique. If Bonaparte had not existed, another man would have arisen to fill the social vacuum. By analogy, it may be expected that if Newton or Lavoisier had not existed their work would have been done by others. In this as in other sociological interpretations of the history of science, there is little if any scope for the unique, the fortuitous and the visionary.

With the publication of Mr Christopher Hill's book *The Century of Revolution* (1961), reinforced by his Ford Lectures given at Oxford in 1962,[8] a sociological interpretation of the

---

P. H. Kocher, *Science and Religion in Elizabethan England* (San Marino, 1953) and M. Curtis, *Oxford and Cambridge in Transition 1558-1642* (Oxford, 1959).

[6] E. Zilsel, 'The origins of William Gilbert's scientific method', repr. from *Jour. Hist. Ideas*, ii (1941), pp. 1-32, in *Roots of Scientific Thought*, eds P. Wiener and A. Noland (New York, 1957), pp. 219-50.

[7] K. Marx and F. Engels, *Selected Works* (London, 1950), ii, pp. 457-9.

[8] Published in abbreviated form in *The Listener* (May-July 1962). Published in full as *Intellectual Origins of the English Revolution* (London, 1965).

Scientific Revolution made its first real impact in the field of general English history, as distinct from specialist studies in the history of science or of literature. In Hill's work, science is treated as a general social phenomenon, analogous and related to the rise of puritanism and the rise of the bourgeoisie. Indeed, Hill regards science along with these as one of the causes of the Civil War. The 'causes' of the rise of science are to be sought in the state of English society at the time. Individual contributions by scientists such as Briggs and Gunter do not go unrecognized, but the main emphasis is upon sociological considerations. If geniuses do exist, they are essentially spokesmen for social movements and trends, which are more important than any single human being.

The great attraction of Hill's interpretation is that it makes the history of science part of general English history and one can easily appreciate why it has had such a favourable reception. It is expounded with great skill. It hangs together as a rational whole. Moreover, Hill is surely correct in thinking that now is the moment to offer explanation, rather than narrative. Nevertheless there are grounds for thinking that in many ways this interpretation carries simplicity to excess and imposes a rational framework more rigid than the complexity of the period will stand.

The central point round which Hill's interpretation develops is the figure of Francis Bacon. On this view, it was Bacon's *Advancement of Learning* and *Novum Organum* which provided a blueprint for the 'forward looking' merchants and artisans of early Stuart England. The self-taught, eager merchants and artisans sought to come to terms with the new astronomy of Copernicus and Galileo, increasingly rejected authority in Church and State and, optimistic for the future, found their spokesman in Francis Bacon, the prophet whom the court rejected. The court, the clergy and the universities looked to the past, accepted authority uncritically and were pessimistic about the possibility of progress. In the future Civil War, the Ancients were to face the Moderns in the field as they had done earlier in the study. 'The civil war', Hill tells us, 'was fought between rival schools of astronomy, between Parliamentarian heliocentrists and Royalist Ptolemaics.'[9]

In elaboration of this view Hill also maintains that Baconian-

---

[9] *The Listener*, 7 June 1962, p. 985. Cf. also Hill, *The Century of Revolution* (Edinburgh, 1961), p. 179.

ism existed before Bacon. He makes a good deal of the action of Sir Thomas Gresham, Elizabeth's adviser in economic matters, in leaving money to endow a college in London, which was to provide the institutional counterpart for Bacon's ideas. Gresham College, founded in 1597, was, it is stressed, under the control of the merchants, not the clergy. It aimed at providing useful knowledge; its expected clientele were to be artisans, seamen, craftsmen; for which reason some of its lectures were to be in the vernacular. It provided a contrast at every point with the clerically-dominated universities, catering for the gentry, based on a Latin curriculum perpetuating the authority of the ancients and exposed to control by the court. Under its first professors, Briggs, Gunter and Gellibrand, Gresham College became the centre of scientific advance as well as popularization. Meanwhile, the universities languished, monuments of the ancient regime. The future was bound up with the lay science of Gresham College, not with the universities.

Bacon's ideas, it is pointed out, also suggest a link between scientific radicalism and religious radicalism. Bacon's method is based on personal observation and personal experience. 'This highly individualistic approach compares with the Puritan demand for first-hand religious experience as against the traditions of men.' Bacon's mother was a Puritan. Pym and other leaders of the puritan party in the Commons invited Comenius over to England in 1641 in order to found a college on Baconian lines. It was only after 1640 that Bacon's writings were published on a wide scale. Most of the merchants who attended Gresham lectures were puritan in sympathy. There was 'an intimate connection between merchants and science'.[10] All in all, Hill has no doubts of the interconnection of the progressive forces of early Stuart England. Science was one of these and it was not surprising that the advance of science should speed up during the Interregnum when puritanism was in power.

There can be no doubt that Hill presents his case attractively and ably. He marshals his evidence imaginatively and writes in a persuasive prose. Nevertheless, I believe that it does not stand up to analysis.

Let us examine each of the key points of the argument in turn: Gresham College, the role of merchants and artisans in the history

[10] *The Listener*, 31 May 1962, p. 946.

of science, Baconian ideas, and the intellectual significance of puritanism and the Civil War.

I

Gresham College occupies a strategic position in the argument. Hill stresses several aspects: first, that it was a lay institution, distinct in kind from the clerically dominated universities; secondly, it was endowed by a merchant and controlled by merchants; thirdly, it provided up-to-date instruction in science in the vernacular for merchants and artisans. Finally he hints that the puritan connections of Gresham College were of some significance. The College seems to provide decisive evidence for his view that puritanism, modern science and the merchant-artisan groups are all interrelated.

Now it is indisputable that in Briggs, Gunter and Gellibrand, Gresham College possessed several distinguished scientists on its staff. But this should not lead too readily to the conclusion that the College was essentially scientific in character. Readers of F. R. Johnson's classic article on Gresham College might well draw this conclusion, but it would be mistaken.[11] In fact, Sir Thomas Gresham endowed an institution which closely resembled the traditional image of a university. It provided for instruction in the three major faculties of divinity, law and physic, and, in the junior faculties of arts, for music and rhetoric[12] as well as astronomy and geometry. If we concentrate our attention on the last two arts of the traditional *quadrivium*, we obtain a misleading impression of Gresham College. It was, in fact, much closer to Oxford and Cambridge in concept than to, say, a technical institute, such as the Casa de Contratación in Seville. When the University of Cambridge objected to its foundation, this was not a simple case of the outmoded attacking the up-to-date, of Ancients against Moderns; rather it was of one of the ancient universities

[11] F. R. Johnson, 'Gresham College: precursor of the Royal Society', repr. from *Jour. Hist. Ideas*, i (1940), pp. 413–38 in *Roots of Scientific Thought*, eds P. Wiener and A. Noland, pp. 328–53.

[12] It seems likely that Ben Jonson was assistant professor of rhetoric c. 1620. Cf. *Poems of Ben Jonson*, ed. G. B. Johnston (London, 1954), p. xxxiii.

scenting the danger to its monopoly of higher learning. Fear of the Great Wen, not defence of the Great Chain of Being, was the motive. The fact that the law taught at Gresham was Civil Law was of great significance, since this reinforces the suggestion that Oxford and Cambridge were the model. Common Law as taught at the Inns of Court was already catered for in London.[13]

Once Gresham College had been set up, the connection between it and the universities could hardly have been closer. It recruited its professors exclusively from the universities. It produced no alumni of its own. Many of its professors combined fellowships at Oxford and Cambridge with their posts at Gresham. Richard Holdsworth was a fellow of St John's College, Cambridge, while at the same time professor of divinity at Gresham, and did not resign his Gresham post when he was elected Master of Emmanuel. John Greaves continued to hold his fellowship at Merton despite his appointment to a Gresham chair in 1630. Peter Turner, who succeeded Briggs at Gresham in 1620, continued to hold his fellowship at Merton—if Briggs came to Greshamize Merton, Turner went to Mertonize Gresham. Thomas Eden combined his Gresham chair of Civil Law with the Mastership of Trinity Hall from 1625. In short, one cannot draw a division between Gresham College and the universities. There were close links between the two.

To regard Gresham teaching as in some way in advance of the universities is equally mistaken. The College was fortunate in having Briggs, a great mathematician by the standards of the day, but it also carried dead wood. The first professor of astronomy, Edward Brerewood (1596–1613), was an Oxford M.A. whose main achievements were in logic and ethics. He wrote textbooks on these and published nothing in astronomy. His successor, Thomas Williams (1613–19), the son of a merchant, showed no aptitude for the post. It was not until Edmund Gunter was appointed in 1619 that the chair had an occupant who was a true mathematician. But Gunter was a student of Christ Church, he was in orders and he was a bachelor of divinity to boot. He is no evidence for the existence of lay science apart from universities. His successor, Henry Gellibrand, was an Oxford M.A. who had

---

[13] There is no full modern study of Gresham College. The standard work is J. Ward, *Lives of the Professors of Gresham College* (London, 1740) from which much of the following information is taken.

been a pupil of Sir Henry Savile there. Nor does the story of the geometry chair under Briggs (1596–1620), Peter Turner (1620–30) and John Greaves (1630–43) offer any evidence for a split between Gresham and the universities. Briggs was a fellow of St John's College and lecturer in mathematics at Cambridge before coming to Gresham, while Turner and Greaves both retained their connection with Merton. Briggs himself was essentially a product of Renaissance Cambridge, where St John's, to judge from its alumni, had a strong mathematical tradition. Even after he came to Oxford, Briggs's services as a consultant were in demand.[14]

Against this background, Gresham College does not appear as an institution cut off from the universities. A Gresham professor such as Briggs is in many ways scarcely distinguishable from a university don. This point also emerges from letters exchanged between James Ussher of Trinity College, Dublin and various correspondents in England including Briggs at Gresham College, and Bainbridge at Oxford, both of them mathematicians. Ussher himself was no mathematician. He was primarily a theologian with historical interests who in the course of his studies of the Old Testament became absorbed in problems of dating. Solar eclipses in Biblical times seemed to him to form a basis for an absolute chronology and this brought him into contact with Briggs and led him to acquire the papers of Bainbridge and Edward Wright.[15] Ussher and Briggs were clearly on friendly terms and Briggs did his utmost to be helpful. In a letter from Gresham College dated 10 March 1615, he mentioned Napier's logarithmic discoveries to Ussher and expressed the hope that these would help in the solution of problems raised by eclipses.[16] Clearly logarithms were not regarded by Briggs as a narrowly practical tool but one which might be put at the service of theology. They were useful but not in the twentieth-century sense of the word. Briggs remained interested in theological matters after he went to Oxford in 1620. Thomas James, who was Bodley's Librarian 1602–20, referred

[14] *Acts Privy Council 1625–6*, p. 361.
[15] W. O'Sullivan, 'Ussher as a collector of manuscripts', *Hermathena*, lxxxviii (1956), p. 42.
[16] *The Whole Works of the most Rev. James Ussher*, ed. C. R. Elrington, vol. xv, (Dublin, 1864) p. 90. Professor Trevor-Roper points out that Napier himself regarded logarithms as a short cut to calculating the Number of the Beast: cf. 'The general crisis of the seventeenth century', *Past and Present*, no. 16 (Nov. 1959), p. 62 n. 3.

to the need for help from Briggs and Bainbridge in certain difficulties of textual criticism.[17] 'I have restored three hundred
citations' he wrote, 'and rescued them from corruption in thirty
quire of paper: Mr. Briggs will satisfy you in this point, and sundry
other projects of mine ...' Several points emerge from this
correspondence. First, with Briggs as with Newton, theological
and 'scientific' interests merged. Secondly, he was in the closest
contact on matters of general scholarship with university scholars,
and his mathematical and other learning was in some demand.
Thirdly, he moved in semi-puritanical university circles. He was
anxious to recommend young men as students from Trinity
College, Dublin, at a time when this foundation was too puritani-
cal for Archbishop Abbott. But his puritanism led him into
theological niceties, not away from them. The Advancement of
Learning in this circle was a concept which included scriptural
truth as well as practical utility. If Briggs was a Puritan, then so
were half the dons of Oxford and Cambridge; and if this is
admitted, what remains of Hill's view that puritanism, science,
Gresham College and the merchants form a meaningful sociological grouping? Violent criticisms of the universities such as
were made by Milton and others during the period 1640–60 may
lead to the false conclusion that all Puritans were somehow
violently antagonistic to university education. This is to generalize
on too narrow a foundation.

Thus Gresham College was not as an institution distinct from
the universities, but one designed to make university learning
readily available to the population of London, not merely
mathematics and navigation, but also rhetoric, divinity, and civil
law. It was an extra-mural college, drawing its intellectual strength
from the universities, yet watched jealously by them to prevent it
developing into independent life of its own.

Any attempt to stress the lay, puritan, and scientific character of
Gresham College, as distinct from the clerical, conservative and
'useless' education provided by the universities will not stand up
to detailed examination. Gresham College, as much clerical as lay,
and more middle-of-the-road protestant than puritan, was a
worthy attempt to provide extra-mural teaching in 1600. It was

[17] Ussher, *Works*, xv, p. 266. Cf. also Bainbridge's letters to Ussher, *ibid.*,
pp. 394, 447. John Greaves, a Gresham professor, also wrote to Ussher
about such matters.

fortunate in having Briggs, as was the W.E.A. in its early years in having Tawney as a tutor. But to regard it as an institution distinct from the universities is to do violence to the facts.

We may conclude these remarks on Gresham College with two quotations, which may be set in contrast with the rapturous verdicts of the two Gresham professors quoted by Hill in praise of that institution. The first of these extracts illustrates the views of George Hakewill, a writer of the 1630s well-known for his advocacy of progress. It may be argued that Hakewill is making a conventional tribute to Oxford, but the same weight may be placed on his words as Hill does upon the inaugural lectures given by Wren and others at Gresham College. Many will find it surprising that Hakewill, who as one of Hill's Baconians would be expected to criticize Oxford, should praise the university so enthusiastically. The second extract is from a 1647 pamphlet, criticizing Gresham College, though this is precisely the moment when on Hill's view, that institution should have been in full flower. Both extracts add to the difficulties which face an interpretation as simple as Hill's.

Hakewill wrote in praise of his alma mater:[18]

> Were I destitute of all other arguments to demonstrate the *providence* of *God* in the *preservation of the World*, and to prove that it doth not *universally* and *perpetually decline*, this one might fully suffice for all, that thou, my *Venerable Mother*, though thou waxe old in regard of yeares, yet in this latter age in regard of strength and beauty, waxest young againe. Within the compasse of this last *Centenarie* and lesse, thou hast brought forth such a number of worthy *Sons* for piety, for learning, for wisedome; and for *buildings* hast bin so inlarged and inriched, that hee who shall compare thee with thy selfe, will easily finde, that though thou bee truly accounted one of the most ancient *Universities* in the World, yet so farre art thou from withering and wrinkles, that thou art rather become fairer and fresher, and in thine issue no lesse happy then heretofore.

Vitruvius, the anonymous author of a pamphlet wrote:[19]

[18] G. Hakewill, *An Apologie or Declaration of the Power and Providence of God* (Oxford, 1630), sig. b2.
[19] *Sir Thomas Gresham His Ghost* (London, 1647).

Worthy Reader:

The consideration of these two things, imboldned me to the writing of these few lines: Considering, first, the great accommodations that might have redounded unto this City, and to all men, had the good-intended Will of *Londons* large and bountifull Benefactor Sir *Thomas Gresham*, been (as in conscience and equity it should have been) rightly performed, in giving his House to seven able Artists to inhabit, to exercise and teach the seven liberall Sciences; for hereby Learning might have been nourisht, Art flourish, Ignorance abandoned, the Ignorant taught, the Artist improved, the Learned established, every man profited. Secondly, considering the bad use that is made of it, the Will abused, Men deceived in their expectations, the City misused, Art neglected, Ignorant rejected, and all things sleighted. Whereas they ought every day to exercise; they have brought it . . . to be Read only in Tearm time; whereas Sea-men and other Artists (that their more necessary business will not permit to be present) are abridged of reaping that profit the Gift was intended for.

Thus Gresham College fits easily into Hill's sociological hypothesis only when carefully trimmed to size. In its rough sixteenth-century fullness, Gresham College appears not as a new educational departure in the interests of a rising capitalist class but an institution which owed a great deal to the past. It represented a reorganizing of academic culture in a London environment, with some recognition of the importance of practical needs. Was it the Nuffield College of its day?

II

We must next examine the second element in Hill's explanation of the rise of science, namely the role of the merchants and artisans, 'the idea of co-operation between the humblest craftsmen and the scientist' and 'the intimate connection between merchants and science'. According to this interpretation of the Scientific Revolution, the merchants and the craftsmen provided the decisive social motive force. How far does this stand up to examination?

Some attempt may first be made at an estimate of the numbers of people involved in science at this time. If we look upon the main achievement of seventeenth-century science as in the fields of dynamics and astronomy, and hence as essentially mathematical in character, the total number of people who can be defined as mathematical practitioners, capable of making a contribution, however slight, was extremely small.[20] Over the period of a century and a half, from 1550 to 1700, it amounted to no more than six hundred, and during the formative period of the late sixteenth and early seventeenth centuries the total concerned was much lower, probably in the region of one hundred and fifty, a number small in modern eyes, but which represented a much higher proportion of the population than ever before. How it compared with European countries at the same date, it is difficult to say.

The day-to-day existence of most of these mathematical practitioners depended upon the patronage of the educated public, and the services which they supplied reflected its needs. In the main these services fell into two main categories, those connected with land surveying, and those connected with the sea and navigation. The mathematicians who specialized in surveying found their patrons among the landed classes. For this reason, surveying was taught at the Inns of Court, attendance at which formed a normal stage in the education of a gentleman. The Irish plantations also created a demand for skilled surveyors in the reigns of Elizabeth, James and Charles. We may conclude that advances made in the art of surveying during this period were due, so far as patronage was concerned, to the landowners. In contrast, navigation and the making of navigational instruments drew patrons from a much wider spectrum of the social scene, crown, gentry and merchants. The crown, for example, in the person of the Controller of the Navy, Sir Henry Palmer, was the patron of the distinguished mathematical practitioner, Henry Bond, who followed up Gellibrand's discovery of the variation of the magnetic variation. Bond was lecturer in applied mathematics in the royal dockyard at Chatham in the 1630s. Members of the court were also patrons. Apart from Leicester, Northumberland and Ralegh,

[20] E. G. R. Taylor, *Mathematical Practitioners of Tudor and Stuart England* (Cambridge, 1954). P. Laslett makes this point in more general terms, in *Scientific Change*, ed. A. C. Crombie (London, 1963), p. 862.

all mentioned by Hill as examples of puritan patronage of science, there were other great courtiers such as Cumberland, Bridge-water, and Cecil himself. Sir Charles Cavendish, younger brother of the earl of Newcastle, was a friend of Oughtred and Wallis, a patron of Pell and Warner and a man keenly interested in science. Sir Francis Kynaston was the patron of a German mathematician, John Speidell. Another member of the gentry, William Gascoigne, killed on the royalist side at Marston Moor, was well known for his work in improving perspective glasses. The group surrounding the Towneleys of Towneley Hall also included many scientists of great merit, including John Flamsteed. Indeed, throughout the sixteenth and seventeenth centuries, from Leonard Digges and John Dee onwards, the gentry played a prominent part in the patronage of the new science. Another group of patrons came from those interested in the practice of astrology and the making of almanacks. This category is less susceptible to clear analysis since its membership ranged from obvious cranks to men who combined astrology with medicine or surveying. But they cannot be ignored among the mathematical practitioners of England during this period. Finally, the patronage which came from the merchants and the great merchant companies may be mentioned. It was the Muscovy Company, for example, which backed the translation from the Spanish of Martin Cortes's textbook on navigation in 1561. The East India merchants, Wolstenholme and Smythe, both friends of the court, endowed a lectureship in navigation in 1604. However, it should also be noted that Edward Wright was refused help by the East India Company when the death of Prince Henry removed his royal patron. Merchants were quite capable of driving a hard bargain in such matters.

The conclusion seems inescapable that patronage for applied mathematics came from no single source. It also appears that merchants counted for much less in this field than might have been anticipated, a reason for which may be sought in the depressed state of the English economy. The years 1560–1640 no longer seem a period of uninterrupted economic advance. The work of Fisher and Supple and others[21] has shown that there was a dark side to

[21] F. J. Fisher, 'Tawney's century' in *Essays in the Economic and Social History of Tudor and Stuart England*, ed. F. J. Fisher (Cambridge, 1961), pp. 1–14. B. Supple, *Commercial Crisis and Change in England 1600–1642* (Cambridge, 1959), p. 23.

the glories of Elizabeth's reign. Contracting markets, endemic underemployment and a depressed economy brought many social difficulties. There was some recovery after the Spanish peace of 1604 up to Cockaigne's scheme, and English merchants, as Mr Davis has shown, displayed a good deal of enterprise in the Mediterranean trade and east of Suez.[22] Even so, we may be sure that it is misleading to consider all English merchants at this time as by definition 'progressive and forward looking'. In the seventeenth century as in the twentieth much depended on the individual firm. In the Levant trade and East India trade it was possible to make great profits, but the names of royalists like Sir Paul Pindar and Sir Henry Garway are not ones which fit at all into Hill's scheme of things. Another name, that of Sir Morris Abbott, shows the difficulty of separating the universities from the commercial world, since two of his brothers were fellows of Balliol and one of his sons was an Oxford graduate. The two great trading companies were 'forward looking', yet their sympathies were right wing politically and religiously, as indeed we might anticipate. All this suggests that there is no clear and obvious link between merchants and political, religious or scientific radicalism. Perhaps we need the same kind of detailed research on the merchant classes as is being done on the gentry, before even tentative generalization is possible.

So far, attention has been focused upon mathematical practitioners and their patrons, but their activity should not be identified with the Scientific Revolution as such. Practical advance went on apace, but this in no way made a theoretical breakthrough inevitable.[23] In many ways, indeed, successful practice might well have impeded fresh theoretical development. Thomas Digges, for example, was shocked by the conservatism of skilled seamen on a four-month voyage which he undertook. Oughtred criticized

---

[22] R. Davis, 'England and the Mediterranean 1570–1670' in *Essays in the Economic and Social History of Tudor and Stuart England*, ed. Fisher, pp. 117–37.
[23] See A. R. Hall, 'The scholar and the craftsman in the Scientific Revolution', in *Critical Problems in the History of Science*, ed. M. Clagett (Madison, Wisconsin, 1959), pp. 3–23. Cf. also Leonardo's remark, 'Practice must always be founded on sound theory': A. Blunt, *Artistic Theory in Italy 1450–1600* (Oxford, 1940), p. 49. Newton expressed a similar view in 1694: *The Correspondence of Isaac Newton*, ed. H. W. Turnbull (Cambridge, 1959–), vol. iii, pp. 359–60.

those 'would-be mathematicians who occupy themselves only with the so-called practice which is in reality mere juggler's tricks and instruments'.[24] Indeed, the theoretical advances which were made were often beyond the capacity of many seamen until education in mathematics became more widespread.

Such major advances as were made during the period under discussion were in fact the achievement of a handful of men, Gilbert, Briggs, Gunter, Gellibrand, Wilkins, Barlow, Wallis, Wright, Oughtred and a few others. None of these was an artisan, although they did find the assistance of instrument-makers essential. All of them were university educated, not in the conventional sense of two or three years, but over an extended period of ten years or more. Edward Wright, whose *Certain Errors in Navigation* was a landmark, was a fellow of Caius for nine years before joining the earl of Cumberland. Some, like Barlow, Gunter, Wilkins and Oughtred, were clergymen. Others like Briggs and Gilbert were physicians. If we seek what these had in common, the secret does not seem to lie in any affiliation of class. For Barlow, whose contribution to science is underestimated by Hill, family connection may supply the answer. He was the nephew of Roger Barlow, the early sixteenth-century explorer. For some, such as Oughtred, the key may well lie in the possession of leisure. For all of them science seems to have been an imaginative rather than a practical activity, something carried on for its own sake, not for merely utilitarian ends. What is certain is that no merchant made any direct contribution to science during this period.

III

Hill's final point, the role of puritanism in the rise of science, must now engage our attention. He makes this in various ways, by reference to the puritanism of the early patrons of science and the puritanism of some of the Gresham professors, by associating 'puritanism and freedom of thought', by comparing Bacon's emphasis on personal observation and personal experiment with the puritan demand for first-hand religious experience and by stressing the fact that science emerged fully only during the

[24] Taylor, *Mathematical Practitioners*, p. 192.

Puritan Revolution. The Baconian sympathies of leaders of the
puritan party also appear significant, and it almost seems no
paradox to associate Pym and the Royal Society. All these points
build up into a formidable case, but once again we may ask whether
the picture is so simple.

We must first quarrel with the view that in essence puritanism
and science are analogous. All general terms are ambiguous, but
puritanism is more ambiguous than most. In Hill's use of the
word, the emphasis seems to fall upon religious experience or
what some in the seventeenth century termed 'enthusiasm'.
Puritanism in this sense found expression in the Independents. In
the intellectual field, it went with a violent hatred of the universities and of the use of learning in religion. In preaching it was
associated with a plain unadorned style, which had no use for
learned allusions and imagery. It found its spokesmen in such
writers as Webster and Hall. If we adopt puritanism in this sense,
then it is true that one or two scientists, Gellibrand for example,
may have been puritan. Briggs, like Ussher, moved in left-wing
protestant circles, but how much he had in common with the
Puritans is open to conjecture. However, when we look at the
general run of the leading scientists, such as William Harvey,
Robert Boyle, John Wilkins and Seth Ward, we find that they
belong to quite another tradition of religious thought, best
described as latitudinarian or moderate. Ward and Wilkins
became bishops after the Restoration. Robert Boyle was sympathetic to the tolerant views of the Cambridge Platonists, who had
reacted strongly against the Calvinist doctrine of predestination.[25]
William Harvey's religious opinions were similarly moderate.
Isaac Newton moved theologically in the same gravitational
field as Henry More, the Cambridge Platonist.[26] In short these
men may be ranked among the greatest opponents of the type of
puritanism described by Hill. It was not surprising that Wilkins
and Ward should be found defending the universities against the
attacks of Webster and Hall. These men emphasized the place of
reason in religion, rather than emotional experience. They stressed

[25] *Anglicanism, The Thought and Practice of the Church of England Illustrated
from the Religious Literature of the Seventeenth Century,* ed. P. E. More and
F. L Cross (London, 1935), p. lix.
[26] E. A. Burtt, *The Metaphysical Foundations of Modern Physical Science*
(London, 1925), p. 258.

what was in common between Christian and pagan learning. Natural theology, and, in the outlook of a man like Boyle, natural science, became a means of studying the wisdom of God as revealed in the Universe. Between these men and Hill's Puritans a great gulf was set.

Any difficulties which remain in elucidating the connection between puritanism and science derive from Hill's view that science and Baconianism were identical. If this is accepted, then the enthusiasm of the puritan leaders for Baconian ideas must be interpreted as enthusiasm for science. 'Baconianism', however, is also an ambiguous term, and the word 'Baconian' is used by Hill in a manner so broad that it includes Sir John Eliot, who cannot be regarded as showing any sympathy in his writings for Bacon. However, the real ambiguity of the word 'Baconian', as Hill himself points out, lies in the ambiguity of Bacon's own position. Bacon was torn between advocating the pursuit of knowledge for its own sake and the advancement of learning for utilitarian purposes. In our terms, he was undecided as to the relative importance of technology and pure science; in his own terms, it was not quite clear which came first, 'fruit' or 'light'.

Of these two attitudes, utility carried the greatest appeal for the Puritans of the seventeenth century. The greatest exponents of the utilitarian attitude were to be found in the pamphleteers, Hartlib, Petty, Hall and Webster. It was also implied in the violent anti-Aristotelianism of many Puritans, since emphasis upon utility was the obvious alternative to the Aristotelian view, which placed the liberal above the practical arts, and contemplation above practical activity. This utilitarian outlook was certainly to be found in Bacon, but it also had a long history behind it, which went back beyond Bacon to the sixteenth-century humanists, Vives and Ramus.[27] The importance of Ramus has come to be increasingly recognized in recent years, though he still remains something of an enigma. What is undeniable is that Ramism was one of the great intellectual influences of the late sixteenth and early seventeenth centuries. Ramus was a humanist but a humanist with a difference. He stressed the importance of those classical authors whose works were useful in practical life, Virgil's Georgics for example.[28] From Aristotelian logic, he removed all features which in his

[27] Randall, *The Career of Philosophy*.
[28] R. Hooykaas, *Humanisme, Science et Reforme* (Leyden, 1958), p. 34.

eyes were useless, and fashioned an instrument which professional men could use, as well as students. Ramus and Ramism particularly influenced the English Puritans from Perkins onwards, and their utilitarian bent may be said to derive from there, rather than from Bacon himself. When Pym and the puritan party invited Comenius to England in 1641 they were turning to a continental Ramist, reared in the Ramist centre of Herborn, and a man whose *Janua linguarum reserata* stressed a utilitarian and simplified approach to the study of languages in the spirit of Ramus. Comenius was an admirer of Bacon but it was Bacon the utilitarian who appealed to him. The Comenian group in England thus gave an impetus to Baconianism in this sense.

What interested them in science was its application to agriculture and the crafts, not the advancement of understanding for its own sake. In fact the 'advancement of learning' for them meant the propagation of useful knowledge.[29] It is thus not surprising that they should be sceptical about the possibility of discovering the truth or falsehood of heliocentric cosmologies. Typically enough, Comenius was anti-Copernican. The Bible provided enough information on these matters, without vainly seeking further. Milton was to express the same view later on in *Paradise Lost*, for which he has been taken to task by Professor Lovejoy in strong language:[30]

> Milton's position . . . is pragmatic, in the most vulgar sense of that ambiguous term, the sense in which it designated an obscurantist utilitarianism hostile to all disinterested intellectual curiosity and to all inquiry into unsolved problems about the physical world.

In the 1640s this combination of religious enthusiasm and utilitarian zeal gave birth to a group known as the 'Invisible College'. Hartlib was prominent among them, so also were Haak and Oldenburg, who were later to be associated with the Royal Society. One of their members, Boate, produced a natural history of Ireland, written, typically enough, not for its own sake, but to

[29] W. E. Houghton, 'The history of trades: its relation to seventeenth-century thought', repr. from *Jour. Hist. Ideas*, ii (1941), pp. 33–60, in *Roots of Scientific Thought*, eds P. Wiener and A. Noland, pp. 354–81.
[30] *Reason and the Imagination: Studies in the History of Ideas 1600–1800*, ed. J. A. Mazzeo (London, 1962), p. 142.

serve the needs of the Cromwellian Plantation. Another man who was once attracted by the group was Robert Boyle, though his enthusiasm waned after a time. The 'Invisible College' was at once Comenian and Baconian, amateurish, enthusiastic and utilitarian, certainly the precursor of the Royal Society in one of its aspects.

It is also clear, however, that a different kind of group can claim to be an ancestor of the Royal Society, namely the scientists who congregated at Oxford in the 1650s. They differed from the 'Invisible College' in several respects. In the first place, they were nearly all skilled mathematicians, and it was in mathematics rather than in experiment that they placed their hopes for the advancement of learning. This certainly put them out of step with Bacon and gave them more in common with Descartes. Secondly they were Aristotelian enough to place discovery above utility, 'Light' above 'Fruit'. Thirdly, in the persons of Wilkins and Ward, they defended the universities and traditional learning against the attacks of the puritan pamphleteers. Finally, as has already been pointed out, in their religious views they tended to identify themselves with a non-puritan outlook. This group, which included many of the leading scientists of the day, was serious and professional in a way that the 'Invisible College' could never hope to be. They and the spirit which they represented were to form the hard core of the Royal Society, the 'players' as distinct from the 'gentlemen'.

The difference between the 'Invisible College' and the Oxford group is to be seen in the movement of Robert Boyle from one to the other. As Professor Boas has pointed out, by 1653 Boyle was becoming less and less the dilettante amateur and more and more the serious scientist. As soon as this change of attitude took place, he moved from London to Oxford. Even then his lack of mathematics and his interest in the experimental side of chemistry made him suspect. In 1660 he wrote:[31]

> some Learned Men . . . thought it strange (if not amisse also) that one of whose studies they were pleas'd to have too favourable an Expectation, should spend upon Chymicall tryalls (to which I then happen'd to be invited, by the

[31] Quoted in M. Boas, *Robert Boyle and Seventeenth-Century Chemistry* (Cambridge, 1958), p. 37.

opportunity of some Furnaces and some leisure) much of those Endeavours which they seem'd to think might be farre more usefully employ'd then upon such empty and deceitfull study.

The Oxford scientists were very critical of the practical aims of mere 'sooty Empiricks'. They poked fun at the 'company of meer and irrational Operators, whose Experiments may indeed be serviceable to Apothecaries, and perhaps to Physicians, but are Uselesse to a Philosopher, that aimes at curing no disease but that of Ignorance'.[32] It was not surprising that the unquiet utilitarian spirit of Petty should find Oxford oppressive and lead him to seek more practical and financially profitable activities in Ireland. All this may lead us to question whether the connection between puritanism and science is as clear as Hill makes out.

One final point remains to be discussed, namely the significance of the Civil War period. Hill clearly attaches great significance to this period. 'In this intoxicating era of free discussion and free speculation nothing was left sacred.' Victory in the Civil War went to the side which supported the new science. 'The civil war was fought between rival schools of astronomy, between Parliamentarian heliocentrists and Royalist Ptolemaics: Ptolemy perished with Charles I.' Moreover 'More of Bacon's works were published in 1640-1 than in all the fourteen years since his death.'[33] Here again the evidence seems to be overwhelming, but here again it is open to criticism of a serious kind.

First, the spread of Bacon's writings. A glance at the standard bibliography reveals that the evidence of this is by no means as clear as one would have expected from Hill's categorical statement.[34] Of the editions of the *Novum Organum*, one was published in 1620 in London, the other three editions in Holland in 1645, 1650 and 1660. What this tells us about the spread of Baconian ideas is a matter for conjecture. Of the editions of *De augmentis scientiarum*, one appeared in 1623, the remaining six were continental.[35] Similarly, of the *Advancement of Learning*, all editions were published before 1640 including two by Oxford University

---

[32] Quoted in M. Boas, *Robert Boyle and Seventeenth-Century Chemistry*, pp. 67-8.
[33] *The Listener*, 7 June 1962, p. 985.
[34] R. W. Gibson, *Bibliography of Francis Bacon* (Oxford, 1950).
[35] 1624, 1635, 1645, 1652, 1654, 1662: Gibson, *op. cit.*, p. xv.

Press in 1633 and 1640. Of the *Sylva Sylvarum*, much the most popular work apart from the essays, the first six editions appeared before 1640 and only three during the Interregnum. Some of Bacon's writings were reprinted in 1641 but their chief attraction was apparently of a political or religious character, for example his discourse concerning Church Affairs and his three speeches concerning Anglo-Scottish matters, obviously of relevance in 1641. This particular piece of evidence does not favour Hill's case. Baconian ideas did spread during the Commonwealth period, but they did so largely in a crude and oversimplified form. The Baconian pamphleteering of Webster, Petty and Hartlib stressed the utilitarian side of Bacon to the exclusion of all others, and tailored the *Novum Organum* to fit their Ramist and Comenian preconceptions.

The idea that the political divisions in the Civil War correspond to divergences in astronomy is an attractive one, and Hill claims Miss Marjorie Nicolson in support.[36] It is doubtful, however, whether her words support the interpretation he places on them. For example, she comes down against the simple view that this was a period of free discussion, of Cromwellian light contrasted with Laudian darkness:[37]

> during this period astrology came again for a time into its own, and comets and eclipses were forebodings of the doom that seemed to overhang the little world of man. In addition, almanacs came to be recognized as valuable tools of propaganda. The majority of their editors naturally sided with the party in power, and their prognostications were drawn less from the conjunctions of the planets than from the editors' desire to curry favour with the rulers.

In other words, in the main parliamentary almanack-makers were no more 'scientific' than their royalist counterparts. Indeed Fairfax had recourse to astrologers at the siege of Colchester, requiring them to predict an outcome favourable to the parliamentary cause, as a boost for the morale of his men. In addition, the simple contrast between Copernican and Ptolemaic theories before the Civil War was tending to give way to a more complex

[36] M. Nicolson, 'English Almanacks and the "New Astronomy"', *Annals of Science*, iv (1939), pp. 1–33.
[37] *Ibid.*, pp. 19–20.

pattern, in which the rival cosmologies were derived from Copernicus and Tycho Brahe. The picture, so far as rival cosmologies is concerned, turns out to be as complex as any other we have examined. It is stimulating to have the matter raised, but to arrive at a simple answer is near to guesswork. If close analysis were undertaken, it might well show that the more biblically-minded of the Parliamentarians tended to support the Tychonic compromise, which was expressly designed to save the literal sense of the Bible.

The conclusions towards which this investigation points are largely negative in character, but not entirely so. It has been shown, in the first place, that there was no simple connection between puritanism and science. But this need not rule out alternative theories of a relationship between religious radicalism and scientific discovery. It is possible, for example, that a more critical attitude towards religious authority created a climate of opinion which predisposed some men to be equally critical of dogma in science. A recent book by Professor van Gelder, *The Two Reformations in the Sixteenth Century*,[38] is relevant here. This suggests that a rival religious movement existed alongside the Protestant Reformation. It developed throughout the sixteenth century and by the close it included among its disciples many important figures in both the Catholic and Protestant Churches, among them such men as Lipsius and Montaigne. To this movement, scientists such as Galileo and Kepler may be said to have belonged, and even Francis Bacon. The religious views of the Cambridge Platonists, of Robert Boyle and Isaac Newton may also be traced back to the same tradition. If we are seeking a connection between the Reformation and the Scientific Revolution, this 'Major Reformation' seems likely to provide it.

Our second conclusion is that there was no direct connection between economic and scientific development. Tempting though it may be to link up the Commercial Revolution of the Sixteenth Century and the Scientific Revolution, no valid body of evidence seems to exist upon which to base a generalization of this kind. The revolutionary discoveries in science had no practical application, any more than Darwin's theory of evolution had. The mathe-

[38] H. van Gelder, *The Two Reformations in the Sixteenth Century* (The Hague, 1961).

matical world of the new science was as abstract in its own way as the world of Aristotelian metaphysics. Yet this need not rule out the possibility that social change did have some effect in making the Scientific Revolution possible. But what kind of social change? It may well be that new wealth in the seventeenth century made possible the existence of a greater number of scholars with leisure than ever before. More men attended the English universities than at any time until the nineteenth century. This meant that more men received a training in abstract thought, particularly in mathematics, than before. Social change of this kind, which is not to be explained merely in economic terms, may well be a decisive factor.

Finally, we have suggested that an attempt to link up political attitudes during the seventeenth century with rival cosmologies is an unprofitable exercise. Fundamentally the main objection here lies in the insularity of any view which treats English politics on the same plane as European intellectual developments. The English Civil War and Commonwealth may have been an English affair, though there are grounds for thinking it was not so exclusively one as is often made out. But the Scientific Revolution was not English, it was a European movement. Newton was a great Englishman, but it was thanks to the work of his fellow Europeans Galileo and Kepler that he achieved success. The same may be said for comparatively minor developments in navigation and surveying. English politics are irrelevant, partly because they are politics but even more because they are English. When all is said Hill's interpretation is too narrowly English in its scope. By leaving Europe out of account, he sharpens the outline of the picture produced but the simplicity of effect is artificial. What is needed is a broad sweep which takes account of the Jesuit Cavalieri and the Jansenist Pascal as much as the puritan Gellibrand. A European approach would also lead us to consider whether the style of continental science was as different from that of England as Racine's tragedies from Shakespeare's, or whether England was relatively backward in any field. It might also suggest that the Renaissance cannot be left out. Renaissance painting may be regarded without paradox as a form of practical science and the absence of a Renaissance school of painting in England may well have affected the development of science in England. These sociological considerations and many others are raised as soon as

English science is looked at in a European context. Thus criticism of Hill's sociological interpretation of the rise of science need not rule out other and wider interpretations of a sociological character. If one agrees that every society gets the kind of science which it deserves, then an examination of English society in the early seventeenth century is surely a relevant consideration. But concepts such as puritanism, merchant classes, even 'the gentry' are much too loose to be really helpful. Seventeenth-century history needs a more critical vocabulary to enable it to escape from a cloud of false problems.[39]

[39] See J. G. A. Pocock, 'History and theory', *Comparative Studies in Society and History*, iv (1962), pp. 525-35.

XVIII

PURITANISM, CAPITALISM AND THE SCIENTIFIC REVOLUTION*

Christopher Hill

It was kind of Dr Kearney to give advance publicity to my *Intellectual Origins of the English Revolution* by criticizing in *Past and Present* a very summarized version of it which appeared in *The Listener*. I shall not attempt to reply to all his detailed criticisms, many of which are dealt with in the full and documented text of my book.[1] But some points of general interest arise.

I

I agree with Dr Kearney's insistence that the Scientific Revolution was a European movement, and that my interpretation is too narrowly English in its scope to be definitive (*K.*, p. 101; p. 241 in this volume). I point this out myself (*H.*, p. 4, chapter 6 *passim*), and I still believe that an analysis in national terms has something to contribute to our understanding of the relations of science and society. But Dr Kearney is right to insist that sociological interpretations of the rise of science must be attempted on a European scale. Whether this wider context will be more favourable to his view than to mine remains to be seen. For what has to be explained is why in the sixteenth and seventeenth centuries

---

* From no. 29 (December 1964).
[1] *K.* signifies H. F. Kearney, 'Puritanism, capitalism and the Scientific Revolution', *Past and Present*, no. 28 (July 1964), pp. 81–101; pp. 218–42 in this volume; *H.* stands for my *Intellectual Origins of the English Revolution* (Oxford, 1965).

the lead in navigation passed from Portugal and Spain to England and the Netherlands, and never returned to a Catholic country; why in science generally the lead passed from Italy to the same two countries; why in Counter-Reformation Italy science survived longest in Venice, 'the one genuine mercantile republic which sought to remain within the Catholic Church', whose theological radicalism caused Venetians like Paolo Sarpi to be regarded by most Englishmen as 'honorary protestants'.[2] We have to explain why science, still flourishing in Spain in the late sixteenth and early seventeenth centuries, slumped tragically thereafter.[3] Why did science disappear from Copernicus's Poland and Kepler's Bohemia as these countries reverted to Catholicism and suffered economic decline? Why did that good Catholic Descartes find greater intellectual freedom in the bourgeois and protestant Netherlands than in his own country? Yet France, with its Huguenots and Jansenists, its government-supported trade and industry, proved more favourable to science than countries dominated by the Counter-Reformation.

In my view science is not a product of protestantism, or of puritanism: both science and protestantism sprang from the shift by which urban and industrial values replaced those appropriate to a mainly agrarian society. In Italy science pre-dates the Reformation. Even in England some protestant attitudes can be detected before the Reformation, especially among artisan Lollards and urbane Erasmians. The Protestant Reformation, by overthrowing traditional authorities, by encouraging criticism of certain aspects of the Catholic tradition, 'created a climate of opinion which predisposed some men to be equally critical of dogma in science' (K., p. 100; p. 240 in this volume). Where protestant churches were established they tried to restrain this process, as the English bishops did by controlling Oxford and Cambridge. But what we may call the logic of protestantism—the dissidence of dissent—was always potentially present in protestant countries, liable to break out as soon as circumstances were

[2] H. R. Trevor-Roper, 'Religion, the Reformation and social change', *Historical Studies*, iv (1963), p. 39; cf. my *Puritanism and Revolution* (London, 1958), pp. 134–5; my article on 'William Harvey and the idea of monarchy', *Past and Present*, no. 27 (April 1964), pp. 70–2; pp. 160–81 in this volume; and *H.*, pp. 276–8.

[3] J. H. Elliott, *Imperial Spain, 1469–1716* (London, 1963), pp. 236, 291, 381.

propitious: as they were in England after the breakdown of the church and its censorship in 1640. 'Mechanics and artificers (for whom the true natural philosophy should be principally intended)'[4] were also those to whom radical protestantism seems to have appealed (*H.*, pp. 22–7, 293–300). This sort of analysis would explain why clock-making, a vital test of skilled craftsmanship, was almost a protestant industry, centering in Switzerland, the Netherlands, the Huguenot areas of France, and England. It would explain why Geneva and Scotland became important in the history of science only after the stricter Calvinist discipline had broken down; why Benjamin Franklin, who personifies the 'capitalist spirit' as well as the scientific spirit in America, sprang from a Calvinist background though he himself had lost the faith of his fathers.

II

Dr Kearney's main disagreement with me, the root of all the others, concerns the relation of 'puritanism' to science. We must begin by defining terms. For me the main stream of puritanism, from Perkins to Baxter, includes all those radical protestants who wanted to reform the church but (before 1640 at least) did not wish to separate from it. After 1640 divisions appear within puritanism, but there is a sense in which even the most radical sectaries descend from the undifferentiated puritanism of pre-1640. I take this usage to be that of most contemporaries, and of the classical tradition of historical writing from Gardiner to Haller.[5]

Historians, like Humpty Dumpty, can make words mean anything they like; but they should aim at being consistent in their usage, and should not be too severe with their colleagues who work consistently with different definitions. Dr Kearney appears at first to accept the traditional definition, when he refers to Briggs's 'puritanism' (*K.*, pp. 88–9; p. 227). But he shifts his ground immediately by referring to Briggs's Gresham College as 'more middle-of-the-road protestant than puritan', without

[4] T. Sprat, *History of the Royal Society*, quoted *H.*, p. 14.
[5] See my *Society and Puritanism in Pre-Revolutionary England* (London, 1964), chap. 1 *passim*, esp. pp. 28–9; and *H.*, p. 26.

telling us what the distinction is (*K.*, p. 89; p. 227). By page 95 Briggs has moved from the middle of the road to 'left-wing protestant circles', which makes the distinction between this and puritanism even more mystifying. But already a new definition has appeared, wrongly attributed to me: puritanism is equated with enthusiasm, and 'puritanism in this sense found expression in the Independents' (*K.*, p. 94; p. 234), though typical Independents like John Owen and Thomas Goodwin do not strike me as the most enthusiastic of men. 'Puritanism in this sense' 'found its spokesmen in such writers as Webster and Hall'. So far as I am aware there are no grounds for calling either Webster or Hall an Independent in religion, nor would they have agreed theologically with one another, Webster being far more radical than Hall. Nor do I know of any grounds for equating the theology of either with that of Gellibrand, to whom Dr Kearney in his next sentence attributes 'puritanism in this sense'. (I can only suppose that Dr Kearney recalled that Laud alleged that Gellibrand was said to 'keep conventicles at Gresham College'—*H.*, p. 57.) If puritanism goes with 'a violent hatred of the universities' (*K.*, p. 94; p. 234), then there were virtually no Puritans, no vocal Puritans at least, before 1640. A page later the touchstone of puritanism becomes 'the Calvinist doctrine of predestination', not enthusiasm: the object being to describe the Cambridge Platonists, most of them staunch Parliamentarians, as 'among the greatest opponents of the type of puritanism described by Hill' (*K.*, p. 95; p. 234; *H.*, pp. 101, 312). On this definition Milton was not a Puritan, nor John Goodwin.

Thus within seven pages Dr Kearney employs at least as many definitions of puritanism. If he would settle for one of them it would make the discussion easier. But let us try to make sense of the definition which he attributes to me on pages 94–5 (p. 234), and which derives from some remarks I made about the parallels between the puritan (in my sense) emphasis on experience as the test of religious truth and the scientists' emphasis on experiment. Dr Kearney says the former 'found expression in the Independents': from what follows we must assume he means 'among the sectaries'. But he need only turn over the pages of a few puritan sermons from Perkins to Sibbes to find that this emphasis was by no means confined to sectaries (or Independents), though they perhaps developed it furthest. Such respectable 'middle-of-the-road Protestants' as Hugh Broughton, Thomas Taylor, George Wither and Richard Baxter make the point for me (*H.*, pp. 113-15, 294-7).

This terminological discussion is not as pedantic as it might appear. It has recently become fashionable, especially in the U.S.A., to deny the existence of any connection between puritanism and science, as it has long been fashionable to deny connections between puritanism and the rise of capitalism. The denial is often accompanied by emotional overtones and an abandonment of normal scholarly methods.[6] It is easiest to prove that no connection exists between A and B by defining A in a way which virtually precludes any connection. Mr Rabb, for instance, has a definition of 'puritan' which would exclude Richard Baxter, John Milton and John Wilkins.[7] Mr Feuer, whom Dr Kearney also cites, goes even farther, though it must be said in his defence that it appears from the internal evidence of his book that he is innocent of historical training. In analysing the Fellows of the Royal Society, Mr Feuer does not contrast Puritans with non-Puritans, or Parliamentarians with Royalists; he contrasts Puritans with Royalists. Since every Parliamentarian who survived 1660 and was not a dedicated sectary had to pretend to be a Royalist, here again the desired conclusion is built into the premises.[8] Very few scientists were Puritans because very few puritan revolutionaries were Puritans.

III

Sometimes Dr Kearney seems to me to erect Aunt Sallies of his own in order to have the satisfaction of knocking them down again. Thus he says 'If Briggs was a Puritan, then so were half the dons of Oxford and Cambridge; and if this is admitted, what remains of Hill's view that puritanism, science, Gresham College and the merchants form a meaningful sociological grouping?'

[6] See for instance K. Samuelsson, *Religion and Economic Action*, trans. E. G. French, and ed. D. C. Coleman (London and Stockholm, 1961), and my review in *Eng. Hist. Rev.*, lxxvii (1962), pp. 765-6.
[7] T. K. Rabb, 'Puritanism and the rise of experimental science in England', *Jl of World History*, vii (1962), pp. 46-67.
[8] L. S. Feuer, *The Scientific Intellectual* (New York, 1963), pp. 420-4.

(*K.*, p. 89; p. 227). I do not think I ever stated such a view; and I doubt very much whether 'half' the dons were as puritan as Briggs; but I agree that there was a minority at both universities which was 'puritan' in my sense of the word, and a minority which had scientific interests and was in favour of modernizing the teaching at Oxford and Cambridge. These minorities did not invariably coincide, but I argue that there was a correlation (*H.*, pp. 309–14). Oxford and Cambridge were not monolithic bodies, whose establishments and curricula pleased all dons: then as now there were conflicts and controversies over what should be taught and how. What I do argue is that all the greatest scientists and scientific writers of the pre-revolutionary period (though sometimes educated at Oxford and Cambridge—where else could they have been educated?) were not at the universities when they did their most important work—Recorde, Dee, the Diggeses, Gilbert, Bacon, Wright, Hariot, Briggs, Gunter, Gellibrand, Foster, Napier, Oughtred, Harvey, Digby, Horrocks, Wilkins, Pell, to name only those in the first rank (*H.*, pp. 15–20, 24, 53, 304). How many names of comparable eminence can be quoted on the other side?

Attempts were made to modernize Oxford and Cambridge, by individuals inside the universities (notably Sir Henry Savile) but mainly from outside (Camden, Sir William Sedley, Richard Tomlins), often by radical Protestants (Sir Thomas Bodley, Sir Fulke Greville). Bacon himself had hoped to found lectureships at Cambridge, but did not leave enough money. These attempts at modernization were often fiercely resisted by those in control of the universities, especially the Laudians (*H.*, pp. 52–6, 175–7, 309). One of the spokesmen of the forward-looking minority was George Hakewill, whom Dr Kearney calls 'a writer of the 1630s', presumably because his *magnum opus* was published in 1627. Hakewill's very carefully worded dedication to Oxford, praising its protestantism and buildings, which Dr Kearney triumphantly quotes, must be read in conjunction with Hakewill's strictures on Oxford's backwardness in anatomy, botany, history and Arabic.[9] Hakewill had reason to be cautious: his career had already languished because of his puritanism. Bishop Goodman, perhaps better placed to judge than either Dr Kearney

---

[9] One reason for wanting to learn Arabic was to study Arabic science and mathematics; it was also useful for Levant traders (*H.*, p. 303).

or myself, thought Hakewill no friend to the universities (*K.*, pp. 89–90, p. 228; *H.*, pp. 11, 28–9, 199–202, 303). Only during the Interregnum was outside support for the minorities in Oxford and Cambridge strong enough to make an effective, though short-lived, purge of the universities. George Hakewill, who had been made Rector of Exeter at a time when Charles I's government was trying to appease his opponents, co-operated with the Parliamentary Visitors; and science and puritanism were introduced into Oxford simultaneously.

Gresham College, founded by a merchant, controlled by merchants, providing adult education for a lay public of mariners and others ignorant of Latin, by methods which deliberately deviated from those applied in Oxford and Cambridge, and with many Puritans among its professors, thus seems to me more than the mere extension of the universities which Dr Kearney suggests (*K.*, p. 89, p. 227; *H.*, chapter 2 *passim*).[10] I accept his analogy with 'the W.E.A. in its early years'. Tawney, like Briggs, was educated at Oxford and ended as a university professor. But Tawney was hardly a typical figure of the university establishment. His turn to the W.E.A. sprang from a revulsion from the form and content of university teaching, and from a desire to reach groups of the population which Oxford and Cambridge then failed to touch. The analogy can be pressed further, since the institutionalization of adult education at Gresham College exposed it to the kiss of death from the court, just as the institutionalization of adult education in our own time has made it something more like a mere extension of the universities than the pioneers would have wished (*H.*, pp. 55–61).

IV

Dr Kearney's second point concerns the role of merchants and artisans in the history of science in England. Let me first disavow some of the ideas attributed to me. I did *not* say 'most of the merchants who attended Gresham lectures were puritan in sympathy' (*K.*, p. 85; p. 223). There is no means of knowing who

---

[10] I deal with Gresham College at some length in this chapter, discussing some at least of the points which Dr Kearney raises.

attended, still less the religious affiliations of audiences; but the evidence suggests seamen and artisans rather than merchants (*H.*, pp. 33–74). I did *not* say that any merchant 'made any direct contribution to science during this period' (*K.*, p. 94; p. 233), though I did argue at some length that 'mechanicians' like Humfrey Cole, Robert Norman, Richard Norwood, William Bourne, John Hester, Thomas Hill, Raphe Handson, Richard Delamain, John Wells, Phineas Pett, John Tapp, Henry Bond, Robert Norton, William Borough, contributed a good deal to the theory and practice of what was to be called the mechanical philosophy (*H.*, chapter 2, *passim*, pp. 88; 292–300)—the -ism of the 'rude mechanicals', as mercantilism was the -ism of the merchants. So, I agree, did almanac-makers (*K.*, p. 92, p. 231; *H.*, pp. 48–51).

Nor did I treat 'all English merchants at this time as by definition "progressive and forward-looking"'. I did point out specific ways in which merchant companies and individual merchants patronized science and mathematics, and contrasted this with the lack of government patronage (*K.*, p. 93, p. 232; *H.*, pp. 17–19, 41, 62, 70–1, 193–9). I was perhaps foolish to assume general agreement that merchants interested in long-distance trade would not be hostile to the arts of astronomy, mathematics and navigation, which made it easier to sail ships across oceans safely. For Dr Kearney thinks that 'the revolutionary discoveries in science had no practical application. . . . The mathematical world of the new science was as abstract in its own way as the world of Aristotelian metaphysics' (*K.*, p. 100; pp. 240–1). I find this an odd way to describe the age of Wright and Hariot, of Napier and Briggs. Has Dr Kearney ever glanced at Commander Waters's *The Art of Navigation in Elizabethan and Early Stuart Times*? There is plenty of evidence that merchants, impressed by the ignorance of mathematics shown by some seamen, were interested in extending popular mathematical education. It was in this context that I stressed that Gresham College was founded and controlled by merchants, and aimed—*inter alia*—at teaching mathematics to navigators (*K.*, p. 93, pp. 232–3; *H.*, pp. 33–5, 45–7, 63). I nowhere suggest, though Dr Kearney seems to imply that I do, that scientists or mathematics teachers were patronized exclusively by merchants. I discuss at length the patronage of the Leicester, Sidney, Northumberland and Ralegh groups, and the use of mathematics for surveying gentlemen's estates (*K.*, pp. 91–2, pp. 230–1; *H.*, pp. 21–2, 28–33, 40–2, 132–145).

Dr Kearney rightly distinguishes between the craft tradition which combines utilitarianism and religious zeal, on the one hand, and the scholarly mathematical tradition on the other. The former appealed to the more radical among the Puritans (*K.*, p. 97, pp. 236–7; *H.*, pp. 119–25, 148–9, 298). This is an important distinction, and one which I wish I had emphasized even more than I did.[11] But it is easier for the historian to distinguish between two trends of thought than it was for contemporaries: men were often influenced by both, as Dr Kearney recognizes in the crucial case of Bacon (*K.*, p. 95, p. 235; *H.*, pp. 14–15, 85–96). I do not think Bacon's successors fall into two classes as neatly as Dr Kearney suggests. Nor can the former tradition be so simply identified with the Invisible College, the latter with the Oxford group led by Wilkins. Boyle, Haak and Oldenburg, who moved from the former group to the Royal Society, have to be laughed off (*K.*, p. 97; pp. 236–7), though Boyle remained so puritan (on my definition) that he refused to become President of the Royal Society because it would have meant taking an oath. Dr Kearney forgets that Wilkins was as utilitarian as any Comenian ('those may justly be accounted barren studies which do not conduce to practice as their proper end'—*H.*, p. 85); and it is surely odd to class Professor Petty and Hartlib (on the committee for Durham College) among enemies of the universities (*K.*, p. 97; pp. 236–7).

Dr Kearney also ignores the Gresham College group of 1645, more important than the Invisible College. The Gresham group brought together Wilkins, Wallis and Goddard with the Emmanuel Puritan Samuel Foster and the Comenian Haak (*H.*, p. 48). Nor should the fact that Wilkins became a bishop after 1660 be allowed to cancel out the fact that in 1646 he published a wholly puritan treatise on preaching; any more than the fact that Sprat too became a bishop should make us forget his panegyrics on Wilkins's brother-in-law, Oliver Cromwell (*H.*, pp. 125–6).[12] Men who were not heroes had to live as they could in those days of defeat; just as they took ideas as they found them. We err if we

[11] A start has been made in an interesting article by P. M. Rattansi, 'Paracelsus and the Puritan Revolution', *Ambix*, xi (1963), pp. 24–32; cf. *H.*, pp. vii–viii.

[12] Contrast Rabb, *op. cit.*, p. 50.

try to impose a retrospective consistency on their thought or actions; we err still more if we accept at its face value Sprat's propagandist *History of the Royal Society*, which was designed to cover up the parliamentarian and puritan background of the leading founders of the Society (*H.*, pp. 64, 121–30).

In reality things were very mixed up. Dr Kearney refers to Boyle's interest in alchemy (continuing Bacon's), and Napier's interest in the number of the Beast (*K.*, pp. 97–8, 88, pp. 237–8, 226; *H.*, pp. 7, 40–1). I whole-heartedly agree that 'with Briggs as with Newton, theology and "scientific" interests merged' (*K.*, pp. 88–9; p. 227), though the fact that seventeenth-century scientists had seventeenth-century ideas does not surprise me as much as it seems to surprise Dr Kearney. One of my main arguments was precisely this convergence of puritanism and science, with an interest in exact chronology as one of the meeting points (*H.*, pp. 7, 22–7, 55–9, 190). Fairfax made propagandist use of astrologers (*K.*, p. 99; p. 239); but years later even Robert Hooke, a scientist of the scientists, noted the unfortunate astrological conjunctions which marked the death of John Wilkins.[13] Miss Yates has recently reminded us afresh of the vitally important contribution of the magical tradition to the evolution of science, and Professor Farrington has rammed the point home in relation to Bacon.[14] It is possible that Miss Nicolson was wrong to suggest the civil war divisions corresponded to rival schools of astronomy, though I have never seen her evidence refuted. But her point is not disproved by pointing out that once the Ptolemaic theory had been defeated with Charles I, disputes for the succession broke out between defenders of Copernicus and Tycho Brahe; or that almanac-makers used astrology for political purposes (*K.*, pp. 85, 99, pp. 222, 239–40; *H.*, p. 118).

There are other points at which Dr Kearney's logic strikes me as odd. On page 96 he appears to argue that if English Puritans were utilitarian, this is due to Ramus, not Bacon; if the Ramist Comenius is a Baconian, this is due to Bacon's utilitarianism, not to his science (*K.*, p. 96, p. 236; for Ramus see *H.*, pp. 31–3, 93, 133–4, 148, 291–3). I am again confused when Dr Kearney's

13 M. 'Espinasse, *Robert Hooke* (London, 1956), p. 113.
14 F. A. Yates, *Giordano Bruno and the Hermetic Tradition* (London, 1964);
B. Farrington, *The Philosophy of Francis Bacon* (Liverpool, 1964), chap. 10;
cf. *H.*, pp. 147–9.

remark (with which I agree), 'it may well be that new wealth in the seventeenth century made possible the existence of a greater number of scholars with leisure than ever before' is followed by the statement that 'Social change of this kind . . . is not to be explained merely in economic terms' (*K.*, p. 100; p. 241). How is new wealth explained in non-economic terms?

Dr Kearney may be right to deny the connections which I (and many before me) have tried to suggest between puritanism and the rise of science, and between the rise of capitalism and both puritanism and science, though there seems to me a formidable amount of evidence on our side. I hope readers of his article will look at my book before assuming that Dr Kearney's charge of over-simplification is proven. I cannot help feeling that Dr Kearney's objection is really to any attempt to establish meaningful connections in history, and I should therefore be uneasy about his underlying assumptions even if some of his detailed criticisms of me proved to be correct. It is easy to slide from 'let us not oversimplify' into a theoretical justification, or a tacit assumption, of history as just one damn thing after another—a historical nihilism which is becoming fashionable today, for obvious sociological reasons. I may not have stated the connections correctly, but I am impenitent in my conviction that it is right to try to see society as a whole, and wrong to consider men's work and thought as though they existed in separate self-contained compartments.

XIX

PURITANISM AND SCIENCE: PROBLEMS OF DEFINITION*

H. F. Kearney

As I hope to make clear, the discussion between Mr Hill and myself about the relationship between puritanism and science hinges largely upon different definitions and assumptions. But I do not see a debate of this kind, as he apparently does, as a conflict between the forces of light and darkness. Mr Hill erects his hypothesis into a species of orthodoxy to be defended by the faithful with every shot in the polemical locker. I do not share his belief that there are no loose ends in history, no gaps for lack of evidence, no surprising contradictions in human behaviour. I cannot follow him in his unhesitating division of seventeenth-century society into forward-looking and reactionary elements.

Of course, this division of opinion is not merely a matter of definition. I think that Mr Hill's use of evidence is also open to criticism. For example, he seems to see a 'scientist' wherever he finds a globe and a pair of compasses. On this basis, the first four provosts of Trinity College, Dublin, are turned into 'scientists' and the college itself into a centre of scientific endeavour.[1] This is indeed viewing the evidence with the eyes of faith. Mr Hill quotes contemporary witnesses when they support his case but not apparently when they do not. He quotes from John Donne's poetry to illustrate conservative reaction[2] but not from his

---

* From no. 31 (July 1965).
[1] C. Hill, *Intellectual Origins of the English Revolution* (Oxford, 1965), p. 277 n. 4.
[2] C. Hill, *The Century of Revolution* (Edinburgh, 1961), p. 95.

letters[3] which seem to give a different impression. In contrasting
the forward-looking Sir John Eliot with the reactionary Donne,
Mr Hill quotes Eliot at length but in a highly selective way.[4] But
a scrutiny of Mr Hill's use of evidence would lead us into an endless discussion of particulars when what logically comes first is
the hypothesis which Mr Hill defends. It is this which I propose
to examine, by looking first at Mr Hill's 'puritanism' and then
his 'science'.

I

Mr Hill is, of course, right to draw attention to the various
meanings I attribute to the word 'puritan'. This point lies at the
heart of the principal difference between us. He thinks that a single
definition can be attributed to the word. For me, in contrast, the
word 'puritanism' is analogous to words such as 'socialism' or
'romanticism'. Their value lies in covering a wide range of
different views; they are impossible to use precisely, much as one
may be tempted to do so. There are as many 'puritanisms' as there
are 'socialisms' and 'romanticisms'. In short, to describe someone
as a Puritan is not really to tell us very much about his specific
views. James Ussher, archbishop of Armagh, and John Milton
were both 'Puritans', yet they differed radically on many points.
Who is to decide who was the more puritan of the two?

On my view, puritanism consisted of various cross-currents of
thought and emotion, generally Calvinist in tone and possessing
a certain continuity from the 1560s to the Cromwellian period and
beyond. It seems to me that much puritan thought was clerical
in colour, much of it anti-clerical. Some of it was academic, some
opposed to learning. Many Puritans were presbyterian, others
were Independent. Some were millenarian, some were not.
Puritanism is nearer a flavour, a tone of voice, a loose set of not-
always-consistent assumptions than a precise and unambiguous
concept which can be sharply defined. If we must have a definition,
I would define puritanism as the growing circle of discontent
both within and without the Established Church from the 1560s

---

[3] J. Hayward (ed.), *John Donne: Complete Poetry and Selected Prose* (London,
1941), p. 674.
[4] Hill, *The Century of Revolution*, p. 95.

onwards. It ranged from the academic puritanism of Cartwright and Greenham to the popular vulgarities of the Marprelate Tracts, which they condemned. It included both the rationalism of the Cambridge Platonists and the anti-rationalism of their critics. Basically I suppose what was common to all of them was a vision of what the Church of Christ ought to be if it were stripped of externals and inessentials. Where they differed (and their differences were not insignificant) was in their view of what was external and inessential. Their vision varied as much as the nineteenth-century socialist vision itself.

Now Mr Hill's definition of puritanism conflicts with this at several points. His book, *Society and Puritanism in Pre-Revolutionary England*, published (London, 1964) since my article was written, makes this abundantly clear. In the first place, Mr Hill confines the phenomenon of puritanism to the period between the 1590s and the Civil War. One can see the attraction of this assumption from his point of view, since it makes it possible for him to attribute a certain unity to puritanism. The movement, he tells us, 'is not to be identified with either Presbyterianism or Independency'. This conveniently rules out the clericalism of the 1570s and 1580s and the sectarianism of the 1640s and 1650s. Puritanism before 1640 is, in Mr Hill's view, 'undifferentiated'.[5] There is 'a main stream of Puritan thought'.[6] Finally, now that presbyterianism has been ruled out of court, it is possible to stress the lay character of puritanism. Its appeal, Mr Hill assures us, was to 'the industrious sort of Englishman'. Indeed, 'There is the very closest connection between the Protestant ideology of hard work and the economic needs of English society.'[7] One might begin by drawing attention to the obvious tautology of Mr Hill's definition of puritanism. If this definition of puritanism largely confines it to beliefs appealing to 'the industrious sort of Englishman', then it is neither surprising nor informative to find that puritanism fulfils an economic need. The sleight of hand is too obvious to be impressive. On this definition, the Puritan can never appear in a purely religious guise; economic overtones are always to be heard rumbling. Certain types of Puritan of course, academics,

---

[5] 'Puritanism, capitalism and the Scientific Revolution', *Past and Present*, no. 29 (Dec. 1964), p. 90; p. 245 in this volume.

[6] *Society and Puritanism in Pre-Revolutionary England* (London, 1964), p. 29.

[7] *Ibid.*, p. 276.

gentry and visionaries, hardly merit the accolade 'industrious sort of Englishman' and these receive only occasional mention by Mr Hill, rarely emphatic salute.

But even apart from this objection, Mr Hill offers a curiously simplified view of puritanism, as we may see from the first chapter of his book *Society and Puritanism*. Drawing on his wide reading, Mr Hill provides the reader with many examples of the uses of the word 'puritan' by contemporaries. Well and good. We draw what seems to be the obvious conclusion, that usage ranged widely, between extremes of obvious absurdities. But Mr Hill draws the opposite conclusion, unwarranted by his own evidence, namely that: 'I agree with contemporaries in thinking that there was in England in the two or three generations before the civil war a body of opinion which can usefully be labelled Puritan.'[8] 'Body of opinion' is a crucial phrase. Before the reader is aware, the body assumes a corporeal unity and is packed and labelled within a paragraph. A body of opinion drawing on a wide variety of views has been transmuted into a consistent, thrusting ideology. On pages 29–30 of his book, Mr Hill cuts puritanism to a shape and size which suits his interpretation. But his readers are not obliged to adopt this particular fashion.

To me, it seems excessively paradoxical to cut off the period 1600–40 from what went before and what came after. Presbyterianism rose from below the waves in 1640, whence we may assume that it led a submerged existence in England before that date. We know from the New England colonists, who carried their religious opinions with them, that puritanism of the 1630s offered a variegated appearance. Do we not find Independency in Massachusetts and elsewhere, and if we do, may we not presume that more existed where it came from? Puritanism is 'undifferentiated' before 1640 only to the eyes of the converted. The tensions and differences which exploded after 1640 were already in existence. For this the puritanism of the New World offers unmistakable evidence.

Of course the view which I have been putting forward has nothing new about it. It is derived very largely from the classical works of William Haller. The story of puritanism, as Haller tells it, does not exclude presbyterianism or Independency. Haller

8 *Ibid.*, p. 28.

begins with Thomas Cartwright and carries on until well into the 1640s. On presbyterianism, he specifically tells us that:[9]

> The main body of the Puritan preachers, it is important to remember, never surrendered the hope of taking over the establishment and running it according to the scheme of the *Book of Discipline*. These men became known in time as the presbyterians and composed the majority of the Westminster Assembly.

Haller also includes Independents, Brownists, Baptists and the host of sectaries in his study of puritanism. I find it exceedingly curious therefore that Mr Hill accuses others of maintaining too exclusive a definition of puritanism when this is precisely the charge which he is open to. As for his claim to be writing in the classical tradition of Gardiner and Haller, the evidence is against him. He certainly quotes from them in *Society and Puritanism*, but only as and when it suits his argument. Essentially, their view of puritanism is quite different from his.

II

We may now turn to science, about the nature of which Mr Hill and I again hold opposite views. Mr Hill sees science as a useful activity, concerned with the collection of facts, and as a movement which involved doctors, seamen, artisans and so on. He writes in *The Century of Revolution*:[10]

> Francis Bacon was the son of an intensely Puritan mother. His programme of industriously collecting facts with the object of ultimately building up a body of knowledge which would help to improve man's lot on earth was entirely in the Puritan tradition.

Leaving Bacon's mother on one side (and I have never seen the relevance of this piece of information), this view of seventeenth-century science does not really stand up to criticism. The Scientific Revolution was surely utilitarian only to a limited degree. The classic experiments were anything but useful in their application.

[9] W. Haller, *The Rise of Puritanism* (New York, 1938), p. 16.
[10] *The Century of Revolution*, p. 94.

Pascal's experiments on the vacuum culminating in the Puy de Dome episode of 1648 were extraordinarily imaginative but entirely useless. The improvement of man's lot on earth was an irrelevant consideration. Nor was Pascal collecting facts. He was answering questions and testing hypotheses, which is a very different matter.

What has been said about Pascal applies equally to Kepler's planetary investigations, Galileo's mechanics, Mersenne's study of music, the Cartesian theory of the universe, Harvey's discovery of the circulation of the blood and Newton's *Principia*. Intellectual curiosity is relevant here, not a crude utilitarianism. The interesting question indeed is how men like these managed to escape from the all-embracing utilitarianism of the European tradition; for it was precisely the growth of intellectual curiosity for its own sake, which transformed the field of scientific enquiry. A sociological investigation therefore must concentrate attention not upon technology and economic need but upon the social and intellectual conditions which favoured the development of originality.

In fact, in my view the historian of science, far from being concerned with 'class' or 'urban values', whatever these may have been in the seventeenth century, is or should be examining the origins of particular milieux or intellectual circles. The group of which Friar Marin Mersenne was the centre may be taken as a case in point. From a convent in Paris, Mersenne (1588–1648) drew into his epistolary network[11] most of the leading scientists of his day, irrespective of religion or nationality, even to the extent of admiring the work of Bacon, Hariot and Oughtred. Though based on Paris, the circle was western European in scope. It connected Descartes in Holland, Gassendi and Peiresc in Provence, Schickard in Tübingen, Hortensius in Leyden, Galileo in Florence and van Helmont in Brussels. Gassendi's journey in 1629 illustrated a similar kind of international contact.[12] It was upon these foundations and not upon economic developments confined to particular geographical areas that scientific research advanced.

Mersenne's correspondence in fact symbolizes the *European* nature of science. Mr Hill's approach, in contrast, is based upon

[11] See P. Tannery and C. de Waard (eds), *Correspondance du . . . Mersenne*, vol. ii, *1628–1630* (Paris, 1936).
[12] *Ibid.*, pp. 242–6.

the categories of the nation state. But 'Kepler's Bohemia' and 'Copernicus's Poland' illustrate a type of nineteenth-century concept from which the seventeenth-century historian must try to escape. The intellectual Europe of the age of Galileo took no account of later national boundaries. Nor, curiously enough, do religious differences seem relevant, despite the shadow of the Thirty Years' War. But even on his own grounds, Mr Hill's interpretation of the puritan origins of science is open to criticism. French Huguenots made no mark scientifically. Jansenism did not encourage science; Pascal was very much the lone wolf who gave up his scientific work as an idle pastime after his conversion. In Holland, Cartesianism came under heavy fire from both Church and State. In seventeenth-century Italy, Torricelli (1608–47) and Malpighi (1628–94) were far from being alone in their scientific work. Malpighi's observation of the growth of the heart of a chick has been praised as 'perhaps the most remarkable observational achievement of any biologist in the seventeenth century'.[13] And yet controversy along these lines misses the point. The development of science is too subtle a process to be explained in crude modern terms of religion, class or nationality. Sociological investigation there should be, but surely with more delicate instruments, with more precisely defined (and more relevant) concepts.

III

In conclusion, then, the case against Mr Hill is that his historical argument is marred by its tautology. Puritanism and science are seen by him as analogous activities because they are narrowly defined in analogous ways. Puritanism appears as the type of religion which appeals to the 'industrious sort of Englishman'; science is described as an activity in which practical utility plays the decisive part. Both then fit neatly into Mr Hill's interpretation of early modern history, in which 'urban and industrial values replaced those appropriate to a mainly agrarian society'.[14] But

[13] *The New Cambridge Modern History*, vol. v, *The Ascendancy of France 1648–88*, ed. F. L. Carsten (Cambridge, 1961), pp. 68–9: A. R. Hall quoting from F. J. Cole, *A History of Comparative Anatomy* (London, 1949), p. 180.
[14] Hill, *Past and Present*, no. 29, p. 89; p. 244 in this volume.

if this interpretation seems plausible, it is because of a highly selective use of the evidence. My original article criticized Mr Hill's description of Gresham College on these grounds. The publication since then of his book *Society and Puritanism* has shown that his views on puritanism are open to similar criticism.

I naturally regret that Mr Hill, who so rarely loses his good humour, should have taken my previous remarks amiss. I owe him an apology for attributing to him a statement about the audience at Gresham College which he did not make. But apart from this, I thought I stated his views fairly. His argument is now available in full in *Intellectual Origins of the English Revolution* (Oxford, 1965), but the outline was already clear in *The Century of Revolution* (London, 1961) which his articles in the *Listener* to some extent only confirmed. Is it unfair to say that latest Hill is but old Hill writ large? Mr Hill also implies that in criticizing his hypothesis, I am striking at the foundations of accepted historical orthodoxy. The role of Urban VIII is ill-suited to any historian, most of all to Mr Hill; but in any case the implication is false. Mr Hill has resurrected and refurbished views which are unfashionable among many historians of science. In recent years, the pace has been set by such men as Koyré and Clagett who are not to be dismissed lightly.[15] Finally, it is difficult to understand why Mr Hill should regard me as a Nihilist, a Kafka-like figure on the Downs, rejecting all meaning in history, when all that I reject is Mr Hill's interpretation of it.

[15] E.g. A. Koyré, *Études Galiléennes* (Paris, 1939); *Critical Problems in the History of Science*, ed. M. Clagett (Madison, Wisconsin, 1959).

XX

RELIGION AND THE RISE OF MODERN SCIENCE*

Theodore K. Rabb

The last section of Mr Christopher Hill's recent article on William Harvey[1] opens with the assumption that modern scholarship has established a connection between protestantism and the rise of science. Since Dr Kearney adopted a rather different interpretation when he discussed the same subject in the following number of this journal,[2] it may be well to inquire what it is that the researches of recent years have in fact demonstrated.

Mr Hill begins by deriding as 'rather smart' and completely unsuccessful those who question 'the relationship between protestantism and the *rise* of science' (italics mine, for reasons which will become apparent). Without informing the reader where the questions can be found, what the objections are, or how they have been overcome, Mr Hill merely refers to two books and two articles which show that the relationship is 'so well established.' The four works are: Candolle's study of scientists from the 1660s to the mid-nineteenth century; R. K. Merton's attempt to give a

* From no. 31 (July 1965). This contribution was first written before the appearance of Mr Hill's Rejoinder to Dr Kearney, 'Puritanism, capitalism and the Scientific Revolution', in *Past and Present*, no. 29 (December 1964), pp. 88–97; pp. 243–53 in this volume, and his book *Intellectual Origins of the English Revolution* (Oxford, 1965). It has since been modified and expanded to deal with certain of the issues raised by this second article (cited as his Rejoinder) and the book.

[1] C. Hill, 'William Harvey and the idea of monarchy', *Past and Present*, no. 27 (April 1964), pp. 70–2; pp. 160–81 in this volume.

[2] H. F. Kearney, 'Puritanism, capitalism and the Scientific Revolution', *Past and Present*, no. 28 (July 1964), pp. 81–101; pp. 218–42 in this volume.

puritan 'ethos' the principal credit for the rise of science in England; J. Pelseneer's investigation of sixteenth-century 'Belgian'
scientists; and S. F. Mason's analysis of certain parallels between
the thought of a few early scientists and the early Reformers.[3]
Since the burden of proof is placed on these studies, it will be
necessary to take a closer look at them before Mr Hill's opening
assumption can be accepted. But first of all the points at issue
should be clarified.

I

Nobody can ignore the links between the reformed religion and
scientific advance from the mid-seventeenth century. The heavy
preponderance of Protestants among scientists after the 1640s is
inescapable, and it is obvious that the descendants of Luther and
Calvin could embrace the new discipline much more readily than
could the Catholics. What is less clear, and much more to the
point, is the situation *before* the 1640s. After all, the *rise* of science
is the topic under discussion. The question is not why protestantism proved to be more flexible in the long run, but rather what
part religion played in stimulating the great advances in anatomy,
physics and astronomy which are known as the Scientific Revolution. Most of these advances had taken place by the end of the
1630s. By 1640, with the work of Galileo, Harvey and Descartes
virtually complete, one can safely say that science had risen. How
it consolidated its gains, spread further, and moved on to new
achievements, is a different matter. The story of its *rise* is clearly
over by the 1640s.

But before 1640, the neat statistical connection is not so easy to
find. In fact, were it not for the subsequent preponderance of
Protestants, one would be inclined to judge the Catholic the more
fruitful of the two churches. Italy was the undisputed centre of
scientific inquiry during this period: almost every one of the

---

[3] A. de Candolle, *Histoire des Sciences et des Savants depuis deux Siècles*
(Geneva, 1873); R. K. Merton, 'Science, technology and society in
seventeenth century England', *Osiris*, iv (1938), pp. 360–632; J. Pelseneer,
'L'Origine protestante de la science moderne', *Lychnos* (Uppsala, 1946–7),
pp. 246–8; S. F. Mason, 'The Scientific Revolution and the Protestant
Reformation', *Annals of Science*, ix (1953), pp. 64–87, 154–75.

great names associated with the discoveries of the time studied there, and the Italians' tradition of leadership in the field reached a climax in the work of Galileo. One might argue that some of the most famous pioneers were not conspicuously devoted to the Church, but their sense of commitment to Catholicism cannot be doubted. Copernicus was a cleric of unblemished orthodoxy, and even Galileo and Descartes, for all their difficulties with the hierarchy, struggled mightily to remain within the fold.[4]

Moreover, as T. S. Kuhn and others have shown, opposition to Copernicanism came equally from both religious camps in the sixteenth and early seventeenth centuries.[5] Luther, Calvin and Melanchthon all derided the notion that the earth circled the sun, while on the other side, Counter-Reformation popes such as Paul III and Gregory XIII at least welcomed the findings of the new astronomy which paved the way for calendar reform. The only well-defined group which seems to have been solidly hostile to the discoveries was the conservative academic community. Professors reluctant to change their way of teaching massed against Vesalius, Kepler and the young Galileo. Many of their criticisms inevitably rested on scripture, but this kind of argument was not peculiar to Catholics. If such reasoning tended to have a special appeal to one of the two sides, it was to the Protestants, who preferred a more literal interpretation of the Bible. Both the

[4] See G. de Santillana, *The Crime of Galileo* (London, 1958); and, for Descartes, Part VI of the *Discourse on Method*, or his letters to Mersenne of 22 July 1633, and 10 Jan. and 15 March 1634: *Œuvres Philosophiques de Descartes*, ed. L. Aimé-Martin (Paris, 1852), pp. 544-7. For a survey of the wide variety of Catholic achievements in this period, see F. Russo, 'Rôle respectif du catholicisme et du protestantisme dans le développement des sciences aux XVIe et XVIIe siècles', *Jl of World History*, iii (1957), pp. 854-80, and the works he cites, notably those of F. de Dainville. Russo undoubtedly goes too far, for he denies that Galileo's trial had any effect, and he refuses to recognize the clear lead the Protestants took in the late seventeenth century. But he certainly presents enough evidence of major Catholic activity to refute any claims for protestant superiority before mid-century.

[5] T. S. Kuhn, *The Copernican Revolution* (Cambridge, Mass., 1957); de Santillana, *op. cit.*; M. Caspar, *Kepler*, trans. C. D. Hellman (New York and London, 1959). These works document the remarks which follow. The fact that Vesalius encountered his principal opposition from university professors and anatomists of both faiths, and not from the Inquisition, as Mr Hill claims, emerges from C. D. O'Malley, *Andreas Vesalius of Brussels, 1514-1564* (Berkeley and Los Angeles, 1964).

major Catholic contribution to pre-1640 scientific advance, and the lack of noticeable difference between protestant and Catholic resistance to change in the sixteenth century, must be explained away if the reformed religion is to be considered inherently more conducive to science, or in any way responsible for the rise of the new form of inquiry.

II

The four works cited by Mr Hill labour under an immediate disadvantage when applied to the issues just outlined. None of them deals with Catholicism in the pre-1640 period. In addition, Candolle's book may be ruled out from the start, because it covers only the years after the crucial century of 1540–1640.

R. K. Merton's study of English puritanism has been the target of such severe and unanswered criticisms that it can no longer be adduced as the final word on the subject. Knappen, Kocher, Conant, Hall and Curtis have all challenged many of Merton's assumptions, and in a recent article I have questioned both the validity of his statistics and his attempt to find inherently puritan qualities which promoted scientific inquiry.[6] These rebuttals of Merton may not have been successful, but they have yet to be refuted. In particular, the denial of any significant connection before 1640 will be overcome only by the disclosure of new evidence which, as we shall see, has not yet been forthcoming. Merton's findings are at best in doubt, and the evidence from the pre-revolutionary period pointedly fails to support his conclusions. Furthermore, in the larger context of the relationship between protestantism and science, Merton's work is to some extent irrelevant. He was not drawing distinctions between

[6] M. M. Knappen, *Tudor Puritanism* (Chicago, 1939), pp. 478–80; P. H. Kocher, *Science and Religion in Elizabethan England* (San Marino, 1953), particularly pp. 14–19; J. B. Conant, 'The advancement of learning during the puritan Commonwealth', *Proceedings of the Massachusetts Historical Society*, lxvi (1936–41) pp. 3–31; A. R. Hall, 'Merton revisited: or, science and society in the seventeenth century', *Hist. of Science*, ii (1963), pp. 1–16; M. H. Curtis, *Oxford and Cambridge in Transition, 1558–1642* (Oxford, 1959), pp. 247–9, 287–8; T. K. Rabb, 'Puritanism and the rise of experimental science in England', *Jl of World History*, vii (1962), pp. 46–67, especially pp. 53–67.

protestantism and Catholicism, but between Anglicanism and puritanism. Even if the Puritans *were* more inclined towards science than the rest of their countrymen, the English discoveries were still all made by protestant scientists. What matters is that before 1640 their achievements were of considerably less importance than those of their Catholic counterparts (and were no more widely accepted by one religious group than another).

Since Mr Hill has argued for the connection between puritanism and science at greater length in his Rejoinder to Dr Kearney and his *Intellectual Origins*, it might be well to make a brief excursion at this point to see whether the links are now better established than they were in Merton's study. As has been mentioned, this is something of a side issue, but it is relevant here because the arguments often parallel those used in discussions of protestantism as opposed to Catholicism. It is striking, for instance, that the evidence Mr Hill uses to support the link between puritanism and the rise of science in England is more concrete after 1640 than before. He complains in his Rejoinder that others have defined puritanism too narrowly to allow the connection to be made in the earlier period (p. 91; p. 247). But surely it is a far more serious 'abandonment of normal scholarly methods' when, as happens repeatedly in his *Intellectual Origins*, arguments rest on innuendo rather than evidence. In the effort to raise the spectre of puritanism at every conceivable opportunity, implications are made which are simply distortions. Due to limitations of space, one example must suffice. The paragraph on page 163 discussing the career of Sir Edwin Sandys rightly points out his importance as a leader of overseas enterprise and parliamentary opposition. But the penultimate sentence of the paragraph leaves this subject and interjects: 'Sandys, son of a Marian exile, was a patron of the Pilgrim Fathers'. The implication is clear. Sandys was not only an opponent of the Crown and a colonizer, but he also seemed to have puritan sympathies. And earlier in the book, on page 63, Sandys is unjustifiably associated with science. Thus a whole group of the characteristics which Mr Hill considers to have paved the way for the Revolution are combined in one man. The flaw in this network of associations is that the crucial sentence could just as accurately have read: 'Sandys, son of an archbishop of York who was Whitgift's ally and who denounced the Puritans, made a speech in the 1593 Parliament attacking separatists (in opposition to Ralegh), was a student and close friend of Richard Hooker, and financed the publication of the *Laws of Ecclesiastical Polity*'.

Both in his Rejoinder and his *Intellectual Origins* Mr Hill condemns historians who, by failing to see society as a whole, compart men's thoughts and actions. But he is guilty of the same distortion. He makes no effort to see a man as a whole, or to inquire whether, without special pleading, a slim connection with puritanism such as Sandys's has any relevance in a brief description of his career. Thus eventually he builds up an elaborate series of associations, often based on nothing more than a host of occasional passing references. But these associations serve only to produce the very effect which Mr Hill deplores: they isolate artificially those few features of thought and society which he happens to consider important. The resultant implication is that these features enjoyed an exceptional inter-relationship (a particularly conspicuous example of this distortion can be found in Mr Hill's treatment of Prince Henry's household). But the English 'establishment' of Elizabethan and Jacobean times was such a close-knit group that connections can be found in almost any direction. As Mr Hill admits, both the Court itself and many undeniable non-Puritans must be included among the most important contributors to the rise of scientific inquiry in England. In effect, there were so many groups, including near-sceptics, Ramists, and fervent Puritans, all prominently involved in early scientific activity, that it is invidious to assign to any one of them a special importance.

A major obstacle to Mr Hill's attempt to emphasize puritanism is the scarcity of 'radical Protestants who wanted to reform the church'[7] among prominent English scientists active before 1640. He has solid evidence in only five cases: Briggs, Horrocks, Napier, Foster and Gellibrand—and the last two were hardly of 'the first rank'. And his setting of Francis Bacon's ideas in a puritan context is almost as contrived as his similar treatment of William Harvey.[8]

[7] This definition of a Puritan by Mr Hill (Rejoinder, p. 90, p. 245 in this volume; *Intellectual Origins*, p. 26) is accepted as the basic description in the paragraphs which follow.
[8] Mrs Whitteridge has dealt with Mr Hill's conjectures about Harvey in *Past and Present*, no. 30 (April 1965), pp. 104–9; pp. 182–8 in this volume.

In 1961, with no more evidence than the puritanism of Bacon's mother, Mr Hill placed Bacon's programme 'entirely in the puritan tradition'. In his *Intellectual Origins* he now refers to Sir Francis's 'pious parents', possibly because B. Farrington has recently shown the importance of Sir Nicholas Bacon as an influence on his son.[9] Yet the evidence is unmistakable that Bacon rejected his mother's puritanism; that his ideas about church reform owed little to theological or doctrinal motives; that his proposals on the subject were merely the typically practical recommendations of a man obsessed by reform itself; that his criticism of Puritans was more severe than his criticism of the bishops; that the church reforms he did propose would have been no more than palliatives for Puritans; and that he was 'a sincere if unenthusiastic Christian', irenic and rational, fairly tolerant of Puritans but not committed to their cause.[10] There is also no evidence, apart from the special case of Bishop Williams, that the Puritans showed any particular interest in Baconian views before 1640—except as a justification for impeachment.[11] Moreover, as

[9] C. Hill, *The Century of Revolution* (Edinburgh, 1961), p. 94; *Intellectual Origins*, p. 91; B. Farrington, *The Philosophy of Francis Bacon* (Liverpool, 1964), pp. 12–13.

[10] E. A. Abbott, in his *Francis Bacon* (London, 1885), pp. 105–11, did call Bacon a Puritan, but the overwhelming evidence to the contrary, outlined in this last sentence, has emerged from more recent studies: viz. C. D. Broad, *The Philosophy of Francis Bacon* (Cambridge, 1926), p. 19, from which the quotation is taken; J. W. Allen, *English Political Thought, 1603–1660*, vol. i (London, 1938), pp. 122, 229–31; B. Farrington, *Francis Bacon* (New York, 1949), which notes Bacon's puritan background, but stresses repeatedly that he himself did not follow his mother's footsteps (see pp. 22, 28–9, 47); and F. H. Anderson, *Francis Bacon* (New York, 1962), especially chap. 5.

[11] This is the most serious difficulty faced by any attempt to connect Baconianism with puritanism before 1640. It is significant that there was no Puritan among the six men Bacon himself considered probable supporters for his scientific schemes (*Intellectual Origins*, p. 99). And there is no evidence in the books by R. F. Young and G. H. Turnbull (cited *ibid.*, p. 100) that the Puritans who supported Comenius, Dury and Hartlib enthusiastically in the 1640s had anything like the same interest in their reform proposals before the Revolution. It is also noteworthy that the post-1640 enthusiasm was inspired as much, if not more, by the trio's activity in the cause of religion as by their scientific concerns. Mr Hill admits the belatedness of the Puritans' appreciation of Bacon (*Century of Revolution*, pp. 179–80; *Intellectual Origins*, pp. 116–19), but he does not seem to realize how critically this impairs his argument. His only

Farrington has shown, Bacon's interest in the Scriptures 'was not primarily theological': the Bible was the agent of the overthrow of Scholasticism, and the repository of 'a world-outlook in which his new conception of science could take root and grow'.[12] It is not difficult to see why puritanism and Baconianism later formed a natural alliance; but in Bacon himself the religious impulse was almost entirely absent. Since Mr Hill cannot prove that Sir Francis was a Puritan, he claims instead that the Lord Chancellor's ideas subsumed and were nurtured by strong protestant traditions. Yet to claim his practical bent of mind for puritanism is to ignore an equally strong similar tradition on the continent. To call Bacon's division of religion from science 'in the best protestant tradition' is to ignore another long-standing continental tradition, which received its most famous expression, not in Bacon's work, but in Galileo's *Letter to the Grand Duchess Christina*. The 'benefit to humanity' view, the relationship with artisans, the interest in fruitful applications of scientific thought, are all as common among Catholics of this period as among Protestants. Even Bacon's vision of progress (which, incidentally, included an acknowledgement of the superiority of the ancients in genius) owed much to that solid Catholic, Louis Leroy, and many earlier Catholic thinkers.[13]

It is only by ignoring the enormous Catholic scientific activity of the period that major claims can be made for the importance of protestantism, let alone puritanism. The many parallels that Mr Hill draws seem to have very little meaning when placed in the

---

explanation of the time lag consists of a few weakly documented implications that Court and Laudian censorship kept science down. (*Intellectual Origins*, pp. 32–3, 119.)

[12] Farrington, *The Philosophy of Francis Bacon*, chap. 3.

[13] Mr Hill outlines the debt Bacon's ideas owed to puritanism on page 49 of his *Century of Revolution*, and on pages 91–6 of his *Intellectual Origins*. For the qualification of Bacon's praise of the moderns, see R. F. Jones, *Ancients and Moderns* (St Louis, 1936), p. 47, and Farrington, *Francis Bacon*, p. 170. For the evidence showing Bacon's use of Leroy, see W. L. Gundersheimer, 'Louis LeRoy's humanistic optimism', *Jour. Hist. Ideas*, xxiii (1962), p. 338. For the many even earlier influences which shaped the seventeenth-century view of the moderns, see H. Baron, 'The *Querelle* of the Ancients and the Moderns as a problem for Renaissance scholarship', *Jour. Hist. Ideas*, xx (1959), pp. 3–22, where the debt of Bacon and Hakewill to Italians and Frenchmen is outlined.

broader context of all the scientific thought of the period.[14] If Protestants and Puritans had all the many advantages Mr Hill suggests, then one can only be amazed that so large a number of Catholics were nonetheless engaged in scientific activity in this period, and that they were actually coming up with many of the most important discoveries from the 1540s to the 1630s. It would seem remarkable, for example, that Kepler relied on the international community of Jesuits to provide him with astronomical observations, or that a Jesuit should have published Galileo's discoveries in Chinese in Peking.[15] Evidently orthodox Catholics somehow managed to develop a great interest in science during this century despite their want of religious encouragement. Could it be that religious stimuli were not enormously important to the *rise* of science, or did the Catholics have the same advantages as the Protestants?

In his wish to emphasize protestant achievements, Mr Hill also exaggerates the importance of English scientific work before 1640. With only a few exceptions (Gilbert, Napier, Briggs and Harvey), most of the people mentioned in his *Intellectual Origins* had little impact on the scientific advances of the day. Only a handful more can be considered first-rate scientific thinkers. Frequently Mr Hill's 'scientists' were merely propagandists, technologists, or virtuosi. And he does not strengthen his case by referring to a widespread belief in Copernicanism and the infinity of the universe at a time when such beliefs still had no firm foundation in scientific observation or method. One can agree that many Englishmen were interested in science, and many turned out to be on the 'right side', but this does not give them any major role in the breakthroughs of scientific thought. Mr Hill also promotes another, more important misconception about the progress of science. He considers the practical applications and

14 The parallels are to be found mainly on pages 109–25 of the *Intellectual Origins*. Emphasis is placed on such characteristics of protestantism as its 'sense of athletic purpose', its reliance on personal experience, and its stress on co-operation: 'Science, like religion, is a co-operative activity: the test of the truth of experiment is social, in the sectarian congregation no less than in the community of scientists' (p. 113).
15 Caspar, *Kepler* (Collier edn, 1962), p. 174; S. Drake, *Discoveries and Opinions of Galileo* (New York, 1957), p. 59. See, too, M. W. Burke-Gaffney, *Kepler and the Jesuits* (Milwaukee, 1944), *passim*; and the article by Russo cited above, in note 4.

'fruitful' results of English work a touchstone of its excellence. (*Intellectual Origins*, chapters 2 and 3, *passim*: e.g. page 47.) But these advances, such as improvements in navigation, belong to the realm of technology, not science. The great scientific (as opposed to technological) breakthroughs of the period were intellectual and conceptual, not material. Galileo consulted artisans, but his greatness as a scientist rests on his theoretical insights, not his practical suggestions about chronometers or pulleys. (See below, note 27; and section 11 of Dr Kearney's contribution to this debate, pp. 107-9; pp. 229-33.) Finally, in the matter of organiza-tion of a scientific community, there was no group in England before 1640 whose significance in the history of science could compare with the Academy of the Lincei in Italy or Mersenne's circle in France.

Of central importance to Mr Hill's case is his emphasis on those features of puritanism which encouraged its adherents to turn to science (see above, note 14). But, like his predecessors in this argument, he stresses only those characteristics which were favourable to science, and ignores such anti-scientific traits as the other-worldly and anti-intellectual tendencies of the movement. Even during the Revolution the Puritans' effective action in edu-cation was to be primarily concerned with religion, not science.[16] It proves nothing to show that puritanism had some charac-teristics which might have promoted science. What needs to be shown is why and when these characteristics came to dominate the movement, and thus to have their eventual effect. In my article on 'Puritanism and the rise of experimental science in England' (cited above in note 6), I argued that the more material interests triumphed only during the Revolution, when puritanism became more than a set of religious beliefs, and when, in the search for a well worked-out social and educational philosophy, Baconianism was conveniently found at hand. A similar con-clusion was reached by S. F. Mason in the article which Mr Hill cited, and which will be discussed below (see pages 273-4). This interpretation at least seeks to explain why it took so many years before Bacon's influence began to be felt, and why the Puritans were for so long indifferent to Baconianism. It thus re-emphasizes the crucial date, the 1640s. Only in the midst of a revolution did puritanism embrace the new discipline, for previously the

[16] See my 'Puritanism and . . . science . . .' (cited in note 6), pp. 61-2.

connection had been haphazard and inconclusive. The five future bishops in the Invisible College reflected a patronage of science which, to use Mr Hill's apt distinction (Rejoinder, page 91; page 247 in this volume), was being provided by the *puritan revolutionary*, not the Puritan. To which one can only add, yet again, that by the time these *puritan revolutionaries* ('very few' of whom 'were Puritans', to quote Mr Hill) finally appeared, the new learning was already a productive and established discipline throughout Europe.

III

The third work Mr Hill cites is J. Pelseneer's two-page article discussing the religious affiliations of 'Belgian' scientists from the 1530s to 1600. Pelseneer's conclusion certainly was that 'modern science was born out of the Reform', but it is less certain that his thesis was proved in so short a space and with such limited material. The evidence he offered was an analysis of scientific works in 'Belgium' during the last seventy years of the sixteenth century. He rightly stressed that this period was decisive if natural links were to be found between protestantism and science. However, his statistics were far from conclusive. In the first place, he gave no definition of a 'scientific' work. During the period in question, the distinctions between what we might recognize as science, and fields such as astrology and alchemy, were frequently unclear, and one must wonder how many of these works do qualify as genuine scientific inquiry. Even if this point is granted, the statistical classifications do not inspire confidence. Pelseneer divided all the scientists about whom he could find information into two groups: Catholics and Protestants. Among the latter he included those whom it is possible 'to suspect regarded the new ideas favourably, and inclined towards Reform without always going so far as to commit themselves openly'.[17] Much more needs to be known about the evidence on which these suspicions were based before the assignment of everyone in this category to the protestant side can be accepted. The total number of people analysed (thirty in one group, sixty in another) was itself rather

[17] Pelseneer, *op. cit.*, p. 247. I have placed his geographic unit 'Belgium' between inverted commas because there was no such entity in the sixteenth century.

small. If this borderline category supplied anything like a majority of those labelled Protestants, the statistics become far less decisive. And at best Pelseneer's figures provide only a mild corrective to Italian Catholic leadership. His short article can hardly be regarded as a firm foundation for the conclusion that protestantism was the parent of science.

Finally, Mr Hill mentions a two-part essay by S. F. Mason. The early pages of Mason's study outlined the connection between protestantism and science that Candolle, Merton, and Pelseneer had suggested. Three reasons were then given for the connection: 'a concordance between the early Protestant ethos and the scientific attitude', the later Calvinists' stress on good works, and 'a certain congruity between the more abstract elements of the Protestant theologies and the theories of modern science'.[18] Mason illustrated the first reason by showing the parallel between the Protestant who interpreted God's word for himself, and the scientist who interpreted nature for himself. Without a doubt certain interesting parallels between early protestant and early scientific thought can be found. But such analogies do not prove the existence of any significant connection between the two movements. It is just as easy to stress the many contradictions, and to conclude that the affinities became more important only at a later date. Mason virtually admitted as much when discussing one of these contradictions: between the strictly literal Calvinist interpretation of the Bible and the Copernican theory. He pointed out that Wilkins eventually overcame the difficulty *in the 1640s* only at the expense of the literal interpretation—that is, at the expense of the religious belief: science affected doctrine, not vice versa. And Mason also acknowledged that the integration of science and Calvinism came about only in the generation of Wilkins, Boyle, and their successors[19]—*after* 1640. He proposed the same time scheme when elaborating the second of his reasons, the stress on good works. He admitted that the doctrine was not particularly important to either Luther or Calvin themselves, and he took all of his examples from the mid-seventeenth century and later. Although he considered this reason for the link between protestantism and science to have been the most important, he did not see it in operation until the generation *after* Kepler and Galileo.[20] He elaborated the third reason in a fashion similar

[18] Mason, *op. cit.*, p. 65.   [19] *Ibid.*, pp. 82–4.   [20] *Ibid.*, pp. 84–5.

to the first, by showing parallels in the Reformers' and scientists' attacks on medieval concepts of hierarchy. Again only parallels were revealed, and there was no attempt to claim that they were more decisive than the simultaneous contradictions. Much the same was true of the second section of the article, which entered the field of iatro-chemistry and the mystical concepts of Paracelsus and others down to the nineteenth century. Here the parallels were more personal, such as the view of the individual held by Luther and Paracelsus. (It might be noted, incidentally, that Paracelsus learned his alchemy and chemistry from a bishop.) But none of these analogies served to prove an inherent connection between the growth of the reformed religion and scientific advance. Indeed, Mason never set as much store by the parallels he traced as he did by the change that came over protestantism in the mid-seventeenth century.

IV

It is thus difficult to agree that these four authorities have 'well established' a solid relationship between protestantism and the rise of science. With this original assumption undermined, it will be seen that Mr Hill's subsequent comments on the subject do nothing but reinforce the framework suggested above. Spanish interest in science during Philip III's reign, for instance, was not at all exceptional, and the contrasting situation as described in 1671 typified perfectly the mid-century transformation of Catholicism. The Servetus case seems irrelevant to a discussion of protestant opposition to science, because surely nobody has questioned that both Calvin and those who led the outcry (presumably Mr Hill means Castellio) were interested only in the punishment of doctrinal heresy. To suggest another issue is to raise a straw man. Nor is there any foundation for Mr Hill's later implication that persecution of heretical religious beliefs entailed the persecution of heretical scientific theories. De Santillana has demonstrated, for example, that doctrinal and spiritual considerations were only minimally responsible for Galileo's trial.[21] Protestant disapproval of the new learning could have been illustrated more aptly by reference to Kepler's difficulties, or the

[21] De Santillana, *op. cit.*, *passim*.

pronouncements of the major Reformers on Copernicus. As for Mr Hill's next point, that there was no protestant parallel to Galileo's enforced recantation, perhaps this was merely because no protestant sect had quite as much power as the Catholics at the appropriate time.[22] Certainly the leading Reformers opposed the heliocentric theory much more openly and vehemently than did sixteenth-century popes; and, although he was not forced to recant, Kepler suffered little short of persecution at the hands of German theologians and professors. It is also worth recalling that until the 1630s there was no parallel to Galileo's trial in the Catholic church either (Bruno can be equated with Servetus in this respect).

The purpose of Mr Hill's reference to Urban VIII's belief in magic is not entirely clear, since many scientists of the time, including Kepler, held a similar belief. More significant was the pope's great admiration and friendship for Galileo which lasted until the fatal confrontation with the Inquisition. The Index, too, became a serious weapon against Copernicanism only at the time of Galileo's trial. Few would deny that this unprecedented official opposition caused the drastic decline of Catholic scientific inquiry. But the chronology is essential to the issue. As de Santillana has shown, the opposition did not begin to appear until the second, third, and fourth decades of the seventeenth century, and it began to have effect only in the last of those decades.[23] Mr Hill recognizes this transformation, but does not seem to realize that it came too late to impede the vital Catholic participation in the decisive advances before 1640. He also overlooks the shift in the attitudes of the Protestants, whose earlier hostility lost its force at the very time that the Roman church forsook its indifference.[24] The roles were thus reversed only when the Scientific Revolution was almost complete. Previously, professors and theologians of every shade of belief had both resisted and encouraged the changes. Not until the 1630s and 1640s, when the two faiths moved towards appreciably different positions, did the progress

[22] This phrase is explained below, pp. 284-5.

[23] De Santillana, *op. cit., passim.*

[24] Examples of this shift have already been noted, above, in the discussion of Mason's article. Another good illustration of the awakening protestant encouragement of new discoveries, after years of relative indifference, is the 'Vesalius renaissance' at the University of Leyden in the 1610s: cf. W. S. Heckscher, *Rembrandt's Anatomy of Dr. Nicholaas Tulp* (N.Y., 1958); p. 76.

of the new learning at last begin to feel the effects of specifically religious forces.

Mr Hill returns to this subject in his Rejoinder to Dr Kearney, but he still produces no evidence which undermines the Catholic contribution to scientific advance before 1640. On pages 88–9 (243–5) of this second article he asks a number of questions which can be summed up by the query: did not the Counter-Reformation destroy Catholic scientific activity? The answer is yes, of course it did, but not until the revolution in science was virtually over. Two of Mr Hill's references on these pages imply that protestantism did somehow affect pre-1640 advances, but in neither instance is the implication valid. He asks why science disappeared from 'Copernicus's Poland' as it 'reverted to Catholicism'. Copernicus was almost fifty before a Protestant appeared in his native land, and during the 1520s the Lutherans were viciously persecuted by Sigismund I, notably in Danzig. There was a flowering of learning in Poland that preceded the Reformation, and it was out of *this* milieu, not protestantism, that Copernicus, a steadfast cleric, emerged. Mr Hill asks the same question about 'Kepler's Bohemia', but with even less justification. The help science received in Bohemia came from the Emperor Rudolf II. Rudolf was raised in Spain, he supported the Jesuits in Prague, and in 1602 he refused toleration to all but Catholics and Utraquists. It was this devoted Catholic who became Brahe's patron when the astronomer had to leave protestant Denmark under a cloud, and it was he who employed Kepler. The two scientists stayed in Bohemia for a very short time: only fourteen years. Their presence was a manifestation neither of Bohemian scientific interest, nor of protestant encouragement, but simply of the patronage of a strongly Catholic Emperor.

In his *Intellectual Origins* (page 27) Mr Hill further suggests that, because of the Counter-Reformation, the Italians' contribution to science (made by 'merchants and artisans') declined after the fifteenth century, except in Padua. Both the chronology and the geography of this interpretation are contradicted by the activity of the seventeenth-century academics (the Lincei in Rome and the Cimento in Florence), and by the work of scientists of the calibre of Cesalpino, Grimaldi, Cavalieri, Steno, Malpighi, Torricelli, Viviani, Borrelli, Redi and Cassini, all of whom had closer connections with Florence, Pisa or Bologna than with Padua. Moreover, Italy's leading scientists were nearly all academics, not merchants or artisans.

Because of his wish to stress religious and political unorthodoxy, Mr Hill naturally emphasizes Padua and the Venetian Republic, a subject to which he returns on pages 276–8. But once again he slights non-Venetian Italy. Perhaps Galileo would have been safer in Padua, but in 1610 he found just as flourishing a scientific circle in Florence, where he preferred to work. And Vesalius was 'safe in his unorthodoxy' in many places in Italy. He was lionized in Bologna and Pisa, his chief patron was the Emperor Charles V, and his principal opponents were conservative academics of both faiths, not the Inquisition (see above, note 5). In the following century Galileo's triumphant reception in Rome in 1611 and 1624 indicates that science was still as respected at the centre of Catholicism as it was in unorthodox Venice.[25] Mr Hill simply fails to realize how late the Counter-Reformation affected science.

V

At the very end of his article on Harvey Mr Hill suddenly seems to deny the importance of the very feature of protestantism which was considered so essential by the four authorities he cites: religious doctrine. He emphasizes the social, political and institutional changes of the period at the expense of doctrine, which merely 'might contribute something' to the development of science, but evidently not much. His interpretation of the breaking of various monopolies, and his stress on the importance of republics, have been treated by Dr Kearney, and need not concern us at length.[26] But the change of emphasis does merit attention. If, as Mr Hill suggests, all that protestantism finally accomplished in the cause of science was the reduction of the power of

[25] In his effort to stress Venice's importance, Mr Hill wreaks further havoc with the career of Sir Edwin Sandys. His statement (*Intellectual Origins*, p. 277) that Sandys's *Europae Speculum* was written in Venice with the help of Sarpi is entirely conjectural and contradicts the little evidence we possess: see my article, 'The editions of Sir Edwin Sandys's *Relation of the State of Religion*', *Huntington Lib. Quarterly*, xxvi (1963), pp. 323–36. Mr Hill's enthusiasm for the freedom of thought in Venice might have been tempered had he recalled Bruno's fate. [26] See below, p. 278.

priests, then why cite works which concentrate on doctrine and 'ethos'? Why refer to them as the ultimate authorities, who have established their case so securely, and then abandon them, proposing instead an entirely different and as yet unsubstantiated interpretation which shares nothing but its conclusions with Candolle and his successors? The same contradiction is apparent in Mr Hill's Rejoinder to Dr Kearney, where he seems to have rejected completely the emphasis on doctrine which informed the work of his predecessors. And yet on page 96 (253) he places himself among the 'many' who 'have tried to suggest' 'connections . . . between puritanism and the rise of science', and claims 'a formidable amount of evidence on our side', even though he himself appears to distrust their fundamental argument, and the evidence before 1640 is meagre at best.

It is interesting to note that Mr Hill's point about the effect of republics on scientific advance is open to precisely the same objection that undermines the connection with protestantism. There were hardly any scientists—certainly not enough to create a 'trend'—who did much important work in republics before 1640. Galileo, for example, spent more productive years in Tuscany than in the Venetian Republic, contrary to Mr Hill's implication. As for the emphasis on the pernicious influence of priests, it is difficult to regard such important churchmen-scientists as Copernicus, Mersenne, Cavalieri, Grimaldi and Mariotte, to name but a few, plus so many Jesuits, as nothing but exceptions. In the end, when he includes within his analysis of the rise of science so many changes in politics, economics and religion, Mr Hill seems to be demonstrating little more than the transformation of European society in the sixteenth and seventeenth centuries. The growth of scientific inquiry was one of these changes; and, towards the end of the period, when the new discipline, the reformed religion, and the capitalist economy were all secure, it may have been natural for a forward-looking man who espoused one to approve of the other two. But to say that three fairly new and revolutionary movements eventually came to have much in common does not prove that they had common origins, or that they influenced each other as they established themselves. To demonstrate this second point, evidence must be produced of a significant connection before the mid-seventeenth century (and this is also true of any link between political change and scientific progress). Yet whenever the argument reaches this stage we encounter a stumbling-block that has not been surmounted.

By turning his attention away from the concerns of his predecessors, and concentrating on non-doctrinal matters, Mr Hill is presumably adding a new dimension to the connection between protestantism and the rise of science. Unfortunately the existence of any significant link at all has still to be proved. Despite all efforts, nothing of consequence has been uncovered which either helps to explain the advances before 1640, or diminishes the importance of Catholic achievements in this period. The later close relationship is indicative of the effect of science on protestantism, rather than the reverse. The mid-seventeenth-century followers of the Reformers were simply flexible enough to espouse a new discipline which had been of minor interest and possibly heretical to their predecessors, and which the Catholic church, hitherto officially unconcerned, was just beginning to suppress. In the story of the rise of science, therefore, religion is a peripheral concern. The search for an explanation of a great intellectual breakthrough; the influence of Weber; the historian's inclination to find causal relationships between simultaneous developments; and the undoubted preponderance of Protestants among scientists in later times; all have made the connection seem plausible. But little evidence in its favour has been produced for the vital pre-1640 period; and now, after so many years, the pursuit of such evidence appears to have outlived its usefulness. Newer theories, such as those of S. Toulmin and T. S. Kuhn,[27] offer more promising means of understanding the origins and nature of the Scientific Revolution.

[27] S. Toulmin, *Foresight and Understanding* (London, 1961), and T. S. Kuhn, *The Structure of Scientific Revolutions* (Chicago, 1962). See, too, the important recent discussions of problems which are currently receiving the attention of historians of science: *Critical Problems in the History of Science*, ed. M. Clagett (Madison, 1959), and *Scientific Change*, ed. A. C. Crombie (London, 1963). On pages 3–29 of *Critical Problems . . .*, and in the article by Hall cited in note 6, there are valuable analyses of the essential differences between the artisan's utilitarian aims and the scientist's conceptual concerns. These distinctions should help to correct Mr Hill's basic misconception about the nature of scientific inquiry and its relation to the practical needs of society (see above, pp. 270–1, and Hill's Rejoinder, pp. 89, 94; pp. 243–53 in this volume).

XXI

SCIENCE, RELIGION AND SOCIETY
IN THE SIXTEENTH
AND SEVENTEENTH CENTURIES *

Christopher Hill

I

I have been allowed so much space in recent discussions in *Past and Present* that I must only comment briefly on the contributions of Dr Kearney and Mr Rabb in No 31 (July 1965). I apologize to the former if my previous reply appeared ill-humoured. His new definition of puritanism (p. 105; pp. 255–6 in this volume) restores my good humour, since it differs substantially from all those he employed earlier and comes closer to that of Gardiner and Haller which I follow. But when I say 'Puritanism is not to be *identified* with either Presbyterianism or Independency', this does not mean that my definition *excludes* members of these sects (pp. 105–6; p. 256): a glance at the names with which I illustrated 'the main stream of puritan thought' would make this clear.[1] Dr Kearney might consider some recent wise words by Professor Dickens and Mr Yule on the existence within the Church of England of non-sectarian Puritans.[2]

But after apologizing for misrepresenting me last time, Dr Kearney really should not keep on doing it. It is fair enough to speak of my 'belief that there are no loose ends in history, no

* From no. 32 (December 1965).

[1] Hill, *Society and Puritanism in Pre-Revolutionary England* (London, 1964), pp. 28–9.

[2] A. G. Dickens, *The English Reformation* (London, 1964), pp. 313–15; G. Yule, 'Developments in English puritanism in the context of the Reformation', *Studies in the Puritan Tradition* (A Joint Supplement of the Congregational and Presbyterian Historical Societies, 1964), pp. 8–27.

gaps for lack of evidence, no surprising contradictions in human behaviour' (p. 104; p. 254) since it is clear from the context that this is polemical hyperbole unsubstantiated by facts. But Dr Kearney seems seriously to suggest that I am *defining* 'seventeenth-century science' or 'the Scientific Revolution' where (as any reader can see from his quotation) I am *describing* Bacon's programme (pp. 107-8; pp. 258-9). The whole of Dr Kearney's second section in consequence tilts at windmills. 'Nor was Pascal collecting facts' is a good thundering phrase: but please, did I ever say he was?

II

Mr Rabb argues at length that many early scientists outside England were Roman Catholics. I was not concerned to deny this. My subject was not the Scientific Revolution, in which Dr Kearney and Mr Rabb are primarily interested; I was looking for origins of the political and intellectual revolution which took place in England in the 1640s. As I explained in the Preface to my *Intellectual Origins*, I should have written a different book if I had been discussing the intellectual history of the period; it would have been different again if my subject had been the history of European science. To isolate one country has obvious limitations, which I pointed out (pp. 3-4, 8, chapter 6); but I could not otherwise have discussed the contribution of English science to the only one of the contemporaneous seventeenth-century revolutions which was successful.

I suggested that a protestant environment was more favourable to the spread of scientific ideas than a post-Counter-Reformation Roman Catholic environment. Is it relevant to retort (p. 112; p. 264) that Copernicus was a pre-Counter-Reformation Catholic, or that subjectively Galileo and Descartes wanted to remain Catholics? Nor was I primarily concerned with the *quality* of science, with 'the great advances in anatomy, physics and astronomy' which interest Mr Rabb (p. 112; p. 263). The best early scientists naturally came from the old cultural centres. But in England, I argued, there was greater *popular* interest in science, a more widespread understanding of science, than in most Roman Catholic countries before 1640. I think this stands, and it is my main point. There was indeed a crucial breakthrough for science, as for so much else, in republican England (and I am grateful to Mr Rabb for reinforcing my argument by reminding us that a similar breakthrough occurred thirty years earlier in the Dutch Republic—note 24). But the spread of popular scientific knowledge and appreciation before 1640 contributed to making possible the English Revolution as well as laying the basis for exceptional scientific progress afterwards.

For the rest, readers must decide between us. They can see for themselves whether I 'consider the practical applications and "fruitful" results of English work *a touchstone of its excellence*' (p. 118, pp. 270–1; my italics) by turning up the page reference which Mr Rabb fortunately gives. They can compare his flat assertion that 'in Bacon himself the religious impulse was almost entirely absent' with pages 85–96 of my *Intellectual Origins* where I try to document the contrary. They can judge from my text whether I in fact 'placed Bacon's programme "entirely in the puritan tradition". . . . *with no more evidence* than the puritanism of Bacon's mother' (p. 115, p. 268; my italics). And they can ponder Mr Rabb's ingenuous argument that 'there was no protestant parallel to Galileo's enforced recantation perhaps [sic!]. . . . merely because no protestant sect had quite as much power as the Catholics at the appropriate time' (p. 122; p. 275). At 'the appropriate time' James I was burning heretics condemned by Anglican bishops, and Gustavus Adolphus was King of Sweden! Mr Rabb regards my remarks about the effectiveness of early Stuart censorship as 'weakly documented' (note 11). It is indeed difficult to establish what would have been written if no censorship had existed. But the censorship itself was not a figment of my imagination: for documentation see the index to my *Century of Revolution* (Edinburgh, 1961) or *Intellectual Origins of the English Revolution* (Oxford, 1965) under that word.[3]

For something that is 'essential to the issue' (p. 122; p. 275), Mr Rabb's chronology is curiously unstable. Roman Catholic opposition to scientific enquiry began to appear in the 1610s, and to have effect in the 1630s (p. 122; p. 275). It was however still

[3] Professor Wickham (like many others) attributes 'the decadence in Jacobean and Caroline dramatic writing' to the censorship: G. Wickham, *Early English Stages, 1300–1660*, ii, *1576–1660*, Part 1 (London, 1963), p. 94.

just beginning after 1640 and in the mid-century (pp. 125–6; pp. 278–9). Unlike Charles II, it was an unconscionable time being born. I gave examples (*Intellectual Origins*, pp. 26–7; *Past and Present*, no. 27, pp. 70–2; pp. 178–81; no. 29, pp. 88–9; pp. 243–5) to suggest that it started well before any of these dates.[4] Again readers will decide between us on the evidence. Finally, I see no contradiction in arguing that protestantism contributed to the rise of science *both* by reducing the power of priests *and* by its doctrine and ethos (p. 124; pp. 277–8). The power of priests was reduced by the central reformation doctrine of the priesthood of all believers, and by doctrinal opposition to magic in most spheres. The doctrine and ethos spread as the authority of conscience and experience supplanted the authority of priests. The working out of these two complementary processes was what I had in mind when I spoke of 'the relationship between protestantism and the rise of science'.[5]

[4] Professor Trevor-Roper, whilst criticizing my interpretation, seems to accept an earlier dating than Mr Rabb's: 'Religion, the Reformation and social change', *Historical Studies*, iv (1963), p. 44.
[5] I fear I must reject the hand of friendship even when Mr Rabb extends it by referring to an 'apt distinction' of mine (p. 119; p. 272). Alas, I made the 'apt distinction', with what I hoped everyone would recognize as heavy irony, in an attempt to reduce an argument to the absurd by summarizing it. Never try to be funny.

XXII

SCIENCE, RELIGION AND SOCIETY IN THE SIXTEENTH AND SEVENTEENTH CENTURIES*

Theodore K. Rabb

As Mr Hill says,[1] readers must decide for themselves—whether he refutes the views I expressed, and whether he meets my main objections.[2] At one point in his rebuttal, though, my meaning is misinterpreted in a manner which my original remark might seem to allow, and I would like to dispel any confusion that may exist.

The word 'appropriate' in my sentence (p. 122; p. 275) about the Protestants having less power than the Catholics 'at the appropriate time' was intended to refer to two different periods: the time when (a) protestant, and (b) Catholic, leaders were predominantly opposed to the new science. (a) spanned the 1540s and 1550s, when Luther, Melanchthon, and Calvin denounced Copernicanism; (b) began some eighty years later. Thus, at the time when Protestants might (appropriately) have wished to suppress scientific investigation, they were scattered and weak; but when the Catholics were similarly inclined they (the Catholics) were a formidable power. I would suggest that this numerical difference between the two, at the times when each opposed the new learning, might help to explain why one, but not the other, could force a scientist into a spectacular recantation. Mr Hill's comment about James I and Gustavus rests on *his* interpretation of 'appropriate', not mine.

* From no. 33 (April 1966).
[1] *Past and Present*, no. 32 (Dec. 1965), pp. 110–12; pp. 280–3 in this volume. For earlier contributions in this debate, see nos. 27, 28, 29, 30 and 31.
[2] *Past and Present*, no. 31 (July 1965), pp. 111–26; pp. 262–79 in this volume.

I had hoped the two sentences following my possibly elliptical remark would make my meaning clear, and I trust the above removes any remaining doubts. It might also be worth recalling that my principal target was the last section of Mr Hill's article on Harvey,[3] the subject of which *was* the Scientific Revolution.

[3] *Past and Present*, no. 27 (April 1964), pp. 54–72; pp. 160–81 in this volume.

XXIII

LATITUDINARIANISM AND SCIENCE IN SEVENTEENTH-CENTURY ENGLAND *

Barbara J. Shapiro

Scholars concerned with the history of science have devoted much attention in recent years to the investigation of the social and intellectual conditions associated with, and thus presumably encouraging, scientific innovation. The attempt to establish a relationship between puritanism and the rapid development of science in seventeenth-century England provides an outstanding example.[1] The puritanism-science thesis has already been sub-

* From no. 40 (July 1968).

[1] Robert K. Merton, 'Puritanism, pietism and science', *Sociological Review*, xxxviii (1938), pp. 1–30; ——, 'Science, technology, and society in seventeenth century England', *Osiris*, iv (1938), pp. 360–632; Dorothy Stimson, 'Puritanism and the new philosophy in seventeenth century England', *Bull. Inst. Hist. Med.*, iii (1935), pp. 321–34; George Rosen, 'Left-wing puritanism and science', *ibid.*, xv (1944), pp. 375–80; R. F. Jones, *Ancients and Moderns: A Study in the Background of the Battle of the Books* (St Louis, 1961); ——, Puritanism, science, and Christ Church', *Isis*, xxxi (1939), pp. 65–7; Christopher Hill, 'Intellectual origins of the English Revolution', *Listener*, May–June 1962, pp. 943–6, 983–6; 'Puritanism, capitalism and the Scientific Revolution', *Past and Present*, no. 29 (Dec. 1964), pp. 88–97 (pp. 243–53 in this volume); *Intellectual Origins of the English Revolution* (Oxford, 1965); L. Solt, 'Puritanism, capitalism, democracy and the new science', *Amer. Hist. Rev.*, lxxiii (1967), pp. 18–29; H. F. Kearney, 'Puritanism and science: problems of definition' *Past and Present*, no. 31 (July 1965), pp. 104–10 (pp. 254–61 in this volume); T. K. Rabb, 'Religion and the rise of modern science', *ibid.*, pp. 111–26 (pp. 262–79); ——, 'Science, religion and society in the sixteenth and seventeenth centuries', *ibid.*, no. 33 (April 1966), p. 148 (pp. 284–5).

jected to searching criticism,[2] and the purpose here is not to elaborate this critique but to suggest an alternative hypothesis: that religious moderation was far more intimately connected than puritanism with the English scientific movement of that period.

Basically the contention, put forward in the 1930s by Robert K. Merton and Dorothy Stimson, that there was an intimate relationship between puritanism and the rise of science is an extension of the Weber-Tawney thesis to show that religious beliefs may affect not only economic but other non-spiritual endeavours as well. Perhaps the greatest difficulty and source of confusion lies in the definitions of puritanism that leading proponents of the theory have adopted. Merton's nearly all-inclusive definition makes precise historical analysis nearly impossible because it fails to distinguish between the significant religious groups in seventeenth-century England.[3] To hold that there is a close correlation between puritanism and science, while including nearly the whole spectrum of English thought under the puritan rubric, is simply to say that a correlation exists between Englishness and English science. This is true but not very helpful. If the object is to show the influence of puritanism, viewed as a unique religious and social ethic, on science, it would seem necessary to arrive at a definition of puritanism that reflects the actual historical division on religious questions in England.[4]

[2] James W. Caroll, 'The Merton thesis on English science', *American Jl of Economics and Sociology*, xiii (1954), pp. 427–32; T. K. Rabb, 'Puritanism and the rise of experimental science in England', *Jl of World History*, vii (1962), pp. 46–67; H. F. Kearney, 'Puritanism, capitalism and the Scientific Revolution', *Past and Present*, no. 28 (July 1964), pp. 81–101 (pp. 218–42); A. Rupert Hall, 'Merton revisited: or, science and society in the seventeenth century', *History of Science*, ii (1963), pp. 1–16. See also Mark Curtis, *Oxford and Cambridge in Transition 1558–1642* (Oxford, 1959); M. M. Knappen, *Tudor Puritanism* (Chicago, 1939); P. H. Kocher, *Science and Religion in Elizabethan England* (San Marino, California, 1953); L. S. Feuer, *The Scientific Intellectual* (New York, 1963).

[3] His conclusions rest on a classification of the whole spectrum of protestantism, with the exception of Lutheranism, as puritan: *Osiris*, iv, p. 416.

[4] Merton's assumption that all groups within his puritan category shared the same social ethic makes it almost impossible to explain a civil war between elements supposedly in essential agreement. Nor does the broad scope of his category correspond with his admission that, the Puritans in fact constituted only a very small proportion of the population: *ibid.*, p. 473. These difficulties are further compounded by his treatment of

Furthermore the alleged puritan contribution to rationalism, empiricism and utilitarianism[5] is open to question. It is unlikely that these elements were fundamental to the puritan movement, and in fact they seem to have entered puritanism at a rather late stage in its development. Indeed proponents of the puritanism and science hypothesis often seem to succumb to the temptation of ascribing characteristics to puritanism which it acquired during a later period or even as a result of its acceptance of science.

Miss Stimson sought to show that moderate Puritans were at the core of the scientific movement.[6] She was then in effect claiming that those 'Puritans' who were least differentiated from Anglicans were most involved in science. In short those men to whom it is least convenient and enlightening to apply the puritan label are those who led Miss Stimson to speak of puritanism and science.

Nevertheless, Christopher Hill, the most recent proponent of the ideas of Merton and Stimson, still insists there is a 'formidable amount of evidence' to support the puritanism-science connection.[7] Like Merton, however, what he is essentially saying is that Englishmen contributed to English science. For he defines puritanism basically in terms of 'doctrine about religion and Church government, aiming at purifying the Church from inside'.[8] Since the Laudians had been moving the church away from its traditional, Elizabethan form, every Englishman who was not a High Churchman or a Roman Catholic favoured purification at least in the sense of eliminating some of the Laudian innovations. Quite typically Hill centres his discussion on the most puritan Puritans, thus creating the impression that there was a distinct puritan group presumably distinguished from its distinctly Anglican counterpart. But when it becomes convenient for his

---

puritanism as a static phenomenon, which sometimes leads to the use of nineteenth-century statistics as indices of seventeenth-century conditions: *Osiris*, iv, pp. 487–90.

[5] *Ibid.*, pp. 467–9; Merton, *Sociological Review*, xxxviii, p. 9.

[6] Stimson, *Bull. Inst. Hist. Med.*, iii, p. 327.

[7] Hill, *Past and Present*, no. 29, p. 96; p. 253.

[8] Hill, *Society and Puritanism in Pre-Revolutionary England* (London, 1964), p. 28. See also Hill, *Past and Present*, no. 29, p. 90; p. 245. Only here does he add the additional concept of 'radical'.

argument, he begins casting his net widely to include persons and ideas that are puritan only in the vaguest 'reform' sense, and ends by labelling as puritan all sorts of men who were simply less High Church than the Laudians and all sorts of intellectual movements in which a broad cross-section of non-Laudian Englishmen participated. Merton, Stimson and Hill then, share a common difficulty that arises from the fact that they all uncritically accept a traditional set of categories, 'puritan' and 'Anglican', which encompass and conceal both a considerable degree of vagueness and a major hiatus in historical research and analysis.[9] It has been customary to equate Laudianism with Anglicanism. There is a certain superficial simplicity about this equation since the High Churchmen do form a relatively distinct group with a relatively distinct ideology. The next step, however, is usually to consider all other non-Roman Catholic Englishmen as Puritans. There is no great philosophical principle that forbids such an all-encompassing usage of the word puritan. Would it not be simpler and clearer, however, to speak of 'all non-Laudian Protestants' when we really mean 'all non-Laudian Protestants', particularly because, to all but the most immediately concerned scholars, 'puritan' calls up the image of a quite separable and distinct group of English Protestants?

More important, the whole process of dividing Englishmen into Puritans and Anglicans, and equating Anglicanism with Laudianism, obscures the fact that there was a broad middle category of divines, scholars, and politicians who wanted mild reforms in the church and sought moderate means of accomplishing them. Some of this group were men who were Puritans in the sense of falling within the stream of thought 'associated with men like Perkins, Bownde, Preston, Sibbes, Thomas Taylor, William Gouge, Thomas Goodwin, Richard Baxter'.[10] Others were Anglicans in the sense of maintaining their basic allegiance to the traditional forms of organization and ceremony in the Church of

[9] Historians of Anglicanism have tended to focus on High Churchmen. There have been few studies of the low church tradition. For a recent attempt to distinguish Anglicanism and puritanism see John New, *Anglican and Puritan: The Basis of their Opposition, 1558–1640* (Stanford, California, 1964). See also T. H. Breen, 'The non-existent controversy: Puritan and Anglican attitudes on work and wealth, 1600–1640', *Church History*, xxxv (1966), pp. 273–87.

[10] Hill, *Society and Puritanism*, p. 29.

England. In short it is possible to speak of moderate Anglicans and moderate Puritans.

It is possible to do so, but is it wise? For attempts to draw the line between moderate Puritans and moderate Anglicans can only lead to endless and largely superficial hairsplitting. Would it not be better, for certain purposes at least, to acknowledge the existence of a group of moderates who cannot be neatly split into Anglican and puritan camps? I would submit that, once this acknowledgement is made, many of the knotty problems in the debate over puritanism and science will disappear, for we shall be able to see that nearly all of the seventeenth-century English scientists and scientific movements are to be found within this moderate category. It is particularly the absence of research on non-Laudian, moderate Anglicans, combined with the extensive work on the puritan movement, that has obscured the fact that moderation *qua* moderation, not the puritanism of puritan moderates, provides the key link between science and religion. The rubric 'moderation and science' or 'latitudinarianism and science' will direct our attention to that core of personalities and modes of thought that religion and science actually held in common. A brief examination of those involved in the scientific movement will, I think, reveal some of the difficulties of the Merton–Stimson–Hill hypothesis and suggest instead a firm alliance between religious moderates and the scientific movement.

One of the most striking patterns that emerges from an examination of the thought of sixteenth- and seventeenth-century English and continental scientists, whatever their particular religious commitments, is a quite universal suspicion of religious disputes accompanied by a pronounced desire for religious compromise and unity. Copernicus, for example, strove for an accommodation between Roman Catholics and Lutherans. Galileo and Kepler were unconcerned with or hostile to dogmatic theology. Campanella was an outspoken critic of religious zealotry. Stevin, who was so important in the development of mechanics, urged that religious disputes be not permitted to disturb the public peace.[11]

English scientists appear to have shared the view of their continental colleagues. Although Francis Bacon, the outstanding spokesman of English science, has been claimed for the Puritans,

11 Feuer, *The Scientific Intellectual*, p. 202.

there is not much profit in so labelling this intensely secular mind. He was as unsympathetic to the quibblings of the theologians of his own time as to those of the scholastics, and his advocacy of a moderate policy toward the Puritans may be attributed to his distaste for persecution rather than to puritan sympathies. Bacon, like the majority of later scientists, made it clear that 'controversies of religion' could only 'hinder the advancement of science'.[12]

Sir Walter Ralegh and the scientific circle that clustered around him have also been enlisted in the puritan cause.[13] Although Ralegh became a puritan idol after his death, his approaches to politics and religion while he was alive hardly warrant the label puritan. Perhaps the most significant thing about Ralegh's religion was that he 'had no strong feelings about dogma', and opposed condemning either Brownists or Jesuits for their opinions.[14] Thus even Christopher Hill, who offers Ralegh in support of the tie between puritanism and science, recognized that 'Ralegh . . . seems to have had the sort of tolerance born of indifference which finally triumphed in 1689'.[15] Nor do his close associates help prove the connection. Thomas Hariot, for instance, was said to have been responsible for influencing Ralegh in a deistic or even atheistic direction.[16] If the Ralegh circle suggests anything, it suggests a wide range of religious speculation, most of which would have been beyond the pale of either puritan or Anglican orthodoxy, and a willingness to countenance a wide range of religious speculation by others. Here again moderation, not puritanism, seems to be the recurrent phenomenon.

There is also some doubt whether the English and European followers of Comenius who were intimately involved in scientific affairs are best characterized as Puritans. If as a group they possessed one distinguishing characteristic, surely it was their desire for religious reunion, and a distaste for the religious warfare which was destroying both Europe and England. Conflict

[12] Hill, *Intellectual Origins*, p. 93, quoting letter of Bacon to Tobie Mathew, 10 October 1609.
[13] *Ibid.*, pp. 22–7, 42–4, 131 *et seq.*   [14] *Ibid.*, p. 171.
[15] *Ibid.* Hill also notes Ralegh's religious writings were 'more compatible with deism than Christianity': *ibid.*, p. 172. Like so many virtuosi he abhorred 'war, massacres, and murders for religion', *ibid.*, pp. 171–2, citing Ralegh, *History*, i, pp. xxix–xxx.
[16] Hill, *Intellectual Origins*, p. 139.

between protestant sects was precisely what they sought to eliminate.[17] When Robert Boyle was a member of the 'Invisible College', dominated by the Comenian Samuel Hartlib, he particularly noted that its members were 'persons that endeavour to put narrow-mindedness out of countenance, by the practice of so extensive a charity that it reaches unto everything called man, . . .'.[18] It is also suggestive that those most attracted to Comenian ideas and to the Comenian circle prior to the outbreak of the Civil Wars were such men as John Gauden, Archbishop Ussher, Bishop Williams, Lord Brooke and John Pym, whose religious views are difficult to fit neatly into either puritan or Anglican categories.

It is, of course, impossible to detail here the religious views of every seventeenth-century English scientist. It is possible, however, at least to illustrate my hypothesis by focusing on one figure, John Wilkins, whose central position in the scientific movement of the period is, I think, indisputable. If there was any single individual who tied the scientific and latitudinarian movement together, it was certainly Wilkins. Not only did he establish a scientific centre at Wadham College, Oxford, during the stormy years of the Interregnum and promote a particularly moderate climate in the College itself, but in the early years of the Restoration he was one of the most important, if not the most important, contributor to the creation of the Royal Society, while at the same time gathering together a circle of young latitudinarian clerics. In both periods Wilkins served as a rallying point not only for those who wished to avoid religious conflict but for those who sought to establish a climate of opinion which would end the conflict itself and lead to calmer, more pragmatic levels of discourse and action. His most striking talent, in fact, was his ability to encourage critical interplay while avoiding the bitter feuding which so often marked the intellectual life of the seventeenth century.

Wilkins's activities and writing have frequently been offered

---

[17] Samuel Hartlib was involved in the English publication of Acontius' *Satans Strategems*, one of the most successful attacks on religious dogmatism.

[18] Hill, *Intellectual Origins*, p. 93 citing Boyle, *Works*, i, p. 20. Hill curiously has offered this statement as evidence favouring the puritan-science connection.

as an important piece of evidence in support of the imputed connection between puritanism and science. Curiously enough Wilkins provides an almost ideal illustration of the difficulties of that hypothesis. In his early life he was under the influence of John Dod, surely a Puritan, but one who, in his later years, emphasized that disputes over doctrine and ritual should be subordinated to church unity and the fostering of practical morality in daily life.[19] Wilkins himself changed religious allegiances as the regimes in London changed. He was intruded as a 'Puritan' in the reformation of Oxford, and then suspected, rightfully, of harbouring Anglicans. He ended his career as a bishop in the Church of England, suspected, again rightly, of harbouring Dissenters. Indeed his religious stance was so consistently moderate that his loyalties were always suspected by both puritan and Anglican stalwarts. His later religious career was entirely devoted to creating and fostering a latitudinarian movement and a theology of natural religion that would eliminate the issues which had divided Anglicans and Puritans. Wilkins is thus a curiously anomalous figure on whom to base a theory of puritanism and science.

His scientific career presents the same anomaly. For the link between Wilkins's 'puritanism' and science is his role in creating a new emphasis on science at Oxford by gathering a scientific circle around him during his Wardenship at Wadham. In the first place it is not clear that the university had been markedly deficient in scientific instruction before his arrival,[20] for he himself had become familiar with the most advanced astronomy and mathematics of the day during his student years at Laudian-dominated Oxford. Second, there is little to indicate that the puritan regimes actively sought to reform the curriculum in the direction of science. Third, and most important, Wilkins's success as a scientific organizer at Oxford must basically be attributed to the

[19] William Lloyd, *A Sermon Preached at the Funeral of John Wilkins* (London, 1675), pp. 47–8; Thomas Fuller, *The Church History of Britain* (London, 1842), iii, p. 478; David Lloyd, *Memoirs . . . of those that suffered . . . in our late Intestine Wars* (n.p., 1668), p. 129; William Haller, *The Rise of Puritanism* (New York, 1957), pp. 120–1.
[20] Curtis, *Oxford and Cambridge in Transition*, pp. 227–60. See also Hill, *Intellectual Origins*, pp. 301–14 and P. Allen, 'Scientific studies in the English universities of the seventeenth century', *Jour. Hist. Ideas*, x (1949), pp. 219–53.

fact that he offered Wadham as a shelter to moderates of both puritan and Anglican identification who came to Oxford and engaged in scientific activities precisely because they wished to avoid the religious factionalism that had engendered and then been fostered by the Puritan Revolution.

Unlike most Oxford dons Wilkins:[21]

> had nothing of Bigottry, Unmannerliness, or Censoriousness, which then were in the *Zenith*, amongst some of the Heads, and Fellows of Colleges in *Oxford*. For which Reason many Country Gentlemen, of all Persuasions, but especially those then stiled Cavaliers and Malignants, for adhering to the King and the Church, sent their Sons to that College, that they might be under his Government.

Matthew Wren, a Royalist and Anglican member of the Wadham group noted Wilkins's 'generous freedome . . . in an Age overrun with passion and soureness . . .' and wrote:[22]

> It is not enough with you [Wilkins], for the ruining a man, to be told that he is of such a party or perswasion. . . . This is the Prerogative of your judgment, which being able to pass sentence upon every particular, is not put to take things in grosse upon the credit of any faction or company of men.

Seth Ward, the new Savilian professor of astronomy, and a known Anglican and Royalist, came to Wadham 'invited thereto by the Fame of Dr *Wilkins* . . .'.[23] Christopher Wren, also a Royalist, came in 1649. The mathematician, Laurence Rooke, later Gresham professor of astronomy, left Cambridge 'for the sake of Dr. Wilkins . . . and of Dr. Ward', bringing several of his

---

[21] Walter Pope, *Life of Seth, Lord Bishop of Salisbury*, ed. J. B. Bamborough (Oxford, 1961), p. 29.
[22] [Matthew Wren], *Considerations on Mr. Harrington's Common-wealth of Oceana* (London, 1657), dedicatory Letter, sig. A3r–A3v. In a period when fear of proclaiming Anglican sentiments was common, Wilkins encouraged at least one Anglican to maintain his beliefs, and used his influence to protect many others. Lloyd, *Funeral Sermon*, p. 48; Thomas Barlow, *The Genuine Remains* (London, 1673), Epistle to the Reader; William Orme, 'Memoirs of his life and writing', in John Owen, *Works*, ed. Thomas Russell (London, 1826), i, p. 19.
[23] Pope, *Life of Seth Ward*, pp. 28–9.

students with him.[24] The mathematician William Neile, son of Sir Paul Neile and grandson of the Archbishop of York, also came 'for the sake of Dr. Wilkins . . .'.[25] John Wallis, although he did not come to Wadham, obtained the Savilian professorship of geometry at least partly through Wilkins's efforts.[26] Robert Boyle, a latecomer to Oxford, also decided to take up residence in Oxford after meeting Wilkins. Thus if we cannot say conclusively that Wilkins's moderate policy drew scientists to Oxford, the evidence suggests that they did not flock there because of Oxford's peculiarly puritan atmosphere.

In fact the more strictly puritan members of the university found Wilkins far too lenient with their opponents and attempted to oust him from the Wardenship in 1654. Both Wilkins and Seth Ward were much criticized in university circles and had become 'liable to the Persecutions of those peevish People, who ceas'd not to Clamour, and even to Article against them, as *Cavaliers in their hearts, meer Moral Men, without the power of Godliness*'.[27] The moderation and emphasis on practical morality which were to characterize not only Wilkins but most scientists during the Restoration period were thus already evident, indeed notorious, during the Oxford period.

Although Wilkins probably offers the most outstanding example of moderation, he was hardly an isolated phenomenon. There was an extremely high proportion of religious moderates in the Wadham circle of scientists. Sir William Petty, for example, rejected all dogmatism and expressed disgust for sectarian squabbles.[28] He finally left England at the outbreak of the war in order to absent himself from 'this ill face of things at home'.[29] Ralph Bathurst, a devoted Anglican, was also known for his

[24] Anthony Wood, *Athenae Oxonienses*, ed. P. Bliss, 4 vols (London, 1813–20), iii, cols 587–8.
[25] Thomas Birch, *History of the Royal Society of London* (London, 1756), ii, p. 460.
[26] Bodleian Library, MS. Convocation Register, fo. 57, 14 June 1649.
[27] Pope, *Life of Seth Ward*, pp. 45–6. The extremist party was 'rigidly and unmercifully Censorious against the Moral Men, . . .' and had attacked them from the university's pulpits: *ibid.*, p. 47.
[28] Richard S. Westfall, *Science and Religion in Seventeenth-Century England* (New Haven, 1958), p. 132; C. E. Whiting, *Studies in English Puritanism from the Restoration to the Revolution, 1660–1688* (London, 1931), p. 495.
[29] Emil Strauss, *Sir William Petty* (London, 1954), p. 21. Petty was variously labelled an atheist, a Jesuit and a Socinian. William Petty,

dislike of religious controversy. Like so many in Wilkins's circle, he was censured for his compliance while at Oxford and his seemingly unsettled religious principles.[30] Robert Boyle, besides being a devout Anglican,[31] intensely disapproved of the religious quarrelling he saw around him. 'It is strange', he wrote to John Dury, 'that men should rather be quarrelling for a few trifling opinions, wherein they dissent, than to embrace one another for those many fundamental truths, wherein they agree'.[32] Boyle not only vigorously opposed 'all severities and persecutions on account of religion',[33] but refused to 'shut himself up within a party, nor neither did he shut any party out from him'.[34]

Still another friend of Boyle and Wilkins who favoured some kind of religious accommodation was John Beale.[35] Jonathan Goddard, also of the Oxford circle, and at the same time closely associated with the Cromwellian government, was nevertheless known, especially while he was the university's representative in parliament, for his willingness to defend scholars of any and all religious parties. Goddard had 'none of that narrowness of mind which was the common failing of the great men of these times'.[36]

There are, it must be admitted, several important figures in the

---

Reflections upon some Persons and Things in Ireland (London, 1660), p. 137. Petty returned to serve the Cromwellian government. Significantly, however, he served the Crown as well and during the Restoration Charles II protected him from those who disliked his latitudinarian ways. See the entry in *Dict. Nat. Biog.*

30 Thomas Warton, *Life and Literary Remains of Ralph Bathurst* (London, 1761), pt I, pp. 180-1; Anthony Wood, *Life and Times*, i, p. 365.

31 Mitchell S. Fisher, *Robert Boyle, Devout Naturalist* (Philadelphia, 1945), p. 140.

32 Quoted in J. G. Crowther, *Founders of British Science* (London, 1960), p. 79. Shortly after the Restoration Boyle asked Dury to write on behalf of religious freedom. Dury's tract, *The Plain Way of Peace and Unity in Matters of Religion* was a typical latitudinarian plea favouring common acceptance of religious fundamentals and the abolition of religious controversy. Dury, from at least 1628 had been involved in efforts to gain protestant reunion on the Continent. Boyle also asked Sir Peter Pett, one of the original members of the Royal Society, to write a similar tract in 1660. Whiting, *Studies in English Puritanism*, p. 482.

33 J. P. Wood (ed.), *Funeral Sermons by Eminent English Divines, 1650-1760* (London, 1831), p. 290.   34 *Ibid.*, pp. 291-2.

35 Royal Society MSS., *Early Letters*, B. 1. 30.

36 M. B. Rex, *University Representation in England 1604-1690* (London, 1954), pp. 186-7.

Wadham circle who cannot be easily described as moderates or latitudinarians. But one, Seth Ward, was a staunch Anglican and became a persecuting bishop. If he was not a moderate, he certainly was not a Puritan.[37] At first glance John Wallis seems to provide support for the Merton–Stimson–Hill thesis, for there can be no question of his puritanism and presbyterianism during the earlier and middle years of his life. Nevertheless Wallis seems to have been affected by the moderate atmosphere at Oxford, for his later years exhibit a growing moderation and a movement toward latitudinarianism.[38] Wallis may not have begun his life as a moderate, but he surely ended as one.[39]

The Oxford circle constituted the most important scientific cluster of its day. Among its members, Wilkins, Petty, Bathurst, Boyle, Goddard, Wallis, and Beale can be counted as both moderates and major contributors to the scientific movement. Matthew and Christopher Wren, Thomas Willis and Ward were Anglicans. While Goddard and Wallis might justifiably be labelled moderate Puritans, there is not a single unambiguous and fully committed Puritan in the entire scientific leadership.[40]

[37] At least for the time he was under the influence of Wilkins at Wadham, Ward responded to Wilkins's plea for moderation. Seth Ward, *In Thomae Hobbii philosophiam exercitatio epistolica* (Oxford, 1656), dedicatory letter.

[38] Wallis noted that he 'purposely waved (as I alwaies do) all nice disputes of Speculative Subtilties in Controversal Points . . . as more tending to disturb the peace of the Church, than to promote Piety. . . . And I heartily wish there were more Zeal for these Great Truths, and less Animosities about little things, which unhappily Divide good Men, Break our Peace, and Gratifie those who seek our Ruine'. John Wallis, *The Necessity of Regeneration* (London, 1682), preface. See also his *Theological Discourses* (London, 1692), p. 6.

[39] John Wallis, 'Account of some Passages of his own Life', in Thomas Hearne, *Peter Langtoft's Chronicle* (Oxford, 1725), i, p. clxix.

[40] A similar pattern appears among the scientifically-inclined at Cambridge. Isaac Barrow, though a staunch Anglican, was also a convinced latitudinarian: P. H. Osmond, *Isaac Barrow: His Life and Times* (London, 1944), p. 78. Francis Willoughby, a student of John Ray's was also known for his comprehensive charity to men of all persuasions: Willoughby, *Ornithology* (London, 1678), preface by John Ray. The latitudinarian and scientific interests of the Cambridge Platonists are well known. When Wilkins became Master of Trinity College, Cambridge he 'joined with those who studied to propagate better thoughts, to take men off from being in parties, or from narrow notions, from superstitious conceits, and a fierceness about opinions': Gilbert Burnet, *History of My Own Time*, ed. Osmund Airy (Oxford, 1897–1900), i, pp. 332–3.

Emphasis on the contributions of the Wadham group should not, however, suggest that no scientific studies existed at Oxford prior to the migration of scientists in 1649. Scientific investigation had been a leading feature of English intellectual life long before mid-century, and the universities had responded to that interest. The Savilian professorships of geometry and astronomy, founded in 1619, had drawn the very best minds in these fields, particularly from among the professors at Gresham College. Nor had the biological sciences been entirely neglected before the Wadhamites advanced them so far. In 1645 when William Harvey accepted the Wardenship of Merton College from the Crown, he found a congenial group who collaborated with him in his experiments and dissections. Several of these men were associated in turn with the London scientific group of the 1640s, the Oxford group of the 1650s and the Royal Society,[41] again indicating the continuity of pre-puritan, puritan and post-puritan science at Oxford.

Furthermore, neither the Visitors nor the Parliamentary committee in London did anything to encourage scientific studies. The regime did maintain the level of appointments to the Savilian professorships, but talented persons held these posts both before the Puritans appeared on the scene and after they ceased to influence the university.[42] The Puritans have been given considerable credit for appointing scientists as heads of colleges. With the exceptions of John Wilkins and Jonathan Goddard, however, no other new head had any particular scientific interest. Most heads, as in the past, were theologians and scholars in the traditional mould. Indeed, if the Puritans can claim Wilkins and Goddard, the Royalists can similarly claim William Harvey and Ralph Bathurst.[43]

[41] E.g., Ralph Bathurst, Charles Scarburgh, Thomas Willis, Mr Highmore and George Ent. Louis Chauvois, *William Harvey* (London, 1957), pp. 145–7.

[42] Political and religious affiliation did not always determine university appointments. Seth Ward, a known Anglican, replaced John Greaves as professor of astronomy when Greaves refused to take the necessary oaths. It was Greaves, however, who insisted that Ward take the post: 'if you refuse it, they will give it to some Cobler of their Party who never heard the Name of *Euclid*, or the Mathematics, and yet will greedily snap at it for the Salaries sake': Pope, *Life of Seth Ward*, p. 21.

[43] Bathurst became head of Trinity College, Oxford after the Restoration. Isaac Barrow became Master of Trinity College, Cambridge during the Restoration period.

When the Commonwealth government considered changing the statutes of the colleges and university, it made no moves or even gestures towards emphasizing science in the university. If, as has been so prominently argued, the Puritans were the great champions of new science against traditional learning, it is strange that they failed to take advantage of this sterling opportunity really to reform the university, and, indeed, expended most of their efforts on enforcing obedience to the old curriculum. The Visitors were basically concerned with a religious reformation. They wanted to eliminate the 'corruptions' of the past, not to alter traditional education. In fact it even appears that 'the new Philosophy was interdicted in some Colleges' by Presbyterians, who feared that it would lead to innovations in religion and that intellectual liberty would inspire religious speculation as well.[44]

Part of the case for puritan encouragement of science at Oxford, of course, rests on the simple logic we have encountered before in a larger arena: the university was puritan, the university did science, *ergo*. . . . Actually the religious complexion of the university was not as uniform as one might expect. Those willing to accept the Covenant and Engagement were permitted to remain. For example, Gerald Langbaine, an Anglican, continued as Provost of Queen's. Puritan forms of religious observance certainly dominated, but Anglican services were held covertly at the home of Dr Thomas Willis, one of the Wadham scientific circle, and were attended by Matthew and Christopher Wren, also members of the group.

Thus if one were not so anxious to impose the puritan-science hypothesis on the actual historical data, it would become apparent, I think, that from at least the early seventeenth century there was a steadily increasing appreciation of the sciences at Oxford. This movement reached its height during the 1650s not because of puritanism but because a group of men with widely differing political and religious beliefs found themselves in a situation conducive to scientific work. This situation was created by the Puritans only in the negative sense that many of these men sought refuge at Oxford precisely because the religious and political

[44] S[imon] P[atrick], *A Brief Account of the New Sect of* Latitude-Men: *Together with some Reflections upon the New Philosophy*, in *The Phenix*, vol. ii, (London 1708), p. 516.

conflicts associated with puritanism had made their positions elsewhere untenable.

It is not difficult to see why scientific activities attracted so many during this period of religious and political upheaval. Science provided a respite, a non-controversial topic of conversation, where men might have 'the satisfaction of breathing a freer air, and of conversing in quiet one with another, without being ingag'd in the passions, and madness of that dismal Age'.[45] As Thomas Sprat wrote:[46]

> For such a candid, and unpassionate company, . . . and for such a gloomy season, what could have been a fitter Subject to pitch upon, then *Natural Philosophy*? To have been always tossing about some *Theological question*, would have been, to have made that their private diversion, the excess of which they themselves dislik'd in the publick: . . . It was *Nature* alone, which could pleasantly entertain them, in that estate. The contemplation of that, draws our minds off from past, or present misfortunes, . . . *that* never separates us into mortal Factions; *that* gives us room to differ, without animosity; and permits us, to raise contrary imaginations upon it, without any danger of a *Civil War*.

In other ways too the political and religious upheaval proved to be a stimulus to the Oxford scientific group. Science provided an outlet for creative energies which could no longer be employed in normal channels. Many men were forced out of their professions and into a position of enforced leisure. This is probably what happened to Matthew Wren who retired to Oxford. After the Restoration he returned to politics. Philosophy and medicine in particular gained many practitioners initially intended for the church.[47] Ralph Bathurst was unable to earn a livelihood as an Anglican cleric and turned temporarily to medicine.[48] With the Restoration he returned to the church, becoming President of Trinity College, Oxford, chaplain to the king and dean of Wells.

[45] Thomas Sprat, *The History of the Royal Society*, eds Jackson I. Cope and Harold W. Jones (St Louis, 1958), p. 53.
[46] *Ibid.*, pp. 55–6. Sprat had been a student at Wadham during Wilkins's mastership and one of his protégés.
[47] Walter Charleton, *The Immortality of the Human Soul Demonstrated by the Light of Nature* (London, 1657), p. 50.
[48] Warton, *Life and Literary Remains of Ralph Bathurst*, pt 1, p. 35n.

Seth Ward too returned to the church becoming bishop successively of Exeter and Salisbury. Isaac Barrow of Cambridge provides a similar instance of an Anglican Royalist who temporarily abandoned a clerical career for medicine.[49] Unlike Bathurst, Barrow, and Ward, John Wallis never returned to a clerical career after becoming Savilian professor of geometry. A good part of the scientific activity of the war and post-war periods, both among stay-at-homes and exiles, seems to have had its roots in a desire to escape from the turmoil of religious fanaticism and the upsets of revolution.[50]

The closer we look at those involved in the Oxford group, and later the Royal Society, the further we are led away from puritanism as a unifying factor. Very few of these men were actually Puritans. The most striking thing about their religious views and the progress of their careers is their ability to make peace with whatever government was in power, their toleration of disparate views, their repudiation of all forms of dogmatic religion and their tendency to move in the direction of latitudinarianism and natural religion.

The acceptance of *de facto* situations by so many of the scientists was frequently not the result of vacillation or expediency but of a particular religious outlook, best designated by the term latitudinarianism. One of the prominent features of this faith was its concept of church government. The latitudinarian rejected both the presbyterian view that forms of church government and discipline were to be found in Scripture, and the toleration of many religious groups desired by the Independents. The civil government had both the power and authority to establish forms of church government and public prayer. The individual's duty was

[49] Isaac Barrow, *Theological Works*, ed. J. Napier (Cambridge, 1859), i, p. xi. The career of John Pell also exhibited some shifts and turns. He was a diplomatic agent for Cromwell yet secured royalist favour for his services to the Church of England. When Anglicanism was restored he took orders in the Church of England.

[50] Sprat, *History of the Royal Society*, p. 53. Robert Moray took up scientific studies during his exile on the continent: Sir Harold Hartley (ed.), *The Royal Society: Its Origin and Founders* (London, 1960), pp. 242, 244. Viscount Brouncker, the royalist first president of the Royal Society, remained in the country quietly pursuing his mathematical studies during the Civil War and Interregnum. He resumed a political career after the Restoration. *Ibid.*, pp. 147, 148, 150.

to submit to the establishment unless the imposed forms were obviously anti-Christian.[51] While the national church was to enjoy a religious monopoly, it was not to demand uniformity of belief or ceremony, since only a few basic tenets were necessary to insure salvation for the individual and peace within the church.

Their feeling that men should be 'ready to comply with all such ... expedients, as may help ... accommodate the differences amongst them'[52] is a clue to the ability of so many scientists to shift allegiances during the Interregnum and to return to Anglicanism in 1660.[53] It also helps to explain their willingness to protect Anglicans during the Civil War and Interregnum years and their equal willingness to shield Dissenters during the Restoration. Thus, although personally partial to episcopal government,[54] latitudinarian scientists could and did readily accept a non-episcopal church during the years of the Civil War and Interregnum.

They also favoured 'a settled Liturgy',[55] yet felt that the current one should be altered to obtain religious unity. Since ceremonies and liturgical forms were, for the most part, established by human authority they desired forms that would include most of the population. The desire to widen the scope of the established church thus led them to advocate comprehension rather than toleration, at least until comprehension proved politically impossible.

Furthermore, the latitudinarian did not possess one of the prime qualities of the staunch Puritan—confidence that his views were correct. Latitudinarians frequently noted that men were naturally

---

[51] Edward Fowler, *Principles and Practices of Certain Moderate Divines of the Church of England, Abusively Called Latitudinarians* (London, 1670), pp. 332–3.
[52] John Wilkins, *Sermons Preached upon Several Occasions* (London, 1682), p. 400.
[53] John Wallis commenting on his career noted: 'It hath been my endeavour all along, to act by moderate Principles, between the Extremities on either hand, in a moderate compliance with the Powers in being, ... without the fierce and violent animosities usual in such Cases, against all, that did not act just as I did, knowing that there were many worthy Persons engaged on either side. And willing whatever side was upmost, to promote (as I was able) any good design for the true Interest of Religion, of Learning, and the publick good; ... And hereby, ... have [I] been able to live easy, and useful, though not Great': John Wallis, 'Account of some Passages of his own Life', *op. cit.*, i, p. clxix.
[54] Patrick, *Brief Account*, p. 503. Patrick may have overestimated their preference for episcopacy.   [55] *Ibid.*

prone to error and that impartiality was a rare quality. Differences of opinion on religious issues were inevitable and insoluble.[56] Therefore hostility stemming from divergent views was intellectually indefensible and socially destructive.[57] While these misgivings did not lead to scepticism, they do suggest why the latitudinarian lacked the fervour and zeal associated with puritanism. Both scientists and latitudinarians suspected any allegiance based on claims of unchallengeable authority.

Thus the keynote is moderation, 'A thing most reasonable and fitting . . . because of the fallibility of human judgment'.[58] It was necessary to:[59]

> Study the moderate pacifick ways, . . . and run not in extremes: both Truth, and Love are in the middle; . . . when we travel in uncertain Roads, 'tis safest to choose the Middle. In this, though we should miss a lesser truth, . . . we shall meet with Charity . . . He that is extreme in his Principles, must needs be narrow in his Affections: whereas he that stands on the middle path, may extend the armes of his Charity to those on both sides.

For the scientists of latitudinarian persuasion the impartial search for religious truth, not the final position reached, was the true mark of piety:[60]

> we are not to think the worse of others for their differences, . . . for though they should be Erroneous and mistaken in

[56] Anon., The Conformists Sayings (London, 1690), pp. 42-3, quoting Isaac Barrow.

[57] Glanvill, for example, noted 'Every vain Opiniator is as much assured as if he were infallible; . . . and the contrary Doctrines Heretical and Abominable. Hence arise Disputes, Hatreds, Separations, Wars, . . .'. Essays on Several Important Subjects in Philosophy and Religion (London, 1676), Essay 1, p. 31.

[58] Anon., Conformists Sayings, p. 42, quoting from Wilkins.

[59] Joseph Glanvill, Catholick Charity Recommended (London, 1669), p. 28.

[60] Anon., Conformists Sayings, p. 11 quoting from Wilkins. Barrow's latitudinarian bent was similar to that of his friend Wilkins. He, like Wilkins, deplored that 'all parties are zealous, stiff, conceited of themselves, allowing no reason or conscience to their adversaries; censorious, calumnious, fiery, etc; hence averse from peace, thinking by struggling to master their opposites, rather than by fair means to confute things. . .': Osmond, Barrow, p. 78.

their judgment in such things, yet if their Conversations be
more just and righteous than ours, if more humble and
peaceable, they are thereupon to be accounted better than
we are, both more acceptable of God, and approved of men.

Still another element in latitudinarian thought which separates its
proponents from most Puritans is a greater emphasis on the moral
aspects of religion. Doctrinal questions were pushed into the
background in order to focus on the moral elements of Christianity and the fundamentals of religion.

One of the factors moving Wilkins and his associates at Oxford
in the direction of latitudinarianism may have been the failure of
their views to fit quite snugly into either the puritan or Anglican
mould. He and others in this intermediate position may have
been peculiarly sympathetic to efforts at reconciliation and especially sensitive to the fact that there was very little to separate the
moderates on both sides. It is perhaps no accident that the
religious backgrounds and commitments of so many latitudinarians and scientists are not easily defined, and that many combined
puritan, or semi-puritan, backgrounds with certain attitudes
associated with Anglicanism.

If many scientists were latitudinarians, not all latitudinarians, of
course, were scientists. Nevertheless the earliest description of the
latitudinarians noted that the latitude men were 'Followers for the
most part of the new Philosophy, . . .'.[61] William Lloyd, Edward
Stillingfleet, Simon Patrick, Joseph Glanvill, John Tillotson and
Gilbert Burnet did not themselves engage in scientific activities
but were enthusiastic about the new philosophy.[62] Joseph Glanvill and Thomas Sprat were propagandists for both science and

[61] Patrick, *Brief Account*, p. 500. See also p. 508. More recently Walter
Simon has noted the connection between the Royal Society and moderate
churchmen: *The Restoration Episcopate* (New York, 1965), pp. 30, 126–8.
[62] Lloyd and Stillingfleet assisted Wilkins in his *Essay Towards a Real
Character and a Philosophical Language* (London, 1668). Tillotson became a
member of the Royal Society. His sermons make it clear that he was more
than sympathetic to his father-in-law's scientific activities. Stillingfleet
while not an active virtuoso greatly admired Boyle's contribution to
experimental philosophy: Robert Boyle, *Works*, ed. Thomas Birch
(London, 1744), v, p. 516. For information on Burnet see T. E. S. Clarke
and H. C. Foxcroft, *Life of Gilbert Burnet, Bishop of Salisbury* (Cambridge,
1907), p. 477 and Richard B. Schlatter, *The Social Ideas of Religious Leaders
1660–1688* (Oxford, 1940), pp. 52–3.

latitudinarianism.[63] Matthew Hale, one of the most prominent latitudinarian laymen, was also very much interested and engaged in scientific experimentation and publication.[64]

In John Locke we again see the combination of liberal religion and scientific interest. Locke, like so many virtuosi members of the Royal Society, not only numbered Boyle, Tillotson, Barrow, Cudworth and Patrick among his intimate friends, but adopted the rational theology typical of the group and supported the comprehension schemes which they promoted.[65]

Among politicians of the Restoration seeking a more liberal religious settlement an unusual number were interested in science and became active members of the Royal Society. Locke's patron, Lord Ashley, provides an outstanding example. Lord Berkeley and the duke of Buckingham, both patrons of John Wilkins, shared his scientific interests as well as his latitudinarian predilections.[66] Certainly many politicians with scientific interests fell into the latitudinarian camp, and it is not surprising that discussion of attempts to topple the Clarendon government were conducted at dinners which followed meetings of the Society.[67]

---

[63] See Jackson I. Cope, *Joseph Glanvill, Anglican Apologist* (St Louis, 1956) and Sprat, *History of the Royal Society.*

[64] Matthew Hale, *The Works Moral and Religious*, ed. T. Thirlwall (London, 1805), pp. 98, 136, 243.

[65] Maurice Cranston, *John Locke* (New York, 1957), p. 40; H. R. Fox-Bourne, *The Life of John Locke* (New York, 1876), i. p. 309; for a discussion of the relationship of his epistemology to that of Tillotson, Wilkins, Boyle, Glanvill and Newton, see Henry G. van Leeuwen, *The Problem of Certainty in English Thought 1630-1690* (The Hague, 1963), pp. 121-42.

[66] [George Berkeley], *Historical Applications and Occasional Meditations on Several Subjects* (London, 1667), pp. 7, 57, 92-3, 97, 100. Wilkins was promoted to the episcopacy largely through Buckingham's efforts. Buckingham was also Sprat's patron. For his religious views see Richard Baxter, *Reliquiae Baxterianae* (London, 1696), Part ii, pp. 21, 22, 31; and George Villiers, d. of Buckingham, *A Short Discourse upon the Reasonableness of Men's Having a Religion* (London, 1685).

[67] Samuel Pepys, *Diary*, ed. Henry B. Wheatley (London, 1893), vii, pp. 193-6. One such dinner party included Hooke, Pepys, Wilkins, Viscount Brouncker and the Earls of Lauderdale and Tivedale: John Evelyn, *Diary*, ed. E. S. de Beer (London, 1955), iii, pp. 369-70. Another included virtuosi Wilkins and John Evelyn as well as politicians Lords Ashley and Lauderdale, Sir Thomas Clifford and Arlington's secretary, Williamson: *ibid.*, iii, p. 526.

The circle seemed to include many high officials of the anti-Clarendon faction who concerned themselves with eliminating the Act of Uniformity and substituting an act of comprehension.

While the virtuosi of a latitudinarian bent were not the sole supporters of the comprehension movement, they did provide a good deal of its leadership. John Wilkins, who was said to have organized a 'club' for comprehension,[68] was the author and chief promoter of the 1668 proposals to broaden the church.[69] He was almost certainly working very closely with the duke of Buckingham. Sir Matthew Hale was responsible for putting Wilkins's proposals into the proper legislative format.[70] Although the 1668 effort failed, latitudinarians such as Tillotson, Stillingfleet, Lloyd and Wilkins[71] continued to promote similar schemes to heal England's religious schisms. Other virtuosi who favoured comprehension were Glanvill and Sir Robert Moray, the latter together with Gilbert Burnet having been leading figures in attempting to obtain comprehension for Scotland in 1668. Although Moray, one of the principal architects of the Royal Society, has often been labelled a Presbyterian, it appears that he, like most of the founders of the Royal Society, was quite willing to conform and was widely known for his latitudinarian sympathies.[72]

In still another area too we can see the connection between latitudinarians and scientists, for both were advocates of a plain and more simplified style of discourse.[73] Here again John Wilkins

[68] Anthony Wood, *Athenae Oxonienses*, ed. Phillip Bliss (London, 1813–1820), iv, col. 513.

[69] Walter Simon, 'Comprehension in the age of Charles II', *Church History*, xxxi (1962), p. 443.

[70] Gilbert Burnet, 'The Life and Death of Matthew Hale', *Works of Matthew Hale*, ed. Thirlwall (1805), p. 32.

[71] As Bishop of Chester Wilkins attempted to bring Nonconformists into the Church and seems to have practised something like comprehension in his diocese. He also vigorously opposed the Conventicle Act of 1670 though the King demanded his support.

[72] A. Robertson, *The Life of Sir Robert Moray* (London, 1922), p. 173.

[73] But see R. F. Jones, 'Science and English prose style in the third quarter of the seventeenth century', *The Seventeenth Century*, by R. F. Jones and others writing in his honour (Stanford, California, 1951), pp. 75–110; George Williamson, *The Senecan Amble* (London, 1951); Harold Fisch, 'The Puritans and the reform of prose-style', *English Literary History*, xix (1952), pp. 229–48; Lawrence Sasek, *The Literary*

ties the two groups together, for he was one of the first scientists to advocate a clear, precise and plain style and to insist that confusion in the search for religious and scientific truth could be eliminated by eliminating rhetorical, mystical and metaphoric language.[74] It was his protégé, Thomas Sprat, working under his direction who announced the Royal Society's advocacy of the plain style.[75] On the clerical side, it was Wilkins's son-in-law John Tillotson, rather than Wilkins himself, who became the most prominent practitioner of the plain style. Tillotson, however, was not alone among the latitudinarians in following Wilkins's stylistic canons. Most latitudinarian divines did.[76] Joseph Glanvill, one of the most active propagandists of both moderate religion and the scientific movement also directed his efforts at promoting a simplified style.[77]

This preoccupation with style did not reflect simply the pursuit of clarity for clarity's sake. Here again the scientist and the religious moderate are linked by their concentration on avoiding methodologies or modes of discourse that would encourage intemperate claims and inhibit the tentative, step-by-step investigation that they saw as the central vehicle for successful scientific and religious investigation. A clear, unpretentious style of discourse might contribute to clearer and less dogmatic philosophic and theological stances among the discoursers.

Thomas Sprat's official apologia for the Royal Society made

Temper of the English Puritans (Baton Rouge, Louisiana, 1961); William Haller, *The Rise of Puritanism* (New York, 1957); Kenneth Hamilton, *The Two Harmonies: Poetry and Prose in the Seventeenth Century* (Oxford, 1963).
[74] John Wilkins, *Ecclesiastes, or a Discourse concerning the Gift of Preaching* (London, 1646), pp. 72–3; John Wilkins, *A Discourse Concerning the Gift of Prayer* (London, 1651), pp. 28, 48.
[75] Sprat, *History of the Royal Society*, pp. 111–13.
[76] Burnet, *History*, i, pp. 339–40. See also Samuel Parker, *A Free and Impartial Censure of the Platonick Philosophy* (London, 1666), p. 41; Edward Fowler, *Principles and Practices of Certain Moderate Divines* (London, 1670), pp. 41, 104, 112, 116–17; A. T. Hart, *William Lloyd, 1627–1717* (London, 1952), p. 222; James Arderne, *Directions Concerning the Matter and Style of Sermons*, ed. J. Mackray (Oxford, 1952), pp. x–xi. Arderne was a member of the Royal Society. The Cambridge Platonists as a group, however, never became enamoured with the plain style.
[77] See Joseph Glanvill, *An Essay Concerning Preaching* (London, 1678); Glanvill, *A Seasonable Defense of Preaching and the Plain Way of It* (London, 1673); Cope, *Joseph Glanvill, Anglican Apologist*.

perfectly plain the open alliance between liberal religion and scientific inquiry, insisting that the quality of the humble Christian and the scientific experimenter were the same. He argued it was 'requisite' that the scientists 'be well practis'd in all the modest, humble, friendly Vertues; should be willing to be taught, and to give way to the Judgement of others'.[78] Able philosophers could never be produced by 'high, earnest, insulting Wits', who could 'neither bear partnership, nor opposition'.[79] Wilkins and Glanvill too noted the parallel between the moderate Christian and the scientific experimenter, particularly emphasizing consciousness of one's own and others' fallibility as the mark of the true Christian and the true scientist.[80]

Many scientists, however, saw more than correspondence between the attitudes of science and religion. Glanvill insisted that scientific inquiry itself provided a remedy for religious dissensions. It 'dispose[d] mens Spirits to more *calmness* and *modesty*, *charity* and *prudence* in the Differences of *Religion*, and even silence[d] *Disputes* there.'[81] For wherever scientific investigation prevailed 'the *Contentious Divinity* loseth ground; and 'twill be hard to find any one of those Philosophers, that is a zealous Votary of a Sect: . . .'.[82] This is true because by:[83]

> open Inquiry in the great Field of Nature, . . . they will find themselves disposed to more *indifferency* toward those *petty Notions*, in which they were before apt to place a great deal of Religion; and to reckon that *all that* will signifie lies, in the *few*, *certain*, *operative* Principles of the Gospel; and a *Life* suitable to such a *Faith*; not in *doting* upon *Questions*, and *Speculations* that *engender strife*.

Sprat noted that the real philosophy bred 'a race of . . . Men' 'invincibly arm'd' against the enchantments of religious en-

---

[78] Sprat, *History of the Royal Society*, pp. 33–4.

[79] *Ibid.* See also pp. 92, 101, 104–5.

[80] See John Wilkins, *Of the Principles and Duties of Natural Religion* (London, 1675), pp. 35–6; Wilkins, *The Discovery of a New World*, Preface to the Reader, in *Mathematical and Philosophical Works* (London, 1708); Joseph Glanvill, *Plus Ultra* (London, 1668), pp. 127–8, 147.

[81] Glanvill, *Plus Ultra*, p. 149.

[82] Joseph Glanvill, *Essays on Several Important Subjects* (London, 1676), Essay 4, p. 27.

[83] *Ibid.*, pp. 13–14. See also Glanvill, *Philosophia Pia* (London, 1671), p. 92.

thusiasm.[84] The meetings of the virtuosi provided the unusual sight of 'men of disagreeing parties, and ways of life, [who] have forgotten to hate . . .'.[85] Their pursuit of natural philosophy would produce religious calm, for '*spiritual Frensies*, . . . can never stand long, before a cleer, and a *deep skill* in *Nature*'.[86]

The alliance between latitudinarianism and science, however, went far deeper than a common core of practitioners and a mutual distaste for dogmatism. For the two movements also shared a common theory of knowledge, and members of both became the principal proponents of a rationalized religion and natural theology. In their respective areas both scientists and theologians sought a *via media* between scepticism and dogmatism. On the scientific side this search resulted in an emphasis on hypothesis and a science without overt metaphysics. In spiritual matters it led to an emphasis on broad fundamentals and the eschewing of any detailed, orthodox theology claiming infallibility.

It was Sebastian Castellio writing nearly a century earlier, who first attempted to deal with theological problems in the way later adopted by Wilkins and his circle of latitudinarian and scientific associates. Castellio suggested that while there was no way of eliminating all doubts concerning the validity of religious knowledge, it was possible to arrive at a type of assurance about basic truths that would suffice. This line of argument was elaborated by Grotius and then by William Chillingworth. Chillingworth distinguished three levels of certainty. The highest was available only to God. The second was based on evidence which virtually excluded the possibility of error. The third, moral certainty, was the level a reasonable person could attain after considering all the available evidence. Aside from those problems that could be solved by clear and unambiguous reference to Scripture, religious matters fell within this third realm of certainty.[87]

Henry van Leeuwen has described the development of this approach to certainty in England from 1630 to 1690 and shown its importance in the evolution of scientific methodology and epistemological theory. He has suggested that this formulation of the concept was first introduced into the religious sphere by Chillingworth and Tillotson in the context of the Rule of Faith

---

[84] Sprat, *History of the Royal Society*, p. 53.
[85] *Ibid.*, p. 427.　　　　　　　　　　[86] *Ibid.*, p. 54.
[87] Van Leeuwen, *Problem of Certainty*, pp. 22–3, 27, 28.

controversy between Protestants and Roman Catholics, and then adopted and secularized by such scientists as Wilkins, Glanvill, Boyle, Newton and Locke. His examination of Restoration thinkers, however, actually suggests simultaneous development of these notions by churchmen and scientists. Wilkins and Glanvill, for instance, were concerned with both religious and scientific methodology, so that it would be unrealistic rigidly to separate religious and scientific movements and suppose a one-way flow of ideas from the former to the latter. Wilkins's treatment of the problem of certainty, and of epistemology more generally, was an attempt to find a means of establishing a level of certainty in both the religious and scientific areas sufficient to avoid the pitfalls of dogmatism and claimed infallibility on the one hand and outright scepticism on the other.

A brief description of Wilkins's views should suggest how this approach to certainty could encompass both religious and scientific truth. After laying out the types of evidence and their source in sense and understanding, Wilkins suggested the several levels of certainty that might be derived from such evidence. There were two basic categories. The first, knowledge or certainty, was derived from evidence that did not admit any reasonable cause of doubt.[88] The second was opinion or probability.[89] Knowledge had three sub-categories, physical, mathematical and moral. The first was derived from sense data.[90] The second was not limited to mathematics alone, but extended to all 'matters as are capable of the like certainty; . . .'.[91] The objects of moral certainty were 'less simple' than the physical or the mathematical for they:[92]

> are not capable of the same kind of Evidence . . . so as to necessitate every man's assent, . . . yet may they be so plain, that every man whose judgment is free from prejudice will consent unto them. And though there be no natural necessity, that such things must be so, and that they cannot possibly be otherwise, . . . yet may they be so certain as not to admit of any reasonable doubt concerning them.

[88] Wilkins, *Natural Religion*, p. 5.   [89] *Ibid.*, pp. 5, 10–11.
[90] Sense data included the inward as well as outward senses, that is, self-awareness as well as the awareness of objects.
[91] Wilkins, *Natural Religion*, pp. 6–7.   [92] *Ibid.*, pp. 7–8.

The first two yielded 'infallible' certainty, the last 'indubitable' certainty.[93] Most things, including the basic principles of religion, were capable only of 'indubitable certainty', that is a certainty that did not admit of any reasonable cause of doubt. In matters of faith and religion it was only possible to render things 'highly credible'.[94] There were, however, conditions under which even indubitable certainty might not be achieved. When the evidence was unclear or did not exclude the possibility of reasonable doubt, it yielded only opinion and probability.[95] Nevertheless, bare possibility was an insufficient reason for doubting weighty evidence.[96] When there was no certainty, the impartial judgment should 'incline to the greater probabilities'.[97] If the probabilities were equal, it was appropriate to suspend judgment.

Wilkins's categorization of evidence and certainty, which was fairly typical of those of his associates,[98] was applied to religious as well as secular knowledge. He was, in fact, attempting to lay down a rational foundation for the truths of religion. From this theory of knowledge Wilkins and those who shared his approach went on to develop the basic principles of a natural theology. Latitudinarians like Tillotson, Stillingfleet and the Cambridge Platonists were leaders among the churchmen, while Charleton, Ray, Ward, Boyle, Wilkins and Newton were among the virtuosi who contributed to the formulation of this natural religion.[99]

One of the basic approaches of the latitudinarians was the distinction between the fundamentals and non-essentials of religion. Emphasis on non-essentials such as ceremonies, obscure doctrines, vestmentary requirements and the forms of prayer was reduced. Real religion did not revolve around fine theological points. Wilkins even argued that if a point was much debated it was not likely to be very important. And while one or another party might be correct on these minor points, possession of the truth in such lesser matters was not a crucial factor in the life of religion. Wilkins was quite willing to allow the controversies

[93] None, however, were 'absolutely' infallible for that was an attribute of God alone: *ibid.*, p. 9.   [94] *Ibid.*, p. 30.
[95] *Ibid.*, pp. 10, 11. Both the senses and understanding at times yielded only opinion and probability.
[96] *Ibid.*, pp. 27–9.   [97] *Ibid.*, p. 34.
[98] See van Leeuwen, *Problem of Certainty, passim.*
[99] See Richard S. Westfall, *Science and Religion in Seventeenth-Century England* (New Haven, 1958).

between Puritans and High Churchmen to be settled at the Day of Judgement.[100]

Thus the theory of certainty permitted both the latitudinarians and scientists who espoused it to direct attention away from traditional theological disputes, for most of these disputes were over matters that fell into a very low category of certainty, and in fact were usually to be placed only in the realm of probability and opinion. Overconfidence and dogmatism on such doubtful matters as the forms of church government and ceremony simply led to persecution over truths which might or might not be true and could not in any event be established with a sufficient level of certainty to justify coercive policies. The inevitable limitations on human certainty that were so clearly operative and significant in science were equally decisive in religion.

Moreover, just as some scientific truths could be established to a high degree of certainty and thus become the foundation for further scientific investigation, so certain fundamental propositions of religion could be similarly established and similarly used to guide the conduct of religious life. There was a core of religious and scientific truth upon which rational agreement could be attained. Beyond that the limits of certainty should establish the limits of dispute, particularly violent dispute:[101]

> It being utterly impossible . . . that we should always agree in the same apprehension of things. If upon every difference men should think themselves obliged to prosecute matters to the utmost height and rigour, such eager persons may easily from hence be induced to have recourse to Arms rather than such precious things as truth and justice shall suffer; and being once thus engaged, it will be impossible . . . to end their differences by any accommodation, they must fight it out to the last till one side be wholly subdued and destroyed. And thus would men grow wild and savage, the benefits of Society would be lost, and mankind destroyed out of the world.

It was thus a theory of knowledge which incorporated the factor of human fallibility that led many of the Royal Society latitudinarians to emphasize natural religion as a core of established truth

---

[100] *Bishop Wilkins' Character of the Best Christian* (Dublin, 1759), p. 5.
[101] Wilkins, *Sermons Preached on Several Occasions*, p. 414.

on which all men could agree and which would be sufficient to guide their spiritual lives without attempts to settle insoluble questions that could only lead to more heat than light.

This scientific commitment to a non-dogmatic religion quite naturally went hand in hand with the scientists' constant need to re-emphasize the necessity of free inquiry and experiment unconstrained by rules accepted *a priori* on the basis of authority. John Wilkins insisted those in 'search of Truth' must 'preserve a Philosophical Liberty', which must be used to make impartial inquiries.[102] The 'indifferent seeker of Truth' must approach his task 'with an equal Mind, not swayed by Prejudice, but indifferently resolved to assent unto that Truth which upon deliberation shall seem most probable . . .'.[103] Robert Hooke seconded Wilkins with the warning that it was poor procedure to 'dogmatically define' or 'fix axioms'. The better course was to 'question and canvass all opinions, adopting . . . none, till by mature debate and clear arguments, chiefly such as are deduced from legitimate experiments, the truth of such experiments be demonstrated invincibly'.[104] If there were 'any Doubt or Obscurity' on one or another point, it was necessary to 'suspend our Assents', and although continuing to 'dispute *pro* or *con*' on the matter, not to settle one's 'Opinion on either Side'.[105]

The scientists were not only reluctant to accept traditional authorities but hesitant to create new ones. Overconfident assertions constrained investigation by presenting hypotheses as unquestionable truths.[106] One of the basic qualities of the scientific attitude was humility before an ever increasing body of facts and willingness to give way to the judgments of others. Their humility was coupled with the intense feeling that freedom to differ and investigate was the most important tool of the scientist. This was not the stance of the zealous Puritan or the zealous Anglican but of the religious moderates who were rejecting dogmatism and the principle of authority in the sphere of religion.

[102] Wilkins, *A Discourse Concerning a New Planet*, p. 145, in *Mathematical and Philosophical Works*.
[103] *Ibid.*, pp. 221, 145.
[104] Quoted in H. Lyons, *The Royal Society 1660–1940* (Cambridge, 1944), pp. 41–2.
[105] Wilkins, *Discourse Concerning a New Planet*, p. 146.
[106] Glanvill, *Plus Ultra*, pp. 127–8.

Scientific discussion required restraint. Wilkins advised that in all matters where '*Victory* cannot be had, Men must be content with Peace'.[107] He further insisted:[108]

> 'Tis an Excellent Rule to be observed in all Disputes, That men should give *Soft Words* and *Hard Arguments*; that they would not so much strive to *vex*, as to *convince* an Enemy. If this were but diligently practised in all Cases, and on all sides, we might be in a good measure be freed from those Vexations in the search of Truth, . . .

The virtues of the scientist are summed up by Joseph Glanvill. He has:[109]

> a Sense of his own *Fallibility* . . . and never concludes but upon resolution to alter his mind upon contrary evidence. Thus he conceives *warily*, and he speaks with . . . *caution* . . . with great defferrence to *opposite Perswasion*, candour to *dissenters*, and *calmness* in *contradictions*, . . . he gives his *Reasons* without *passion* . . . discourses without *wrangling*, and *differs* without *dividing*. . . . He . . . *suspends* his judgment when he doth not clearly *understand*.

The Royal Society and its predecessors insisted that the approach of Wilkins and the virtues described by Glanvill rule their meetings. Thomas Sprat wrote of the Society's 'singular sobriety of debating, slowness of consenting, and moderation of dissenting'[110] and compared the 'so yielding, so complying' temperament of the scientists to that of 'Bold, and haughty Assertors'.[111] Nature, he insisted, 'never separates us into mortal Factions; *that* gives us room to differ, without animosity; and permits us, to raise contrary imaginations upon it, without any danger of a *Civil War*'.[112] To avoid the possibility of such 'civil war' both the 1645 group and the Royal Society excluded political and religious

[107] Wilkins, *Discourse Concerning a New Planet*, p. 140.
[108] *Ibid*. Cf. 'Soft words and hard arguments being the most effectuall way to convince.' *Ecclesiastes*, p. 16.
[109] Glanvill, *Plus Ultra*, p. 147.
[110] Sprat, *History of the Royal Society*, p. 91.
[111] *Ibid*., p. 34. See also Charles R. Weld, *A History of the Royal Society* (London, 1848), i, pp. 218–19.
[112] Sprat, *History of the Royal Society*, p. 56.

discussion and confined themselves strictly to the 'business of philosophy'.[113]

The virtuosi's lack of sympathy for those who thought they possessed the unquestionable truth in any but the most general and fundamental questions of religion, more than any other quality, separates them from the Puritans of both the pre- or post-Restoration periods. In fact, their approach to religion, with its emphasis on reason, was probably more congenial to Anglicans than Puritans who placed immense confidence in the infallibility of their authorities and dogmatic methods. The outlook of the scientists had a great deal more in common with that of Acontius, one of the earliest religious liberals, than that of Luther or Calvin, for Acontius, after insisting that no man was immune from error and that the chief ally of Satan was spiritual or intellectual pride, concluded with the necessity of free inquiry. The scientists were essentially Erasmian. Not only did they emphasize the unity between piety and learning and focus on practical morality, but they were unsympathetic with the bickerings over dogma and ceremony that they felt resulted in the neglect of true piety. Luther's criticism of Erasmus could surely have been made by the critics of the latitudinarians, both puritan and High Church. 'He is thinking of peace, not of the cross'.[114] It was Erasmus who wrote, 'I merely want to analyse and not to judge, to inquire and not to dogmatize. I am ready to learn from anyone who advances something more accurate or more reliable, . . .'.[115] And it was Luther who replied, 'Not to delight in assertions is not the mark of a Christian heart. Indeed one must delight in assertions to be a Christian at all'.[116] The same exchange might have occurred between the leading members of the Royal Society and their critics.

Thus it is not surprising that so many scientists espoused the new latitudinarian currents of the Restoration. For the co-operative and tentative attitudes of the scientists were easily translated into the sphere of religious discourse and resulted in a

[113] John Wallis, *A Defence of the Royal Society* (London, 1678), p. 7. See also Sprat, *History of the Royal Society*, pp. 33, 82, 104–6, 347.
[114] Quoted in Herschel Baker, *The Dignity of Man* (Cambridge, Massachusetts, 1947), p. 269.
[115] E. G. Winter (trans. and ed.), *Erasmus-Luther, Discourse on Free Will* (New York, 1961), p. 7. [116] *Ibid.*, p. 101.

reduction of the temperature of religious debate. Perhaps even more significant, however, were the mutually reinforcing elements of latitude, moderation, and modest, tentative rationality that the spokesmen of the Royal Society advocated in both the religious and scientific spheres. Not only was science a haven from religious dogmatism and conflict, but the methods of science, if instilled in the public mind, could contribute to improvement in the religious climate. The virtuosi hoped that eventually science and a moderate, latitudinarian, natural religion might serve as the two pillars supporting an intellectual life in which the calm, friendly and practical pursuit of truth and goodness could replace abstract debate and ideologically motivated civil strife.

There is then an intimate connection between religion and science in seventeenth-century England, but it is hardly a simple cause-and-effect relation between puritanism and scientific innovation. The innovators were largely drawn from the ranks of the religious moderates, and the great impetus to science in the Wilkins period at Oxford seems to have been largely a function of the purposeful establishment of a scientific haven from the dogmatic religious conflict associated with the Puritans. Indeed in the last analysis the new science and a new latitudinarian theology became inextricably interconnected in an effort to provide a substitute for the perilous certainties of the puritan divines.

XXIV

CIVIL WAR POLITICS, RELIGION AND THE ROYAL SOCIETY*

Lotte Mulligan

Writers who see the development of science in seventeenth-century England as an integral part of the social and political world have established a long tradition of linking it with the other great seventeenth-century intellectual movement—puritanism. From Merton[1] in 1938 to Christopher Hill in 1965[2] a subtle and intricate web has been woven which draws the student into an appealing synthesis of social conflict, political and religious ideology and scientific innovation.

Attempts have been made by critics not so much to unravel the web as to change its pattern by altering the woof. Rabb[3] has argued that it was not puritanism which triggered off scientific innovation, educational advances and political change, but rather that all four factors were the product of a 'revolutionary' outlook prevalent among politicians, intellectuals, preachers and among the gentry and the urban merchant classes. An attitude developed which sought a 'root and branch' change in politics, religion, education and science and as a result radical thinkers in one or more of these areas found themselves in alliance. Radical

---

* From no. 59 (May 1973).
[1] R. K. Merton, *Science, Technology and Society in Seventeenth Century England* (New York, 1970) reprinted from *Osiris*, iv (1938), pp. 360–632.
[2] Christopher Hill, *Intellectual Origins of the English Revolution* (Oxford, 1965).
[3] T. K. Rabb, 'Puritanism and the rise of experimental science in England', *Jl of World History*, vii (1962), pp. 46–67 and ——, 'Religion and the rise of modern science', *Past and Present*, no. 31 (July 1965), p. 111; p. 262 in this volume.

puritanism as a theological system was, if anything, antagonistic to scientific change.[4]

Kearney[5] suggested that the elusive connection between science and other intellectual and social attitudes was not through radical puritanism but through radical reformist thinking *within* the established church. He traces an Erasmian approach through Montaigne, Galileo, Bacon and the Cambridge Platonists. Trevor-Roper[6] had already picked out a thread of this kind, in tracing the influence of protestantism on the Enlightenment, and Kearney is able to put up a good *prima facie* case for a rational theology having had more to contribute to the advance of science than had fideistic puritanism.

The most recent contributor, Barbara Shapiro,[7] has developed this interpretation further and sees a positive link between religious latitudinarianism and science. She has shown that some important scientists and propagandists of science were not hardline Anglicans or Puritans but believers in religious accommodation, compromise, and submission to civil authority in matters of faith. These men had no dogmatic belief in the infallibility of their views; they stressed moral rather than doctrinal issues, and they shared an epistemology which provided for a rational religion and a natural theology.[8] Such men could be found among both Puritans and Anglicans, and their presence in either camp explains the number of well-known Puritans who became Anglican bishops or important church officials after the Restoration.[9] Not only is this link said to explain such biographical vagaries; it is said to have provided a religious rationale for scientific activity which helped science to become respectable.

So much for the attempts to link science with religion. But Merton and Hill have tried to align science with a social move-

4 Rabb, 'Puritanism . . .', *passim.*
5 H. F. Kearney, 'Puritanism, capitalism and the Scientific Revolution', *Past and Present,* no. 28 (July 1964), p. 100, p. 240 in this volume.
6 H. F. Trevor-Roper, 'The religious origins of the Enlightenment', *Religion, Reformation and Social Change* (London, 1967), pp. 193–236.
7 Barbara Shapiro, 'Latitudinarianism and science in seventeenth-century England', *Past and Present,* no. 40 (July 1968), pp. 16–41; pp. 286–316 in this volume; ——, *John Wilkins 1614–72* (Berkeley, Los Angeles, 1969), chaps 4 and 8.
8 Shapiro, 'Latitudinarianism . . .', pp. 19–35; pp. 290–309 in this volume.
9 In particular, John Wilkins and John Wallis.

ment—to present interest in science as peculiarly bourgeois. Merton simply noted[10] that there was a correlation between puritanism, the merchant classes, and an interest in science and especially in technology. He also argued that scientists of the day were drawn to technological problems by those social forces which otherwise governed their lives. He suggested that the bourgeoisie promoted and encouraged interest in science and that their puritanism provided social attitudes conducive to scientific advance. Hill extended Merton's thesis by arguing that the basis of scientific advance in England was laid by the 'middling sort of men'[11] and that the work of craftsmen and the co-operation of practical puritan merchants were indispensable to scientific advance in the seventeenth century. Francis Bacon, who promoted the view that the crafts had a vital role to play in setting science on the right path, was seen by Hill as imbued, in a special way, with the puritan ethos and with political radicalism. He is used in Hill's argument as a key figure linking radicalism, puritanism and practical science.

This view is criticized in detail by Rabb[12] and in more general terms by Kearney.[13] Hall agrees that specific technological advances were due to the skills of craftsmen but argues that the real work of revolutionizing science was a conceptual task far beyond the capacities of practical and unlearned men.[14] The revolution required and received tough theoretical thinking by academics who may have used instruments but whose achievement owed little to the rule-of-thumb methodology of the workshops.

Most of the arguments linking science with puritanism and the middle classes have relied both on a few key men who exemplified the connections to be established, and on the harmony between the streams of thought they wished to connect. Hill is able to cite very few puritan middle-class scientists, and Bacon was certainly not one of them. Shapiro's work is based on the biography of one

[10] Merton, *Science, Technology and Society*, p. 81.
[11] Hill, *Intellectual Origins*, chap. 2.
[12] Rabb, 'Puritanism . . .', *passim*.
[13] Kearney, 'Puritanism . . .', p. 85 (p. 223 in this volume), and 'Puritanism and science: problems of definition', *Past and Present*, no. 31 (July 1965), pp. 104–10; pp. 254–61 in this volume.
[14] A. R. Hall, 'The Scholar and the Craftsman in the Scientific Revolution', *Critical Problems in the History of Science*, ed. Marshall Clagett (Madison, 1959), p. 21.

man, although a dozen other allegedly latitudinarian scientists and enthusiasts are mentioned. Rabb's theoretical argument introduces a 'revolutionary' character common to reformers in religion, politics, education and science. Although he denies any specific connections between science and puritanism, Rabb sets up an essentially tautological proposition—that people who wanted reform in social, political or intellectual spheres shared a common 'revolutionary' streak.

Only Merton's work attempts a detailed and wholesale analysis of the social and intellectual attitudes associated with an interest in science, but he describes a parallel, and not necessarily related, simultaneous growth of practical and pure science, mercantile interests and puritan allegiance in the society as a whole.

The present paper looks at the problem of the relationship between interest in science and political and religious attitudes in a simple quantitative way. If interest in science were in any way related to other intellectual and social factors, one could take groups who were interested in science, trace their religious, political and social background, and look for correlations. What part, for instance, did men interested in science play in the Civil War? Were they supporters of political reform on the parliamentarian side? Were they aligned with the Puritans? Were they predominantly from one social class—the mercantile class for instance? Was their education and experience practical rather than academic?

The years of the war and of the Interregnum during which most educated people were forced in one way or another to declare publicly their political and religious positions, are an appropriate starting point for investigating the relation between science and other social factors. During this time of political and religious turmoil sizeable groups met to discuss scientific matters and to conduct experiments, while actively dissociating themselves from the prevailing conflicts. But they were too small and too shifting in membership to act as a good test of any general theory about the relation of science to religion or politics. Nevertheless membership of these groups is worth analysing, if only because they can be compared with a far larger scientific group which collected in 1660.[15]

[15] Other discreet scientific activity occurred, of course, during this period, on the part of individuals and groups such as the Towneley circle. See

In 1645 a group of scientists met at Jonathan Goddard's London lodgings to experiment and to discuss scientific subjects.[16] Given the place and time of these discussions it is not surprising that those who came were mainly supporters of the parliamentary side.[17] London in 1645 was not a safe harbour for peaceful scientific royalists. We do not know of everyone who attended these discussions but it is unlikely that John Wallis, who recalled the membership of the group in later life, should have remembered only the parliamentarians and forgotten the royalists.

Charles Webster, 'Richard Towneley (1629–1707); the Towneley Group and seventeenth century science', *Trans. Hist. Soc. Lancs and Cheshire*, cxviii (1965), p. 51.

[16] John Wallis, 'Account of some Passages of his own Life', in Thomas Hearne, *Peter Langtoft's Chronicle* (Oxford, 1725), i, p. clxi; see also C. J. Scriba, 'The autobiography of John Wallis, F.R.S.', *Notes and Records*, xxv (1970), pp. 17–46.

[17] John Wilkins, John Wallis, Jonathan Goddard, Christopher Merrett, Samuel Foster, Theodore Haak, and George Ent, a possible parliamentarian. Francis Glisson was the only royalist. The following biographical sources were used to provide information for classification: *Dictionary of National Biography*, 22 vols (London, 1908–9); J. Venn and J. A. Venn, *Alumni Cantabrigienses*, Pt I, 4 vols (Cambridge, 1922–7); G. E. C., *Complete Baronetage*, vol. iv, *1665–1707* (Exeter, 1904); Anthony a' Wood, *Athenae Oxonienses*, ed. P. Bliss, 4 vols (Oxford, 1813–20); John Aubrey, *Brief Lives, chiefly of Contemporaries*, ed. A. Clark (Oxford, 1898); Joseph Foster, *Alumni Oxonienses*, early series, 4 vols (London, 1891–2); *Biographia Britannica*, 6 vols (London, 1747–66); H. A. C. Sturgess, *Register of Admissions to the Honourable Society of the Middle Temple*, 3 vols (London, 1949); C. H. Hopwood, *Calendar of Inner Temple Records* (London, 1903); *Records of the Honourable Society of Lincoln's Inn. Admissions from 1420 to 1799* (London, 1896); Joseph Foster, *A Register of Admissions to Gray's Inn, 1521–1881* (London, 1889); A. G. Matthews, *Walker Revised* (Oxford, 1948); ——, *Introduction to Calamy Revised* (London, 1959); *Calendar of the Proceedings of the Committee for Compounding with Delinquents 1643–1660* (London, 1889); Robert Baillie, *Letters and Journals . . . 1637–1662*, ed. D. Laing, 3 vols (Edinburgh, 1841); William Bulloch (compiler), Bulloch's Roll, MS. Royal Society Library; E. G. R. Taylor, *The Mathematical Practitioners of Tudor and Stuart England* (Cambridge, 1954); R. W. Innes Smith, *English-Speaking Students of Medicine at the University of Leyden* (Edinburgh and London, 1932); John Ward, *The Lives of the Professors of Gresham College* (London, 1740, Johnson Reprint Corp. edn, 1967); Thomas Thomson, *History of the Royal Society* (London, 1812); W. Munk, *The Roll of the Royal College of Physicians of London*, second edn, 3 vols (London, 1878). These sources were supplemented by specific works on individuals.

In 1651 a group meeting in Oxford contained both parliamentarians who had moved to academic appointments there[18] and a number of royalists who were living in Oxford.[19] When the locus shifted back to London and to Gresham College in 1659, committed parliamentarians were notably absent and royalists were joined by a number of younger men who had not taken part in the turmoils of the early 1640s.[20] This group met during 1659 and 1660 and in November 1660 those present decided formally to set up a college for experimental learning.[21] They named thirty-nine other prospective members of whom only a few were parliamentarians.[22]

These scientific gatherings, then, were evidently not predominantly puritan or parliamentarian. After 1645 more and more royalists joined. The Restoration did nothing to alter the composition of the group, which suggests that after the end of the first stage of war in 1646 political factors did not affect its membership.

John Wallis could not recall everyone who attended these meetings; attendance was shifting and flexible. A much larger and more stable group was that which eventually became the Royal Society. As evidence of who was interested in science it is therefore more suitable for analysis than the more casual earlier gatherings.

The men who joined the 'college' in 1660 were not all scientists but they all clearly wanted to be associated with scientific activity. Many of the early Fellows had been through the war. If religion, politics or social class had any bearing on an interest in science

[18] Wilkins, Wallis, Goddard. They were joined also by William Petty.
[19] Seth Ward, Thomas Willis, Ralph Bathurst and Robert Boyle.
[20] The royalists were Christopher Wren, Sir William Brouncker, Sir Paul Neile, John Evelyn, Thomas Henshaw, Henry Slingsby and Timothy Clark. Abraham Hill, William Balle, William Croone, and William Brereton were too young to be classifiable, and Laurence Rooke cannot be positively classified in either political group. George Ent was the only possible parliamentarian.
[21] William Petty was the only parliamentarian. Royalists were Boyle, Wren, Brouncker, Neile and Sir Robert Moray. Balle, Hill, Croone and Bruce were too young and Rooke was unclassifiable.
[22] There were nineteen royalists (including nine from earlier groups), fourteen younger men and only six parliamentarians, of whom two had been members of the earlier groups.

an analysis of the histories of these men should demonstrate such a link.

Some 162 eventual Fellows of the Royal Society were over the age of sixteen in 1642—old enough to have taken part in, or have been aware of, the issues in the war. Of these, seventeen were foreigners not in England during the war years, twenty-two cannot be placed firmly on the politico-religious scale, either for lack of information or because they were deliberately neutralist, thirty-eight fought for or supported parliament at least initially and eighty-five were royalists in 1642. The study deals with the last two categories and attempts to compare the political, religious, educational, social, personal, occupational and scientific background and interests of their members.

Needless to say not *all* English scientists joined the Society in 1660[23]—but those who did not, appear to have formed no identifiable group.[24] It seems unlikely that anyone was actually excluded from membership for not being scientifically respectable or for social, political or religious reasons.[25] It has been suggested that one active puritan Commonwealth supporter—Samuel Hartlib[26]—was excluded on politico-religious grounds, but men with similar connections and interests[27] were among the original Fellows.

The decision to use Fellows of the Royal Society as a focus for studying the relation between interest in science and prior religious and political attitudes raises several problems which must be dealt with before proceeding to the analysis. It might be argued, for example, that more royalists than parliamentarians would be likely to join the 'Royal' Society because ex-parliamentarians might not have felt free to join such an 'establishment' institution after the Restoration.

[23] Well-known scientists who were not Fellows but who nevertheless corresponded with the Society included men like William Sherard, Edward Llwyd, Christopher and Charles Towneley.
[24] Quentin Skinner, 'Thomas Hobbes and the nature of the early Royal Society', *Hist. Journal*, xii (1969), pp. 217–39.
[25] *Ibid.* Skinner demolishes the argument that Hobbes was excluded for being atheistic, non-scientific or Cartesian or for having the wrong connections. He shows that Hobbes and other scientists who were not Fellows cannot be classified in any of these ways and suggests that there were no doctrinaire reasons for exclusion.
[26] Charles Webster, *Samuel Hartlib and the Advancement of Learning* (Cambridge, 1970), pp. 69–70.
[27] Such as Hartlib's friends, Theodore Haak and William Petty.

But three factors militate against such an objection. First, nearly everyone conformed at the Restoration[28]—very few, other than strongly puritan ministers ejected from their livings, were penalized. Even so, there were three ejected Puritans and one compromised parliamentarian among the early Fellows.[29] Erstwhile Republicans apparently had no difficulty in joining the Society even in the first few years after the Restoration.[30] This was quite appropriate, given the explicit intention of the Society to shun controversial political or religious issues.

Second, the Society was not at first associated with the court or the king. Although there were some courtiers among those who met in 1660[31] and those who were asked to join,[32] they were, with perhaps one exception,[33] interested in science. Those who joined the Society before it was granted its final charter and well before the king became a member[34] were predominantly royalist.[35] There seem to be no special reasons why courtiers should have joined the Society in the early years.

Third, if the royalist Fellows had been merely court hangers-on they would probably have been less scientific than the rest. But the proportion of non-scientific royalists was similar to that of non-scientific parliamentarians both in the first years[36] and over

[28] At least 65 per cent of the parliamentarians adapted themselves to the restored monarchy once it was established and more may have done so. On some there is no specific information about this critical period.

[29] William Harrington, Charles Hotham, Robert Wood and Thomas Blount. The first three were ejected ministers, the last was imprisoned for parliamentary loyalty in 1660.

[30] John Aubrey and Edmund Wylde had been members of 'Rota'. Edward Montagu (later the Earl of Sandwich) and Peter Pett had been loyal Protectorate officials to the last and all were original Fellows. Altogether 23 (60 per cent) of the parliamentarians and 16 (20 per cent) of the royalists had held office and 8 had been MPs in the Commonwealth or Protectorate.

[31] Alexander Bruce, Sir Robert Moray and Sir Paul Neile were associated with the Restoration court but they were reputable scientists.

[32] Lord Hatton, Sir Kenelm Digby, John Denham and Sir Alexander Frazier were rewarded by Charles II in 1660.

[33] Sir John Denham the poet was nevertheless trusted by Charles with surveying the royal works.

[34] Those who joined before June 1663 are called original or founder Fellows. Charles II and many of his court joined early in 1665.

[35] Forty-three royalists and 22 parliamentarians.

[36] Royalists 45 per cent, and parliamentarians 37 per cent.

the whole time span.[37] The early Fellows—whether friendly to the court or not—were solidly scientific and they presumably joined mainly because of their interest in science. Perhaps five of the non-scientists were friends of the court.[38]

It therefore seems unlikely that many royalists of 1642 who joined the Royal Society between 1660 and 1663 did so for political reasons. On the other hand there can be no doubt that the number of non-scientists rose after 1663, and rose more steeply among the royalists.[39] These non-scientists included a high proportion of courtiers or people rewarded by pensions, titles and jobs.[40] The courtly hangers-on joined the Society at an average annual rate of 3·2 until 1663 and at the rate of 5 a year from 1664 to 1668.[41] Many of these non-scientific courtiers were important Anglican clerics who joined with the king in 1664, or soon after.[42]

Despite all this, one might want to argue that the royalists of 1642 were more likely to remain identified with the Stuart cause and to emerge as supporters of a society founded in the year of the Restoration—associating themselves, if not logically, then psychologically, with the new regime. Even if the king did not

[37] Royalists 10/43 (23 per cent royalists), and parliamentarians 4/22 (18 per cent parliamentarians).

[38] Three royalists—Sir Nicholas Stewart, Sir Thomas Nott and Sir John Denham; two parliamentarians—Lord Lindsay, Edmund Waller.

[39] A further 30 non-scientific royalists and 10 non-scientific parliamentarians joined after 1663, i.e. 70 per cent of the total non-scientific group in each case.

[40] Of the non-scientists 24 royalists and 6 parliamentarians were rewarded i.e. 80 per cent of the non-scientific royalists and 60 per cent of the non-scientific parliamentarians.

[41]

				Date of election				
1660	1661	1662	1663	1664	1665	1666	1667	1668
				(Calendar years)				
2	6	2	3	6	9	2	5	3

Non-scientific courtiers

3·2   5   Average per annum

[42] They included Bishops Dolben, Burnet, Pearson, Parker, Sheldon and Stearne, who joined between 1664 and 1666, and other Anglican clerics Benjamin Woodroffe, James Arderne and Anthony Horneck who joined in 1668. This group stands in contrast to the clerics among the founder-Fellows who were all scientists or enthusiasts: Wallis, Wilkins, Holder, Pell, Barrow, Bathurst and Beale were scientists, Sprat a lively apologist.

patronize the Society from the start, the fact that it was set up in London, in the shadow of Westminster, just a few months after the Stuarts' triumphant return, may have disposed loyal old supporters of the crown to join whilst Commonwealth or Protectorate supporters might have avoided *any* public association for a time.

It is therefore useful to look briefly at the Interregnum history of our royalists and parliamentarians. The royalists were much more loyal to their side than were the parliamentarians,[43] though proportionally more of the parliamentarians actually fought in the war.[44] The majority of parliamentarians had been won over to support the Restoration by 1660.[45] A third of all the royalists and parliamentarians held office of one kind or another during the Interregnum,[46] associating themselves positively with the revolutionary regime. A few withdrew to study after having earlier identified with one or the other side.[47] Some committed royalists kept out of the way by living abroad[48] and others joined the exiled court.[49] Very few parliamentarians were penalized by ejection from ecclesiastical or other office in 1660.[50] Many from both camps were rewarded by the king or allowed to resume their places and entitlements.[51]

These group biographies suggest that the scientists of the 1660s were no ivory-tower scholars who kept out of affairs during the critical and dangerous war years or the uncertain period that followed. They took part in events both by fighting on either side and by holding office for parliament or supporting the king. Nor does it seem as if it were in any way embarrassing or inappropriate for men who had been parliamentary soldiers, Commonwealth officials or friends of the Protectorate to join the Society in 1660. Personal friends of Cromwell like Jonathan

---

[43] Two royalists—Anthony Ashley Cooper and Sir Anthony Morgan—changed sides in the fighting but six parliamentarians came over to the king.
[44] Royalists and parliamentarians fought as follows: royalists 24 (30 per cent) and parliamentarians 17 (45 per cent).
[45] Parliamentarians 25 (65 per cent).
[46] Royalists 16 (20 per cent), and parliamentarians 23 (60 per cent). Eight were Interregnum MPs.
[47] Royalists 15 (18 per cent), and parliamentarians 6 (16 per cent).
[48] Royalists 8 (19 per cent).
[49] Twelve (14 per cent) royalists joined the court in France.
[50] Three ministers and a state official were ejected.
[51] Royalists 65 (76 per cent), and parliamentarians 23 (70 per cent).

Goddard, Sir James Long and John Wilkins, Protectorate officials like Jonas Moore and Thomas Blount, 'Commonwealthmen' like John Aubrey and Edmund Wylde, and physicians with official Protectorate positions like George Bate had no difficulty in joining. Taken together with the assumption that there was no alienated 'radical' group of scientists excluded from joining,[52] one is led to the conclusion that the Royal Society was not disposed to accept members from one camp to the exclusion of the other. Further, the evidence would suggest that the Commonwealth and Protectorate was singularly unsuccessful in wooing scientists to its side since only one third of the group under consideration identified positively with that regime. On the other hand more than two-thirds were recognized and rewarded by the Restoration. One might conclude from this that the scientific enthusiasts reflected the general trend towards royalism that helped to make the Restoration successful. More significantly, one begins to feel uneasy about the congruence seen by Hill and Rabb between science and the revolutionary political attitude of parliament's supporters. Hill argued[53] that the promotion of interest in science by radical supporters of parliament's cause was so successful that, although they were defeated *politically*, science itself became 'established'. The political activities and affiliations of the scientists looked at in this study would appear to present a different picture. They tempt one to conclude, not that royalism (and Anglicanism) necessarily favoured science, but that parliamentary radicalism (and puritanism) did not do so.

The early Royal Society, then, contained many royalists and parliamentarians who appear to have been free from political or religious pressures in deciding whether to join. Before the Society was honoured by the king's membership there was no special court connection and the great majority of Fellows joined apparently for no 'ulterior' motive. If the major criterion for joining the Society—at least before 1664—was that of having an interest in science, rather than a particular social, political or religious bias, then one can use an analysis of the membership to ask if there was a significant relationship between the Fellows' affiliations during the revolution, and their scientific interests.

[52] Eighty-eight royalists and parliamentarians were favoured during or soon after 1660 by titles, rewards, offices or promotion.
[53] *Intellectual Origins*, p. 125.

The analysis which follows deals with *all* Fellows who could be identified as royalists or as parliamentarians. Wherever relevant, this large group will be compared with the behaviour of the smaller group of founder-Fellows. The first and overwhelming factor in the analysis is the difference in size of the two groups— the royalists being more than twice as numerous as the parliamentarians.[54] It has already been argued that there were no special political or social reasons for this disparity, and therefore one must accept the appeal which science had for 'conservative' supporters of the royal cause in 1642. Moreover among the founder-Fellows who joined before June 1663, that is, before the Society received its final charter, the ratio of royalists to parliamentarians was then, as later, two to one.[55]

Now, in what ways did the royalists and parliamentarians differ in their scientific interests and in their social and intellectual backgrounds? First, Fellows can be divided into those who had no known interest or expertise in science; those who specialized in archaeology, history, antiquarian pursuits and genealogy;[56] those whose interests stretched over the wide area of 'applied' science; and those who were concerned with 'pure' science— mathematicians, theoretical physicists and other theoreticians. Table I[57] indicates that the royalists were proportionally stronger in every category except that of applied science. The non-scientific members were mostly nobles, soldiers and politicians,[58] supplemented by poets, *littérateurs*,[59] lawyers,[60] merchants,[61]

[54] Royalists 85, and parliamentarians 38.

[55] Forty-three (50 per cent) of the royalists and 22 (57 per cent) of the parliamentarians were original Fellows.

[56] These 'humanistic' interests have been classified as scientific while literary, political or theological interests and writings were excluded because the Royal Society discussed and published matters in the former category but not in the latter.

[57] See pp. 340–1. Fellows with more than one interest have been counted in each relevant category.

[58] Among the royalists 17/38 belonged to this category; 9/14 of the parliamentarians. All but two of the parliamentarians (Titus and Vermuyden) were probably connected with the court.

[59] Royalists 2/38, parliamentarians 1/14.   [60] Royalists 3/38.

[61] Royalists 5/38, parliamentarians 1/14. These included 4 mercers who joined in November 1673 when Gresham College was returned to the Royal Society by the Mercers' Company. Thomas Birch, *History of the Royal Society*, 4 vols (London, 1756–60), iii, p. 110.

clerics and scholars.[62] It has already been shown[63] that there were more non-scientific royalists due to the number of clerics who joined the Society with the king.[64]

The Royal Society concerned itself quite unselfconsciously with archaeology, antiquarianism, history and genealogy. These studies were part of the topographical approach to local studies used in the 'natural histories' of various counties sponsored by the Society.[65] Founder-Fellows like Francis Willoughby and John Aubrey, and later Fellows like Robert Plot, John Ray and Ralph Thoresby collected information about plant and animal life, soil structure, natural curiosities, mining, archaeological remains and family genealogies on their travels, very much assuming the legitimacy, relevance and unity of purpose of these areas of observation. The men classed here as historians, antiquarians and classical scholars were not exclusively historians for they combined these interests with other scientific pursuits. The preponderance of royalist humanists cannot be explained in social or educational terms, because, as this paper goes on to show,[66] there were no significant social or educational differences between the two groups. Perhaps one might argue that a concern for genealogy, history and antiquity demonstrates a conservative backward-looking attitude more typical of the constitutionalists who followed the king in 1642 than of the revolutionaries who justified their rebellion by an appeal to the rights of the people. But historical precedents (albeit different ones) were as compelling for the Independents and some Levellers as they were for Charles I's supporters. In any case, the numerical difference between the two groups in this area is probably too small to justify any close analysis.[67]

An apparent difference exists between the two groups' interest

---

[62] Royalists 11/38, parliamentarians 1/14.

[63] See p. 325.

[64] There is here an apparent difference in the composition of the two sides —a difference which throws into relief the royalist, courtier component which followed the king into the Society. However, the difference between the percentages of royalist and parliamentarian Fellows who had no scientific interests is not statistically significant by the Chi-square test.

[65] John Aubrey's *Natural History of Wiltshire* and Robert Plot's *Natural History of Oxfordshire* for example.

[66] See below, pp. 330–2.

[67] Royalists 12/85 (14 per cent); parliamentarians 4/38 (10 per cent).

in theoretical and applied science.[68] The distinction made here between theory and application is a very general one. Among theoretical scientists included here are all mathematicians, theoretical physicists, astronomers, theoretical chemists and other theoreticians. Among the applied scientists are the medical practitioners, inventors, applied physicists, experimentalists, observers and collectors of natural histories, gardeners and so on. More theoretical thinkers, other than mathematicians, were to be found among the royalists. They included men such as Robert Boyle and Sir Kenelm Digby.[69] Physicians, instrument makers, naval experts, agricultural and horticultural reformers and general applied scientists were more often to be found among the parliamentarians.[70] There was only one 'pure' scientist among them— John Wallis. Sir William Petty, John Wilkins and Robert Wood had theoretical interests but they were mainly practical men.

These figures suggest that the parliamentarians concentrated more on utilitarian science while the royalists were comparatively more theoretical. This might indeed be seen as support for Hill's thesis; that is, parliamentarians appear here to be displaying a middle-class orientation to technology and to the useful applications of science. However, as we shall see, the parliamentarians were socially no more plebeian than were the royalists. About one quarter of these practical scientists were known Puritans,[71] and one-fifth came from a plebeian background or were merchants.[72]

[68] Theoretical science—royalists 11/85 (13 per cent), parliamentarians 4/38 (10 per cent). Applied science—royalists 37/85 (43 per cent), parliamentarians 21/38 (55 per cent). The difference is not significant by the Chi-square.

[69] Royalists 13/85 (15 per cent), parliamentarians 6/38 (16 per cent).

[70] Physicians: royalists 12/85 (14 per cent), parliamentarians 8/38 (21 per cent). Agricultural and horticultural reformers: royalists 11/85 (13 per cent), parliamentarians 10/38 (25 per cent). Instrument makers and inventors: royalists 8/85 (9 per cent), parliamentarians 8/38 (21 per cent). Timber, navy, sea: royalists 3/85 (4 per cent), parliamentarians 6/38 (15 per cent). Again, however, the difference between the percentage of royalists and that of parliamentarians who were interested in applied science is not significant statistically by the Chi-square test.

[71] Goddard, Graunt, Hotham, Montagu, Oldenburg, Petty, Wallis, Wilkins, Winthrop, Wood, Pell, Haak, among the parliamentarians and Moray among the royalists, i.e 13/59.

[72] Among the royalists, 5 had plebeian fathers and 2 others were merchants; among the parliamentarians, 3 had plebeian fathers and three were merchants, i.e 13/59.

Only one in every ten could be described as a middle-class Puritan and one in twenty a utilitarian scientist of puritan middle-class background.[73]

The Society's members were nobles, gentlemen or sons of nobles and men of merchant or artisan origins.[74] The social composition of royalists and parliamentarians was almost identical.[75] There were slightly more parliamentarian merchants, traders and craftsmen or sons of craftsmen, of whom three out of the seven were Londoners. These talented individuals worked their way up through the ranks of the church, the medical profession, by means of patronage or just plain hard work, perseverance and talent.[76] The plebeian royalists were of an exactly similar composition.[77]

The presence of so many nobles reflects, of course, how

[73] Wilkins, Petty, Oldenburg, Graunt, Goddard, Bate.

[74] As usual in classifying men by class in the seventeenth century, there is the difficulty of how to separate the gentry and nobility. 'Nobles' here means arbitrarily those who inherited or had noble titles bestowed upon them while their sons who did not inherit the title are put among the gentry. Sons of clerics, lawyers and 'esquires' are labelled gentry. As nearly all who joined the Royal Society could be regarded as gentlemen, it seemed necessary to differentiate between their social *origins* rather than between their contemporary social positions.

[75] The percentages of 'unknowns' in the two groups were similar enough to enable comparison with percentages of those whose social origins were known. Thirteen per cent royalists and 8 per cent parliamentarians were 'unknown' socially. The nobles formed 20 per cent of the 'known' sectors among both royalists and parliamentarians; 63 per cent of the royalists and 20 per cent of the parliamentarians were gentry; 17 per cent of the royalists and 20 per cent of the parliamentarians were merchants or artisans by trade or background.

[76] Peter Pett, Sir Thomas Player and John Graunt were Londoners, the former a shipbuilder and the latter two merchants. Wilkins was the son of a silversmith and became a bishop, Goddard became a doctor, Henry Oldenburg, of German merchant origins, was tutor to Lady Ranelagh's sons and William Petty worked his way up through a variety of occupations to a position of great prestige and social honour.

[77] They included 4 London merchants—Daniel Colwall, Sir John Lawrence, Sir Thomas Nott and Sir Richard Ford; 3 clerics—Humphrey Henchman and Gilbert Sheldon became bishops and Thomas Smith gained a high preferment—all from humble origins; George Bate, Ralph Bathurst and Thomas Willis worked their way up through university and medical careers; Elias Ashmole and Sir John Birkenhead became a scholar and a court journalist respectively.

respectable science had become by 1660. Most nobles on both sides were men with minimal scientific interests[78] and very few of them had been founder-Fellows.[79] More than half the royalist and parliamentarian nobles joined with or after the king.[80] The social composition of the two sides therefore does nothing to support the view that science was more appealing to 'middling sort' parliamentarians. Only one-sixth of the whole group were of plebeian origin. The two sides' social similarity suggests that class had little to do with predisposing one group rather than the other towards science. By far the majority of scientists and enthusiasts on both sides were gentry.

The Fellows' occupations and training were typical of the seventeenth-century gentry and bourgeoisie. Men have been classified here as 'clergy', 'lawyers' or 'physicians' according to their university training, but many of them would have been landed proprietors and lived the life of country gentlemen[81] or office-holders as well.[82]

Royalist clerics were more numerous because of the influx of Anglican bishops and others who trailed the king into the Society.[83] There was a solid core of 'scientific' clerics on both sides who joined earlier but only three ministers among the Fellows were puritan enough to be ejected from their livings after 1660.[84] This would suggest that science held little appeal for strong Puritans. Proportionally more parliamentarians were to be found among the medical men and, conversely, more royalists among the lawyers. This may reflect a tendency of the politically radical to take up a practical or empirical profession, while the

[78] Nobles who had scientific interests are found in the following proportions: royalist 5/15, and parliamentarian 2/7.
[79] Original Fellows were in the following proportions: royalist nobles 4/15, parliamentarians 1/7.
[80] Nobles who joined during or after 1665: royalists 9/15, parliamentarians 4/7.
[81] It is impossible to classify men under an occupational label such as 'country gentleman' because many FRS's lived part of their lives in London, many practised their professions or changed life-styles frequently. The instability of the Interregnum and interruption of normal life-patterns also helped to make such a classification meaningless.
[82] Where a man had more than one form of academic training or held office as well as a degree he is classified in both categories.
[83] See above, p. 325.
[84] Charles Hotham, William Harrington and Robert Wood.

more conservative royalists were perhaps attracted to the back-ward-looking, precedent-governed common law. Although the differences are not great[85] they do perhaps underline the earlier finding[86] that royalists were more interested in history.

The most striking difference in the occupations of royalists and parliamentarians is the large number of parliamentarian academics.[87] Perhaps this is due to the number of teachers at the early meetings of scientists at Gresham College and Oxford. Since most academic appointments during the Interregnum went to parliamentary supporters, it is not surprising that those academics who took part in the meetings of the 1640s and 1650s and who subsequently joined the Society were parliamentarians.[88] Of the whole group, only one royalist—Seth Ward—was able to get an academic appointment during the Interregnum. Many academics, too, kept quiet about politics and applied themselves to their studies throughout these troubled times.[89] In 1660, when the tide turned, the men who rallied to the Society tended to be men of affairs in public life like Lord Hatton, Henry Slingsby, Sir William Brouncker, Sir Paul Neile and Sir Robert Moray, who were talented and interested scientists but not academics. Men too young to have been in the war, like William Croone and Christopher Wren, became the next generation of university teachers.

The number of parliamentarian university teachers is accentu-ated by comparison with the generally lower level of academic education among their colleagues.[90] The royalists were better

---

[85] Medicine—royalists 14 (16 per cent), parliamentarians 8 (20 per cent); law—royalists 21 (25 per cent), parliamentarians 7 (18 per cent).

[86] See p. 329. Humanities—royalists 14 per cent, parliamentarians 10 per cent.

[87] Academics—royalists 11 (16 per cent), parliamentarians 12 (32 per cent).

[88] The parliamentarian academics who were among the 1645 London group or the later Oxford one included Goddard and Whistler from Gresham, Coxe from the College of Physicians and Wilkins, Petty and Wallis who had Oxford jobs after 1648. With the exception of John Pell who taught at Breda, all eleven parliamentarian academics were appointed by the parliamentary visitors or lectured at the College of Physicians during the Interregnum.

[89] Henry Power, Laurence Rooke and Henry Clark—some were deliberately neutralist, others equivocal.

[90] Seventy-four per cent of royalists whose educational training is known went to English universities compared with 65 per cent of

represented both at the universities and at the Inns of Court.[91] Since the class composition of the two groups was so similar, it cannot account satisfactorily for the educational difference between them. For it would be wrong to see the unacademic strain among the parliamentarians as a sign of practicality or of radical utilitarianism. The majority of the non-academic parliamentarians were nobles or very high-ranking gentry.[92] Only three of those who attended neither university nor Inn of Court might be called practical men of affairs with no time for abstract philosophizing or logic-chopping.[93] Among the non-academic royalists, on the other hand, there were proportionally *more* such practical men.[94] The proportionally larger group of non-academic parliamentarians consisted of a greater percentage of noblemen than of businessmen.

On the whole, then, the royalists were academically well-qualified men of affairs, out in the world, holding court and government positions, interested in science as well as in history; many of them were trained at the law or in the church, and some were London businessmen. The parliamentarians were proportionally less formally educated. Their graduates were either practical medical men or less worldly academics.

The parliamentarians were more likely to be *members* of parliament, at least between 1642 and 1660.[95] Fewer members of the Long Parliament supported the king in 1642 and royalists were less likely to have sat in a Protectorate parliament.[96] On the other

---

parliamentarians. Forty-three per cent of the royalist 'knowns' were at Inns of Court and 37 per cent of the parliamentarians. Thirty-eight per cent of the royalists and 40 per cent of parliamentarians were in the unknown category. Some of these went to overseas universities; many, especially the aristocracy, were privately educated. Most of the Londoners were not university men. The category includes all these groups.

[91] This follows from the greater number of royalist clerics and lawyers, while the smaller number of medical men does not make up the difference.

[92] Men like the Earl of Manchester and Sir John Clotworthy. These made up 9/15 of the group.

[93] John Graunt, Peter Pett, Sir John Player.

[94] There were 12 such royalists including Sir Thomas Nott, Sir James Langham and Sir Richard Ford.

[95] Eight of 13 parliamentarian MPs had sat in the Long Parliament.

[96] Sir James Long had sat in the 1654 parliament, 5/18 royalists had sat in the Long Parliament.

hand, parliamentarians of the 1640s were not barred from sitting in post-Restoration parliaments.

The rewarding of old loyalists by promotion or sinecure after the king's return accounts for their higher proportion among Restoration office-holders[97] but many parliamentarians also profited from the Restoration. Charles rewarded less ardent supporters for reasons of expediency—hence the high honours heaped, for instance, on Edward Montagu.[98]

Neither side had many merchants or craftsmen, and together they account for less than one-tenth of the whole sample.[99] These figures do not suggest either that merchants and craft-trained men predominated on the revolutionary side or that they were more likely than others to be interested in science. Moreover, there is no reason to suspect that merchants were not socially acceptable in the Society—perhaps they were simply too busy to indulge in the delights of science.

The religious affiliations of Fellows naturally followed their politics closely—three out of four royalists were Anglicans and the same proportion of parliamentarians were Puritans.[100] There were a few reputed sceptics on both sides[101] and a sprinkling of Catholics among the royalists. This demonstrates the nice correlation between religion and politics in the Civil War but it adds nothing to the thesis that puritanism encouraged an interest in science. In any case, only one quarter of those whose religion was

---

[97] Royalists 54 (64 per cent), parliamentarians 18 (49 per cent). This category includes reinstated clergy who were given back their livings or promoted to bishoprics, and nobles and others who received high government appointments.

[98] Montagu had been an active supporter and high officeholder under Cromwell and only accepted the Restoration at the last moment. He was at once rewarded by a knighthood and made Master of Trinity House, and honours continued to accrue to him.

[99] Royalists 8 (95 per cent), and parliamentarians 3 (8 per cent). All but Peter Pett, the shipbuilder, were rich London guild members. Total, 11/123.

[100] Those whose religion could not be determined were 38 per cent of royalists and 24 per cent of parliamentarians. Of those whose religion was known, the Anglicans made up 77 per cent of the royalists and the Puritans 77 per cent of the parliamentarians. The foreign members included 6/17 Protestants but these could not be classified with either English religious party.

[101] There were 2 reputed sceptics on both sides, and 6 royalist Catholics.

known were Puritans.[102] The behaviour of the clerics strengthens this negative conclusion. There were eighteen royalist Anglican clerics and six parliamentarian puritan ones. Only three of the Anglicans collaborated with the Commonwealth and Protectorate while four of the Puritans conformed after 1660. The Anglicans were therefore relatively 'strong' while the Puritans were more latitudinarian.[103] The behaviour of these clerics bears out the impression that puritanism was not strongly correlated with science.

The typical background of a science enthusiast in the 1660s was not middle-class, mercantile, puritan, politically radical, unacademic or utilitarian. Rather, our typical Fellow was a royalist, Anglican, university-educated gentleman. Royalists always made up two-thirds of the membership of the Royal Society, even in the early years. Anglicans were not only more resolute but accounted for three out of four Fellows. Nearly three-quarters of the Fellows were university-educated and one-third attended Inns of Court. Two out of three Fellows were members of the gentry. There were very few merchants or people trained in practical non-academic skills.

So much for the 'typical' science enthusiasts. When one comes to look at the parliamentarians and royalists as separate groups to see whether they differed significantly from one another in other than political ways, one finds surprising similarities. Socially, the groups were practically identical. There was no significant mercantile, puritan, parliamentarian group—among the merchants royalist Anglicans with no academic training predominated.

The parliamentarians did however differ from the royalists in a number of ways. They were more interested in applied science and less interested in humanistic studies; there were proportionally more parliamentarian medical practitioners and academics and fewer parliamentarian lawyers and clerics. This may argue for a difference in intellectual outlook—that parliamentarians were more practical, utilitarian and progressive than their opposite numbers who took up studies in more conservative, historical,

---

[102] There were 4 puritan royalists and 20 puritan parliamentarians.
[103] One of the characteristics of latitudinarians noted by Dr Shapiro was that they tended to conform to the temporal authorities on religious forms. The behaviour of the clerics looked at here apparently makes latitudinarianism stronger among the Puritans than among the Anglicans.

less practical areas. Although this may give support to the Merton–
Hill thesis, it must be remembered that the difference between the
two groups on all these scores was small and not statistically
significant, and that *numerically* there were more *royalist* physicians,
applied scientists, and academics. Only six out of 123 could be classified as puritan, non-academic, utilitarian 'middling sort of men'.

Other differences between the two groups follow naturally
from the political dichotomy. The greater number of parliamentarians who held academic appointments has been shown to
be due, at least in part, to the policies of the Commonwealth.
More parliamentarians too, sat in parliament, especially during
the Interregnum. More royalists were post-Restoration office-
holders because they were rewarded for loyalty though a surprisingly large proportion of erstwhile enemies were rewarded
with appropriate carrots. And there were more royalist clerics
because important Anglican clergy tended to follow the king into
the Society. The religious differences between the two groups
are an obvious concomitant of the political division.

This survey does not enable one to conclude that there is a
positive link between an interest in science on the one hand, and
radical political and religious activity or non-academic, utilitarian mercantile backgrounds on the other. Rather it suggests
that science did *not*, in fact, appeal to convinced hard-line Puritans, as the number of Fellows who conformed with the Restoration showed. Even 'ordinary' Puritans were apparently less
captivated by the scientific activities of the Society as the numbers
later expelled in its lean years indicate—Anglican royalists
stayed the course better.[104]

Barbara Shapiro argued for a significant relationship between
latitudinarianism and science and cited a number of writers who
tried to reconcile scientific activity with moderate rational theology. This view suggests that there were serious tensions in
people's minds between their faith and their science. The composition of the Royal Society does not suggest any great religious
difficulties. Anglican bishops, puritan divines, latitudinarians,
Catholics, simple pious men and sceptics collaborated and found,
apparently, no great difficulty in reconciling their religion and
their science. The latitudinarians—Sprat, Wilkins, Glanvill and

[104] Royalists 6 (7 per cent) and parliamentarians 6 (16 per cent) were
expelled.

others—who wrote at length about the compatibility of science and religion might be matched by the eight non-latitudinarian Anglican bishops[105] who joined the Society between 1665 and 1667 and who found it unnecessary to justify their membership. Their presence alone suggests that science had already become respectable and needed no religious justification.

Science certainly did appeal to 'conservative', well-educated Anglican gentry. Douglas Kemsley, indeed, sees a peculiar affinity between Anglicanism and science.[106] He has argued, on the basis of Sprat's comments, that the methodology of Anglican biblical interpretation resembled the scientific method propounded by the Royal Society.[107] Careful, unprejudiced empiricism and criticism—but not annihilation—of tradition were common to Anglicanism and the Royal Society. 'The Church of England therefore may justly be styl'd the Mother of this sort of Knowledge.'[108]

Kemsley argues that Anglican methods of biblical interpretation differed significantly from those of other Protestants and of Catholics 'in a closely similar way'[109] to that in which the scientific method of the Royal Society differed from Cartesian or scholastic methods. Despite his eagerness to establish a congruence between Anglicanism and new science, Sprat was unable to distinguish Anglican from protestant or humanist methods of biblical criticism, since all worked by 'passing by the corrupt Copies and referring themselves to the perfect Originals for their instruc-

[105] Sheldon, Stearne, Henchman, Dolben, Parker, Laney, Morley and Pearson.

[106] Douglas S. Kemsley, 'Religious influences in the rise of modern science: a review and criticism, particularly of the "Protestant-Puritan Ethic" theory', *Annals of Science*, vol. xxiv (1968), pp. 199–226.

[107] Thomas Sprat, *History of the Royal Society*, eds Jackson I. Cope and H. W. Jones (St Louis, 1956), p. 132. Sprat, it is true, made it his purpose to show a basic compatibility between the Church of England and the new science. He pointed to the patronage which the established church had conferred upon the Society, and, rather deviously, called on the Anglican doctrine of obedience to the ruler to support the study of nature as a means of honouring and obeying the 'Divine Majesty'. Since Anglicanism is based on rational exegesis of the scriptures the Church must support all rational activity.

[108] Sprat, *History of the Royal Society*, p. 372.

[109] Kemsley, 'Religious influences . . .', p. 226.

tion'.[110] Sprat's attempt to make a comparison between the Anglican reverence for authority, and Baconian scientists, who were not noted for their reverence to Aristotle, shows up the weakness of the analogy. It is difficult to see Sprat as anything other than an Anglican apologist for the Royal Society. Until it can be shown that Anglican biblical scholarship was more empirical and critical, and less dogmatic, than that of other protestant or Catholic reformers, the case for a special affinity between Anglicanism and the new science cannot be established. There is certainly no reason to suggest that Catholic or Calvinist biblical study was in any way comparable with Cartesian or scholastic rationalism.[111]

The predominance of Anglicans in post-Restoration society may be due, at least in part, to religious indifference—a natural consequence of the religious turmoil of the preceding years. The Anglicanism of the Fellows of the Royal Society may speak as much for their lack of interest in religious issues as for their affection for the Church of England. The Society's avoidance of religious controversies and disputes, and the range of affiliations represented among its members—Catholicism to scepticism—strengthen this view. Perhaps the apologetics of the latitudinarians did less to justify science through religion than to give meaning to religion in an increasingly secular world. The fact that few Anglicans conformed to Presbyterianism in the 1640s while erstwhile Puritans were prepared to accept the Restoration settlement twenty years later may be an aspect of growing religious indifference. The negative results of this study indicate, therefore, that science correlated less with puritanism or latitudinarianism than with the waning role of religion.

[110] Sprat, *History of the Royal Society*, p. 371.
[111] Kemsley, 'Religious influences . . .', p. 226.

TABLE I   *FRS Royalists and Parliamentarians—Scientific Interests and Background Factors*

Total Membership aged 16+ in 1642: 162
Royalists (R)   85 = 52% = 70% of R + P
Parliamentarians (P)   38 = 23% = 30% of R + P
Unclassifiable   22 = 13%
Foreigners   17 = 10%

	Rs Total 85			Ps Total 38		
	No.	%	% of Known	No.	%	% of Known
Science						
No science	38	45		14	37	
Applied science	37	43		21	55	
Theoretical science	11	13		4	10	
Humanities	12	14		4	10	
Social Rank						
Noble	15	18	20	7	18	20
Gentry	46	55	63	21	55	60
Merchant or Artisan background	12	14	17	7	18	20
Unknown	11	13		3	8	
Occupation						
Clergy	18	21		6	16	
Law	21	25		7	18	
Medicine	14	16		8	20	
Academic	11	13		12	32	
MP	18	21		13	34	
1660 + office-holder	54	64		18	49	
trade-craft	8	9		3	8	
Education						
University	39	48	74	15	40	65
Inn of Court	23	27	43	9	24	37
Private or unknown	32	38		15	40	
Religion						
Anglican	41	49	77	6	16	20
Puritan	4	5	7	20	60	77
Catholic	6	7	11	—		
Sceptic	2	2	4	2	6	8
Unknown	31	38		8	24	

Total Membership aged 16+ in 1642 : 162
Royalists (R)   85 = 52% = 70% of R + P
Parliamentarians (P)   38 = 23% = 30% of R + P
Unclassifiable   22 = 13%
Foreigners   17 = 10%

	Rs Total 85			Ps Total 38		
	No.	%	% of Known	No.	%	% of Known
Civil War History						
Fought for King	24	30		6	16	
Fought for Parliament	1	1		17	45	
Commonwealth Official	16	20		23	60	
Studied	15	18		6	16	
Commonwealth MP	—			8	21	
Change to royalism 1660	—			25	65	
Penalized 1660+	—			4	10	
Rewarded 1660+	65	76		23	70	
Abroad—travel in war	8	9		2	5	
Exile with Court	24	30		—		
When joined R.S.						
Original Fellow	43	50		22	58	
Late 1633	12	14		3	8	
1664–9	25	29		10	26	
1670–9	8	9		1	3	
1680–9	1	1		2	6	
Expelled	6	7		6	16	

APPENDIX
FELLOWS OF THE ROYAL SOCIETY

1 *Royalists*

Name	Birth date	Date of election to the Society
Ashmole, Elias	1617	OF*
Atkyns, Sir Robert	1621	1664
Aubrey, John	1626	OF
Austen, John	(? d. 1667)	OF
Baines, Sir Thomas	1622	OF
Baker, Thomas	1625	1684
Bate, George	1608	OF
Bathurst, Ralph	1620	1663
Berkeley, Sir Maurice	(d. 1690)	1667
Birkenhead, Sir John	1616	1663
Blount, Sir Henry	1602	OF
Boyle, Richard	(d. 1665)	OF
Boyle, Robert	1627	OF
Brouncker, Sir William	1620	OF
Bruce, Robert		
Earl of Ailesbury	1626	1663
Campbell, Archibald,		
Earl of Argyle	(d. 1685)	1663
Cartaret, Sir Philip	1623	1665
Cavendish, William,		
Earl of Devonshire	1617	OF
Chamberlayne, Edmund	1616	1668
Charleton, Walter	1619	OF
Churchill, Sir Winston	1620	1664
Clarke, Timothy	(d. 1672)	OF
Clutterbuck, Sir Thomas	1624	1676
Cock, George	(d. 1679)	1665
Colwall, Daniel	(d. 1690)	OF
Compton, James,		
Earl of Northants.	1622	OF
Conway, Lord Edward	1623	1667
Cooper, Anthony Ashley,		
Lord Shaftesbury	1621	1663
Cotton, Edward	1616	OF
Denham, Sir John	1615	OF
Digby, Sir Kenelm	1603	OF
Dolben, John	1625	1665
Evelyn, John	1620	OF
Ford, Sir Richard	(fl. 1670s)	1672

* OF .. Original Fellow, elected before June 1663.

Name	Birth date	Date of election to the Society
Frazier, Sir Alexander	1610	1663
Gascoigne, Sir Bernard	1614	1667
Glisson, Francis	1597	OF
Gomeldon, William	?	1663
Harvey, John	1604	1664
Henchman, Humphrey	1592	1665
Henshaw, Thomas	1618	OF
Holder, William	1616	OF
Howard, William, Viscount Stafford	1609	1665
Hyde, Edward, Earl of Clarendon	1609	1665
Isham, Sir Justinian	1610	1663
King, Sir Andrew	(d. 1679)	OF
Laney, Benjamin	1591	1664
Langham, Sir James	1620	1678
Lawrence, Sir John	1607	1673
Leighton, Sir Elisha	(d. 1685)	1663
Long, Sir James	1617	OF
Moore, Sir Jonas	1617	1674
Moray, Sir Robert	1608	OF
More, Henry	1614	1664
Morgan, Sir Anthony	1621	OF
Morley, George	1597	1666
Neile, Sir Paul	1613	OF
Nott, Sir Thomas	1606	OF
Oudart, Nicholas	1610	1667
Packer, Philip	1620	OF
Pearson, John	1613	1667
Persall, Sir William	(fl. 1620–70)	OF
Pettus, Sir John	1613	OF
Pierrepont, Henry, Marquess of Dorchester	1606	OF
Potter, Francis	1594	1663
Rupert, Prince Palatine	1619	1665
Sackville, Richard, Earl of Dorset	1622	1665
Scarburgh, Charles	1616	OF
Sheldon, Gilbert	1598	1665
Slingsby, Henry	1621	OF
Smith, Thomas	1615	1677
Stanley, Thomas	1625	OF
Stearne, Richard	1596	1666
Stewart, Sir Nicholas	1616	OF
Strangways, Giles	1615	1673

Name	Birth date	Date of election to the Society
Stuart, Charles (King Charles II)	1630	1665
Stuart, James, Duke of York	1633	1665
Talbot, Sir Gilbert	1607	OF
Tuke, Sir Samuel	(d. 1674)	OF
Villiers, George, Duke of Buckingham	1628	OF
Ward, Seth	1617	OF
Waterhouse, Edmund	1619	1663
Wentworth, William, Earl of Strafford	1626	1668
Willis, Thomas	1621	OF
Wyndham, Thomas or William?	?	1677

2 *Parliamentarians*

Name	Birth date	Date of election to the Society
Annesley, Arthur, Earl of Anglesey	1614	1668
Beale, John	1605	OF
Blount, Thomas	1606	1665
Bysshe, Edmund	1615	OF
Clerke, Henry	(d. 1687)	1667
Clotworthy, Sir John, Viscount Massereene	(d. 1665)	OF
Coxe, Thomas	1615	OF
Dorislaus, Isaac	(d. 1688)	1681
? Ent, Sir George	1604	OF
Goddard, Jonathan	1617	OF
Graunt, John	1620	OF
Haak, Theodore	1605	OF
Harley, Sir Edward	1624	1663
Harrington, William	1623	1666
Hay, John, Earl of Tweedale	1626	1664
Hotham, Charles	1615	1668
Lindsay, John, Earl of Crawford	1596	OF
Merrett, Christopher	1614	OF
Monck, George, Duke of Albemarle	1608	1665
Montagu, Edward, Earl of Manchester	1602	1665

344

Name	Birth date	Date of election to the Society
Montagu, Edward, Earl of Sandwich	1625	OF
Mordaunt, Henry, Earl of Peterborough	1624	1663
Oldenburg, Henry	1618	OF
Palmer, Dudley	1617	OF
Pell, John	1611	OF
Pett, Peter	1610	OF
Petty, Sir William	1623	OF
Player, Sir Thomas	(d. 1686)	1673
Robartes, Lord John	1606	1666
Titus, Samuel	1623	1669
Vermuyden, Cornelius	1626	OF
Waller, Edmund	1606	OF
Wallis, John	1616	OF
Whistler, Daniel	1619	OF
Wilkins, John	1614	OF
Winthrop, John	1606	OF
Wood, Robert	1622	1681
Wylde, Edmund	1616	OF

3 *Politically unclassifiable*

Name	Birth date	Date of election to the Society
Alleyn, John	1622	OF
Castell, Edmund	1606	1674
Collins, John	1625	1667
Cutler, Sir John	1608	1664
Dickenson, Edmund	1624	1678
Ford, Sir Henry	1619	1663
Hammond, William	1614	OF
Harley, Thomas	?	1667
Lane, Sir George	1621	1662
Le Hunt, William	?	1668
Murray, David, Viscount Stormont	(d. 1668)	1666
Murray, Mungo	1595	OF
Needham, Jasper	1623	OF
Nelthorpe, Edmund	1604	1666
Povey, Thomas	1615	OF
Power, Henry	1623	OF
Quatremain, William	1618	OF
Rooke, Lawrence	1622	OF

Name	Birth date	Date of election to the Society
Smith, Edward	?	1664
Street, Thomas	1621	OF
Terne, Christopher	1620	OF
Winn, Rowland	1609	1673

4 *Foreigners*

Name	Birth date	Date of election to the Society
Auzout, Adrien	1622	1666
Beunighen, Constantine	1622	1682
Bullialdus, Ismael	1605	1667
Hevelius, John	1611	1664
Justel, Henry	1620	1681
Le Febure, Nicolas	(d. 1669)	OF
de Lionne, H. L.	1611	1665
Mercator, Nicholas	1620	1666
Petit, Pierre	1594	1667
Schroter, William	(d. 1684)	OF
Slusius, R.	1622	1674
Sorbiere, Samuel	1615	1663
Stiernhelm, Gustaph	1598	1669
Vabres de Fresurs, Victor Beaufort	?	1663
Villermont, E. C.	1617	1685
Viviani, Vicenzo	1622	1696
Vossius, Isaac	1618	1664

XXV

THE DECLINE AND FALL OF
RESTORATION SCIENCE*

Margaret 'Espinasse

At the very end of his life, in 1700, Dryden wrote a rather melancholy greeting to the eighteenth century:

> 'Tis well an Old Age is out.
> And time to begin a New.

But Dryden was belated—the new age had already begun. In the
history of science, the years immediately after 1688 mark the
beginning of a new era, 'the transitional or latent phase leading
up to the Industrial Revolution'. In literature, the same moment
is a turning-point towards the Augustan Age: after 1688 'the very
key-note of English literature . . . is changed'.[1] Some of these
changes in literary attitudes between 1660 and the post-Revolutionary years have a curious similarity to the changes within
science. In both fields the Restoration age pursued some ideas
and some interests which were then abandoned for a century or
more. Sometimes the shift of attitude is consonant enough with
general social and economic developments; but sometimes the
changes are unexpected and not easy to understand.

Some scientific contrasts will illustrate both kinds of change,
the expected and the odd. In the first age of modern science, after
1660, the distinguishing attitude is the enthusiasm and hopeful-
ness expressed by so many writers and marking their feeling of

---

* From no. 14 (November 1958).
[1] J. D. Bernal, *Science in History* (London, 1954), p. 356; E. Legouis and
L. Cazamian, *A History of English Literature*, revised edn (London, 1951),
p. 603.

belonging to a revolutionary movement which had a new aim of
social usefulness and a new weapon in the experimental method.
A cardinal characteristic of this new science was its unitary
nature, and among the causes of this unity the new factor was the
exaltation of the experimental method. 'It is certain', says the
historian of the Royal Society, Sprat, 'that *Experimenting* is . . .
that, by which all our Actions are to be fashion'd'[2]—'all our
Actions', however various their objects. Boyle and Hooke, for
example, devised experiments with the air-pump which led not
only to the enunciation of Boyle's Law but also to Hooke's
theories of combustion and respiration. A good experimenter
would expect to range widely, and there was little specialization.
Newton's application to chemistry was 'long and constant';[3]
Hooke contributed to half a dozen branches of science.

But in spite of this feeling of unity, the distinction was of course
apparent between the mathematical and mainly deductive sciences,
which dealt with inanimate matter and where the chief problems
of the age were set; and on the other hand those sciences in which
mathematics was not yet important and which depended mainly
on observation and induction—chemistry at this stage, and the
sciences of life. Nevertheless the distinction between the two
kinds was not pressed; they were not regarded as basically separat-
ate. The mechanical scientist Hooke made a mechanical approach
to biological problems in his *Micrographia*. He and his colleagues
supposed that the living creation would ultimately be found
amenable to the same laws as governed inanimate matter.

The great synthesis of Newton perhaps checked that hope. At
all events, from the time of the *Principia*, approximately, division
becomes noticeable. The scientific interest which then came to
dominate was the attempt to describe and explain the behaviour
of the inanimate universe, and the living creation was in a sense
given up as insusceptible of mechanical handling.[4] A hiatus be-

[2] T. Sprat, *The History of the Royal-Society of London* (London, 1667), p. 90.
[3] William Stukeley, *Memoirs of Sir Isaac Newton's Life* (1752), ed.
A. Hastings White (London, 1936), p. 60.
[4] Cp. John Ray, *Wisdom of God in the Creation* (1691), quoted from 1701
edn, by B. Willey, *The Eighteenth Century Background* (London, 1940),
p. 36: 'These mechanick Philosophers being no way able to give an
account thereof from the necessary Motion of Matter, *unguided by Mind for
Ends*, prudently therefore break off their System there, when they should
come to Animals.'

came apparent between the lofty Newtonian sciences and the humble non-mathematical sciences, and these began to lose social prestige. In 1697 the Royal Society's chosen defender William Wotton commented bitterly on 'the *public ridiculing* of all those who spend their Time and Fortunes in seeking after what some call useless Natural Rarities; who dissect all Animals, little as well as great; who think no part of God's Workmanship below their strictest Examination, and nicest Search'.[5]

And the earlier unity of science was being split along another plane: not only were the sciences which were mathematical and deductive, remote and abstract, becoming separated from the others which were more inductive, concrete and particular; but 'pure' science was also becoming distinct from applied science 'for the use of life'. By the end of the century the social attitude to useful science had undergone a striking change.

The general practical aim of Restoration science is well known. But there is one particular aspect which is not always made enough of. This is the importance of the scheme for a history of trades, which was insisted upon by Bacon, and which passed from Bacon to Petty and Hartlib, to Boyle and the pre-Royal Society groups.[6] In the 1650s Evelyn was collecting material for such a history. His disgust with the slumming which it entailed made him abandon the project as a whole[7] (though most of his published works are to be understood as contributions to it), and the undertaking

---

[5] William Wotton, *Reflections Upon Ancient and Modern Learning*, 2nd edn (London, 1697), p. 419.

[6] For early Royal Society estimates of the importance of the trades to science, see Boyle's essay of 1671, 'That the Goods of Mankind may be much increased by the Naturalist's Insight into Trades', *Works*, ed. T. Birch, 6 vols (London, 1772), iii, p. 449; Sprat, *Hist. Roy. Soc.* (1667), Second and Third Parts, particularly pp. 257–311 and 378–403, and pp. 117–18 where he says that it is for '*Mechanicks*, and *Artificers*' that 'the True *Natural Philosophy* should be principally intended'; Walter E. Houghton Jr, 'The history of trades . . .', *Journal of the History of Ideas*, ii (1941), pp. 33–60; G. N. Clark, *Science and Social Welfare in the Age of Newton* (Oxford, 1937), chap. 1; T. Birch, *History of the Royal Society* (London, 1756–7), entries for 1661 and 1662 *passim*.

[7] The reasons Evelyn gave were his 'great imperfections for the attempt, and many subjections, which I cannot support, of conversing with mechanical capricious persons, and several other discouragements'— Evelyn, letter to Boyle 9 August 1659, in Boyle, *Works* (1772), vi, pp. 287–8.

passed to the newly formed Royal Society. In 1661 and 1662 Petty discussed it with the King and some noblemen, and both he and Evelyn read papers to the Society on plans and methods, and on the histories of particular trades. Other members also contributed, including Boyle, who throughout his life was a steady supporter of the idea. The Society hoped that the tradesmen themselves would put on record some of their special knowledge, but although there were a few gestures—for instance, according to Evelyn, William Faithorne the engraver was going to translate du Bosse's work on the rolling press—the craftsmen on the whole seem to have been reserved.[8] But the Society persevered, and the special committees which it set up in 1664 included a committee for the histories of trades. By 1667 it had made some progress, as can be seen from Sprat, who in the Second Part of his *History of the Royal Society* sets out the general proposals, lists between forty and fifty histories already gathered, and prints three specimens. He devotes ten sections of his *Third Part* to expounding the ways in which experimental philosophy can benefit manual or mechanical arts.

Yet in spite of this brave beginning, the history of trades made little further headway, and the connection between Royal Society science and industrial practice steadily dwindled during the rest of the century. Two well-known illustrations of this decay are the histories of the chronometer and the steam engine. Restoration scientists working on the problems of navigation produced almost a new industry with the immense development of clockwork. By the 1670s Huygens and Hooke had made great advances in their efforts to design a time-keeper for ascertaining the longitude at sea. But in the later period, although a few Fellows like Derham were good amateur horologists, the scientists made no notable contribution to the craft, and the chronometer was finally realized, in the eighteenth century, by a carpenter, Harrison. Similarly, the foundations for a practical steam-engine were laid by the Restoration scientists. Boyle's air-pump was improved not

---

[8] Evelyn, *Sculptura* (London, 1662), note at end. The passive resistance or 'discouragements' offered by the tradesmen to co-operation with the scientists is implied by Evelyn's following remark that he wishes more workmen would imitate Faithorne; and it is stated explicitly in the anonymous translation of Pancirollus, *The History of Many Memorable Things Lost* (London, 1715), appendix, p. 431.

only by Hooke but also by his colleague Denis Papin, who designed a pump of his own in the 1680s. Yet the steam-engine was finally developed in a commercial form by Savery and Newcomen, a military engineer and a blacksmith. They developed it outside the Royal Society, outside organized science, and this although the Society had actually had opportunities to join in their efforts: in the later 1680s Newcomen had a correspondence with Hooke about atmospheric engines in general and in particular about Papin's pump; and in 1699 Savery demonstrated his engine to the Society.[9] The contribution made by science in the later period appears to have been limited to what Newcomen may have learned from this correspondence with the doyen of mechanical scientists, Hooke; no younger Fellow was stimulated to action. And when Papin returned from Marburg in 1707 with the model of a new engine, Boyle and Hooke being dead, the Society gave him no encouragement.[10]

There was, however, one new link, in the end of the seventeenth century, between science and very important practical applications. Statistics—of population, of land, of trade, of life expectation—political arithmetic, as it was called, had been one interest of a group of Fellows in the early Royal Society; but it was the post-Revolutionary period which brought the great development of practical applications, with the rise of insurance (which was a government as well as a private concern) and the establishment of 'the first special statistical department successfully created by any western European state',[11] the office of the inspector-general of imports and exports, whose findings were reported to the new committee of Trades and Plantations set up in 1696. So, although science had lost its connections with industrial practice, it was contributing something to the new financial and commercial developments of the age. But the science which was contributing was not exactly contemporary science. The scientific bases of statistics were the publications of the pioneers Petty and Graunt, and Halley's life-tables, together with the work of Gregory King.

[9] See article on Newcomen's bicentenary in the *Daily Telegraph*, 7 August 1929; for Savery's demonstration see *Phil. Trans.*, vol. xxi, no. 253 (1699), p. 228.
[10] See H. W. Dickinson, 'Tercentenary of Denis Papin', *Nature*, 27 September 1947, pp. 422–3.
[11] G. N. Clark, *op. cit.*, p. 138.

Petty and Graunt belonged to the Restoration Royal Society, in which by 1675 the precocious Halley (born in 1656) was already active and an intimate of older Fellows like Petty, Hooke and Wren; King was older than Halley, and he was not connected with the Royal Society—with organized science.

Statistics was a respectable pursuit, remote from lower-class contamination. Industrial connections, which were not genteel, seem to have been abandoned altogether by the Royal Society before the end of the century. Swift, notoriously, charged the scientists of his day with perfect uselessness. Contrasted with the abstracted Laputans and the chimerical projectors of Lagado are the Brobdingnagians, whose mathematical science was 'wholly applied to what may be useful in life, to the improvement of agriculture and all mechanical arts; so that among us it would be little esteemed'. Satire is special evidence; but Defoe is not being satirical in the introduction to his *Essay on Projects*, and he conveys concisely the change which had come over science when he assumes as a matter of course that its function was restricted to making 'new discoveries in the works of Nature' and when these are explicitly contrasted with 'new discoveries in trade, in arts and mysteries'.

Actually, in the end of the century even 'discoveries in the works of Nature' were few. It was an uninspired period in English science, and there was a marked deterioration in the organ of science, the Royal Society itself. About the time of the Revolution it was already in a dangerous way, with only one or two new Fellows elected annually and with the *Philosophical Transactions* suspended from 1687 to 1691. By the 1690s most of the early Fellows were dead, and although there were a few gifted younger men besides the great Halley, yet the Society as a whole was in a languid state; under an administration which was often mediocre and seldom much interested in science, it seemed to be waiting for the time when Newton should occupy the Presidential chair and dominate its proceedings for a quarter of a century.

Yet even the prestige of Newton could not obviate the contempt which had come to be the stock attitude of many influential writers by the early eighteenth century. We may pass over Swift as being peculiarly hostile, but we might expect Addison to speak with respect of a body of scientists presided over by Newton. For Newton had not only constructed a new world, united one kind of science with religion and provided the basis for a philosophy; he had also been knighted for scientific achievement, had sat in parliament as a Whig, and was Master of the Mint; so that he and his Society might surely be identified with the most respectable elements in the community. Yet Addison, a Whig Secretary of State, a moralist, and a devout Christian Gentleman, asserted (as the terrible Stubbe had declared in 1670)[12] that the Society was first established not, as the ingenuous might think, to promote natural knowledge, but to keep out of politics 'many of the greatest Geniuss [sic] of that Age' (Newton's own age), who otherwise 'might have set their Country in a Flame'. This is an odd enough distortion of what the founders themselves said about the relation of their group to politics, but Addison continues even more oddly: 'The Air-Pump, the Barometer, the Quadrant, . . . were thrown out to those busy Spirits, as Tubs and Barrels are to a Whale, that he may let the Ship sail on without disturbance, while he diverts himself with those innocent Amusements'.[13] (Unfortunately for common sense, the tubs and barrels were in this case spouted up by the whale, to the benefit of the ship.) Newton's scientific work belongs to the seventeenth century, and all of it up to and including the *Principia* was published under the auspices of the Royal Society. Yet it is with this careless figure of speech that an influential writer of the next age dismisses the work of that century and that Society in physics and on instruments—work which was not only of direct use to a maritime people but which also culminated in the great Newtonian synthesis.

The scientists were often ridiculed in the Restoration period, by Butler, Shadwell, Stubbe and many more. But science was not then open to be sneered at in quite the Addisonian tone. By its enemies, the foundation of the Royal Society was not regarded as a means of providing 'innocent amusements' for dangerous thinkers, but on the contrary was felt to have unfortunately united them in a group which was formidable as often as contemptible; *fratres asini* but also *fratres lupi*;[14] atheistic, subversive and dissenting. The universities and their churchmen were

[12] H. Stubbe, *Campanella Revived* (London, 1670).
[13] Addison, *Spectator* 262, 31 December 1711.
[14] H. Stubbe, quoted I. D'Israeli, 'The Royal Society' in *Miscellanies of Literature* (Paris, 1840), ii, p. 112.

alarmed. A large part of the third book of Sprat's *History of the Royal Society* is devoted to a detailed refutation of charges that the new science 'will injure Education', 'Makes men presumptuous and obstinate', is 'dangerous to the Christian religion'—seventeen pages are given to rebutting this important and most damaging accusation. It was of course mechanistic theories of the universe, associated with the dreadful names of Hobbes and Descartes, which sounded the alarum. About biology and microscopy, taken by themselves, there was nothing especially terrifying, but they employed the sceptical approach and were part of the dangerous new whole. In the next age, however, these branches attracted all the ridicule (usually; not always, not in Swift) as they became dissociated from the Newtonian sciences, which were now being regarded with a new eye, no longer of fear, as a rule, but of religious respect. Thinking about the universe was positively an act of worship, and the literature of the late seventeenth and early eighteenth century resounds with physico-theological paeans on the Creator's *mighty* works.

Outside the religious function of Newtonian physics, the social function of science had by this time undergone a sea change. Those are pearls that were its eyes. Instead of being directly useful to the social body, some parts of it were now a precious cultural commodity, a gentlemanly ornament. An early statement of this new conception came from Locke, philosopher, friend of Newton, and FRS. In this learned age, he said in 1693, only a year after the death of Boyle, a gentleman should 'look into' some of the modern systems of natural philosophy, in order 'to fit himself for Conversation'.[15] Addison was another exponent of the contribution which science can make to the assembling of a gentleman. Among the methods which he proposes 'to fill up our time' he lists, along with conversation and the arts, certain kinds of science, with a certain limitation: planting, gardening, farming, flower-growing, 'when they are only as Accomplishments to the Man of Fortune, are great Reliefs to a Country Life'.[16] Biological and microscopical studies, however, were barely conducive to religious feeling, and had a deplorable tendency to become too interesting:[17]

[15] Locke, *Some Thoughts concerning Education* (London, 1693), p. 230.
[16] Addison, *Spectator* 93, 16 June 1711.
[17] Addison, *Tatler* 216, 26 August 1710.

I would not discourage any Searches that are made into the most minute and trivial Parts of the Creation. However, since the World abounds in the noblest Fields of Speculation, it is, methinks, the Mark of a little Genius to be wholly conversant among Insects, Reptiles, Animalcules, and those trifling Rarities that furnish out the Apartment of a Virtuoso . . . Observations of this Kind are apt to . . . make us serious upon Trifles, by which Means they expose Philosophy [science] to the Ridicule of the Witty, and contempt of the Ignorant. In short, Studies of this Nature should be the Diversions, Relaxations, and Amusements; not the Care, Business, and Concern of Life.

Many similar passages embody this common view that some acquaintance with science—even with non-Newtonian science—was not undesirable so long as there was no danger of its being taken seriously or being in any serious degree useful.

This genteel restriction sometimes appears to be almost the only unifying principle left in the later period of fissure, when the Newtonian sciences had come to be thought of as fundamentally different from the others, when pure science was separated from applied science, and when social prestige accrued chiefly to the pure and the Newtonian kinds.

There are equally striking differences in some of the literary and linguistic views of the two periods. The mid-seventeenth-century rebellion against the ancients included a revolt against the domination of the Latin language. This recoil from Latin had a complex of causes and is found among people of various groupings and interests. The dissenters inherited a hatred of it as the language of Popery and obscurantism, and as a cultural mark of their ruling-class antagonists. The early scientists, many of them dissenters, added to these motives the wish to make their findings as public as possible, available to people not trained in the classical discipline. Moreover they soon noted the unsuitability of Latin as a vehicle for modern ideas.[18] Some literary men were influenced by all this recoil from Latin—for instance, Dryden. Of course it is *a priori* improbable that the best writer of his age should despise the language which was his medium; throughout

[18] See, for instance, John Wilkins, *An Essay towards a Real Character, and a Philosophical Language* (London, 1668), Pt. 4, chap. vi.

his life Dryden showed his consciousness of the virtues of English. But the most enthusiastic of his eulogies belong to his earlier life. At that time he was eager to praise the rich vocabulary and the musical sound, the ease and the flexibility of our 'noble, full and significant' language. He was happy, too, in the reflection that the credit for much of this prosperous condition of English belonged to his own times, when 'our language is improved', and there has been 'an alteration for the better'. Those who deny this, he said in 1672, 'have not a just value for the age in which they live'.[19]

In his later years Dryden no longer held these progressive and optimistic opinions. The state of English alarmed him: 'far from making any progress in the improvement of our tongue', the present age was more likely to produce 'a declination of the language'.[20] And—after all—Latin was superior. Dryden's tender reference to English in 1664—'speaking so noble a language as we do'—had turned into conventional depreciation by 1697—'I, who . . . write in a language so much inferior to the Latin'.[21] Dryden had joined the reaction. His shift of outlook was doubtless due in part to the common conservatism of old age (he was by this time between sixty and seventy); but it was very probably also an effect of the real changes in the standing and characteristics of the vernacular at the end of the century. The English of the 1690s was not the English of the 1660s; and perhaps Dryden did not think it better. The adulation of Latin was not good for English, and although he finally joined in it, Dryden may have felt uneasy about its consequences.

From the middle of the seventeenth century the concentration of interest on the vernacular tongue combined with the spreading scientific temper to produce both new kinds of linguistic studies and new methods in older kinds. One new kind which had an extraordinary flowering was the study of language as a symbolic system of communication. Stimulated by the great developments going on in mathematical symbolism, scientists addressed themselves to the business of inventing an artificial classificatory language, to embody the concepts of experimental science and to replace Latin as its international medium. The centre of the Royal

[19] Dryden, *Essays*, ed. W. P. Ker (Oxford, 1900), i, pp. 104, 164.
[20] *Ibid.*, ii, pp. 12, 110.
[21] *Ibid.*, i, p. 5 and ii, p. 231.

Society group working on this was Wilkins, and Wilkins's *Real Character* (1668) is one of the least forgotten of the numerous but ephemeral languages devised at this time. It was admired and publicized by his colleagues, and the Royal Society group continued to think about 'universal language' for a decade or two; but towards the end of the century interest died away.

Most of the linguistic thinking of the period, however, involved the vernacular in some form. Its earliest form, Old English, had for political and religious reasons long been an object of interest to Reformed clergymen intent on finding a protestant prototype in the Anglo-Saxon church, and to Common Lawyers looking behind the Norman Conquest for a native and primitive 'freedom'.[22] But from the middle of the seventeenth century, although these two traditions remained, yet the study of Anglo-Saxon acquired a new quality and new standards of scholarship. It became an academic pursuit. Cambridge University had the Spelman lectureship, and the Parker MSS. (at Corpus); Oxford, coming to the fore later, had the Junius MSS. (after 1678) and the Queen's College lectureship founded in 1679 by Sir Joseph Williamson—it may be noted that Williamson was at that time President of the Royal Society. This new serious study culminated in the work of Hickes and Wanley and the other scholars whom Hickes drew in as contributors to his *Thesaurus*. This monument of scholarship began to be printed in 1698 and to be published in 1703. It is therefore in a sense true to say that in the field of Anglo-Saxon studies (including the comparative philology of the Germanic languages) the Restoration period was less brilliant than its successor. But we may observe that the excellence of the latter was due in a very great degree to one man. Hickes was the focus of activity and the great source of influence; and Hickes was born in the same year as Newton, growing to maturity, therefore, in the Restoration era. In him the vitality and brilliant intellectual qualities of that age were carried on to illuminate the post-Revolutionary period—and the Augustan age as well; for Wanley, thirty years younger than Hickes, was his pupil and protégé. Wanley's death in 1726 ended this extra-

---

[22] See Christopher Hill, 'The Norman Yoke' in *Democracy and the Labour Movement: Essays in Honour of Dona Torr*, ed. J. Saville (London, 1954), pp. 11–66; David C. Douglas, *English Scholars 1660–1730* (London, 1939), chaps 3–5.

ordinary epoch in Anglo-Saxon studies, and for almost a century nothing further was done.

In the Augustan Age, men who were 'for polite learning' tended almost necessarily to despise antiquarian studies, but the work of these Saxonists could not fail to command respect, and they were on the whole excluded from that Augustan hostility to 'enthusiasm' which is as often turned against the 'pedant' (Hearne, Bentley) as against the 'virtuoso'.

As in Anglo-Saxon studies, so in work on contemporary English a new quality is apparent in the later seventeenth century. The observational and practical method of science appeared in works on grammar which founded their rules on good usage (for example, Wallis's celebrated grammar of the English tongue) and in phonetic studies. Wallis, Wilkins, Holder, Lodwick were all admirable phoneticians. They were all, also, members of the Royal Society. It may be significant that the last good phonetician, Cooper, who published his work in the 1680s, was not a Fellow. After Cooper, the standard of linguistic analysis fell; the phoneticians of the eighteenth century were much inferior.[23]

A large part of this work in phonetics and grammar was aimed at recording the facts of English usage. Naturally enough, there was wider interest in the living vernacular than in an artificial language, and many people hoped that English could be made into a vehicle fit to carry modern scientific ideas. The special committees set up by the Royal Society in 1664 included one for this very purpose of improving the English tongue 'and particularly for philosophical purposes'.[24] Among its members were Dryden, Waller, Evelyn and Sprat, and Cowley was connected with it. Evelyn suggested as part of their programme the collection of technical and dialectal words—'terms of art', including the art of agriculture—which might profitably be incorporated into educated English.[25] One result of this notion was a pioneer work— Ray's *Collection of English Words not generally used*, published in 1674 (1673) with a revised edition in 1691. Skeat has called this the most important book on English dialect before the nineteenth

[23] See E. J. Dobson, *English Pronunciation 1500–1700* (Oxford, 1957), i, pp. 310–11.
[24] Birch, *History of the Royal Society*, i, pp. 499–500.
[25] Evelyn, letter to Wyche 20 June 1665, in J. E. Spingarn (ed.), *Critical Essays of the Seventeenth Century*, 3 vols (Oxford, 1908-9), ii, pp. 310–13.

century.[26] It was a novelty which was not followed up; the study of dialect was not resumed till a hundred years later. But Ray would probably not have thought of himself as pioneering in an entirely new country; he would rather have regarded his whole book as contributing simultaneously to the suggested collection of 'terms of art' and to the Royal Society's histories of trades, for he includes, as one of his supplements, an account of nearly a dozen industrial processes, described in highly technical terms.

The notion that English should be enriched with these terms was not confined to the scientific group. Technical terms are obviously necessary to scientists, but so distinguished a literary group as the Pléiade had long before both used them in poetry and recommended them to poets as providing them with beautiful and lively comparisons. In Dryden's youth, Davenant was supporting the idea both in theory and practice, in his heroic poem *Gondibert* and its preface; and in his Royal Society period Dryden did the same. *His* heroic poem, *Annus Mirabilis* (1667) includes technical descriptions (of naval activities) of which he made a characteristic defence in the Preface: 'And certainly, as those who, in a logical dispute, keep in general terms, would hide a fallacy; so those, who do it in any poetical description, would veil their ignorance. . . . For my own part, if I had little knowledge of the sea, yet I have thought it no shame to learn'.[27]

So in the 1660s Dryden was able to accept and feel 'terms of art' as belonging to the 'natural way of English' sought after by the age. But the times changed. In the 1670s Hobbes, who had opposed Davenant on this point in 1650 and who continued to hold the same view, was joined by Rymer, and both of them castigated poets who (in Rymer's words) 'labour to appear skilful with that wretched affectation, they dote on the very terms and *jargon*'.[28] By 1697 Dryden himself was saying the exact opposite of what he said thirty years before. In his *Dedication of the Æneis* he not only apologizes for using some 'cant words' to make a

<hr>

[26] W. W. Skeat, *English Dialect Society, Series B Reprinted Glossaries XV–XVII* (London, 1874), Introduction, p. [v].
[27] Dryden, *Essays*, ed. Ker, i, p. 13.
[28] Rymer, *Preface to Rapin* (1674) in Spingarn, *Critical Essays of the Seventeenth Century*, ii, p. 170. Cp. Hobbes, *Answer to Davenant* (1650), *ibid.*, ii, p. 64, and *Preface to Homer's Odysses* (1675), *ibid.*, ii, p. 68.

critical point but then proceeds to say about the translation itself: 'I will not give the reasons why I writ not always in the proper terms of navigation, land-service, or in the cant of any profession. I will only say, that Virgil has avoided those proprieties [i.e. terms peculiar to a trade], because he writ not to mariners, soldiers, astronomers, gardeners, peasants, etc., but to all in general, and in particular to men and ladies of the first quality, who have been better bred than to be too nicely knowing in the terms'.[29]

Dryden is here joining Hobbes and Rymer in expressing one of the tenets of neoclassicism. But in practice he ignored this piece of restrictive theory, and his *Æneid* suffered the ironic fate of being attacked by Addison for its use of unintelligible '*Technical Words*' (such as 'tack' and 'starboard'!).[30]

In his earlier years Dryden had 'thought it no shame to learn' the terms, and at that time writers would not commonly have agreed to any form of the proposition that it is illbred to be too nicely knowing. The wits of Charles's court notoriously regarded themselves as above the ordinary requirements of good breeding on occasion, and these did not inhibit the play of their lively intelligence. Not many of them were so versatile as to practise science as well as literature, but some did, for instance Buckingham and Rochester (like Sedley, Rochester had been for a short time at Wadham College when it was under the scientific influence of Wilkins). Other literary men gave at least some thought to science; the interests displayed in Dryden's *Essay of Dramatic Poesy* (1668), an imaginary dialogue between Buckhurst, Howard, Sedley and Dryden himself, must have had some basis of actuality. The *Essay* is a discussion on literary topics, but it avowedly borrows from scientific procedure: Dryden described it as 'sceptical, according to that way of reasoning which . . . the best of the Ancients followed, and which is imitated by the modest inquisitions of the Royal Society'.[31] Science makes several appearances in the *Essay*. Crites (Howard) is upholding ancient against modern drama, yet he proceeds by way of a panegyric on the modern experimental philosophy: 'Is it not evident . . . that almost a new Nature has been revealed to us?'[32] His opponent

[29] Dryden, *Essays*, ed. Ker, ii, pp. 208, 236.
[30] Addison, *Spectator* 297, 9 February 1712.
[31] Dryden, *Essays*, ed. Ker, i, p. 124.   [32] *Ibid.*, i, pp. 36-7.

Eugenius (Buckhurst) takes up this point for poetry: 'if natural causes be more known now than in the time of Aristotle, because more studied, it follows that poesy and other arts may, with the same pains, arrive still nearer to perfection'.[33] Neander (Dryden) is full of the same enthusiastic hope: 'We see revived Poesy lifting up its head, and already shaking off the rubbish which lay so heavy on it'.[34] In 1672 Dryden again specifically linked poetry with the progress of science: 'I profess to have no other ambition . . . than that poetry may not go backward, when all other arts and sciences are advancing'.[35]

The influence of scientific method is further seen in the new technique—exhibited by Rymer and Dryden, for instance—of collecting from the literature under discussion passages for analysis and generalization. If it may be questioned whether this innovation of the Restoration period was due to the influence of inductive science, Dryden at least justifies the attribution by using the words 'inductive' and 'induction' about his own critical procedure.[36]

Altogether, the scientific temper was especially congenial to Dryden, who speaks repeatedly of his own 'scepticism', his 'natural diffidence' (which is the same thing), his dislike of an 'Ipse dixit' in poetry as well as science.[37] Moreover, he insists frequently that a good poet must be something of a scientist— 'It requires Philosophy, as well as Poetry, to sound the depth of all the passions; . . . and in this science the best poets have excelled'.[38]

Besides Dryden, the older poets Waller, Denham and Cowley were members of the Royal Society group; and when the interests of some of the Court wits are added to the account, it is clear that a number of literary men took cognizance of what the new science had to offer to literature, whether it was the sceptical approach or

[33] Ibid., i, p. 44.   [34] Ibid., i, p. 89.
[35] Ibid., i, p. 163.   [36] E.g., ibid., i, p. 195; ii, p. 250.
[37] Ibid., i, pp. 260, 138; see also i, p. 163.
[38] Ibid., i, p. 183. See also, i, p. 214. The most detailed expression of this poetic ideal is to be found in 'Preface to Notes and Observations on the Empress of Morocco: Postscript' (1674), Works of John Dryden, ed. W. Scott, 18 vols (London, 1808), xv, p. 411. The Postscript was written by Dryden himself or else involved Shadwell and/or Crowne, his collaborators. In the latter case Dryden's notion of a poet was shared by other literary men.

the inductive method, improvements in prose or a fund of new terms and imagery for poetry. And this influence of science was dynamic. Science was not a body of knowledge but a method, applied progressively to a universe which was not felt to be a closed system. The new sceptical and inductive procedure held out hopes of great advances in literature and language too. But as the influence of this procedure waned, the achievement of science ceased to be looked up to as an example to be emulated in literary and linguistic affairs. The change in the relations with science may be observed in Temple's *Essay upon the Ancient and Modern Learning*. Sir William Temple was an eminent supporter of the ancients in the battle of ancients and moderns which raged intermittently in the later seventeenth century. He gives, of course, an occasional point to the moderns: the English are supreme in dramatic poetry; the French have lately refined their language 'to a degree that cannot be well exceeded'. But his Essay is the Credo of a traditionalist; all the things that men possess or pursue 'are Bawbles, Besides Old Wood to Burn, Old Wine to Drink, Old Friends to Converse with, and Old Books to Read'. Temple was also a notable epitome of the well-bred ideal of polite attainments, and in this ideal science had come to play a remarkably trivial role. For what it is worth, however, Temple deals with it, as a partisan of the ancients. A part of the rhetorical method he uses is the ingeniously simple device of making modern discoveries seem inferior by relegating them to subordinate clauses: 'There is nothing new in Astronomy to vye with the Ancients, unless it be the Copernican System', etc. But Temple seems to feel that this really will not do, for he goes hurriedly on with alternative pleas: these apparently new discoveries are actually derived from the ancients; even if new, they are probably not true, as being contrary to sense; and in any case, they are 'of little use to the World'.[39] The *Essay* appeared in 1690, twelve years after the last of Hooke's *Cutlerian Lectures* in mechanics, and three years after Newton's *Principia*; but the modern physicist whom Temple selects for comparison with Archimedes is Wilkins, who belonged to the pre-Newtonian and pre-Hookean age of physics (he died in 1672). To say that Temple was not much of a scientist is to be generous. He was, however, an influential pattern of the lettered gentleman, and his *Essay*, which had great

[39] Spingarn, *Critical Essays of the Seventeenth Century*, iii, pp. 66, 72, 55-6, 62.

vogue, is a measure of the heavy change in the relation of science and letters since the *Essay of Dramatic Poesy* in 1668.

This is not to deny that in the new century the effect of science on literature was very marked.[40] But the view of the universe derived from science was very different from the seventeenth-century view—and much more in consonance with neo-classic ideals. The earlier excitement over the exploration of God's creation—Nature—was replaced by a soberer contemplation of the Great Machine and the Divine Mechanic. This Machine and the laws which governed it were commonly apprehended as stable and perfected, a body of generalized and authoritative conclusions about a closed system. The connections between such apprehensions and the generalized authoritarian views of neo-classicism are obvious.

So in the fields of literature and language, many interesting starts made in the Restoration period came to nothing. The revolt against Latin became a reaction back towards it, and attention ceased to be focused either on the bases of language in general or on the vernacular tongue. If English was discussed, it was in negative and conservative terms: in place of suggestions for enriching it (for instance, with technical words), we have Swift's insistence on the need for purgation.[41] As the influence of the sceptical and inductive procedures died down, the relation of science and letters was altered, not for the better.

The changes in literary and linguistic attitudes may be explained fairly well by the effect of Newton, combined with some general social developments. An aristocracy has not always great reason to be cautious in its intellectual attitudes. It is above the rules—it makes them. Since the fashionable literature of the Restoration period was prevailingly aristocratic, patronized and led by the Court wits, we are not surprised to find it uninhibited, vigorous and inquisitive. In the age after the Revolution some noble patronage continued, but literary men now found their chief supports not at Court but rather in the government (which employed and subsidized them) and in the new kind of publishers

---

[40] See John Butt, *The Augustan Age* (London, 1950) and bibliography, especially to chap. 6.

[41] Swift, *A Proposal for Correcting, Improving and Ascertaining the English Tongue* (London, 1712); see also Swift, *Tatler* 230, 28 September 1710, Addison, *Spectator* 135, 4 August 1711.

and book-sellers. By this time the public demand for books had widened—more of the middle classes had become readers—and writers adapted themselves to this wider audience, which now included people who were educated, but not so much; gentlemanly in aspiration but not by birth. In their interest the instructive and refining periodical was started, and new plays became more decent (though the old continued to be acted). This rising middle class would naturally adhere to what they apprehended as the culture of the upper classes, with zeal and with anxiety. Such of these changes in opinion as are signs of conservatism and caution are not unexpected—in particular, the dominance of classical and authoritarian and gentlemanly (dilettante) attitudes. This dominance entailed both the re-establishment of Latin as the superior language and the diversion, therefore, of vigorous thinking away from the problems of English; hence the disuse of the inquiring approach to the vernacular as a thing whose structure may be investigated like that of any other creation. It entailed also the distaste for low and particular terms of art in poetry and the preference for a neutralized and abstract vocabulary.

But where science is concerned, some of the later attitudes both among scientists and among literary men are rather odd. It is to be expected, certainly, that the veneration for mathematical physics should carry with it some contempt for biological studies and for applied industrial science. And early eighteenth-century men of letters do on the whole despise natural history and revere Newtonian physics—on the whole; but not consistently; there are strange anomalies and vacillations. Anxiety may battle with veneration so that Pope presents the consequences of Newton as being both beneficent ('All was *Light*') and blasphemous ('we doubt of God . . . Thrust some Mechanic Cause into his place').[42] And again, though Addison usually joins in the popular pastime of ridiculing naturalists 'employed in the gathering of Weeds and the Chase of Butterflies', yet he is also found quite seriously urging the Royal Society to compile 'a body of Natural History'. 'It would be one of the best Services their Studies could do Mankind', he says.[43] And in the midst of all the contempt for applied

[42] Pope, *Epitaph Intended for Sir Isaac Newton; Dunciad* IV 472–5.
[43] Addison, *Spectator*, 21, 24 March 1710/11; 120, 121, 18 and 19 July 1711.

science, Swift transformed earlier attacks on the uselessness of some Royal Society studies into a climactic indictment of 'pure' science as a wicked absurdity.[44]

Applied science, however, was generally depreciated, among scientists as well as men of letters, and it is this attitude which is so difficult to understand. Several explanations have been proposed for the decay of the scientific interest in industry. One is the mere progress of science itself. Bacon had regarded workshops and factories as laboratories for scientists; but—it is suggested—as real laboratories multiplied, and as experiment became more engrossing than the collection of existing information, the crafts and trades became less useful to scientists. This may be quite true. But it is not obvious why scientists should not have gone on hoping to be useful to the trades, and the older men at least did so: in the 1680s Boyle, Hooke and Wren were still experimenting with inventions which would be useful to industry or commerce.[45] But the younger scientists did not apparently follow their example.

It has also been suggested[46] that the technological work of the Royal Society suffered along with its other scientific work from the wars and catastrophes of 1665–8, and from some of their long-term consequences. But in fact the years between 1669 and 1680 saw the publication of brilliant achievement, both in pure science —Newton's work on light, Hooke's law of spring—and in technology, with such inventions as Hooke's universal joint, the anchor escapement, and the balance spring watch. And although the Fire of London provided years of building work for Wren and Hooke and accelerated Wren's absorption into architectural practice, yet the years when Hooke was working indefatigably as City Surveyor were in science his most prolific. Moreover, the building work of these two friends, while it was of little direct use to science, would hardly have the effect of discouraging their Baconian interest in trades, but on the contrary would reinforce

[44] See p. 352 above.
[45] For examples of inventions by Wren see Hooke, *Diary* (1672–1680), ed. H. W. Robinson and W. Adams (London, 1935), entries for 6 February 1674/5, 21 August 1678; for experiments by Hooke in cloth-printing and -dyeing, and in glass-making and -grinding, see Margaret 'Espinasse, *Robert Hooke* (London, 1956), p. 149 and notes 14–17 to chap. 7; for Boyle's investigations into the production of fresh water from sea-water on a commercial scale see G. N. Clark, *op. cit.*, p. 81 and footnote 4.
[46] See, e.g., G. N. Clark, *op. cit.*, p. 17.

it. As may be supposed, and as can in fact be seen from Hooke's Diaries, both men had constant conversation with tradesmen in large numbers and of very various kinds; they discussed with them and with each other the application of scientific principles to building and design, the qualities and effects of materials, and scores of other practical topics. One would require more evidence that the decay of the connection between science and the trades was due to the distraction of the scientists.

But Wren's departure from science recalls one point: the number of important scientists being absolutely small, the number of those who took the connection of science with industry as a matter of course was smaller still. Any loss would have a marked effect; and while the losses from 1660 to 1680 were not many, by 1692 they were considerable: Petty, Wilkins, Boyle were dead. In fact, of the well-known Baconian scientists in this sense, only Hooke and Ray were alive and active.

Finally, it is often pointed out that in the seventeenth century most of the branches of science were not advanced enough to be regularly useful to industry. Although this is in general true, yet we have seen that the mechanical scientists were enormously useful to the clock- and watch-makers by the 1670s, and it is difficult to see why this particular usefulness ceased.

Altogether, the relationship between science and industry in the last four decades of the seventeenth century seems to have a degree of chronological topsiturviness: a close connection might be expected after the Revolution which introduced a period of commercial and industrial expansion, rather than in the Restoration age when several social factors were against it. Government and high society were then monarchical and aristocratic. It is true that Charles himself had democratic manners and that his attitude to science was eminently practical. But even so, and in spite of the considerable power of the merchants and capitalists, and in spite of government concern with the organization of the nation's commercial affairs, the social attitude of the court was highly exclusive. And the early Presidents of the Royal Society were courtiers, officials or statesmen (Moray, Brouncker, Williamson) and so were most of the first Council. Court connections would have done little to promote industrial conversation, and most Fellows (the physicians might be exceptions) would have had to make some effort in their daily lives in order to cultivate it.

Although some of the best of the Fellows had no difficulty in doing this, yet some of the others shrank uncontrollably from tradesmen. The statistician Graunt was the only person of this class who was elected as an original Fellow—and he was a royal nominee.[47] There seem to have been no more elections of the kind for about twenty years. Joseph Moxon became a Fellow in 1678 and John Houghton in 1680,[48] but the great clock-maker Tompion was never elected, though he was intimate with many Fellows, notably with Hooke. In short, the Society seems to have been open to all classes rather in the same way as the law-courts and the Ritz.

But although it was not pervaded by lower-class Fellows, in its formative years it was much encouraged and assisted by people whom Hooke and Sprat call men of traffic—merchants and manufacturers.[49] This social group included the majority of middle-class dissenters, both native and Huguenot; and the early Royal Society also included a large dissenting element: nearly two-thirds of the Fellows of 1663 had or had had puritan leanings, and such distinguished members as Wilkins, Wallis, Petty, Goddard, More had Cromwellian connections. Yet in spite of this dangerous past, and although chartered by the King and permeated by bishops and other clergy of the establishment, the Society nevertheless stuck to its policy of admitting Fellows who were practising non-conformists,[50] from the Catholic Graunt to the Quakers Lower and Penn, Ray, who had refused to subscribe to the Act of Uniformity, and the Huguenot Papin. It is these long-lasting connections with the dissenting and the mercantile groups which give an odd appearance to the Society's social attitude after the Revolution. *Pace* Ray ('the favour of princes smiles' etc.),[51] the

[47] Sprat, *op. cit.*, p. 67.
[48] Moxon was among other things map-printer and -seller to the King; Houghton was an economic journalist, apothecary, and dealer in tea, coffee and chocolate.
[49] Sprat, *op. cit.*, pp. 129–30; Hooke, *Micrographia* (London, 1665), Preface. Examples, of very different kinds, are Francis Lodwick and the egregious Sir John Cutler.
[50] Sprat, *op. cit.*, p. 63.
[51] 'Philosophy and all sound learning, now that the favour of princes smiles upon the efforts and stimulates the industry of scholars, show promise of wonderful advances.' Ray, Preface to *Synopsis stirpium Britannicarum* (1690) quoted by C. E. Raven, *John Ray, Naturalist: his Life and Works* (Cambridge, 1942), p. 252.

court had ceased to be important as a patron of science; and society had begun to assume a middle-class air. This was the moment when organized science might be expected to adhere to the mercantile people for whom the way had been cleared towards great commercial and technological developments; but on the contrary, the Royal Society seems to have linked itself firmly with the more aristocratic element. Or, to put it the other way, the mercantile people had apparently dissociated themselves from the scientific movement. At all events, they were unwilling or unable to prevent the shift of scientific interest away from the useful and the comprehensible, the failure of interest in applied science. So in the end of the century we find science contributing to only one important utilitarian activity, the development of statistics.

Part of the reason for the strange apathy of the middle classes towards useful science may have been the widening gap between the wealthy mercantile and industrial employers and the classes just below them—their employees, and the smaller men generally. By 1688 this upper stratum was identifying itself with the aristocracy more markedly than in 1660; and the Royal Society apparently went with it.

All the same, it is difficult to feel that the changes in scientific attitudes are adequately explained by the merging of the wealthy middle class in the ruling class from the 1680s and by the intellectual consequences of the Newtonian achievement; and it is particularly hard to see how the industrial and dissenting element came to be dissociated from organized science to such a degree that Defoe, the mouth-piece of the technical and commercial vigour of his age, regards science proper as alien to his interests.

XXVI

THE AUTHORSHIP AND
SIGNIFICANCE OF *MACARIA**

Charles Webster

The ideals and aspirations of every age have been reflected in its
utopian literature. Utopias provided a safe vehicle for the social
critic or innovator; current practices could be subtly undermined
or new models of society advocated under the shield of a literary
device concerned with fictional communities in far-distant lands.
There was never a shortage of perceptive readers able to detect
cryptic political messages. Hence utopias provided an important
inducement to social reconstruction and intellectual innovation.
Not surprisingly pioneers of the new science in the seventeenth
century found utopia an ideal location in which to explore and
articulate their programmes. By adopting the utopian genre in
societies suspicious of social change and vigilant to guard against
religious heresy, the new science could be vindicated as an un-
exceptionable element in societies organized according to the
highest moral standards.[1] Furthermore natural philosophy could
be transformed from an intellectual pursuit of limited dimensions
into a central preoccupation, with ramifications affecting all
aspects of communal life. By underlining the great potentialities
of science, the utopian writers were able to fire the imagination

* From no. 56 (August 1972). I should like to thank Mr A. J. Turner for
his comments on this paper.

[1] For present purposes it is not necessary to recite the extensive literature
on utopias. A general bibliography of primary and secondary literature for
the sixteenth and seventeenth centuries is given in R. W. Gibson, *St.
Thomas More: A Preliminary Bibliography* (New Haven and London, 1961),
pp. 291–412. For a more recent, but most unsatisfactory general study, see
Nell Eurich, *Science in Utopia: A Mighty Design* (Cambridge, Mass., 1967).

of their contemporaries and stimulate active dedication to the 'advancement of learning'. The utopian goal was never far from sight in the movements leading to the formation of the first permanent scientific societies.

Francis Bacon provided an auspicious inauguration for English scientific utopias with *New Atlantis* (1626).[2] This fragment was introduced by the customary voyage, storm and description of the Island of Bensalem. But Bacon's patience with fiction was soon exhausted. The fictional elements soon gave way to a description of an ideal scientific institution, Solomon's House, which epitomized Bacon's views on the social role of science and was possibly animated by enthusiasm for the applied scientists of his day, including perhaps Gresham College, but also the more exotic inventors, Cornelius Drebbel and Salomon de Caus.[3] The state was expected to become a considerable beneficiary by exploiting the research of its laboratories. In a society beset by religious persecution, sectarian dispute, suppressed political institutions and economic decline, Bacon's utopian community might have assumed a cynical remoteness. But its optimistic worldview attracted devoted adherents. Although there was little immediate opportunity to promote grandiose scientific institutions or apply science systematically to social reconstruction, Bacon's ideal was cultivated by a growing community of experimental philosophers, who were increasingly able to convince politicians and entrepreneurs that science had an important role to play in an expanding economy and well-ordered society.

Their opportunity to regain the initiative came with the establishment of the Long Parliament, which assembled for its second session on 20 October 1641. Five days later the members were presented with an anonymous tract, *A description of the famous kingdome of Macaria*,[4] consciously designed to appear as the

[2] *New Atlantis* was published as an appendix to *Sylva Sylvarum*; there were eleven editions between 1626 and 1676; R. W. Gibson, *Francis Bacon: A Bibliography* (Oxford, 1950), pp. 147–54. The date of the first edition is conventionally given as 1627, but see Gibson, *op. cit.*, and *STC* no. 1168.

[3] F. M. Jaeger, *Cornelis Drebbel en zijne Tijdgenooten* (Groningen, 1922); R. L. Colie, 'Cornelis Drebbel and Salomon de Caus: two Jacobean models for Salomon's House', *Huntington Lib. Quarterly*, xviii (1954–5), pp. 245–60.

[4] *A Description of the Famous Kingdome of Macaria; shewing its Excellent Government: wherein The Inhabitants live in great Prosperity, Health, and*

lineal descendant of More's *Utopia* and Bacon's *New Atlantis*.[5] By skilfully advocating political and religious policies congenial to the puritan leaders in parliament, the author sought to engender receptivity to a comprehensive social policy and to proposals for economic reform based on the exploitation of experimental science. For the purposes of clarity the fictional element, already greatly reduced in Bacon, was further attenuated. Political circumstances no longer necessitated shrouding reform proposals in protective utopian clothing. Thus *Macaria* became the herald of a vast series of hard-headed reform tracts which appeared during the puritan revolution.

In view of the historical significance of *Macaria* it is highly desirable to establish its authorship, and thereby the author's relationship to the incipient Baconian movement and to the social policy-making of the puritans in parliament. It might also be possible to gain a fuller impression of the sources used by the author. While *New Atlantis* provided an obvious inspiration, much of *Macaria* was either original, or derived from sources not previously detected. Having attempted a solution of these problems in the present paper, it will be possible to re-examine current estimates of *Macaria*.

At no point in the text is any hint of the author's identity given. When the tract was first reprinted, the editors of the *Harleian Miscellany* made no attempt to establish authorship.[6] The problem appeared to have been solved satisfactorily in 1847 by James Crossley, who found frequent references to 'Macaria' in letters composed by Samuel Hartlib in 1659 and 1660.[7] Hence it appeared likely that Hartlib was the author, the utopian tract being a natural development of his earlier proposal for a community of scholars which had been named 'Antilia'. In the 1630s it was hoped to establish a utopian Antilian colony in the Baltic states or

---

Happinesse; the King obeyed, the Nobles honoured; and all good men respected,
Vice punished, and virtue rewarded. An Example to other Nations. In a Dialogue
between a Schollar and a Traveller (London, printed for Francis Constable,
1641): Brit. Mus. E173(28); preface dated 25 October 1641.
[5] 'having for my pattern Sir *Thomas Moore*, and Sir *Francis Bacon*':
Macaria, Preface, sig. A2v; see also p. 9.
[6] *Harleian Miscellany* (London, 1744), vol. i, pp. 564–9; 1808 edn, vol. i,
pp. 580–5.
[7] *The Diary and Correspondence of Dr. John Worthington*, vol. i, ed. James
Crossley (Chetham Society Remains, xiii, 1847), p. 163.

Virginia. When a similar scheme was introduced in 1659, the new community was called Macaria.[8]

Crossley's attribution has received general acceptance. Although G. H. Turnbull's meticulous survey of the Hartlib papers failed to produce positive evidence on the question, our detailed picture of Hartlib's views and associations in 1641 is quite consistent with his authorship.[9] Hartlib was intimately involved with the puritan party and he was a known advocate of technological innovation. *Macaria* established a framework of constitutional proposals calculated to appeal to a puritan audience, in which maximum emphasis was placed on social improvement by means of economic planning and scientific research. A slight note of hesitation is introduced by the absence of reference to educational reform in *Macaria*. Also, in view of Hartlib's tendency to collect copies of title-pages of works produced under his aegis, it is somewhat surprising that the title-page of *Macaria* is absent from his papers.

Hartlib's cosmopolitan associations appear to reinforce his connection with *Macaria*. Not only had he been involved in utopian societies, but he was also familiar with a wide range of utopian literature. While the obvious debt of *Macaria* was to *New Atlantis*, the scientific, social and religious standpoint was also consistent with Johann Valentin Andreae's *Christianopolis*.[10] This was a source known to Hartlib but to few others in England at this time. Another previously overlooked model is Caspar Stiblinus's *Commentariolus de Eudaemonensium Republica*.[11] In this brief essay the island of Macaria was visited after the customary shipwreck. Its capital, Eudaemon, had a devout, well-educated

---

[8] For an account of Antilia, see C. Webster, '*Macaria*: Samuel Hartlib and the Great Reformation', *Acta Comeniana*, xxvi (Prague, 1970), pp. 147–64.

[9] G. H. Turnbull, *Hartlib, Dury and Comenius* (London, 1947), pp. 73, 76, 90.

[10] J. V. Andreae (1586–1654), *Reipublicae Christianopolitanae descriptio* (Strassburg, 1619); English translation edited by F. Held (New York, 1916). Two other utopian writings by Andreae were translated by John Hall at Hartlib's instigation as *A Modell of a Christian Society* and *The Right Hand of Christian Love Offered* (Cambridge, 1647).

[11] Appendix to *Coropaedia, sive de moribus et vita virginum sacrarum* (Basel, 1555). The only copy of this work currently located in England by the present writer is in Emmanuel College, Cambridge. See also above, p. 9 n. 22.

protestant community exhibiting many features in common with the later version. For instance, public disputes about religion were strongly discouraged. General agreement on religious matters was obtained by private discussions among reputable scholars. In Eudaemon factious churchmen were expelled, while in Macaria they were executed. In both societies deserving public servants were maintained by the state, the later work placing the emphasis of patronage on 'all such as shall be able to demonstrate any experiment for the health or wealth of men'.[12] Like *Christianopolis*, Stiblinus's book must have been very rare, but Hartlib's universal correspondence was likely to detect any specimen of utopian literature.

Identification with *Macaria* was probably welcomed by Hartlib. Gradually his correspondents may have come to share our assumption that he was directly responsible for its composition. Indeed the precise attribution of authorship was of little concern to Hartlib's tightly-knit community of reformers. In the interests of the rapid diffusion of information, identities were usually suppressed in their writings. Consequently recent close investigation has shown that almost every work published by Hartlib was drafted by his colleagues.

The above evidence has been sufficient to suggest that Hartlib was familiar with *Macaria*, perhaps even from the earliest stages of its composition, but it is now clear that he was not its primary author. I have elsewhere drawn attention to the similarity of outlook between *Macaria* and the writings of Gabriel Plattes, as well as indicating direct links between the texts.[13] It is now apparent that Plattes had an even closer involvement. Incidental references to *Macaria* in his writings make it obvious that he was the author of the utopian tract. With this reattribution, *Macaria* remains the property of the Hartlib circle, but a slightly different perspective is introduced, affecting current estimates of its intentions.

Plattes was one of the numerous, impecunious but ambitious innovators whose cause was taken up by Hartlib. Already in the 1630s Hartlib had worked on behalf of the Moravian inventor Johann Christoph de Berg, who was commended to John Pym as

---

[12] *Macaria*, p. 5.
[13] '*Macaria . . .*', p. 156; *Samuel Hartlib and the Advancement of Learning* (Cambridge, 1970), p. 203.

a drainage expert. Plattes emerged into the public view in 1639 with two able technical treatises on agriculture and mining.[14] They impressed Hartlib, who quickly attracted their author into his orbit. Sir Thomas Roe was informed that:[15]

> the author of the Schedule of Divers New Inventions is the Plattes who a year ago published two profitable treatises concerning husbandry and mining. He is now busy contriving other tracts which will more particularly instruct all sorts of people how to procure their own and the public good of these countries.

The association was of advantage to both partners; Plattes would gain access to patrons, while Hartlib saw the public usefulness of a craftsman who was anxious to disseminate technical knowledge. Plattes was encouraged to undertake further experiments and to compose more ambitious tracts. This association developed until Hartlib was supporting the inventor from week to week in the

[14] *A Discovery of Infinite Treasure, Hidden since the Worlds Beginning* (London, 1639; 2 issues, STC. 19,998 and 19,999). *A Discovery of Subterraneall Treasure, viz. Of all manner of Mines and Mineralls, from the Gold to the Coale; with plaine Directions and Rules for the finding of them in all Kingdomes and Countries* (London, 1639; STC. 20,000). From Plattes's writings it may be assumed that he was aged about forty-five in 1640. He had little formal education, being probably taught by the engineer and inventor William Engelbert, to whom he dedicated both of the above works. For the later editions of Plattes's works see G. E. Fussell, *The Old English Farming Books from Fitzherbert to Tull 1523 to 1730* (London, 1947), pp. 36–44; W. Harte, *Essays on Husbandry* (London, 1770), vol. i, p. 35; J. Ferguson, *Bibliotheca Chemica* (Glasgow, 1906), i, p. 170; ii, pp. 207–8.

Engelbert (or Ingelbert) is a little-known figure. As a gentleman of Chelsea he was involved in fen drainage schemes in Lincolnshire and East Anglia between 1597 and 1618: Eric Kerridge, *The Agricultural Revolution* (London, 1967), pp. 229–30. He was described as an 'excellent ingenor' by John Norden, *Surveiors Dialogue* (London, 1610), p. 145. Some authorities regarded him as the true originator of the New River Project, designed to provide a new supply of drinking water to London. According to Aubrey 'there ought to have been erected a statue for the memory of this poore-man from the city of London': *Brief Lives*, ed. A. Clark (Oxford, 1898), ii, pp. 1, 60; J. W. Gough, *Sir Hugh Myddelton* (Oxford, 1964), pp. 32–3. According to a petition by Plattes, Engelbert's engine for coining pence and half-pence was deposited at the mint: Hartlib Papers, Sheffield University Library, LXXI 4.

[15] Letter from Hartlib to Roe, 10 August 1640: *Cal. State Papers Domestic, 1640*, p. 568.

period before the latter's tragic death in late December 1644.[16] According to one report, the martyr for science was 'suffered to fall down dead in the streets for want of food, whose studies tended to no less than the providing and preserving food for whole Nations'.[17] His teacher Engelbert had died in similar poverty.

The unfortunate death of Plattes is a reflection of the low fortunes of the Hartlib circle during the distractions of war. Comenius, having arrived in England in the autumn of 1641, left in the following spring, convinced that state patronage would not be available. Once stable conditions returned various short essays by Plattes were incorporated in Hartlib's works, but expectations of major writings were not fulfilled. One of Plattes's compositions, 'A Caveat for Alchymists', provides the clue to the composition of *Macaria*.[18] The Caveat was included in Hartlib's *Chymical, Medicinal and Chyrurgical Addresses* of 1655. This rare collection of essays has recently attracted notice for the discovery that it contains Boyle's first published work.[19] Plattes's contribution was primarily designed to warn those wishing to embark on transmutation experiments that they must obtain complete familiarity with the techniques of practical chemistry, as well as background knowledge of other sciences. Otherwise they will fall victim to uncritical knowledge and be exploited by cheats. In the course of this discussion he noted in passing:[20]

for the truth is that the world is unhappy, only for want of wit, which I have demonstrated in a little book lately

---

[16] G. H. Turnbull, 'Some correspondence of John Winthrop Jr. and Samuel Hartlib', Massachusetts Historical Society, *Proceedings*, lxxii (1961), pp. 36–7, 43. Letter from Sir Cheney Culpeper to Hartlib, 4 January 1644/5, Hartlib Papers, Sheffield University Library, XIII.

[17] S. Hartlib, *His Legacy of Husbandry*, 3rd edn (London, 1655), pp. 183–4: introductory letter by Cressy Dymock to Plattes's 'Certain Notes, and Observations concerning Setting of Corn, and the great benefit thereof', pp. 184–216.

[18] S. Hartlib, *Chymical, Medicinal and Chyrurgical Addresses: Made to Samue Hartlib, Esquire* (London, 1655), pp. 49–88. The Caveat is partly reprinted by D. Geoghegan in *Ambix*, x (1962), pp. 97–102. Its Preface is dated 10 March 1643/4.

[19] *Chymical Addresses*, 'Philaretus to Empyricus', pp. 113–50. For the identification, M. E. Rowbottom, 'The earliest published writing of Robert Boyle', *Annals of Science*, vi (1950), pp. 376–89.

[20] *Chymical Addresses*, p. 63.

printed, which sheweth how any Kingdome may live in great plenty, prosperity, health, peace and happiness, and the King and Governours may live in great honour and riches, and not have half so much trouble, as is usual in these times.

Although *Macaria* is not mentioned by name, this description of an earlier writing exhibits close verbal similarity to the title-page of the *Description of Macaria*.[21] Furthermore none of the title-pages or headings of Plattes's other works bear resemblance to this description, although they express similar general sentiments. Absence of direct reference to the key word *Macaria* may have caused contemporaries to overlook Plattes's meaning. After all, by 1655, the 1641 tract would not have been fresh in memory. Indeed in 1641 it may not have been widely circulated outside Hartlib's immediate circle of political associates. With further passage of time, the *Chymical Addresses* themselves lapsed into obscurity, rendering it unlikely that Plattes's incidental reference to *Macaria* would be noticed, except by a reader recalling the subtitle of the utopian tract. Plattes's claim must have been obvious to Hartlib, who presumably took no exception to this reference. Otherwise, as editor of the Caveat, he would have had every opportunity to expunge the incidental reference to *Macaria*.

Plattes's authorship is supported by various verbal and conceptual parallels between *Macaria*, the Caveat and other writings by the innovator. The introductory epitome of *Macaria* is even more like the above quotation than is its title-page:[22]

In a Kingdome called *Macaria*, the King and the Governours doe live in great honour and riches, and the people doe live in great plenty, prosperitie, health, peace, and happinesse, and have not halfe so much trouble as they have in these European Countreyes.

Likewise, one quotation from the Caveat is a particularly effective summary of the central themes of *Macaria*:[23]

But now I have been a Petitioner to the High and Honourable Court of Parliament, that I may demonstrate my ability, to do the Common-wealth of *England* service, which service

---

[21] See above, note 4.   [22] *Macaria*, p. 2; see also pp. 7 and 9.
[23] *Chymical Addresses*, p. 87; see also pp. 51–2.

consisteth in three things principally; to wit, to shew how
the husbandry of this Land may be so improved, that it may
maintain double the number of people, which now it doth,
and in much more plenty: also to shew how the Art of
Physick may be improved: and lastly, to shew the Art of
the Transmutation of Mettals, if I may have a Laboratory,
like to that in the City of *Venice*, where they are sure of
secrecy.

Each of the above three proposals is developed in *Macaria*.
First, the Traveller in the dialogue is asked to suggest his contribution to the new order. He replies:[24]

I will propound a book of Husbandry to the high Court of
Parliament, whereby the Kingdome may maintaine double
the number of people, which it doth now, and in more
plenty and prosperity, than now they enjoy.

Exactly similar terms were used to publicize his projected
'Treasure House of Nature Unlocked', undoubtedly the book
which the Traveller intended to present to parliament.[25]

Secondly, the book is read by the Scholar, who especially
commends 'that you shew the transmutation of sublunary bodies,
in such manner, that any man may be rich that will be industrious'.
This project was expected to be particularly attractive to parliament.[26]

Plattes's third objective is covered by the proposal for a 'Col-
ledge of experience, where they deliver out yeerly such medicines
as they find out by experience'.[27]

This three-point programme announced in *Macaria* and the
Caveat was ultimately derived from Plattes's books on husbandry

---

[24] *Macaria*, p. 11.

[25] Plattes, 'Mercurius Laetificans' in Hartlib, *His Legacy*.
pp. 173–82; p. 175. 'The summe of the Book consisteth in shewing how
this Kingdom may maintain double the number of people which it doth
now, and in farre greater plenty' (p. 175). This tract had been published
earlier as *The Profitable Intelligencer* (London, 1644).

[26] *Macaria*, pp. 11–12. Compare with the opening of the Caveat: 'Whereas
I am shortly to demonstrate before the High and Honourable Court of
Parliament in *England*, that there is such as thing feisible as the
Philosophers Stone': *Chymical Addresses*, pp. 51–2.

[27] *Macaria*, p. 5.

and mining, *A Discovery of Infinite Treasure* and *A Discovery of Subterraneall Treasure*. The latter devoted a brief chapter to methods of preparing gold from compounds of iron, copper and mercury.[28] Of the five Councils devised to superintend social and economic development in *Macaria*, the most emphasis was given to the Council of Husbandry, by which 'the whole Kingdome is become like to a fruitfull Garden'. Similarly *The Discovery of Infinite Treasure* was designed 'to make this Countrey the Paradise of the World'.[29]

Even the political tone of *Macaria* finds expression in the Caveat. Plattes urges his readers to adopt a critical attitude in scientific enquiry. This is regarded as analogous to distrust of tyranny in civil life. He adds, 'I know where I am, to wit, in a free State, where the subjects know so well their own Liberties and Priviledges, that they will never suffer any Tyrannical Government to prevail in this Nation'. This echoed the sentiments expressed two years previously: 'the common people, knowing their own rights and liberties, will not be governed by way of oppression; and so, by little and little, all Kingdomes will be like to *Macaria*'.[30] Plattes's tone throughout the Caveat was strident and aggressive. He petitioned the state to recognize an obligation to play an active role in social and economic planning, involving patronage of its specialist advisers. With the introduction of regulation of industry and agriculture, recalcitrant landowners, physicians or technicians would be punished as traitors if unresponsive to innovation. He was confident that only disaffected members of the community would resist the attractions of economic planning. His 'Treasure House of Nature Unlocked' was expected to receive the parliamentary imprimatur and provide the blueprint for future policies.

The evidence presented above indicates such a close verbal and conceptual integration between *Macaria* and the writings of Plattes, that there is no reason to doubt this authorship of the utopian tract previously ascribed to Hartlib. But the latter's role was probably significant. By the time of its composition, Plattes was intimately involved with the Hartlib circle and familiar with their political and religious alignments. Hartlib's precise part in

[28] *Discovery of Subterraneall Treasure*, pp. 40–3.
[29] *Macaria*, p. 4; *Discovery of Infinite Treasure*, sigs A3v–A4r.
[30] *Chymical Addresses*, p. 86; *Macaria*, pp. 13–14.

the composition of *Macaria* must remain conjectural, but it is almost certain that he was active at some stage. Plattes confessed to having had little education.[31] This impression is supported by his writings, which indicate unfamiliarity with classical languages. It is also probable that he would have been ignorant of the extensive continental utopian literature. Consequently Hartlib may have played a more than usually active part in framing the text. He perhaps suggested the use of the utopian medium, selecting Stiblinus's Macarian state for the framework. In addition he may have transmitted other literary elements and introduced political doctrines congenial to their allies. Plattes gave the work a distinctive character by underlining the potentialities of experimental science to advance social policies. At this crucial stage Plattes successfully canvassed the claims of science to be considered as an integral component of a puritan religious and social programme. By the intelligent cultivation of science the nation was offered a solution for unemployment, prosperity in its colonies, even wealth based on mining precious metals and the transmutation of base metals into gold. The possibilities appeared limitless. Crucial to the credibility of these proposals were Plattes's writings and reputation. His sound practical experience, enthusiasm for experiment and original outlook created considerable interest in the further progress of his work. The Civil War produced a temporary setback, but Hartlib took over his objectives; the social application of science became the preoccupation of a group of enthusiasts ranging from craftsmen to the more influential public figures Boyle, Petty and Worsley. The natural heir to *Macaria* was the 'Invisible College', which focused on husbandry, metallurgy and pharmacology, precisely the three spheres of scientific involvement propounded in *Macaria*.[32] The 'Invisible College' and Hartlib's Office of Address reinforce the relevance of *Macaria* to the formation of attitudes on social policy during the puritan revolution.

Historians of science tend to judge *Macaria* according to altogether different standards. They are primarily interested in detecting 'progressive' tendencies which contributed to the

[31] *Discovery of Infinite Treasure*, p. 4.
[32] See my forthcoming article 'New light on the Invisible College: the social relations of science in the mid-seventeenth century', *Trans. Roy. Hist. Soc.*, xxiv (1974).

'Scientific Revolution' of the seventeenth century. Out of the complex spectrum of debate on natural philosophy, attempts have been made to detect those elements most relevant to the emerging scientific movement. Considerable divergence of opinion has been engendered by the adoption of conflicting conceptions of the nature of scientific activity. On the whole there is a preference for a narrow and exclusive definition of science, dictated by current views on scientific methodology. There has been a tendency to eliminate from consideration, on the one hand intellectuals engaged in metaphysical debates relating to theology; on the other those engaged in the utilitarian application of science. Thus history of science is seen entirely in terms of classic works of a small élite involved in self-sustaining scientific enquiry, bearing only incidental relationship to the general intellectual and social environment. This restrictive approach is productive if it successfully isolates the central agencies of scientific change, but if a range of relations fundamental to the understanding of scientific development is arbitrarily excluded by such techniques, its value is fundamentally impaired.

Macaria, as an important indicator of puritan scientific attitudes, provides an ideal illustrative example to test the workings of restrictive history. As a minor work by a minor author, stressing the social relations of science, utilitarianism and utopianism, with attitudes dominated by religious and political preconceptions, reflecting the views and aspirations of an amorphous and partly anonymous community of puritan craftsmen and philanthropists, it does not present science in a form congenial to the techniques of restrictive history. At this point it is relevant to summarize attitudes to *Macaria* and its author in order to illustrate the anomalies introduced by the restrictive point of view.

The recent historian of the early Royal Society describes a temperamental barrier which prevented Hartlib and his associates from understanding Bacon's true intentions: their 'view of the physical universe which was vague, distorted, and, above all, incapable of correction or progress because it was not rooted in scientific method'.[33] This worldview has been aptly apostrophized as 'vulgar Baconianism' in which 'Bacon's study of Nature had been subordinated to the Protestant pantheism of the puritan

[33] M. Purver, *The Royal Society: Concept and Creation* (London, 1967), p. 209.

sects, his anti-Aristotelianism to their social radicalism, his new "metaphysic" to the millenarism [sic] of their prophets. His *experimenta lucifera* had degenerated into the *Via Lucis* of Comenius'.[34] A very similar attitude is given authoritative expression by A. R. Hall. In Hall's extensive writings on seventeenth-century science and technology, Hartlib has received occasional mention, usually with mild approbation. It is recognized that Hartlib's personal 'charm' was instrumental in attracting young intellectuals into the study of experimental science, while in 'his hopes for the foundation of a great philosophical college, and for the advancement of technology, he was at one with aspects of the Baconian tradition'. The Hartlib circle is acknowledged as one of the three major groups in English science at this period, their bias being 'to social and ethical reform and more occupied with technology than abstract science'.[35]

In a recent impressionistic essay reappraising the scientific implications of seventeenth-century utopian literature, Hall reverts to a more critical point of view.[36] An overtly unsympathetic attitude is adopted to utopian writings and the intellectual aspirations of their authors. Damning judgments are hazarded without detailed reference either to original works or the extensive modern commentaries so necessary for the understanding of such elusive figures as Andreae, Campanella or Hartlib. *Macaria* is singled out for particular censure. Even the 'very sketchy' or 'short and incoherent dialogue' form of *Macaria* causes distaste.[37] It is overlooked that brevity and reduction of the fictional element were adopted intentionally to increase the practical effect of *Macaria*, designed as a 'discourse, which is briefe and pithy, and easie to be effected, if all men be willing'.[38] This was the form of utopia most suited to the political circumstances of 1641. This elementary point reinforces the necessity of relating utopian writings to their general historical context. They are more meaningful when seen in this light than when compared arbi-

[34] *Ibid.*, Introduction by H. R. Trevor-Roper, pp. xvi–xvii; H. R. Trevor-Roper, *Religion, the Reformation and Social Change* (London, 1967), pp. 289–90.
[35] A. R. Hall in *Cambridge Economic History of Europe*, vol. iv (Cambridge, 1967), pp. 118–19; ——, *From Galileo to Newton* (London, 1963), pp. 141–2.
[36] 'Science, technology and utopia in the seventeenth century', in *Science and Society 1600–1900*, ed. P. Mathias (Cambridge, 1972), pp. 33–53.
[37] *Ibid.*, p. 37.   [38] *Macaria*, p. 9.

trarily with other representatives of the genre. Certainly in the writings of Bacon, Andreae, Campanella and Hartlib (Plattes), the genre was merely a vehicle for conveying views about nature and human society, which must be seen as part of a wider debate.

The scientific element in *Macaria* is described by Hall as 'puffing discussion of a "book of husbandry" written by the author'. It is thought significant that rewards were given for technical ingenuity rather than science. On further consideration, Hartlib was not even aiming at a 'technological Utopia'. Neither invention, nor technological progress were of more than incidental importance to the author of *Macaria*.[39] As a sympathizer with 'the German school of practitioners of esoteric or Hermetic arts' or 'elements of transcendentalism and mysticism' Hartlib was debarred from involvement in constructive scientific work.[40] In view of the irrefutable evidence about Hartlib's personal influence it is admitted that he 'might be said to have caused religion, social aspiration, mystical idealism and science to unite in a few people's minds—they are not incompatible—though in my own opinion this has little or nothing to do with the development of science in mid-seventeenth-century England'.[41] In view of the dominance of religious motivation and social ethic in the utopian writings, Hall feels that reference to 'the promotion of material riches or the attainment of a technological Utopia' has only the significance of a literary device.[42] Having established a fundamental disregard for science and technology in *Macaria* and to a great extent in other utopian works, the way is cleared for declaring their irrelevance to the nascent scientific movement—'this particular link between science (or technology) and victorious Puritanism vanishes'.[43] By this tortuous route the desired goal of restrictive history is achieved. If *Macaria* appears to display scientific concern, it is assumed to be unproductive because of the affiliation with Hermeticism, mysticism or pansophism. Alternatively, as a technological utopia, its technology excludes science; then on closer examination, recognition of the dominance of religious and social ideas is thought to exclude serious concern for technology.

Whatever the logical defects of such procedures, the unrealistic

[39] Hall, 'Science, technology . . .', p. 40.
[40] *Ibid.*, pp. 37, 40.
[41] *Ibid.*, pp. 40–1.
[42] *Ibid.*, pp. 41, 43.
[43] *Ibid.*, p. 43.

qualities of this analysis become apparent with close attention to the evidence. By adopting a less restrictive attitude, it becomes apparent that *Macaria* has a much greater scientific relevance. This case does not depend on the reattribution of authorship, but with the recognition that *Macaria* is integrally related to the scientific writings of Plattes, the divorce between this utopian work and science becomes even more difficult to sustain. Only by adopting absurdly narrow criteria for science and technology could Plattes's concern with these subjects be denied. His writings were terse and fragmentary, but their brief was undoubtedly scientific. Besides the anticipated practical hints and accounts of inventions, Plattes expressed methodological principles in sympathy with the experimental philosophy of Bacon; he conducted a range of experimental studies in such subjects as refining metals and the use of indicators for chemical analysis. Finally, he proposed theories to explain geological phenomena.[44] His writings have a freshness resulting from limited education and unfamiliarity with the major literary traditions of natural philosophy. Hence he was not particularly concerned to elaborate complex Hermetic theories. His view of nature was not mechanistic, but this involved no necessary impediment to experimental science. Even his interest in transmutation, exploited in *Macaria* to attract interest in his work, was expressed in disciplined and experimental terms in his metallurgical writings. The emphasis was strongly towards refining rather than actual transmutation. It is not claimed here that his technical improvements or scientific insights are of spectacular importance, but only that they fulfil

[44] A. G. Debus, 'Gabriel Plattes and his chemical theory of the formation of the Earth's crust', *Ambix*, ix (1961), pp. 162–5; ——, 'Solution analyses prior to Robert Boyle', *Chymia*, viii (1962), pp. 41–61; J. R. Partington, *A History of Chemistry*, vol. ii (London, 1962), p. 103.
  C. S. Smith and R. J. Forbes regard Plattes as the first to compose a useful treatise in English on metallurgy: 'Metallurgy and assaying' in C. Singer *et al.* (eds), *A History of Technology* (Oxford, 1954–5), iii, p. 63. R. E. Prothero (Lord Ernle) thought that 'men like Gabriel Plattes or Sir Richard Weston were suggesting new agricultural methods, or introducing new crops which were destined to change the face of English farming': *English Farming Past and Present*, 4th edn (London, 1927), pp. 106–7 and *passim*. In addition, W. K. Jordan regards Plattes's work as a 'contribution of considerable importance to both political and economic theory': *The Development of Religious Toleration in England*, vol. iii, Part 2, *1640–1660* (London, 1940), p. 345, see also pp. 84–5.

the essential conditions of science and technology. If the definition of these subjects is restricted to exclude such figures as Plattes, other implied exclusions would be so extensive that the terms would no longer be meaningful. It is much more realistic to accept the serious scientific and technological aims of *Macaria* and its author.

Thus *Macaria* may be reaffirmed as a technological utopia, providing its technology is emancipated from anachronistic connotations. Its technology assumed a sound scientific foundation and direction according to a social ethic derived from religious premises. There is every reason to believe that this model provided a direct incentive to the Hartlib circle. Furthermore, its outlook was reflected in an even wider group of puritan intellectuals, whose scientific and technological enterprise continued to be informed by religious ideals. Restrictive history has determined that this tradition has no relevance to the nascent scientific movement. It must now be considered whether its procedures lead to patently false conclusions as in the case of *Macaria*, by excluding factors which provided necessary conditions for the formation of English scientific attitudes in the later part of the seventeenth century.

Macaria warns against the application of restrictive premises. Productive science was not necessarily ruled out by its intimate relations with religious speculation, social policy or technological innovation. Adherence to Hermeticism, pansophy or other complex metaphysical systems could under certain circumstances enliven scientific activity.[45] Transmutation, universal medicines or perpetual motion, although ultimately bypassed by advanced science, were not inherently unscientific hypotheses. Neither was an animistic worldview less conducive to scientific progress than the mechanical philosophy. The seventeenth-century mind was not capable of identifying with the watertight compartments imposed by modern historians. The scientific community comprised men with fluctuating and wide-ranging interests; their minds moved rapidly and naturally from religious doctrine to scientific theory and technical innovation. It is quite arbitrary to

[45] P. M. Rattansi, 'The social interpretation of science in the seventeenth century' in *Science and Society*, pp. 1–32; J. E. McGuire and P. M. Rattansi, 'Newton and the "Pipes of Pan" ', *Notes and Records of the Royal Society*, xxi (1966), pp. 108–43.

assume *a priori* that any one of these facets of thought was irrelevant to the individual's scientific accomplishments. Restrictive history also ignores the sociological factors involved in the formation of scientific opinion and recruitment to the scientific community. Minor works by minor authors may be highly significant indicators of intellectual change. Attitudes are the property of social groups rather than of individuals operating *in vacuo*. In the scientific movement of puritan England, it is necessary to assess the importance of various communities of practitioners in order to gain an impression of the balance between individual scientific creativity and the individual's role as the exponent of the opinions of his colleagues. Just as *Macaria* was a legitimate expression of the aspirations of the Hartlib circle in 1641, Boyle's scientific classic, the *Usefulness of Experimental Philosophy*, was its expression a decade later.[46] Examined from this point of view, 'victorious Puritanism' will undoubtedly prove to have played an integral and significant part in the English scientific movement of the seventeenth century.

[46] *Some Considerations touching the Usefulnesse of Experimental Naturall Philosophy* (Oxford, 1663). According to the introduction, Part I of this work was composed about 1650. Part II was composed later, but bears a strong imprint of his earlier interests.

XXVII

GODLY RULE AND ENGLISH MILLENARIANISM*

Bernard Capp

The role of millenarianism has, to date, received more attention from the anthropologist than from the historian. Professor Norman Cohn's *Pursuit of the Millennium* (London, 1957) did much to rectify this situation for medieval Europe, but millenarianism in early modern Europe is a field unexplored and largely ignored. For England, however, a change of attitude seems to be signalled by a cluster of recent titles. They share a common theme in seeking to dispel the 'twilight world . . . where . . . millenarianism is fanaticism',[1] and to stress instead its importance and its normalcy. In *Pulpit in Parliament* (Princeton, 1969), Professor John F. Wilson has provided a study of the Fast Sermons of the Long Parliament, with a detailed analysis of the role of millenarianism within them. The title of Dr J. A. de Jong's book, *As the Waters Cover the Sea: Millennial expectations in the rise of Anglo-American missions 1640–1810* (Kampen, 1970), indicates its particular viewpoint. *Puritans, the Millennium, and the Future of Israel* (Cambridge and London, 1970), edited by Dr Peter Toon, is a collection of brief essays covering the academic rediscovery of millenarianism and its role in the presbyterian, Independent, Fifth Monarchist and Quaker movements. The most ambitious work is that of Dr W. M. Lamont. In his article, 'Puritanism as history and historiography' (*Past and Present*, no. 44, August 1969), Dr Lamont advanced the theory that millenarianism, derived largely from John Foxe,

* From no. 52 (August 1971).

[1] William M. Lamont, *Godly Rule: Politics and Religion, 1603–1660* (Macmillan, London, 1969), p. 6. Page references in the text refer to this book, which is cited in the footnotes as Lamont.

represented the 'common denominator' of English puritanism before and in the first years following the outbreak of the Civil War. In *Godly Rule: Politics and Religion, 1603–1660*,[2] he ascribes to millenarianism a still greater role. It represented 'not alienation from the spirit of the age but a total involvement with it' (p. 13), and as such it embraced not only Foxe, Bishop Jewel and seventeenth-century puritanism but even Laudianism and King James I. As its cover promises, *Godly Rule* is a 'provocative study' challenging many basic assumptions about the period, and it deserves a close scrutiny.

As a concise discussion of various concepts of godly rule—*iure divino* episcopacy, the godly prince, presbyterianism—Dr Lamont's book can be welcomed as a useful and succinct account. But as the vehicle for his thesis of an all-pervading millenarianism it is open, I believe, to a number of fundamental objections. Dr Lamont leads us out of the 'twilight world' but leaves us in a mist in which certain key concepts are blurred misleadingly. He defines millenarianism, following Dr Sylvia Thrupp, as 'any conception of a perfect age to come' (p. 9). Since it fails to distinguish between millenarianism, that is belief in a perfect society to be established through divine intervention, and utopianism, a perfect society to be created by man's unaided efforts, this definition is indeed open to criticism, as the author anticipates. But the real complaint must be that he has not adhered to his own definition. For throughout the book he equates any interest in the prophecies of Revelation, and in particular the belief that they are currently being fulfilled, with millenarianism. Such an assumption confuses the two vitally different conclusions which Revelation produced—the pessimistic belief in an imminent doomsday, and the optimistic expectation of an earthly paradise. His thesis rests on the further false assumption that any godly, disciplinarian rule must be based on a millenarian vision. The Calvinist regime at Geneva provides an obvious but convincing refutation, Calvin being totally unmoved by millenarian dreams, as Dr Lamont himself observes (p. 22).

The effect on the book of these two assumptions is enormous; for when advancing the novel claim that Laudianism was inspired by a millenarian impulse (pp. 67–81), Dr Lamont feels his point is proved when he has documented merely a Laudian

2 *Ibid.*

concern with imposing true faith and discipline. His chapter on Laudianism runs to about twenty pages, mostly discussing its preoccupation with discipline and its elevation of divine-right episcopacy above the divine right of kings. Only a couple of pages are devoted to Laudian interest in eschatology, and the evidence is far from impressive. For he shows that Montague and Cosin *rejected* the identification of Antichrist with the Papacy, and thus, implicitly, the whole concept of the Reformation as an apocalyptic struggle between Christ and Antichrist. As positive evidence, he refers only to an unpublished comment by an unnamed Laudian that the Beast would be destroyed by divine-right episcopacy (pp. 66–8). And that is all. On this evidence, one can only conclude that the Laudian concept of godly discipline owed nothing to millenarian beliefs, and that Laudianism was remarkable for its *lack* of eschatological interest.

In studying the advocates of the 'Godly Prince' (chap. 2), notably John Foxe and Bishop Jewel, Dr Lamont is on stronger ground. Foxe certainly regarded the entire span of Christian history as the gradual fulfilment of the Biblical prophecies, and believed that their completion was near. Jewel, in his more rhetorical moments, could proclaim that 'God's kingdom, my brethren, is even now come upon us'.[3] But Foxe and Jewel were never millenarians, and thus could not be founders of a millenarian school. For despite their eschatological preoccupations, neither held the belief that an enduring period of supernatural perfection was dawning on earth. On the basis of the political and religious upheavals in England and abroad, both believed themselves to be living in the last and worst days of the world. Bliss could be expected only in Heaven after the impending Last Judgement. In the conclusion of the *Acts and Monuments*, Foxe reflected that 'the elder the world waxeth, . . . the nearer it hasteneth to its end, the more Satan rageth'. Elizabethan England was for Jewel a second Jerusalem when compared with Marian England, but this fruit of divine mercy was precarious and likely to be short-lived, for 'We are almost fallen into the lowest pit: . . . unless we repent, the kingdom of God shall be taken away from us . . . Jerusalem shall be overthrown . . . this noble realm shall

[3] J. Jewel, *Works*, ed. J. Ayre (Parker Soc., xxvi, Cambridge, 1847), ii, p. 1083.

be subject to foreign nations'. 'Likewise St. Paul . . . said', he observed, ' "In the last days there come perilous times . . ." '.[4]

The idea that they were living in the last and worst days of the world was widespread amongst Elizabethan and indeed earlier English Protestants. Hugh Latimer thought in 1552 that the end of all things 'may come in my days, as old as I am'. John Bradford, the Marian martyr, concluded from Daniel's prophecies that the end was near, and that 'wicked empires shall continue until the last day'. The belief was reflected in prayers authorized by the Elizabethan church, thanking God for preserving England from the 'unnatural wars' and 'great iniquity which aboundeth in these latter days'. The arguments were summarized in 1574 by Edwin Sandys, later archbishop of York:[5]

> Christ hath set down certain tokens of the end, which all are fulfilled; and amongst others he saith, 'Iniquity shall abound: charity shall wax cold: the gospel shall be preached in all the world; and then shall come the end'. Never more iniquity; never less charity; the gospel never so liberally taught: behold the end.

The belief spread far among both clergy and laity, and was re-inforced by the turmoils of the Civil War. It was held at that time by (among others) Joseph Hall, former bishop of Norwich, and a belated Laudian. But far from proving the existence of Laudian millenarianism (as Dr Lamont might argue), Hall felt the belief was a convincing refutation of the millennial creed, which was, he argued, merely a fond delusion by which men contrived to ignore the terrible reality of the imminent Last Judgement.[6]

What of the godly princes themselves? Dr Lamont says little of Elizabeth, though as far as can be seen she was quite close to Foxe and Jewel in regarding her reign as set in 'these last and worst days of the world'.[7] James I, however, had clearly a far

[4] J. Foxe, *Acts and Monuments*, ed. J. Pratt (London, 1877), viii, p. 754; Jewel, *Works*, ii, pp. 1014, 1073.
[5] H. Latimer, *Sermons and Remains*, ed. G. E. Corrie (Parker Soc., xx, Cambridge, 1845), ii, p. 53; *The Writings of John Bradford*, ed. A. Townsend (Parker Soc., li, Cambridge, 1853), ii, p. 361; *Liturgies . . . of Queen Elizabeth*, ed. W. K. Clay (Parker Soc., xxvii, Cambridge, 1847), p. 644; E. Sandys, *Sermons*, ed. J. Ayre (Parker Soc., ii, Cambridge, 1841), p. 172.
[6] J. Hall, *The Revelation Unrevealed* (London, 1650), pp. 224–7.
[7] F. Chamberlin (ed.), *The Sayings of Queen Elizabeth* (London, 1923), p. 108.

greater interest in eschatology. His *Fruitefull Meditation* on Revelation xx was designed to prove that Rome was Antichrist, and that the last days were at hand. But Dr Lamont produces no evidence to show that James was interested in the role of Emperor of the Last Days (p. 32) or believed in any form of future millennium. James conceded only an indeterminate but 'short space' between the fall of Rome and the end of the world, and placed the thousand years of Satan's binding firmly in the past.[8]

Finally, there is Dr Lamont's thesis that the various stages of puritanism were linked together by a common denominator, namely millenarianism.[9] Puritan millenarianism did not begin in 1641, but was transformed then from a 'centripetal' creed, that is, one which stressed the role of the monarch, as an 'Emperor of the Last Days', in establishing the millennium, into a 'centrifugal', anti-royalist doctrine, anticipating the imminent destruction of all existing regimes to make way for Christ's kingdom. The thesis, in fact, is confined to the Stuart Puritans who, he says, took Foxe and Jewel rather than their Elizabethan predecessors as their mentors (p. 44). The early Stuart Puritans were indeed anxious to bring about the completion of reformation through the godly magistrate: it was the only hopeful tactic left to them after the Elizabethan puritan failure to pressurize or by-pass the crown. But a reference (p. 46) to John Preston's connection with the duke of Buckingham proves only that Preston recognized this tactical need, not that he ascribed millennial roles to Buckingham or James. The prime figure in Dr Lamont's thesis of millenarian 'shift' is Henry Burton. His *Seven Vials* (London, 1628) argued that Elizabeth, James and Charles had a major role in the downfall of Antichrist,[10] while in the early 1640s he was noted as an able champion of the right of Parliamentary resistance. It is not clear, however, of whom Burton was typical. There is no attempt at quantification, and no evidence is produced to justify placing the foremost Puritans of the time, such as Gouge, Preston, Sibbes, Perkins and so on, in a band of 'centripetal millenarians'. Burton's *Seven Vials* is certainly proof that 'belief in the imminence of the Last Judgement' could be 'a stimulant

[8] James I, *A Fruitefull Meditation* (London, 1603), sigs A7–8v., B6v.
[9] Lamont, 'Puritanism as history and historiography: some further thoughts', *Past and Present*, no. 44 (August 1969), p. 145.
[10] *Ibid.*, p. 142.

to an Emperor Cult'.[11] But Dr Lamont fails to appreciate the distinction that in England, while belief in the imminent Last Judgement could have a 'centripetal' character, glorifying the monarchy, millenarianism itself was fundamentally 'centrifugal'. Burton's career illustrates the point: during his royalist phase (in 1628) he argued that the end of the world would follow promptly on the fall of Antichrist. His disillusion with the monarchy and adoption of millenarianism (from Brightman) went hand in hand.[12] Burton thus was not a 'centripetal millenarian'; indeed the species did not exist in pre-war England. Millenarianism did exist and was spreading amongst pre-revolutionary Puritans, but it was always 'centrifugal' in character and derived from Thomas Brightman and Joseph Mede,[13] not from Foxe.

Certain other criticisms of *Godly Rule* may be covered more briefly. The implausible attempt to make millenarian puritanism the cause of English witchcraft persecutions—'after Thomas Brightman, Matthew Hopkins' (pp. 98–100)—is barely documented and appears conceivable only when all earlier and later persecutions are ignored (as they are by the author). There is no attempt to show whether Hopkins did have millenarian beliefs or that (if so) they were responsible for his preoccupation with witchcraft. There is a suggestion of over-hasty writing when Dr Lamont uses *Certain Quaeres*, the Norfolk declaration of 1649 which is generally accepted as the opening salvo of the Fifth Monarchist movement, to prove and illustrate an alleged rapprochement of Independents and Presbyterians on a millenarian basis (p. 144). The assertion that Cromwell's quarrel with the Levellers at Putney in 1647 signalled his retreat from millenarianism (pp. 137–9) rests on a doubtful identification of the Levellers as a millenarian movement. It would need, too, a whole series of 'euphoric lapses' (p. 139) to explain away Cromwell's speech to Barebones in 1653, steeped in the prophecies of Revelation and Daniel. Barebones was hailed as 'the door to usher in the things that God has promised; which have been prophesied of . . . it is our duty to endeavour this way; not vainly to look at that prophecy in Daniel . . .'. If Dr Lamont is right, how does

---

[11] *Ibid.*, p. 137.
[12] H. Burton, *The Seven Vials* (London, 1628), p. 141; Lamont, 'Puritanism as history and historiography', p. 142.
[13] For whom see below, pp. 396–7.

one explain the alliance with Major-General Harrison which led to Barebones, or Cromwell's endorsement of the extravagantly millenarian army declaration of Musselburgh in 1650 as a 'plain simple spiritual one'?[14] Cromwell rejected the political radicals in 1647 when he recognized the social implications of their programme. He rejected millenarian dreams only in the latter part of 1653 when he perceived the social radicalism which the more extreme sectarians had grafted on to millenarianism. Distrusted by the Levellers from 1647, Cromwell was seen as a second Moses by many sectarians until late 1653.[15]

It is perhaps only a foible that, having stressed the normalcy of millenarian beliefs, Dr Lamont should continue to follow seventeenth-century prejudices by including the Fifth Monarchists among the 'cranks' and 'fanatics'. Since he has accepted that the millenarian ideology was normal, he is presumably following the seventeenth century in regarding social radicalism as proof of eccentricity. It is a more serious point, though, that Dr Lamont treats the rise of millenarianism as a purely English phenomenon. English Protestants always saw the Biblical prophecies as being fulfilled on a wider, European plane, and to ignore the effect of continental writers and events, especially the Thirty Years' War, on English eschatology, is to provide a misleading perspective.

Before leaving *Godly Rule*, it is necessary to turn, finally, to Dr Lamont's claim that Thomas Hobbes comes 'within the mainstream of post-millennial belief' (p. 8), on the basis of the third and fourth books of *Leviathan*. Dr Lamont cites, in support of this assertion, an essay by Professor John Pocock, since published as 'Time, history and eschatology in the thought of Thomas Hobbes' in *The Diversity of History: Essays in honour of Sir Herbert Butterfield*, edited by J. H. Elliott and H. G. Koenigsberger (London, 1970). Professor Pocock, in a complex but brilliant argument, does indeed establish convincingly that Hobbes believed in a future personal reign of Christ on earth. But Hobbes had no belief in the *imminence* of this messianic reign, which I (with Dr Lamont, p. 7)

---

[14] W. C. Abbott, *The Writings and Speeches of Oliver Cromwell* (Cambridge, Mass., 1937–47), ii, p. 302, iii, p. 64.
[15] A. H. Woolrych, 'The calling of Barebone's Parliament', *Eng. Hist. Rev.*, lxxx (1965), pp. 492–513; see also my Oxford D.Phil. thesis (1969), now published as: *The Fifth Monarchy Men: A Study in Seventeenth-century English Millenarianism* (London, 1972), chap. 3.

hold to be a basic part of the millenarian creed. Hobbes adopted a millenarian structure of thought but, as Professor Pocock shows, had no interest in Daniel and Revelation or the date of Christ's return, and rejected the identification of Antichrist as the Papacy or any existing person or institution. Hobbes was interested not in the millennium itself but in the millenarian *doctrine* which he used as a weapon against clerical power and pretensions— whether papal domination or the theocratic claims of the radical millenarian sects, set out, for example, in the *Certain Quaeres* of 1649. Christianity was presented by Hobbes as concerned essentially with prophecy and eschatology. By defining salvation as participation in Christ's future kingdom, and saving faith as merely willingness to believe in God's power and prophecies, Hobbes was able to reduce the role of the church—any church— to insignificance. He was pursuing ends diametrically opposed to those of the mass of contemporary millenarians: pushing New Jerusalem into the indefinite future, he rejected any attempt by a self-proclaimed Elect to establish a disciplinarian holy commonwealth. It is indeed testimony to the prevalence of millenarian ideas that Hobbes, even while living abroad, should adopt a millenarian structure of thought absent from his earlier work. But the contents and purpose of Books Three and Four of *Leviathan* place Hobbes firmly outside the millenarian 'mainstream'.

Godly Rule, then, leaves unsupplied the need for a history of the rise of English millenarianism, and of the role and importance of eschatological interest in general in this period. It offers no reasons why Foxe's scheme of history, with its belief in an imminent Last Judgement, was so popular, nor why rival, millenarian eschatological schemes came to challenge and partly supersede it.

One of the fundamental problems facing early protestantism was to explain why God had allowed Antichristian Rome to flourish and to persecute the true believers for so many centuries. Two obvious answers were equally unpalatable—either Satan had triumphed over God, or Rome must be the true church. Foxe provided a third solution by interpreting the whole of history as the fulfilment of the Biblical prophecies. Rome's triumph was thus merely a part of God's divine (if inscrutable) plan, and God had pre-ordained Rome's downfall as the plan unfolded. God's ways were just, and 'justifiable to men' since the Antichristian tyranny, according to James I, 'shall tend . . . to the double Crowne of glory, to the perseverers or standers out to the end'.[16]

The general philosophy of history expounded by Foxe and Jewel was undoubtedly pessimistic, expecting troubles until the imminent end of the world, and indeed it needed to be to appear relevant to the precarious situation of the early years of Elizabeth. As such, it complemented the widespread belief in universal decay and degeneration.[17] Nevertheless, it contained an element of consolation and even limited optimism which probably explains much of its popularity. What was needed was a guarantee of English security in the midst of the European religious-political turmoil. Foxe's theory that England was God's elect and favoured nation provided this security at the same time as appealing to the vigorous force of English nationalism.[18] John Aylmer made the point clearly in 1559: 'Think not that God wil suffer you to be foyled at their [i.e. the Pope's and Turks'] handes, for your fall is hys dishonour, if you lose the victory: he must lose the glory'.[19] The point of the frequent comparisons of Elizabeth with Constantine was that she too was providing security after persecution and was promoting the true faith. Elizabeth herself thanked God for making her His 'instrument, to set forth the glorious Gospel' and that 'when wars and seditions with grievous persecutions have vexed almost all Kings and Countries round about me, my reign hath been peaceable, and my Realm a receptacle to the afflicted church'.[20] The tone was defensive in most Elizabethan references to the elect nation concept. Foxe was anxious lest 'the Turk do give some attempt against England by the seas'; Aylmer declared that his 'trust is in God, thoughe the French and scots, and the deuil him selfe' conspired against the land. His greatest hope was the limited wish that Elizabeth might 'cutt of the head of that Hidra, the Antichrist of Rome, in such sort, as it neuer

[16] Cf. T. F. Torrance, 'The eschatology of the Reformation', *Scottish Jl of Theology*, Occasional Paper no. 2 (n.d.), pp. 36–62; James I, *Fruitefull Meditation*, sig. B4v–5.

[17] See, for example, V. Harris, *All Coherence Gone* (Chicago, 1949), *passim*; H. Baker, *The Wars of Truth* (London and New York, 1952), pp. 65–78.

[18] W. Haller, *Foxe's Book of Martyrs and the Elect Nation* (London, 1963), chap. 7.

[19] J. Aylmer. *An Harborowe for Faith-full and Trewe Subiectes* (Strassburg, 1559), sig. P4v.

[20] Chamberlin, *Sayings of Queen Elizabeth*, p. 108.

growe againe *in this realme of England*'.[21] In later years, as the early sense of insecurity receded, the role of the elect nation became progressively more ambitious. In *The Ruine of Rome* (1603), the Essex clergyman, Arthur Dent, envisaged England taking part in the physical destruction of Rome—in alliance, however, with France, Italy and Spain which would have accepted the protestant faith.[22] In the seventeenth century the theory of the elect nation fused with millenarianism, and was in large part the basis of the wish to carry the English Revolution into Europe.[23]

The firm establishment of protestantism in England, and the progress of Calvinism in France, the Netherlands and Germany constituted a major improvement in the general European religious situation. Dent's confidence that 'the Protestants shall have the day' throughout Europe was far removed from Aylmer's limited aspirations at the outset of Elizabeth's reign.[24] Dent was fully in line with earlier Elizabethan eschatology, however, in denouncing millenarianism as a 'foolish error' and regarding the fall of Rome and the end of the world as virtually simultaneous events—indeed he argued that the defeat of the Armada in 1588 represented the beginning of Armageddon [25] But with the spread of protestantism in the second half of the sixteenth century, the hope was born of overthrowing Antichrist by the preaching of the Gospel. This new hope was developed into an academic eschatological system by Thomas Brightman (1562–1607), minister of Hawnes, Bedfordshire, and a critic of the Anglican church from a presbyterian and possibly separatist position. Though ascribing to Elizabeth and Cecil an honourable role as the agents of two of the divine vials of wrath poured on Antichrist (Revelation xvi), Brightman condemned Anglicanism as the 'luke-warm' Laodicea of Revelation iii. 14–18. His eschatological scheme retained the traditional view of Satan's binding (Revelation xx. 2) as from 300 to 1300, but this was to be followed by a second millennium in which the saints would reign on earth in a purified Church. This millennium had begun around 1300 with Marsilio and later Wyclif,

---

[21] Foxe, *Acts and Monuments*, iv, p. 114; Aylmer, *An Harborowe*, sigs O4r, R3r (my italics).
[22] A. Dent, *The Ruine of Rome* (London, 1607), pp. 250-1.
[23] C. Hill, *Puritanism and Revolution* (London, 1962), pp. 130 ff.; cf. my *The Fifth Monarchy Men*, pp. 37-8, 151-4.
[24] Dent, *Ruine of Rome*, p. 238.   [25] *Ibid.*, pp. 218, 268.

and increasing steadily in glory would soon, with the fall of Rome, reach perfection.[26] The European situation which shaped Brightman's thinking gave rise to similar expositions on the continent, including those of Daniel Cramer, Lutheran professor at Stettin, in 1618, the French Calvinist, Matthieu Cottière (fl. 1604–55) and later the Dutch Calvinist Jacobus Koelman (1633–95).[27]

Brightman's millenarian exposition was to have immense and enduring influence in England, but its monopoly was soon challenged by a still more radical theory. Shortly after 1600 the European situation changed rapidly for the worse, and the Thirty Years' War threw in doubt the very survival of protestantism. Schemes of a millennium spreading gradually over a lengthy period by evangelical efforts became increasingly difficult to reconcile with political reality. A more relevant system was produced by the celebrated encyclopaedist, Johann Heinrich Alsted, professor at Herborn. Alsted initially expounded a 'gradualist' system, but under the stress of the war which forced him into exile, he began to teach that the millennium was wholly future, and that it would be established imminently by a cataclysmic series of events. The most systematic English expositor of the 'cataclysmic' school was Joseph Mede, a Cambridge theologian. Mede, who suggested a millennium to begin abruptly with the fall of Rome, was almost certainly influenced extensively by Alsted's writings.[28]

It is difficult to measure the extent of millenarian ideas in England derived from Brightman, Mede and Alsted, but in the 1640s they were certainly both widespread and expanding rapidly. An analysis of the writings of over a hundred of the foremost ministers supporting Parliament in this period suggests a figure of roughly 70 per cent expressing such beliefs with varying

[26] T. Brightman, *The Revelation of St. John* (London, 1644), pp. 824–5 and *passim*. There is a useful summary of his eschatological system in P. Toon (ed.), *Puritans, the Millennium and the Future of Israel: Puritan Eschatology 1600–1660* (Cambridge, 1970).

[27] See my *The Fifth Monarchy Men*, Conclusion.

[28] J. H. Alsted, *The Beloved City* (London, 1643), esp. pp. 13–19; J. Mede, *The Key of the Revelation* (London, 1643), *passim*. For the development of Alsted's thought and its influence on Mede, see R. G. Clouse, 'The Influence of John Henry Alsted on English Millenarian Thought' (Univ. of Iowa, Ph.D. thesis, 1963), pp. 108–205; there is a summary by Dr Clouse in Toon, *op. cit.*, chap. 3.

degrees of emphasis.[29] Professor John Wilson, in *Pulpit in Parliament*, has not ventured to give statistics, but after analysing the fast sermons of the 1640s he has concluded that belief in the millennium was 'the most striking and fundamental characteristic of the formal preaching before the Long Parliament'.[30]

Dr Nuttall remarked some years ago that millenarianism was so common among Independents that to 'go through the country' making 'a list of names would be tedious'.[31] Professor Wilson goes further in suggesting that the founding of a gathered church was a 'specific anticipation of a broader reign of Christ', and that millenarianism was part of the definition of Independency, one of its 'differentiae' from traditional puritanism[32]—where he is clearly at odds with Dr Lamont. He wisely does not insist that all or only Independents were millenarians, among whom he includes such figures as Henry Wilkinson and the more equivocal Stephen Marshall. But it is not made clear whether the Presbyterians are included in the category of traditional puritanism, and if this is the case, it would seriously underestimate presbyterian interest in the millennium as a period of 'latter-day glory'. The presbyterian ideal was of a gradual, spiritual development, leaving largely untouched the social and political system. It was summarized by the Scottish Presbyterian, James Durham, in the remark that 'the Kingdom of our Lord is come, when . . . Religion is countenanced, and Kings become nursing fathers to the Church; all the Saints do not become Magistrates, but God maketh Magistrates Saints'.[33] In practice, however, English millenarianism in the 1640s and 1650s was of a notably composite character, in which the 'gradualist' and 'cataclysmic' models were merged. Many Presbyterians, in accepting Stephen Marshall's interpretation of the Civil War as an apocalyptic struggle to decide 'whether *Christ*, or *Anti Christ*, shall be *Lord* and *King*', were leaving Durham's position far behind.[34] At the other end of the spectrum, the Fifth Monarchists, whose professed readiness to set up

[29] For details see *The Fifth Monarchy Men*, pp. 38–9, 46–9.
[30] J. F. Wilson, *Pulpit in Parliament* (Princeton, 1969), p. 195.
[31] G. F. Nuttall, *Visible Saints: the Congregational Way 1640–1660* (Oxford, 1957), pp. 146, 148.
[32] Wilson, *op. cit.*, pp. 229 and 223.
[33] J. Durham, *A Commentarie upon the Book of the Revelation*, 3rd edn (Amsterdam, 1660), p. 712.
[34] R. L'Estrange, *Dissenters Sayings: the Second Part* (London, 1681), p. 73.

Christ's Kingdom by the sword makes them the most likely 'cataclysmic' group, accepted some kind of gradual process. Their most gifted expositor, John Tillinghast, rector of Trunch in Norfolk, interpreted the vials of wrath leading to the fall of Antichrist as a long-extended series of events beginning with Luther's first declaration of the truth. Tillinghast synthesized Brightman and Mede by dividing the millennium into two parts, a 'gradualist' prologue in which the saints lay the foundations of Christ's Kingdom, to be brought to a 'cataclysmic' perfection by Christ's triumphant and dreadful return in 1701.[35]

Now that millenarianism is no longer identified solely with the sectarians, it has become clear that its peak was in the 1640s, not later, and Professor Wilson and Dr Lamont both make this point. The 1650s witnessed a retreat from a doctrine which had become the ideology of a radical social change.

The decline of millenarianism was itself, however, an extended process. Such beliefs remained an important, if diminishing, aspect of nonconformist thought for the remainder of the century, and continued to be championed by such prominent sectarians as Hanserd Knollys. Moreover, the evangelical impetus given by the millenarian yearning to bring the whole world under Christ's rule continued for centuries rather than decades. It was the millenarian aspects of the Propagation of the Gospel in Wales which made it so dear to the saints, and failure there was followed by prolonged efforts in foreign lands, a theme which is traced in the work of Dr de Jong, *As the Waters Cover the Sea*.[36]

The books reviewed here still leave a need for a history of English millenarianism and of Reformation preoccupation with eschatology. Dr Lamont's book is indeed designed rather as an attempt to 'provoke . . . to thought and occasionally to violent disagreement'. Together, these works should have secured the primary achievement of moving the subject away from the neglected wings of historical research and writing and nearer the centre of the stage.

---

[35] J. Tillinghast, *Knowledge of the Times* (London, 1654), and *Generation-Work* (London, 1653–4).

[36] For an interesting Catholic parallel of apocalyptic and evangelical fervour in the sixteenth century, see J. L. Phelan, *The Millennial Kingdom of the Franciscans in the New World*, 2nd edn (Berkeley and Los Angeles, 1970).

XXVIII

RICHARD BAXTER, THE APOCALYPSE AND THE MAD MAJOR*

William Lamont

In 1686 Richard Baxter was actively engaged in millenarian research. This discovery is doubly upsetting. It is the wrong man at the wrong time. Dr Christopher Hill, in his recent book on the subject, has Antichrist dying in England by 1660.[1] Dr Capp, in his review article in this journal, is more cautious. He speaks of the decline of interest in millenarianism in England as 'an extended process'. But he recognizes that it *is* in decline and looks for its residual champions to sectarians like Hanserd Knollys rather than to mainstream Protestants like Richard Baxter.[2] In Dr Hill's formidable parade of seventeenth-century Englishmen who were involved with Antichrist, Baxter only squeezes in one appearance: and that for a parenthetical cynicism.[3]

In this article I want to make three points that arise from this discovery. First, I shall argue that it raises doubts about Dr Capp's approach to millenarianism. The schematic rigour which he brings to the study in depth of one committed theological school —the Fifth Monarchists—may not be the way to understand less committed groups or individuals. Mr Edward Thompson has urged on his fellow historians of a later period of English history

---

* From no. 55 (May 1972).
[1] Christopher Hill, *Antichrist in Seventeenth-Century England* (London, 1971), p. 164: but his theology is latitudinarian enough to allow for a post-1760 resurrection.
[2] Bernard Capp, '*Godly Rule* and English millenarianism', *Past and Present*, no. 52 (August 1971), p. 117; p. 398 in this volume.
[3] Hill, *op. cit.*, pp. 136–7.

the importance of a generous approach to the problem of millenarianism: above all, the need to be sensitive to the *imagery*—of Babylon and Egyptian exile and the Celestial City and contest with Satan—'in which minority groups have articulated their experience and projected their aspirations for hundreds of years'.[4] Baxter's notes in prison in 1686 show an involvement with the Apocalypse that is intelligible on Mr Thompson's premises, but which is not easy to reconcile with Dr Capp's categorizations. Second, I shall argue that this involvement does not mark a radical departure in Baxter's thought—a senile aberration—but is one which flows from earlier concerns. I shall try to show that his encounter with a Mad Major was particularly fruitful in this respect. Third, I shall argue that Baxter's doctrinal evolution is more closely related to these millenarian explorations than has commonly been supposed. Much more work needs to be done before either of the last two points can be substantiated: this is in the nature of an interim report which will, nevertheless, I hope, reopen some questions about seventeenth-century English millenarianism.

Dr Capp has drawn our attention to a number of recent works on this subject which have succeeded in moving millenarianism 'away from the neglected wings of historical research and writing and nearer the centre of the stage'.[5] The stereotype of the millenarian as a fanatic died hard. Englishmen in the seventeenth century found it difficult to talk about millenarianism without talking about the excesses of a John of Leyden. Those who attacked millenarianism exploited the stereotype; those who defended it dissociated themselves from it. It was something of a landmark when J. H. Alsted cheerfully admitted that, on three out of six basic points, he *agreed* with the wild men of Munster.[6] No less when

---

[4] E. P. Thompson, *The Making of the English Working Class* (London, 1963), p. 49.   [5] Capp, *op. cit.*, p. 117; p. 398 in this volume.
[6] J. H. Alsted, *The Beloved City* (London, 1643), pp. 70-1. Alsted sides with them on three points: that Antichrist will be destroyed *before* the Millennium; that *during* the Millennium the Church will be free from persecutions; that *after* the Millennium the War of Gog and Magog shall begin. But he disapproves of: their preference for carnal pleasures over spiritual joys; their belief that Christ will reign visibly on earth; their readiness to join this Millennium to the end of the sixth Millennium of the World.

Cromwell memorably squashed the intolerant Crawford: 'Ay; but the man is an Anabaptist. Are you sure of that? Admit he be, shall that render him incapable to serve the Public?'[7] Now most Englishmen at that time would have thought three out of six an inflationary agreement and would have shared Crawford's misgivings about the Anabaptists. What we have learned from the works which Dr Capp cites[8]—and from others which he does not[9] —is to mistrust such reflexes as our guide to how Englishmen viewed the Apocalypse. The pursuit of the millennium could take routes undreamed of by John of Leyden. This knowledge makes it possible for the subject to move away from the wings and nearer the centre of the stage.

But it may soon return to the wings if Dr Capp has his way. He draws his categories with confidence. There are two vitally different conclusions which Revelation produced: 'the pessimistic belief in an imminent doomsday, and the optimistic expectation of an earthly paradise'.[10] Millenarianism is quite distinct from utopianism: the belief in a perfect society to be established through divine intervention from one created by man's unaided efforts.[11] Belief in the imminence of the millennium leads a self-proclaimed Elect to establish a disciplinarian holy commonwealth.[12] The difficulty comes in relating these categories to individual figures. Not to J. H. Alsted for whom the optimistic expectation of an earthly paradise *is* quite distinct from the coming of doomsday;[13] in others—even Mede—the distinction is blurred. In their

---

[7] Thomas Carlyle (ed.), *Oliver Cromwell's Letters and Speeches* (London, 1897), i, p. 182.

[8] In particular: John F. Wilson, *Pulpit in Parliament* (Princeton, 1969); P. Toon (ed.), *Puritans, the Millennium and the Future of Israel: Puritan Eschatology 1600–1660* (Cambridge and London, 1970); J. A. de Jong, *As the Waters Cover the Sea: Millennial expectations in the rise of Anglo-American missions 1640–1810* (Kampen, 1970).

[9] In particular: Hill, *Antichrist in Seventeenth-Century England*; William Haller, *Foxe's Book of Martyrs and the Elect Nation* (London, 1963); P. Toon (ed.), *The Correspondence of John Owen (1616–1683)* (London, 1970); Marjorie Reeves, *The Influence of Prophecy in the Later Middle Ages: A Study in Joachism* (Oxford, 1969).

[10] Capp, *op. cit.*, p. 107; p. 387 in this volume.

[11] *Ibid.*

[12] *Ibid.*, p. 112; p. 393 in this volume.

[13] Alsted, *op. cit.*, p. 77: 'No place of Scripture teacheth us that the last Judgement is at hand'.

sermons to the Commons in the early 1640s the London ministers *combine* a utopian vision of reform through human agency with an equal confidence in a millennium that will come without such efforts.[14] The message varied with the mood—or, rather, the strategy—of the moment. Holmes and Symonds were rare birds[15] among the London ministers in spelling out the details of their millenarian hopes: most of the others remained pegged at generalities about the downfall of Antichrist and the building of a New Jerusalem. To call these 'prophetic hopes' is one way out of the impasse, but this is as weak a term for describing those eschatological expectations that the ministers shared with their less reticent colleagues as Dr de Jong found it for his similarly placed seventeenth-century missionaries.[16] Other Protestants are even further outside Dr Capp's categories. Certainly Foxe and Jewel are, who 'thus could not be founders of a millenarian school'.[17] But even Brightman is a doubtful case: three hundred years of his future millennium have already passed. The discovery that Hobbes adopted a millenarian structure cannot save him since he failed to believe in the *imminence* of a messianic reign.[18] And there is no evidence that the witch-hunters of the 1640s read Brightman.[19] Whom then are we left with? Mede, Alsted, Tillinghast: not quite the centre of the stage. Has the historian rescued millenarianism from the exclusive claims of the anthropologist only to surrender it into the hands of the theologian?

This is not quite fair to Dr Capp. Much of his rigour is welcome. Given his premise, his arguments are developed in a logical way. He has some suggestive remarks about the influence of Cramer, Cottière and Koelman on the continent. He makes good my neglect of Mede and Alsted. He finds unconvincing my efforts to fit the Laudians into the millenarian framework of my *Godly Rule*: I think now that he is right.[20] But his other

---

[14] See my article, 'Episcopacy and a "Godly Discipline", 1641-6', *Jl of Ecclesiastical History*, x (1959), pp. 76-7.
[15] The details are in Holmes rather than in Symonds, but it is clear that they were working in concert: Nathaniel Holmes, *The New World, or the New Reformed Church* (London, 1641), p. 9.
[16] De Jong, *op. cit.*, p. 2.
[17] Capp, *op. cit.*, p. 108; p. 388 in this volume.
[18] *Ibid.*, p. 112; p. 393 in this volume.
[19] *Ibid.*, p. 110; p. 391.
[20] *Ibid.*, pp. 115, 107, 108; pp. 403-4, 387, 388.

criticisms show that he has not understood my purpose in writing
Godly Rule. It was not intended—as I made clear explicitly in an
introductory note—to provide 'a systematic analysis of millenarian thought in the seventeenth century'.[21] I agree with Dr Capp
that that still has to be written but I look for rigorous studies—
like his own work on the Fifth Monarchists[22]—on specialized
aspects of the period to hasten that day. In the meantime I was
concerned with the more modest aim of tracing the extent to
which millenarian assumptions influenced many men whom we
too readily assume to be outside that influence. One such was
William Prynne. My account of this Puritan, published in 1963,
was based upon a detailed study in depth of all his writings. I
had learned from them that his dependence upon Foxe had given
way by 1641 to a dependence upon Brightman.[23] I could hardly
be unaware that this change involved a different way of looking at
the Apocalypse. I even quoted Robert Baillie's sour perception
that English radicalism—presbyterian or Independent—distanced
itself from its Scottish counterpart precisely by its millenarian
commitment. Even with all these advantages in my favour I
found myself using almost every epithet bar one to describe
Prynne's position in 1641: 'ethical craving', 'expectant rejoicing',
'radical', 'messianic recklessness'. But I shrank from the word
'millenarian'.[24]

There were two reasons for doing so in 1963. One was that—
following Norman Cohn's brilliant study[25]—I associated the
term with radical fanaticism. And I knew that the pamphleteer
of 1780 who saw Prynne in such terms was talking nonsense.[26]
Ergo, Prynne was no millenarian. The other was the absence, in
Prynne, of such a detailed apocalyptic programme as could be
found in Mede and Alsted, Holmes and Symonds. While Dr
Capp would argue the falsity of the first position, he would
accept the logic of the second. I would argue that they are equally

---

[21] William Lamont, *Godly Rule: Politics and Religion 1603-60* (London,
1969), p. 8.
[22] Toon (ed.), *Puritans, the Millennium and the Future of Israel*, pp. 66-90,
contains an interesting essay by Dr Capp on 'Extreme millenarianism'
which whets our appetite for his forthcoming study on Fifth Monarchists.
[23] William Lamont, *Marginal Prynne* (London, 1963), pp. 59-84.
[24] *Ibid.*, pp. 62, 79, 76, 84.
[25] Norman Cohn, *The Pursuit of the Millennium* (London, 1957).
[26] [Anon.], *Equitable Representation Necessary . . .* (London, 1780), p. 23.

distorting: they both push millenarianism into the wings of historical research. I would argue that my technical correctness in 1963 masked a failure of imagination: I had not succeeded in bringing out to the full the extent to which Prynne was moved by millenarian impulses that were articulated more convincingly by some of his colleagues. Dr Pocock's recent essay on Hobbes showed that my attempt to redress the balance, even in 1969 with *Godly Rule*, did not at times go far enough. Thus my fifth chapter may have shown that the Erastians of the 1640s also had their millenarian dreams, but I contrasted them throughout with the cynical Hobbes. Dr Pocock makes us think afresh about Hobbes.[27] Dr Capp remains curiously unexcited by what he admits to be 'testimony to the prevalence of millenarian ideas: the discovery that Hobbes, even while living abroad, adopted a millenarian structure of thought absent from his earlier work'. For Dr Capp the important point is that Hobbes 'rejected any attempt by a self-proclaimed Elect to establish a disciplinarian holy commonwealth'.[28] But this was equally true of Coleman, Prynne and the other chiliast Erastians who opposed the attempts of *antichiliast* presbyterian divines, like Robert Baillie, to establish a disciplinarian holy commonwealth.

Dr Capp sees Henry Burton as a prime figure in my thesis of millenarian 'shift'.[29] I had argued that Burton—like Prynne—had not in 1628 pursued a fascination with Brightman to its logical conclusion; only in 1641—with the rejection of Foxe—did 'centripetal' millenarianism become 'centrifugal'. Dr Capp sees a simpler solution. Burton's 'royalist phase' in 1628, when he argued that the end of the world would follow presently on the fall of Antichrist, is contrasted with his adoption of millenarianism (from Brightman) in 1641 once he had rejected monarchy. But the truth is more complex. *Both* pamphlets show a striking debt to Brightman. But in 1628, as a critic noted, Burton was unconvincingly selective: he quoted the most that he could from

[27] J. G. A. Pocock, 'Time, history and eschatology in the thought of Thomas Hobbes', *The Diversity of History: Essays in Honour of Sir Herbert Butterfield*, ed. J. H. Elliott and H. G. Koenigsberger (London, 1970), p. 180: 'Neither the use of apocalyptic in *Leviathan*, nor its mortalism and materialist literalism, suffice to place Hobbes outside the mainstream of Protestant thinking.'

[28] Capp, '. . . English Millenarianism', p. 112; p. 393.

[29] *Ibid.*, p. 110; p. 390.

Brightman without damaging the Foxeian Christian Prince.[30] In 1641 he had no such scruples. The apocalyptic 'coincidence' of seven trumpets, seals and vials that fascinated him in 1641 was already fascinating him in 1628: the difference was that he made open acknowledgement to Mede in only the later pamphlet for that insight. And he was just as coy in 1641 as he had been in 1628 about extending his speculations beyond the fall of Antichrist.[31]

Whether witch-hunters read Brightman or not would only matter if my attempt *was* 'to make millenarian puritanism the cause of English witchcraft persecutions'.[32] Dr Macfarlane, in his scrupulously undramatic investigation of witchcraft, did not find an explicit millenarian commitment among the leaders of the witch-hunting movement in East Anglia in the 1640s. However he stressed that villagers 'already imbued with millenarian concepts, viewed the witch-finders with considerable excitement'.[33] It is a point to which he returns in his re-creation of the family life of Ralph Josselin: 'This mental world, so full of omens and symbolic nuances, contained few barriers against rumours of witchcraft and the millennium, of monstrous births and meetings with the devil.'[34]

Josselin, the sceptic-parson, is no millenarian in the Mede-Alsted-Tillinghast mould, but he has intimations in common with Prynne, Burton, Coleman and Hobbes. This is not obvious at a first glance. Dr Macfarlane speaks of his 'commonsense scepticism'. Josselin dismissed as fantastic a book of 'Welsh prophecies, which asserts that Cromwell is the great Conqueror that shall conquer Turke and Pope'. He noted in his diary for 1656 that

[30] Hugh Cholmley, *The State of the Now-Romane Church* . . . (London, 1629), pp. 3–4.
[31] Henry Burton, *The Seven Vials* (London, 1628), *passim*; *The Sounding of the Two Last Trumpets* (London, 1641), p. 2. Note in the latter pamphlet, written as late as 1641, his self-denying ordinance on the twentieth chapter of Revelation: 'because they be very obscure, and will require longer time and stronger Prayers for assisting and illuminating grace in the opening of them: therefore I will here put an end for the present, till it shall please God to give a further opportunitie' (p. 93).
[32] Capp, '. . . English Millenarianism', p. 110; p. 391.
[33] Alan Macfarlane, *Witchcraft in Tudor and Stuart England* (Harper Torchbooks, 1970), p. 141.
[34] Alan Macfarlane, *The Family Life of Ralph Josselin* (Cambridge, 1970), p. 189.

'some think their very world would end in 56'. A few months later he spoke of 'that stupendous yeare of 1656, of which men have had strange thoughts' but added that he 'was not of their minde'. Josselin may not have been of their mind, but he did add that he too expected 'notable effects'. And there are other passages in his diary which indicate that 'commonsense scepticism' is not all that one can say about Josselin's views on the Apocalypse. Dr Macfarlane notes that the first record of his meditations on the subject was on 17 November 1650 when his thoughts were 'much that god was beginning to ruine the kingdom of the earth, and bringing christs kingdom in'. Dr Macfarlane does not make the point, but it is an important one, that Josselin's first vision coincides with the date of Elizabeth I's accession to the throne. For a Puritan, reared on Foxe and the cult of Astraea, the date was not fortuitous. And we know that Josselin supplemented Foxe by reading both Brightman and Mede. In 1653 he was urged by an uncle to carry on with his 'apocaliptiq studdies'; earthquakes in England and floods in France in 1650, he thought, must 'portend something'; a year later he noted that apocalyptic rumours about the date 1655 were rampant in Poland. Most remarkable of all is the entry for 2 March 1651 in which he records the dream of his five-year old daughter, that:[35]

> Jesus Christ was in our church, and went up into my pulpitt, and that he stayed a while, and then he came down and came into bed to her; she sayd to him, why dost you come to me, and he answered her, to sleep a little with thee, and he lyd downe and slept; and again she dreamd that Jesus Christ told her that he should come and rayne upon the earth 10000 years.

The challenge posed to historians by Josselin—and, it will be argued, by Baxter—is to do justice to the genuine horror that the Millennium inspired in the socially conservative and to the subversive spell which it wove over the theologically adventurous and—most difficult task of all—to recognize that *both impulses could, as often as not, be found in one and the same person.* Josselin could dismiss Welsh prophecies, but not those of his five-year-old daughter; James I could arrest Finch and Gouge in 1621 for demanding the return of the Jews into England to fulfil the

[35] Macfarlane, *The Family Life of Ralph Josselin*, pp. 189, 190, 185.

Apocalypse but debate with Selden on the precise significance of the number 666.[36] This is the context in which we must try to reassess Richard Baxter's thought.

The case for a reassessment of Baxter is not self-evident. He is a much-researched figure: in his own right—and not merely as a football in the Weber-Tawney controversy[37]—he has earned two major studies by F. J. Powicke and G. F. Nuttall.[38] But Dr Nuttall's important work is a narrative of his career rather than an analysis of his thought. And Powicke was disarmingly frank about the limitations of *his* analysis. He commented on the *Baxter Treatises* in the Dr Williams's Library:[39]

> The existence of these has been no secret. They have long been known, and, to some small extent, have been used. But thirteen folio volumes of close writing, often not easy to decipher, and quite as often concerned with things utterly dead and done with, may well have seemed rather a forbidding task; nor do I pretend to have had either the time or the will to explore the whole mass. I have simply looked it through with more or less care.

Ostensibly it is even less likely than with Josselin that a study of Baxter's manuscript collection would reveal the Apocalypse high among the list of things 'utterly dead and done with' that had preoccupied him. And this for several reasons: he avoided the subject in his published writings; he disliked the way that Brightman and his followers 'Englished' Scripture to suit their interpretations; he was a moderate in the Ussher tradition; he was horrified by the Munster excesses. If we look at each of these objections in turn we will see that they are less formidable than they look.

[36] John Selden, *Table Talk*, ed. F. Pollock (London, 1927), p. 158.
[37] E.g. Lawrence Stone, 'Social mobility in England, 1500–1700', *Quantitative History*, ed. D. K. Rowney and J. Q. Graham (Illinois, 1969), p. 261, on the Puritan ethic: 'There is some reason to believe, however, that this ideological factor did not become fully operative until the 1630s, for its best theoretical expression comes from Richard Baxter'.
[38] F. J. Powicke, *A Life of the Reverend Richard Baxter 1615–1691* (London, 1924) and *The Reverend Richard Baxter Under the Cross 1622–1691* (London, 1927); G. F. Nuttall, *Richard Baxter* (London, 1965).
[39] Powicke, *A Life of the Reverend Richard Baxter* ,preface

First, Baxter did write little on chiliasm. His boast to Harrington was that, on the subject of the Millennium, 'I am myself as merely neutral in it as in almost any point of so great moment so often propounded to my consideration'.[40] In his great flood of controversial writings there seems to be little more than a tiny trickle on the Apocalypse. This is where the discovery of his 1686 notes among his manuscript material is of such importance: I shall return to this later in the article.

Second, he held no brief for Brightman and his school:[41]

> I loathe such expositions as Brightman's that say (This Angel was Thomas Cromwell, and that Angel was Cranmer etc.). He that will figure that I meane English when I expound Gods words that speake of all or other Churches, will judge his own words and not mine.

Clearly he finds Brightman's technique at fault, but it is easy to exaggerate the distance between them. A more important point may be Brightman's inclusion in a very special category of Baxter's :the precious Few whom Baxter looks forward to meeting in Heaven.[42]

Third, while there is certainly no distance between Baxter and Archbishop Ussher, the latter's influence on him may not have been to encourage a blanket rejection of Revelation. Baxter's hero-worship of the Archbishop inspired such unmemorable verse as:[43]

> If but three such in all our times
> As USHER, GATAKER and VINES.

But Ussher's involvement with the Apocalypse agitated Baxter to the extent of an interview with him on the subject:[44]

> I had heard of his Predictions that Popery would be restored in *England* for a short time, and then fall for ever. And asking him of it, he pretended to me no prophetical Revelation

[40] R. B. Schlatter, *Richard Baxter and Puritan Politics* (New Brunswick, 1957), p. 84.

[41] (Doctor Williams's Library), *Baxter Treatises*, i, fo. 82.

[42] Richard Baxter, *The Saints Everlasting Rest* (London, 1677), p. 82.

[43] Baxter, *Poetical Fragments* (London, 1681), p. 124.

[44] Baxter, *Reliquiae Baxterianae*, ed. M. Sylvester (London, 1696), pt ii, p. 206.

for it, to himself, but only his Judgment of the Sense of the Apocalyps.

The distinction may have satisfied Baxter but is blurred in at least one of Ussher's disciples, Pierre Jurieu. Baxter elsewhere had denounced the 'marvellous confidence' of Jurieu in such matters, but it is striking how indebted Jurieu's chiliast pamphlet of 1687, *The Accomplishment of the Scripture Prophecies*, is to Ussher:[45]

the famous *Prophecy* of Usher Arch-bishop of Armagh, who fore-tells *a most terrible Persecution at hand*, the most dreadfull of any which the Church hath suffer'd hitherto; but withall, the *shortest*: after which shall come the *fall* of the *Antichristian Empire*.

Fourth, John of Leyden may have been a more powerful figure than Ussher in encouraging a blanket condemnation of Revelation. Certainly the stock clichés recur in Baxter's autobiography:[46]

It was such Dreams that transported the *Munster* Anabaptists, and the Followers of *David George* in the Low Countries, and *Campanella*, and the *Illuminati* among the Papists, and our English Anabaptists and other Fanaticks here, both in the Army and the City and Country. When they think the Golden Age is come, they shew their Dreams in their extravagant Actions: And as our Fifth Monarchy Men, they are presently upon some unquiet rebellious Attempt, to set up Christ in his Kingdom whether he will or not.

Among the unpublished material in the Baxter collection is a remarkable letter which he wrote on 30 May 1654, which enables us to penetrate behind the clichés to what Baxter really thought about chiliast fanatics.[47] It is worth discussing at some length because it throws light upon the 1686 apocalyptic material that has recently been discovered among Baxter's papers.

[45] *Baxter Treatises*, vi, fo. 356v; Pierre Jurieu, *The Accomplishment of the Scripture Prophecies* (London, 1687), sig. 4r; for Jurieu's important influence on the Camisards, see D. P. Walker, *The Decline of Hell* (Chicago, 1964), pp. 253–63.

[46] Baxter, *Reliquiae . . .*, pt i, p. 133.

[47] *Baxter Treatises*, iii, fos 302–9.

The letter was written to Henry Bromley—a man like so many at that time, who had become infected by Ranter and Fifth Monarchist heresies. Baxter believed that men like Bromley were vulnerable to the chiliast prophets through their melancholia: 'Excessive solicitousnesse and thoughtfulness doth habituate some of them to Melancholly which gives the Tempter advantage to possess them with Deluding phantomess.'[48] The tragedy was that good men were especially susceptible to melancholia. Baxter has drawn elsewhere a striking contrast between two good puritan ministers whom he loved: jolly Simeon Ashe and James Nalton 'the Weeping Prophet', who wept his way to a premature grave.[49] Baxter wanted to be an Ashe, and fought those impulses in his nature that drew him to Nalton. An exchange he recorded with Hyde at the time of the Savoy Conference had left its mark on him:[50]

At our first entrance he merily told us, (*That if I were but as fat as Dr* Manton, *we should all do well*). I told him, if his Lordship could teach me the Art of growing fat, he should find me not unwilling to learn, by any good means. He grew more serious, and said, That I was severe and strict, like a Melancholy Man, and make those things *Sin* which others did not.

Baxter wanted to underline the dangers of melancholia by a personal example. He told Bromley of his experiences when he was staying in Coventry during the Civil War. There he met a Scot, Major Wilkie, 'who came from Northampton to fortifye the citty, being excellent at the worke'. Baxter and Wilkie lived in the same house, and Baxter soon knew him well. He respected Wilkie's linguistic gifts and his knowledge of Scripture. For a month Wilkie lived an orderly life and was a regular church-goer. It was in this period that Wilkie told Baxter about 'the first of his Revelations' that had come to him as a student in Paris. Wilkie was accustomed to sleepless nights and rising 'in his shirt and walking about the chamber'—Baxter makes an aside to Bromley at this point: 'You may see by that he was melancholy'—and one night he saw out of the window a remarkable sight:

[48] *Baxter Treatises*, iii, fo. 302v.
[49] Baxter, *Reliquiae . . .*, pt ii, p. 431.
[50] *Ibid.*, pt. ii, pp. 364-5.

In a Constellation the perfect similitude of a Lyon Rampant
at the Moone: which while he beheld one foote broake of and
turned to the liknes of a cocke: and then broke of a 2nd, and
then a 3rd, and then the 4th . . . while he was admiring at
this, there stood up . . . the similitude of a crowned glorious
prince and the moone did shine in its fullest glory.

Wilkie went back to bed, and in his sleep the significance of his
vision was revealed to him. The cloud was the darkness that
would engulf the Church; the lion was King Charles I who would
persecute the Church; the feet that broke off were the Church in
Ireland, England, Scotland and Wales; the 'crowned glorious
prince' was one called 'the prince of the Nations'. Baxter went on:

Of this Prince he interpreted many prophesies which we
commonly Interpret of Christ. . . . It was Revealed to him,
that Christ should come and raigne on Earth personally a
1000 yeares and the Prince must prepare the World for his
2nd comeing, as John Baptist did for the first: that persone
should be a Northerne man of meane parentage (he thought
a Knight) and have a Certain Mark on his Cheeke: and he
should conquer and subdue the Nations, France, Spain,
Italy, and so pull down the Pope, and remove the Impedi-
ments of the Jews Coming, and then at the end of his raigne
Christ should come and himself convert the Jews and destroy
the Mahometans. There were yet he said, three changes to
be expected (1) the signe of the prince (2) Christs comeing
to raigne 1000 yeares: It he called the time off the Restitution
of all things (3) The end of the 1000 yeares which he called
the time of the New Creation.

Baxter noted that, after thunder, Wilkie rejoiced since it presaged
a victory for Parliament in the Civil War. He had other visions at
certain times. The last one he confided to Baxter was at Easter:

In the morning he told me that on the night (on good
friday) it was revealed to him that the Warre should last a
yeare and halfe longer; 3 yeares and a halfe in all: and then
the parliament would have the better and warre cease: But
by reason of Dissensions and quarrels among ourselves we
should not be settled till 1648 and then we should see the
beginning of a glorious Church and State.

Baxter injects here a sardonic note:

> But many garrisons were long after that untaken and two
> more warres have already ensued, which the prophet knew
> nothing of. And 1648 is past, without any such glorious
> change as he foretold.

Throughout the narrative Baxter is a sceptical observer. For
instance, Wilkie hears spirits crying 'and in the morning he
professed he made a chamber pott full of blood'. Baxter corrects
Wilkie with scientific know-how: 'I told him the motion of the
blood might stir his phantasye, and cause that dreame which he
called a voice.' When Baxter leaves for Shropshire he makes a
pact with Wilkie. Baxter promises to believe him if Wilkie's
spirit will maintain communion with him. But Baxter heard
nothing. And what became of the Mad Major? Baxter proceeds
to tell Bromley with some relish:

> If you aske me now, what he was, and what became of him,
> I will tell you that you may see what Spirits he had commu-
> nion with. He was a constant Drunkard (after a few months
> of Civill life) and would spend whole days in Darknes and
> lye in bed on the Lords day, and say he knew more than we
> could teach him. . . . The next newes I had of him was that
> he was carried bound starke madd to his friends into Scotland,
> and what became of him since I cannot tell. But I remember
> one of his Revelations was, that he should live until Christ's
> Second Comeing, to raigne visibly at Jerusalem: and if that
> be true he is yet alive.

Baxter, sardonic then to the end, now draws the moral of the
episode: 'You may ask why I wrote the tedious Story. I will tell
you why.'[51] We know why. Baxter, the rationalist, is pointing out
to Bromley the dangers of chiliast fantasies. We could not be more
wrong. There is a sting in the tail.

Dr Clifton noted, in a recent number of this journal, that
anti-Catholic panics never involved supposed conspiracy against
the King's life 'With the exception of William Prynne who
believed that the Jesuits had executed the King in 1649'.[52] He

[51] *Baxter Treatises*, iii, fo. 306v.
[52] Robin Clifton, 'The popular fear of Catholics during the English
Revolution', *Past and Present*, no. 52 (August 1971), p. 54, and note.

was seriously underrating the dimensions of that fear. It was not Prynne only who believed it: so did Peter du Moulin, Sir William Morice, Bishop Bramhall and Richard Baxter. The Catholic apologist, Davenport, knew it as a commonplace among ordinary people since the time of the king's execution; he only began to suspect the worst when he saw it 'confirmed by two sober and eminent persons, Mr. Prynne in his *Good Old Cause* and Mr. Backster in his *Key for Catholicks*'.[53] Baxter was not then in 1654 denouncing, from a rationalist position, the hysteria of the irrational; rather he was denouncing, from a protestant position, yet another Popish Plot:

> The Jesuits are subtill and wicked, able to outreach 100 young men and make them believe that they converse with Angells, when they are but befooled by these Juglers. . . . He is blind that sees not the hand of Rome, where is so much of the Interest of Rome involved. . . . Their maine drift is to Disgrace the Scripture as Insufficient which is the master point of our difference with them. If they gett this they thinke they gett the day.

What better way to discredit Scripture than the bait of a 'perfecter Revelation' which 'is to be expected'? What better way to confuse men than to persuade them of a new kind of Babylon and Antichrist? Baxter comments:

> . . . don't you see the Popish interest in all. I confesse some learned Divines have doubted whether the Pope be Antichrist. Zanchy denied it. But the Jesuites well know that if they could roote the opinion from the minds of the people, the day were halfe won. Its not the cleare Evidence and Reason of the matter that so much takes with Vulgar minds, even in best causes, as the Reputation of the matter with those whom they honor. The common opinion that the

---

[53] Brit. Mus., Stowe MS. 755, fo. 14; Peter du Moulin, *A Vindication of the Sincerity of the Protestant Religion* (London, 1671), p. 64; 'Sancta Clara' Davenport, *A Clear Vindication of Roman Catholicks from a Foule Aspersion* (London, 1659), p. 3; White Kennett, *A Register* . . . (London, 1659), pp. 504, 615; James Ussher, *Whole Works*, ed. C. R. Elrington (Dublin, 1847), i, pp. 262–5; Baxter, *Reliquiae* . . ., pt ii, p. 373; *Baxter Treatises*, iii, fos 261v–262v.

Pope is Antichrist doth prevaile more with the Vulgar that can't dispute against particular doctrines of Rome, than all the direct Arguments that are used.

The Jesuits well know this and seek to discredit the thesis that Rome is Antichrist:[54]

And at least they are confident that if they do no more, they shall certainly do this much: they shall make that so seeme a doubtfull controversy, which before seemes to the people past question, when tis seen that so many are of another minde, they will have the advantage of deriding our change and will tell us how many opinions about Babylon and Antichrist are among us—tis more than probable that there is some blacke Jesuiticall Art that doth dreame up the whole designe.

Far from finding the apocalyptic insight that Rome is Antichrist absurd, Baxter seeks to defend it: his quarrel with the fanatics is not for *asserting* the doctrine but for *subverting* it.

We return to the first and most telling objection to linking Baxter with the Apocalypse: that his writings support his claim to Harrington 'to be as merely neutral in it as in almost any point of so great moment'. This is not true. The lie has come to light with the rearrangement of the catalogue of Richard Baxter papers in the Doctor Williams's Library.[55] The Librarian, Roger Thomas, brought together a group of papers which he described in his Introduction to the catalogue as 'the product of the anxious enquiries Baxter undertook into the Book of Revelation during his prison sentence in 1686'. Thomas thought that 'Age probably prevented his publishing this sobering challenge to the wild men of his day.'[56] At which we must ask: which wild men? Isaac Newton? Henry More? Thomas Beverley? Christopher Hill is surely right in arguing that by the 1680s and 1690s the occasional wild chiliast is seen as a challenge to medicine rather than to

---

[54] *Baxter Treatises*, iii, fo. 306v.

[55] Roger Thomas, *The Baxter Treatises* (Dr Williams's Library, Occasional Paper, no. 8, 1959). See also G. F. Nuttall, *The Manuscript of the Reliquiae Baxterianae* (Dr Williams's Library, Occasional Paper, no. 1, 1954). All of us who step gingerly into Baxter territory are permanently in debt to these two scholars for their masterly organization of the Baxter manuscript material. [56] Thomas, *op. cit.*, p. 2.

Church and State.[57] If Baxter's papers merely represented his repudiation of John of Leyden then one could fault his timing: they would have made more impact earlier. Baxter himself offers an explanation. In 1685 he published his *Paraphrase of the New Testament* and admitted his ignorance of the Book of Revelation.[58] The notes of 1686 could simply be his attempt to shore up these deficiencies. Thomas said of the manuscript collection as a whole that 'Much of the material Baxter must have intended to publish; that he never did so is of interest; indeed an interesting study could be made of the books Baxter did not publish and of the reasons why he did not publish them'.[59] But we have seen that Thomas terminated speculation about the non-publication of the apocalyptic material: age had conquered Baxter.

Thomas was wrong. It was not chance that prevented publication of Baxter's papers. He wrote above some of his notes the following words: 'Some generall thoughts on the Revelations . . . set down for my own memory and not for the sight of any other'.[60] Why was he being so secretive? If what he was saying was nothing more than a curse on Fifth Monarchists, why should he fear publication? The answer was that he was saying much more than that: he was developing insights which were hinted at in his letter, thirty years earlier, to Bromley.

Baxter distinguished five sorts of exposition of Revelation: literal, cabalistical, conjectural, rational and revelational. The first three were bogus, and could be dismissed out of hand. The fourth was legitimate: by this process Ussher had arrived at apocalyptic truths. The fifth was the controversial point and Baxter tried to keep an open mind about it: 'Revelationall; By propheticall Inspiration or Vision':[61]

> This last John Fox sweareth by an Appeal to God that he had and some others too have bin as confident as if they had visions: I can boast of no such thing.

Here was the dilemma for Baxter. He himself could boast of no such visions. Those who could, like Major Wilkie, were knaves

[57] Christopher Hill, 'John Mason and the end of the world', *Puritanism and Revolution* (New York, 1964), pp. 323–36. But note the violent reaction to the Camisards in 1707: Walker, *op. cit.*, p. 254.
[58] Baxter *Reliquiae* . . ., pt iii, p. 198.   [59] Thomas, *op. cit.*, p. 2.
[60] *Baxter Treatises*, ii, fo. 102.   [61] *Ibid.*, ii, fo. 103v.

or fools, depending upon whether they were consciously or unconsciously advancing the Jesuit cause. But Foxe could not be pigeon-holed into that category. In 1690 Baxter expressed his gratitude to More and Beverley for drawing him in his last years into a deeper study of Revelation than he had ever undertaken before. He mentioned with pride the authorities he had consulted: among them, Peter du Moulin, Napier, Forbes, Lee, Thomas Goodwin, Stephens and Potter. None came closer to satisfying him than Foxe:[62]

> And of any one I have read John Fox cometh nearest my judgment of the *Five Times and halfe* and of the *42 months* . . . and of that thousand yeares binding of the dragon, and of the *greatest Antichrist*, but not of the *time of his fall*.

Baxter was well aware of the supreme value of Foxe as a demonstration of the falsehood of Popery:

> Foxe's Book of Martyrs will tell you of many undeniable remarkable judgments on those adversaries of pure Religion, the Papists, whose greatest wickedness is against these Scriptures. . . . Yea our own times have afforded us most evident examples . . . such that might silence an Atheist or an Antiscripturist.

When Wilkie read in the clapping of thunder an omen for Parliamentary victories Baxter was amused. This does not prevent Baxter from making an earnest marginal note while in the process of recording some of these 'evident examples':[63]

> About the time of the silencing of Ministers, how many Churches in *England* were torn at once with terrible lightning, and almost no place else, but Churches were touched, especially in the lower part of *Devonshire*, where many were scorched, maimed, and some their brains struck out as they sate in Church.

Lightning significant, thunder not: this is a good example of Baxter's double-think on such matters. Visions and omens in the context of Foxe's insights were invested with a significance denied to the dreams of Major Wilkie.

[62] *Baxter Treatises*, iv, fo. 246v.
[63] Baxter, *The Saints Everlasting Rest* . . ., p. 246.

Baxter could not persuade himself into a total concurrence with
Foxe. But he was aware of the perils of parading too publicly his
differences with Foxe. The Protestant Cause in England seemed
to pivot around Foxe and the martyrs, and the thesis that Rome
was Antichrist. How eagerly the Jesuits would pounce on any
protestant backsliding on such matters! No wonder Baxter had to
veil his scruples, keep 'not for the sight of any other' his agonies
over the Apocalypse. As Baxter himself frankly explained:[64]

> But the main cause is, that so many Martyrs and Protestants
> have been of this opinion (drawen much by sufferings and
> similitude) that now a man that doth but doubt of it is
> accused of a forerunner of Popery; and the beliefe and trust
> of men is become like an Article of Divine Faith; and men
> dare not think otherwise for feare of censure and being lost
> among a party.

Hence the paradox: if millenarianism had been merely a lunatic
fringe activity, Baxter would have had to indulge an *attraction*
towards it furtively. Because it was not, because it was in the
mainstream, Baxter could be drawn to it in the same way as were
his beloved Ussher and Brightman. What Baxter had to be furtive
about—even in the late 1680s—was the range of his *scepticism*.
Baxter could weigh in with gusto against millenarianism in
'literal', 'cabalistical' or 'conjectural' form—in the activities of
the Captain Venners and the Major Wilkies. His argument, it will
be remembered, was that it was he, not they, who was defending
the thesis that Rome was Antichrist. But his argument did not
stop there. When apocalyptic interpretation found 'rational' or
'revelational' expression Baxter's response, like Josselin's, was
ambivalent and troubled. Appalled, he tried to check—in public
at least—a growing scepticism that struck at the eschatological
foundations of the English Reformation itself: the Foxeian
mission to destroy the Roman Antichrist.

Baxter's scepticism about identifying Antichrist with Rome was
no more incompatible with his authorship of *A Key for Catholicks*
than his rejection of Major Wilkie had been. In neither case did
it imply rationalism or a softening of attitudes to Popery. Baxter,
indeed, as part of his 'humble search into the sense of the Revelations' recited at great length a catalogue of Papist atrocities. He

[64] *Baxter Treatises*, vi, fo. 357.

commented wearily: 'And when and where it will stop God knoweth'! But for Baxter the important point is this: 'I do not believe that any text of Scripture tells us that any Antichrist should shed so much blood.'[65] It is not so much that the Papists are not bad enough to be identified with Antichrist; in respect of blood-shedding *they are too bad*. And, no more than Hobbes did, will Baxter allow a detestation of Popery to obscure his rational perception that Rome does not equal Antichrist. But Baxter reaches that conclusion by very different routes from Hobbes. I have only summarized very briefly some of the conclusions of highly involved and closely wrought arguments about the Apocalypse, which are developed at great length in these unpublished papers and which must be dealt with in much more detail at some later date. But they do reveal that Baxter is not arguing from the outside but from the inside: from a commanding familiarity with the controversial literature around the subject. And from the inside he is sensitive—in a way that Hobbes is not—to the damage that could be done to the Protestant Cause by the public discrediting of Foxe's identification of Antichrist with Rome. In the technical sense Dr Capp may be correct in arguing that Foxe was not a millenarian and thus could not be founder of a millenarian school, but it is striking how Baxter cannot—any more than Prynne, Josselin or Burton—avoid taking up an attitude to Foxe when speculating about the Millennium.

We have only begun to scratch the surface of Baxter's involvement with the Apocalypse. A number of questions spring to mind. What impact is made upon Baxter by his arguments with Beverley and More in the 1670s and 1680s? How *does* Baxter discriminate between 'literal', 'cabalistical' and 'conjectural' interpretations of the Apocalypse on the one hand, and those that were 'rational' (like Ussher's) and 'revelational' (like Foxe's) on the other? How do his thoughts on Revelation relate to his views on prodigies—too credulous even for credulous Wesley[66]—as expounded in his *The Certainty of the World of Spirits?* A notable gap at present is the paucity of evidence on what Baxter thought about the Millennium in the 1640s as opposed to what he later *thought* he thought (as in his letter to Bromley). Much more work

[65] *Baxter Treatises*, vii, fo. 277.
[66] John Wesley, *Journal*, ed. N. Curnock (Capricorn Books, 1963), p. 313.

then needs to be done before we can put these contributions of
Baxter in a proper context. Perhaps the case against Dr Capp
is that the rigidity of his categorizations discourages us even from
making a start. What we might lose in the process may best be
made clear by a closer look at one aspect of Baxter's thought:
his growing revulsion from Calvinist dogma.

The Wilkie affair had many morals. One was explicitly drawn
by Baxter himself when he quoted approvingly one critic's
retort:[67]

> Major Wilkie these things seem strange to me; but for my
> part I cant believe that they are of Gods: for if God would
> reveale his will so extraordinarily it would surely be to some
> better man than you; for you know how badd a life you lead.

Two disagreeable consequences of over-emphasizing Grace—a
trait which the older Baxter deplored in his younger self[68]—were
the complacency it inspired in those who saw themselves as the
Elect and the melancholia it inspired in those who saw themselves
as damned. The Mad Major at one end of the spectrum: the
'Weeping Prophet' at the other. Baxter hit at both views in an
attack on the Quakers in 1675:[69]

> I was present in Worcestershire when a Quaker at the
> Assizes walked through the High Street starke naked: as a
> propheticall Act (as others did in other places). In
> Worcester one of them by whimsies grew melancholy, and
> when he had debilitated himself by abstinence went out and
> was found drowned in so small a water as that it was
> supposed he did it voluntarily.

From neither the antinomian nor the manic-depressive[70] could
come the practical pastoral concern that counted for so much
with Baxter.

[67] *Baxter Treatises*, iii, fo. 303v.
[68] Baxter, *Reliquiae . . .*, pt i, p. 129: 'And nothing pleased me so well as
the Doctrine of Regeneration, and the Marks of Sincerity; which was
because it was suitable to me in that state: but now I had rather read, hear
or meditate, on God and Heaven, than on any other Subject.'
[69] *Baxter Treatises*, vi, fo. 8v.
[70] Powicke, *The Reverend Richard Baxter Under the Cross*, pp. 58–9,
shrewdly noted the distance of the mature Baxter from the preoccupations
that tormented Bunyan.

In a recent essay Mr Michael Walzer has explored the revolutionary uses of repression.[71] He quotes Baxter's claim that discipline in his congregation was enforced by 'the zeal and diligence of the godly people of the place, who thirsted after the salvation of their neighbours and were in private my assistants'. Walzer argues that the ultimate bias of the revolutionary is that nobody is incapable of being stirred. He marvels at the paradox of how this belief is yoked in Baxter to rigid Calvinist dogma:[72]

> Even among the Puritans, whose doctrine of predestination would seem to make inequality permanent and inevitable, the actual practice of collective repression in the congregation could produce the extraordinary hope that all men join in the good work and England become 'a land of saints, and a pattern of holiness to all the world'.

But this is not a paradox; in Baxter's case, this just is not true. The practice did not produce the hope in defiance of the doctrine, the practice and the hope produced a different doctrine.

The practice of collective repression, the hope of a land of saints, grew incompatible in Baxter's eyes with adherence to a belief in the Predestination of the Elect. He tried himself to obscure this development. He had, on his own admission,[73] been too rude about the Arminians in Laud's day to be happy to be called one later. At the least he could now denounce the zeal of those 'that cryed *An Arminian, A Devile: The doctrine of Arminians, the doctrine of the devill'*.[74] And, while denying in 1690 that *he* was an Arminian, he could utter—from a Calvinist point of view—such damaging statements as 'I cannot grant that any man truly loving God and perfect holynes can be damned'.[75] He once confessed that he had planned *The Saints Everlasting Rest* in three

---

[71] Michael Walzer, 'The revolutionary uses of repression', *Essays in Theory and History*, ed. M. Richter (Cambridge, Mass., 1970), pp. 122–36.
[72] *Ibid.*, p. 128. Walzer is correctly quoting from Baxter, but elsewhere Baxter rebuked Eliot: 'The Rich will rule in the World, and few rich Men will be Saints' (Baxter, *Reliquiae . . .*, pt ii, p. 297).
[73] *Baxter Treatises*, i, fo. 261: 'I did ignorantly think that Arminianisme (which Dr. Heylyn maketh the chiefe matter then of the Strife) had bin a more intollerable pernicious evill to the Church, and part of Popery, than since I found it'. Cf. also *Baxter Treatises*, i, fo. 67v: 'Parliaments also crying down Arminianisme that know not what it was'.
[74] *Ibid.*, v, fo. 25.   [75] *Ibid.*

columns: two extremes and the truth in the middle.[76] This was how he saw his doctrinal navigation: steering a passage between John Goodwin and Twisse. There is something in the claim, but the logic of controversy led him increasingly to emphasize the points which divided him from Calvinist Twisse rather than from Arminian Goodwin.[77] And won for him the cruel nickname of 'Bellarmine Junior'.[78]

The controversy over free admission to the Sacrament of the Lord's Supper exposed Baxter's distance from orthodox Calvinism. There were two logical—but contradictory—inferences which Calvinists could draw from their doctrine of Grace. One was that God was Inscrutable and that an attempt to discriminate the Elect from the Reprobate was a blasphemy. This was the orthodox Presbyterian argument for free admission as voiced by the Scot, Robert Baillie. The second was that the Elect must withdraw from the company of the ungodly in order to establish a pure communion. Baillie was correct to read millenarian implications into the second position:[79]

> Scripture makes the Church of God so long as it is upon earth
> to be a mixed multitude of Elect and Reprobate, good and
> bad. . . . But, the doctrine in hand [the millennium] changes
> the nature of the Church, and makes it for a thousand
> yeares together to consist onely of good and gracious
> persons, without all trouble, without all Ordinances, without
> any need of Christs intercession.

Dr Dallison, in one of the essays on millenarianism edited by Mr Peter Toon, wonders how far 'the Independents' doctrine of Churches composed only of "visible saints" influenced their

---

[76] Baxter, *The Saints Everlasting Rest* . . ., dedicatory epistle.

[77] This did not pass unnoticed by contemporaries. See W. Eyre, *Vindiciae iustificationis gratuitae* (London, 1654), dedicatory epistle, 'To the Christian Reader', sig. A3r: 'how highly he magnifies *J. Goodwin*, with others of his notion, and how slightingly he mentions Dr. *Twisse*, and all our Protestant Divines that differ from him'.

[78] *Baxter Treatises*, i, fo. 81v: 'These filled the City with the murmurs that I had written that the Pope is not the Antichrist, that not Papall but Heathen Rome is the Babilon, and the Heathen Empire the beast mentioned Revel. 13 etc.'.

[79] Quoted by A. R. Dallison in Toon (ed.), *Puritans, the Millennium and the Future of Israel* . . ., p. 106.

eschatological position'; he suggests that it rendered the concept of the millennium more acceptable to them than it could ever be to the Presbyterians.[80] Such speculation is reinforced by the researches of Dr Wilson, who suggests that the founding of a gathered church was a 'specific anticipation of a broader reign of Christ'.[81] Dr Capp is worried if this leads to an underestimation of Presbyterian interest in the millennium as a period of 'latter-day glory'.[82] Dr Dallison and Dr Wilson are both probably right to think that the man who was anxious to keep the communion pure was also more likely to be a millenarian than one who favoured open admission, but equally Dr Capp is probably right to think that Independents had no monopoly of such concern for purity of communion. That is the significance of the phenomenon which I emphasized in *Godly Rule*: of the defection of so many *Presbyterians* from Baillie's position in the controversy over admission to the Sacrament of the Lord's Supper. Baillie—aware that most of his English colleagues, and not merely the Independents, were 'expresse Chiliasts'[83]—was therefore not surprised, but was displeased, to see so many English Presbyterians joining with Independent ministers in the search for a pure communion. It is a commonplace that Scottish Presbyterians failed to impose their will on English Puritanism. Not enough attention has been paid to the impact the other way round: of English Puritanism upon Scottish Presbyterianism. That it was a profound one (and not for the good) has been argued by Professor J. B. Torrance:[84] a view which receives some contemporary support in the bitter attacks made by advocates of free admission like Thomas Coleman and Henry Jeanes upon a Presbyterian turncoat like George Gillespie.[85]

Baxter was an opponent of Gillespie, it is true, on this issue and yet he was equally unhappy with free admission. He insisted on the search for 'order and decencye' as a protection from

[80] Toon (ed.), *Puritans, the Millennium and the Future of Israel*, p. 106.
[81] Wilson, *op. cit.*, p. 229.
[82] Capp, '. . . English millenarianism', p. 116; pp. 397–8 in this volume.
[83] Robert Baillie, *Letters and Journals*, ed. D. Laing (Edinburgh, 1841–2), ii, p. 313.
[84] J. B. Torrance, 'Covenant or contract? A study of the theological background of worship in seventeenth-century Scotland', *Scottish Jl of Theology*, xxiii (1970), pp. 51–76.
[85] Lamont, *Godly Rule . . .*, pp. 146–8.

antinomianism.[86] This was too lax for those who stipulated a 'deeper discoverie'[87] in the communicant, but too austere for those who wanted free admission:[88]

> affrighted the poor soules from all hope of entring . . . no prophane or unclean person hath right to meddle with this Grace. No, first they must have such heart-preparations, purifications and prejacent qualifications, before they draw neer to partake of mercy; must first cleanse and cure themselves, and then come to Christ afterwards; must be cloathed with an inherent Righteousnesse first, and then expect to be cloathed upon with a Righteousnesse imputed.

Baxter had committed the unforgivable sin: in this Calvinist civil war, he had opted for neutrality.

So had others. Christopher Hill calls the breakdown of Calvinism in the mid-seventeenth century 'one of the great turning-points in intellectual history'. He contrasts the 'old Arminianism of the Laudians' with 'the new Arminianism of John Goodwin and Milton and the Quakers'.[89] What do Goodwin, Milton and the Quakers have in common with Baxter?

John Goodwin began in the early 1640s with a vision of the destruction of Antichrist and 'executing the judgments of God upon the Whore', moved on in 1646 to a denunciation of the 'unpolitic Christians' who 'catch at the spiritual privileges of New Jerusalem before it comes down from heaven', and arrived five years later at the point where he was asserting the goodness and rationality of Man.[90] The young Milton looked to the establishment of a New Jerusalem in five weeks; the mature Milton

[86] (Doctor Williams's Library) *Baxter Correspondence* 59.1, fo. 253. Cf. Baxter, *Reliquiae* . . ., pt ii, p. 406: 'If the Pastors will not differ between the precious and the vile, by necessary regular Discipline; tender Christians will be tempted to difference by irregular Separations'. Also *Baxter Treatises*, i, fo. 40—attacking a supporter of free admission—'I hope the Christian Church will keepe the safe middle way between yours and unwarrantable separation'.

[87] *Baxter Correspondence* 59.3, fo. 196: the phrase is Philip Nye's, in a letter to Baxter; it is echoed in the Declaration that the Independent ministers drew up at the Savoy Conference of 12 October 1658 (Benjamin Hanbury, *Historical Memorials*, London, 1844, iii, pp. 525–6).

[88] John Crandon, *Mr. Baxters Aphorisms* . . . (London, 1654), sig. C2v.

[89] Christopher Hill, *God's Englishman* (London, 1970), p. 215.

[90] Lamont, *Godly Rule* . . ., p. 180.

extolled the patience of Job. Mr Fixler convincingly argues that Milton's Arminianism arises in protest at the rule of 'Saints' who were patently unworthy.[91] The Messianic blasphemy of James Nayler was a gift to opponents of Quakerism; less often emphasized is the stimulus which it gave to Quakers themselves—and, not least among them, to Nayler—to reappraise their theology.[92]

Baxter did not become an Arminian merely because of the antics of Major Wilkie. But among the forces that drew Baxter away from rigid Calvinism was a perception of the mischievous social consequences of such a belief. John Crandon, for one, believed that Baxter's horror of the Antinomians' teaching that 'no more required to the perfect irrevocable Justification of the vilest Murtherer or Whoremaster, but to believe that he is justified' had driven him fatally into the arms of the Arminians.[93] We do not need to accept such a simplistic explanation to see the advantages of exploring the relationship between such attitudes and his views on the Apocalypse. Two things in the past have stood in the way of such exploration. One is Baxter's public posture of cold neutrality: the outsider who can view with detachment the excesses of Munster Anabaptists. The other is the restriction, by Dr Capp and others, of millenarianism to clearly defined limits: Baxter does not belong to the categories that confine Brightman, Mede and Alsted. The new evidence of Baxter's interest in the Apocalypse does not totally remove both of these objections. The private Baxter remains opposed to the social fanatics and, on the big questions raised by Brightman, Mede and Alsted, he retains a broad scepticism. The revisionism operates at a more subtle level. *Baxter rejects Major Wilkie, it is true, but from the inside*, with an insider's sympathy for many of the premises held by Wilkie, but not for the consequences drawn from them. And ultimately this leads to a questioning of the premises themselves. And yet the very sympathy that he has with those premises is a barrier against prematurely publicizing his disenchantment.

The new Arminians of the 1650s were the old chiliasts of the

[91] John Milton, *Selected Prose*, ed. W. M. Wallace (Oxford, 1963), p. 314; M. Fixler, *Milton and the Kingdom of God* (London, 1964), *passim*.
[92] G. F. Nuttall, *James Nayler: A Fresh Approach* (Friends' Historical Soc. Jl Suppl., no. 26, 1954), *passim*.
[93] Crandon, *op. cit.*, Preface.

1640s. Why should the excesses of a Nayler or a Wilkie have had such a traumatic effect upon them? *Because Nayler and Wilkie were not peddling lies, but were parodying truths*. They took truths acceptable to most Protestants—the Predestination of the Elect; the equation of Rome with Antichrist; the imminence of the New Jerusalem—and made of them something monstrous. Baxter had said briskly of witches: 'Cheats are numerous, but realities also very sure'.[94] His long letter to Bromley in 1654 is really a sermon on that text. But we have seen that it was in practice no easier for Baxter than it was for John Goodwin, Milton and the Quaker leaders to maintain that distinction: an attack on the cheats broadened to an attack on the realities. Arminius, for example, never provided a more solid argument for the value of good works than did the Mad Major. Baxter's notes on the Apocalypse in 1686 show how far he had broadened his attack since 1654; his determination, on the other hand, to keep them 'not for the sight of any other' shows the constancy of his fear that Popery would be the ultimate beneficiary of a scepticism that was pushed too far.

In 1686 Baxter was in prison: old and ailing. Throughout his life he had attacked the chiliast cheats; now he was not even sure of the realities which they had distorted. Baxter's determination, nevertheless, to keep these scruples 'not for the sight of any other' is as remarkable a testimony to the central pull of the Apocalypse on protestant loyalties as that provided by the other recent research that we have discussed in this article. To renounce openly the Apocalypse—even as late as 1686—was to dishonour the memory of the protestant martyrs. As much for Protestants in the seventeenth century, as for their predecessors in the sixteenth century, Foxe had the last word.[95]

[94] *Baxter Treatises*, iv, fo. 357.
[95] How happy Foxe would have been with this distinction is, of course, another matter. A good recent study of Foxe by V. N. Olsen—which, I hope, will soon find publication—emphasizes the gap between Foxe's *objectives* in writing his *Acts and Monuments* and their subsequent *effect*. Olsen criticizes both Professor Haller and myself for confusing the two on occasions.

Since this article was written I have found, tucked away in an epilogue to some of his prison writings, the fullest personal statement from Baxter of how he came to be involved with the Apocalypse (*Baxter Treatises*, vii, fos 294v–302v). Particularly important are his instructions to his literary executors about his millenarian writings. He asked that they be referred to an 'impartiall Godly Divine' and, if found inadequate, burned. If not, he asked that they be kept 'utterly secret till the Designe of papall prevalency be blasted by the providence of God'. This is not inconsistent with my view that Baxter was, at this time, primarily concerned not to upset the orthodox Foxeian case against 'papall prevalency', whether by arguments that were relevant but weak, or by ones which were strong but irrelevant. But he does not mention Foxe, other views are clearly possible, and the need to set my tentative hypotheses very carefully beside Baxter's own statement of his position is obvious. Baxter remains maddeningly opaque about his earlier commitment—'I was once allmost drawn to the Millenary opinion' (*ibid.*, fo. 296)—but there is rich additional material about the nature of his later commitment.

THE MILLENNIUM AND ESCHATOLOGY IN ENGLAND*

Bernard Capp

Anyone who has followed the course of a seventeenth-century pamphlet controversy would be reluctant to revive the genre. In recent numbers of this journal and elsewhere, Dr Lamont and I have set out differing sketches of the role of millenarianism in early modern England.[1] This is still a relatively new field of study, and there remain too many gaps in our knowledge to make prolonged theorizing at this stage very productive. We are agreed, I think, on the fundamental point—the importance of millenarianism in this period—and I trust that differences over its interpretation will not obscure a more general recognition of this. Before leaving the debate, I would like in this note to correct some mistaken conclusions drawn by Dr Lamont from my article, to spell out the areas on which we can agree as well as those where we still differ, and to place my earlier very brief sketch of English millenarianism[2] in the wider context of general eschatological interest.

The distance between us can be narrowed, first, by removing the misconceptions arising out of my review article. Thus, in

---

* From no. 57 (November 1972).

[1] W. M. Lamont, Godly Rule: Politics and Religion 1603-60 (London, 1969); ——, 'Puritanism as history and historiography: some further thoughts', Past and Present, no. 44 (August 1969), pp. 133-46; ——, 'Richard Baxter, the Apocalypse and the Mad Major', ibid., no. 55 (May 1972), pp. 68-90 (pp. 399-426 in this volume); B. S. Capp, 'Godly Rule and English millenarianism', ibid., no. 52 (Aug. 1971), pp. 106-17 (pp. 386-98); ——, The Fifth Monarchy Men (London, 1972), esp. chap. 2.

[2] Capp, 'Godly Rule', pp. 112-17 (pp. 395-8).

recalling the distinction between utopia and millennium, I was *not* implying that English millenarians expected New Jerusalem to appear by divine action alone.[3] Almost all accepted that God worked through human agents: demands for reform by parliament in the 1640s were the more insistent because parliament was seen as God's instrument and the reforms as part of the divine plan. Despite Dr Lamont's confidence, I certainly would *not* insist on the composition of a detailed exposition of a chiliastic creed as part of the definition of a millenarian.[4] Of course most men expressed their beliefs in the turn of a phrase or a short passage rather than a systematic, prolonged analysis of the prophecies. These misconceptions led to the charge that my approach would relegate millenarianism 'to the wings'.[5] I am not sure how this could be reconciled with my (possibly rash) assertion in the review that roughly 70 per cent of leading clergy supporting parliament during the Revolution, many of them moderate Presbyterians, held millenarian ideas—though statistics cannot, of course, record variations in the character of the millenarian beliefs or strength of commitment.[6] Two further earlier points of difference can also be resolved. Dr Lamont has now withdrawn his thesis that millenarianism played an important role among the Laudians. Moreover I am sure he was right to challenge my rather loose claim that the 'mass of contemporary millenarians' were preoccupied during the puritan revolution with creating a disciplinarian theocracy.[7] Though this was understandably the brand which most alarmed the ruling classes, it was only one of many forms the doctrine could and did take.

We are agreed on the importance of millenarianism, and several of the points of disagreement can thus be reconciled. But two major differences remain. First, Dr Lamont believes there was only a 'technical' distinction, little noticed even by contemporaries, between what I will call the 'apocalyptic' approach (expecting an imminent doomsday) and the 'millenarian' (expect-

[3] Lamont, 'Richard Baxter', p. 70 (p. 401); Capp, *'Godly Rule'*, p. 107 (p. 387).

[4] Lamont, 'Richard Baxter', pp. 70, 72 (pp. 402, 403).

[5] *Ibid.*, p. 70 (p. 401) in this volume.

[6] Capp, *'Godly Rule'*, p. 115 (p. 396); for details see my *Fifth Monarchy Men*, pp. 38–9, 46–9.

[7] Lamont, 'Richard Baxter', pp. 70, 71 (pp. 402, 403); Capp, *'Godly Rule'*, p. 112 (p. 393).

ing an age of perfection on earth).[8] Secondly, partly as a result, I believe that he ascribes too ubiquitous a role to millenarianism, which he sees as embracing the extremes of King James and Cromwell, Hobbes and the sectarians, acceptable to 'the orthodox mainstream of . . . religious thought' and influencing 'the *mainstream* of political thought until the time of the Civil War'.[9]

My own view is rather different: that on the whole contemporaries *did* preserve an awareness of the distinction between millenarian and non-millenarian eschatology, and that modern analyses should be correspondingly specific. I believe there *was* a consensus among English Protestants that current events were the fulfilment of the Biblical prophecies of the latter days; but that this consensus did not extend to agreement on an imminent millennium, a doctrine which remained suspect (though widespread) until the Revolution in the 1640s. The Reformation, stressing the Bible as the literal Word of God, made almost inevitable a literal rather than allegorical interpretation of the scriptural prophecies. Several responses, however, were possible. One could argue that the prophecies, though genuine, were so 'dark and dubious' that they were best ignored until God chose to make clear their meaning. Or, secondly, it could be argued, as by Foxe, Jewel and others, that the prophecies referred to the Reformation and subsequent events, and proved that the end of the world was at hand. Thirdly, the prophecies could be seen as foreshadowing the fall of existing world-orders, not the world itself, and heralding an age of perfection on earth. The second line of interpretation, elaborated by Foxe, enjoyed almost universal acceptance among Elizabethan Protestants. Dr Hill has documented the general acceptance of the belief that Rome was Antichrist,[10] accompanied usually by an expectation of its downfall amidst the dissolution of the world. This gloomy vision of the approaching end contained nevertheless several important elements of comfort. Protestants were assured of their orthodoxy and their salvation in the next life. The idea of Elizabeth destroying Antichrist in England appealed to English jingoism, fanned

[8] Lamont, 'Richard Baxter', p. 83 (p. 418).
[9] Lamont, *Godly Rule*, pp. 19, 25.
[10] Christopher Hill, *Antichrist in Seventeenth-Century England* (London, 1971), chap. 1.

further by the concept of the elect nation, which implied a reworking of Calvinism, all the more popular for branding foreigners as the reprobate.[11] The elect nation theory coexisted and no doubt sometimes fused with the literary cults of Elizabeth as Gloriana or Astraea, reviving a golden age based on classical rather than Biblical sources.[12] But Foxe himself (and probably most contemporary writers, beneath the literary flourishes) was preoccupied with the problem of political and religious insecurity: the danger to Protestant England when a disputed succession and religious differences gave France and Spain ample justification for invasion. As the elect nation, England had a special role as God's champion, implying also a special degree of protection. But there was an awareness that this was a David-and-Goliath situation, and that absolute security would come only through God's intervention at the last day. Moreover, the literary symbolism of the golden age coexisted with the widespread but contradictory belief in universal decay.[13] Though religious truth was preached, Archbishop Sandys (like Jewel) felt that it was an age not of gold but of unparalleled corruption and degeneracy. Afflictions, he told a congregation at Paul's Cross, would end only with 'the end of all things, [which] is at hand'.[14]

Foxe's interpretation remained widespread up to and beyond the Civil War, but by that date it no longer represented a Protestant consensus. At a semi-popular level, eschatology was often linked with astrology, and Professor Stone has suggested that the failure of the great conjunction of 1583 to produce the predicted cataclysm foreshadowing the world's end led to a reaction against Biblical as well as astrological prophecies.[15] Perhaps more important were changes within the Anglican Church. An emphasis on eschatology is essentially a dynamic attitude, concerned with major transformations in the world. The religious upheaval of 1558–9 made this appropriate for the early Anglican Church,

[11] Cf. W. Haller, *Foxe's Book of Martyrs and the Elect Nation* (London, 1963).

[12] F. A. Yates, 'Queen Elizabeth as Astraea', *Jl of the Warburg and Courtauld Institutes*, x (1947), pp. 27–82.

[13] See, for example, V. Harris, *All Coherence Gone* (Chicago, 1949).

[14] E. Sandys, *Sermons*, ed. J. Ayre (Parker Soc., ii, Cambridge, 1841), p. 387.

[15] W. B. Stone, 'Shakespeare and the Sad Augurs', *Jl of English and Germanic Philology*, lii (1953), pp. 457–79, esp. p. 467.

especially as many of the first bishops sympathized with the more radical Protestant movements abroad, and hoped for further changes in England. But the gradual rise of a generation of bishops who regarded the Elizabethan settlement as permanent made an eschatological emphasis much less attractive. Determined to preserve the *status quo* at home, and suspicious of the church systems of the Huguenots and Dutch Calvinists, the Anglican Church rapidly shed any dynamic outlook. The eschatological preoccupations of Jewel, the first major champion of Anglicanism, are conspicuously absent from the works of the second, Richard Hooker, a generation later. The Church did not abandon the idea that the end of the world was approaching, and that Rome was Antichrist—which was, after all, a basic guarantee of Protestant orthodoxy. But an emphasis on the prophecies slowly became identified with the sector of English Protestantism which still sought change, the Puritans and separatists. Jacobean and later satires—by Ben Jonson, Richard Corbet, Abraham Cowley and Samuel Butler—ridiculing Puritan preoccupation with Biblical predictions only make sense if the earlier consensus no longer existed.

With the growing breach in the later Elizabethan Church, more extreme Puritans sought to justify their position, and guarantee their success, by stressing the elements of Antichrist remaining within the episcopal church. The bishops themselves were denounced as 'limbs of Antichrist'. Whitgift remained constant to his earlier belief that the Pope was Antichrist, but was stung in the 1570s to denounce Cartwright and the Presbyterians as the 'tail . . . of Antichrist' and the means by which the Church was most threatened.[16] This attempt to adapt the struggle of Christ and Antichrist to the Elizabethan *via media*, with Antichrist representing both extremes, was not altogether successful; a more natural, and satisfactory response was to minimize eschatological speculations. Whitgift, for example, warned the Puritan, Richard Rothwell, to cease preaching almost exclusively from Daniel and Revelation.[17]

Professor Collinson has marked the emergence among Elizabethan Puritans of belief in 'some kind of apocalyptic victory

[16] J. Whitgift, *Works*, ed. J. Ayre (Parker Soc., xliv, xlviii, l, Cambridge 1851–3), ii, p. 182; iii, p. 495; Hill, *op. cit.*, chap. 2.
[17] Capp, *Fifth Monarchy Men*, p. 32.

which would bring in the discipline', though despite the wealth of recent work on the movement, this process has not been fully documented.[18] Probably it reflected in part disillusion with appeals to parliament to pressurize Elizabeth into further reforms, and was strengthened later by the failure of appeals to the Stuart kings to reverse the trend towards a *iure divino* episcopacy. Developments on the continent certainly had a major impact: Huguenot and Dutch Calvinist successes in the late sixteenth century bred hopes that a league of Protestant nations might overthrow Antichrist without the physical reappearance of Christ. The turmoils of the Thirty Years' War transformed this 'gradualist' millenarian belief into a more 'cataclysmic' approach.[19] Millenarian ideas were primarily a Puritan phenomenon, and while there were sometimes appeals to the crown against episcopal trends, the general approach was of criticism towards the Stuart regime.

The early seventeenth-century Church did not promote any counter-doctrine advancing the Stuarts as messianic emperors. As suggested above, its approach was to reduce eschatological debate, and Archbishop Laud and his supporters even dared to question whether the Pope really was Antichrist.[20] Such a step undermined doctrines accepted since the beginning of Elizabeth's reign: for if Antichrist was not even positively identified, it was futile to expect his imminent overthrow, and there was no longer a basis for believing the world to be in its last stages, witnessing the unfolding of the prophecies. Royalist, Anglican beliefs in a messianic monarchy only became of any importance during the Interregnum, when royalism itself had become a doctrine of change.[21] It witnessed a revival in the 1690s, focusing on hopes that William III, having overcome the forces of Antichrist in England, would sweep them aside on the continent.[22]

Two final points. Dr Lamont reproaches me for being 'curiously

---

[18] P. Collinson, *The Elizabethan Puritan Movement* (London, 1967), pp. 389–90.

[19] P. Toon (ed.), *Puritans, the Millennium and the Future of Israel: Puritan Eschatology 1600–1660* (Cambridge, 1970), *passim*; Capp, *Fifth Monarchy Men*, chap. 2.

[20] Hill, *op. cit.*, pp. 36–9.

[21] Capp, *Fifth Monarchy Men*, pp. 41, 194.

[22] Much of this was of a semi-popular, astrological character; I hope to discuss this aspect elsewhere.

unexcited' by Hobbes's use of a millenarian structure of thought. Dr Pocock's discovery—of the prominent role of eschatology in Hobbes—is indeed of major importance, but the point remains difficult to interpret satisfactorily. Hobbes was perhaps unique as a millenarian who seems to have been fundamentally uninterested in either the coming or the nature of the millennium. His major attraction to the doctrine may well have lain in its ulterior use as an anti-clerical creed. Dr Pocock argued that Hobbes was not outside the 'mainstream of Protestant thinking', but noted that Hobbes's position was nevertheless 'visibly enigmatic'.[23]

Lastly, Dr Lamont's interesting recent findings on Baxter have led him to wonder if the generally-accepted belief in the decline of millenarianism after 1660 might be mistaken.[24] This is a very neglected area, and I would not care to prejudge the issue. But it is worth recalling that after 1660 millenarians—Presbyterians as well as sectarians—were suspect as having sanctioned rebellion in the 1640s as the fulfilment of Biblical prophecies. Roger L'Estrange elaborated the point at length in 1681: that millenarianism was to be linked with fanaticism and political subversion.[25] Baxter was, of course, a product of the Revolution. Dr Lamont's suggestion could only be verified by examining the extent of millenarianism among the generation which reached maturity *after* the period of apocalyptic excitement in the 1640s. There is certainly some evidence to support the traditional thesis of a period of slow decline. It is difficult, for example, to envisage before 1660 an incident which occurred in 1679, when the millenarian enthusiasm of a sectarian minister was rudely rebuffed by a request from his congregation to study 'more profitable subjects'.[26]

Our debates have revealed a number of major gaps in knowledge as well as differences in interpretation. To summarize, Dr Lamont sees millenarianism as a doctrine generally accepted (or acceptable) in Elizabethan and Stuart England, appearing in

[23] Lamont, 'Richard Baxter', p. 72 (p. 404); J. G. A. Pocock, 'Time, history and eschatology in the thought of Thomas Hobbes', in J. H. Elliott and H. G. Koenigsberger (eds), *The Diversity of History: Essays in Honour of Sir Herbert Butterfield* (London, 1970), p. 180.
[24] Lamont, 'Richard Baxter', p. 68 (pp. 399–400) and *passim*.
[25] R. L'Estrange, *The Dissenter's Sayings*, 1st edn (London, 1681).
[26] Capp, *Fifth Monarchy Men*, p. 217.

both a 'centripetal' character (focusing on the messianic claims of the monarch) and, especially after 1640, a 'centrifugal', anti-monarchical form. I would agree that a consensus existed in early Elizabethan England, regarding the Bible as prophesying the approaching downfall of Antichristian Rome and the end of the world. This belief, developed by Foxe, was to remain popular until the time of Newton; but it no longer represented a Protestant consensus. This had been undermined on the one hand by Puritan emphasis on elements of Antichrist within the English Church, and the subsequent puritan development of millenarianism, and on the other hand by the Laudian rejection of the basic certainty that Rome really was Antichrist. What resulted, to oversimplify, was a polarization by which the Foxeian line was held by both Anglicans and Puritans, but with the Anglican position extending towards a general scepticism as regards eschatology and a wish to minimize its role, while the much more vociferous puritan interest extended to millenarianism proper. After 1640 many, probably most, Presbyterians, Independents and sectarians accepted millenarianism. How long they continued loyal to it remains one of the major questions.

INDEX

439

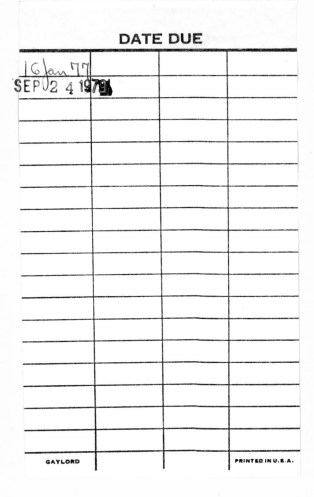